CHILDREN AND FAMILIES ACT 2014 (UK)

Updated as of March 26, 2018

THE LAW LIBRARY

TABLE OF CONTENTS

Introductory Text	4
PART 1. Adoption and contact	4
PART 2. Family justice	11
Repeal of uncommenced provisions of Part 2. of the Family Law Act 1996	18
PART 3. Children and young people in England with special educational needs or disabilities	20
Application of Part to detained persons	61
Disapplication of Chapter 1. of Part 4. of EA 1996. in relation to children in England	62
Interpretation of Part 3	62
PART 4. Childcare etc	64
PART 5. Welfare of children	66
PART 6. The Children's Commissioner	81
PART 7. Statutory rights to leave and pay	85
PART 8. Time off work: ante-natal care etc	111
PART 9. Right to request flexible working	125
PART 10. General provisions	127
Schedules	129
Schedule 1. The Adoption and Children Act Register	129
Schedule 2. Child arrangements orders: amendments	131
Schedule 3. Special educational needs: consequential amendments	151
Schedule 4. Childminder agencies: amendments	169
Schedule 5. Children's Commissioner: minor and consequential amendments	192
Schedule 6. Repeal of requirement to appoint Children's Rights Director: transfer schemes	195
Schedule 7. Statutory rights to leave and pay: further amendments	197
Open Government Licence v3.0	213

Introductory Text

Children and Families Act 2014

2014 CHAPTER 6

An Act to make provision about children, families, and people with special educational needs or disabilities; to make provision about the right to request flexible working; and for connected purposes.
[13th March 2014]
Be it enacted by the Queen's most Excellent Majesty, by and with the advice and consent of the Lords Spiritual and Temporal, and Commons, in this present Parliament assembled, and by the authority of the same, as follows:—
Modifications etc. (not altering text)
C1. Act applied (1.9.2014) by The Children and Families Act 2014 (Transitional and Saving Provisions) (No. 2) Order 2014 (S.I. 2014/2270), art. 20. (1)

PART 1. Adoption and contact

PART 1 Adoption and contact

1. Contact between prescribed persons and adopted person's relatives

(1) In section 98 of the Adoption and Children Act 2002 (pre-commencement adoptions: information), after subsection (1) insert—
"(1. A)Regulations under section 9 may make provision for the purpose of facilitating contact between persons with a prescribed relationship to a person adopted before the appointed day and that person's relatives."
(2) In each of subsections (2) and (3) of that section, for "that purpose" substitute " a purpose within subsection (1) or (1. A) ".
(3) In subsection (7) of that section, after the definition of "appointed day" insert—
""prescribed" means prescribed by regulations under section 9;".
Commencement Information
I1. S. 1 in force at 25.7.2014 for E. by S.I. 2014/889, art. 6. (a)
I2. S. 1 in force at 19.10.2015 for W. by S.I. 2015/1808, art. 2

2. Placement of looked after children with prospective adopters

(1) Section 22. C of the Children Act 1989 is amended as follows.
(2) In subsection (7), after "subject to" insert " subsection (9. B) and ".

(3) After subsection (9) insert—
"(9. A)Subsection (9. B) applies (subject to subsection (9. C)) where the local authority are a local authority in England and—
    (a) are considering adoption for C, or
    (b) are satisfied that C ought to be placed for adoption but are not authorised under section 19 of the Adoption and Children Act 2002 (placement with parental consent) or by virtue of section 21 of that Act (placement orders) to place C for adoption.
(9. B)Where this subsection applies—
    (a) subsections (7) to (9) do not apply to the local authority,
    (b) the local authority must consider placing C with an individual within subsection (6)(a), and
    (c) where the local authority decide that a placement with such an individual is not the most appropriate placement for C, the local authority must consider placing C with a local authority foster parent who has been approved as a prospective adopter.
(9. C)Subsection (9. B) does not apply where the local authority have applied for a placement order under section 21 of the Adoption and Children Act 2002 in respect of C and the application has been refused."
Commencement Information
I3. S. 2 in force at 25.7.2014 by S.I. 2014/889, art. 6. (b)

3. Repeal of requirement to give due consideration to ethnicity: England

(1) Section 1 of the Adoption and Children Act 2002 (considerations applying when making decisions about the adoption of a child) is amended as follows.
(2) In subsection (5) (due consideration to be given to religious persuasion, racial origin and cultural and linguistic background), for "In placing the child for adoption, the adoption agency" substitute " In placing a child for adoption, an adoption agency in Wales ".
(3) In consequence of the amendment made by subsection (2)—
    (a) in subsection (1), for "This section applies" substitute " Subsections (2) to (4) apply ";
    (b) in subsection (6), for "The court or adoption agency" substitute " In coming to a decision relating to the adoption of a child, a court or adoption agency ";
    (c) after subsection (8) insert—
"(9)In this section "adoption agency in Wales" means an adoption agency that is—
    (a) a local authority in Wales, or
    (b) a registered adoption society whose principal office is in Wales."
Commencement Information
I4. S. 3 in force at 25.7.2014 by S.I. 2014/889, art. 6. (b)

4. Recruitment, assessment and approval of prospective adopters

(1) In Chapter 2 of Part 1 of the Adoption and Children Act 2002 (the Adoption Service) after section 3 insert—
"3. ARecruitment, assessment and approval of prospective adopters
(1) The Secretary of State may give directions requiring one or more named local authorities in England, or one or more descriptions of local authority in England, to make arrangements for all or any of their functions within subsection (3) to be carried out on their behalf by one or more other adoption agencies.
(2) The Secretary of State may by order require all local authorities in England to make arrangements for all or any of their functions within subsection (3) to be carried out on their behalf by one or more other adoption agencies.
(3) The functions are their functions in relation to—

(a) the recruitment of persons as prospective adopters;
(b) the assessment of prospective adopters' suitability to adopt a child;
(c) the approval of prospective adopters as suitable to adopt a child."
(2) In section 140. (3) of that Act (statutory instruments containing subordinate legislation that are subject to the affirmative procedure), before paragraph (a) insert—
"(za)under section 3. A(2),".
(3) The Secretary of State may not make an order under subsection (2) of section 3. A of the Adoption and Children Act 2002 (as inserted by subsection (1)) before 1 March 2015.
Commencement Information
I5. S. 4 in force at 13.5.2014 by S.I. 2014/889, art. 5. (a)
Prospective

5. Adoption support services: personal budgets

In Chapter 2 of Part 1 of the Adoption and Children Act 2002 (the Adoption Service) after section 4 insert—
"4. AAdoption support services: personal budgets
(1) This section applies where—
(a) after carrying out an assessment under section 4, a local authority in England decide to provide any adoption support services to a person ("the recipient"), and
(b) the recipient is an adopted person or the parent of an adopted person.
(2) The local authority must prepare a personal budget for the recipient if asked to do so by the recipient or (in prescribed circumstances) a person of a prescribed description.
(3) The authority prepare a "personal budget" for the recipient if they identify an amount as available to secure the adoption support services that they have decided to provide, with a view to the recipient being involved in securing those services.
(4) Regulations may make provision about personal budgets, in particular—
(a) about requests for personal budgets;
(b) about the amount of a personal budget;
(c) about the sources of the funds making up a personal budget;
(d) for payments ("direct payments") representing all or part of a personal budget to be made to the recipient, or (in prescribed circumstances) a person of a prescribed description, in order to secure any adoption support services to which the budget relates;
(e) about the description of adoption support services to which personal budgets and direct payments may (and may not) relate;
(f) for a personal budget or direct payment to cover the agreed cost of the adoption support services to which the budget or payment relates;
(g) about when, how, to whom and on what conditions direct payments may (and may not) be made;
(h) about when direct payments may be required to be repaid and the recovery of unpaid sums;
(i) about conditions with which a person or body making direct payments must comply before, after or at the time of making a direct payment;
(j) about arrangements for providing information, advice or support in connection with personal budgets and direct payments.
(5) If the regulations include provision authorising direct payments, they must—
(a) require the consent of the recipient, or (in prescribed circumstances) a person of a prescribed description, to be obtained before direct payments are made;
(b) require the authority to stop making direct payments where the required consent is withdrawn.
(6) Any adoption support services secured by means of direct payments made by a local authority are to be treated as adoption support services provided by the authority for all purposes, subject to any prescribed conditions or exceptions.

(7) On the occasion of the first exercise of the power to make regulations under this section—
    (a) the statutory instrument containing the regulations is not to be made unless a draft of the instrument has been laid before, and approved by a resolution of, each House of Parliament, and
    (b) accordingly section 140. (2) does not apply to the instrument.
(8) In this section "prescribed" means prescribed by regulations."

6. Adoption support services: duty to provide information

In Chapter 2 of Part 1 of the Adoption and Children Act 2002 (the Adoption Service) after section 4. A (as inserted by section 5) insert—
"4. BAdoption support services: duty to provide information
(1) Except in circumstances prescribed by regulations, a local authority in England must provide the information specified in subsection (2) to—
    (a) any person who has contacted the authority to request information about adopting a child,
    (b) any person who has informed the authority that he or she wishes to adopt a child,
    (c) any person within the authority's area who the authority are aware is a parent of an adopted child, and
    (d) any person within the authority's area who is a parent of an adopted child and has contacted the authority to request any of the information specified in subsection (2).
(2) The information is—
    (a) information about the adoption support services available to people in the authority's area;
    (b) information about the right to request an assessment under section 4 (assessments etc for adoption support services), and the authority's duties under that section and regulations made under it;
    (c) information about the authority's duties under section 4. A (adoption support services: personal budgets) and regulations made under it;
    (d) any other information prescribed by regulations."
Commencement Information
I6. S. 6 in force at 25.7.2014 by S.I. 2014/889, art. 6. (c)

7. The Adoption and Children Act Register

(1) The Adoption and Children Act 2002 is amended as follows.
(2) In section 125 (Adoption and Children Act Register)—
    (a) in subsection (1)(a), after "children who are suitable for adoption" insert " , children for whom a local authority in England are considering adoption ";
    (b) in subsection (3), after "search" insert " (subject to regulations under section 128. A) ".
(3) In section 128 (supply of information for the register), in subsection (4)(b), after "children suitable for adoption" insert " or for whom a local authority in England are considering adoption ".
(4) After section 128 insert—
"128. ASearch and inspection of the register by prospective adopters
(1) Regulations may make provision enabling prospective adopters who are suitable to adopt a child to search and inspect the register, for the purposes of assisting them to find a child for whom they would be appropriate adopters.
(2) Regulations under subsection (1) may make provision enabling prospective adopters to search and inspect only prescribed parts of the register, or prescribed content on the register.
(3) Access to the register for the purpose of searching and inspecting it may be granted on any prescribed terms and conditions.
(4) Regulations may prescribe the steps to be taken by prospective adopters in respect of information received by them as a result of searching or inspecting the register.
(5) Regulations may make provision requiring prospective adopters, in prescribed circumstances, to pay a prescribed fee to the Secretary of State or the registration organisation in respect of

searching or inspecting the register.

(6) On the occasion of the first exercise of the power to make regulations under this section—

(a) the statutory instrument containing the regulations is not to be made unless a draft of the instrument has been laid before, and approved by a resolution of, each House of Parliament, and

(b) accordingly section 140. (2) does not apply to the instrument."

(5) In section 129 (disclosure of information), in subsection (2)(a) after "suitable for adoption" insert " or for whom a local authority in England is considering adoption ".

(6) In section 140. (7) (power for subordinate legislation to make different provision for different purposes) after "purposes" insert " or areas ".

(7) In section 97 of the Children Act 1989 (privacy for children involved in certain proceedings), after subsection (6) insert—

"(6. A)It is not a contravention of this section to—

(a) enter material in the Adoption and Children Act Register (established under section 125 of the Adoption and Children Act 2002), or

(b) permit persons to search and inspect that register pursuant to regulations made under section 128. A of that Act."

(8) Schedule 1 (amendments to the Adoption and Children Act 2002 to provide for the Adoption and Children Act Register not to apply to Wales and Scotland and to remove the requirement to make provision for that register by Order in Council, and other related amendments) has effect.

Commencement Information

I7. S. 7 in force at 13.5.2014 by S.I. 2014/889, art. 5. (b)

Contact

8. Contact: children in care of local authorities

(1) Section 34 of the Children Act 1989 (parental contact etc with children in care) is amended as follows.

(2) In subsection (1), after "subject to the provisions of this section" insert " and their duty under section 22. (3)(a) ".

(3) After subsection (6) insert—

"(6. A)Where (by virtue of an order under this section, or because subsection (6) applies) a local authority in England are authorised to refuse to allow contact between the child and a person mentioned in any of paragraphs (a) to (c) of paragraph 15. (1) of Schedule 2, paragraph 15. (1) of that Schedule does not require the authority to endeavour to promote contact between the child and that person."

(4) In subsection (8), before paragraph (a) insert—

"(za)what a local authority in England must have regard to in considering whether contact between a child and a person mentioned in any of paragraphs (a) to (d) of subsection (1) is consistent with safeguarding and promoting the child's welfare;".

(5) In subsection (11) after "Before" insert " making, varying or discharging an order under this section or ".

Commencement Information

I8. S. 8 in force at 25.7.2014 by S.I. 2014/889, art. 6. (d)

9. Contact: post-adoption

(1) After section 51 of the Adoption and Children Act 2002 insert—

"Post-adoption contact

51. APost-adoption contact

(1) This section applies where—
(a) an adoption agency has placed or was authorised to place a child for adoption, and
(b) the court is making or has made an adoption order in respect of the child.
(2) When making the adoption order or at any time afterwards, the court may make an order under this section—
(a) requiring the person in whose favour the adoption order is or has been made to allow the child to visit or stay with the person named in the order under this section, or for the person named in that order and the child otherwise to have contact with each other, or
(b) prohibiting the person named in the order under this section from having contact with the child.
(3) The following people may be named in an order under this section—
(a) any person who (but for the child's adoption) would be related to the child by blood (including half-blood), marriage or civil partnership;
(b) any former guardian of the child;
(c) any person who had parental responsibility for the child immediately before the making of the adoption order;
(d) any person who was entitled to make an application for an order under section 26 in respect of the child (contact with children placed or to be placed for adoption) by virtue of subsection (3)(c), (d) or (e) of that section;
(e) any person with whom the child has lived for a period of at least one year.
(4) An application for an order under this section may be made by—
(a) a person who has applied for the adoption order or in whose favour the adoption order is or has been made,
(b) the child, or
(c) any person who has obtained the court's leave to make the application.
(5) In deciding whether to grant leave under subsection (4)(c), the court must consider—
(a) any risk there might be of the proposed application disrupting the child's life to such an extent that he or she would be harmed by it (within the meaning of the 1989 Act),
(b) the applicant's connection with the child, and
(c) any representations made to the court by—
(i) the child, or
(ii) a person who has applied for the adoption order or in whose favour the adoption order is or has been made.
(6) When making an adoption order, the court may on its own initiative make an order of the type mentioned in subsection (2)(b).
(7) The period of one year mentioned in subsection (3)(e) need not be continuous but must not have begun more than five years before the making of the application.
(8) Where this section applies, an order under section 8 of the 1989 Act may not make provision about contact between the child and any person who may be named in an order under this section.
51. BOrders under section 51. A: supplementary
(1) An order under section 51. A—
(a) may contain directions about how it is to be carried into effect,
(b) may be made subject to any conditions the court thinks appropriate,
(c) may be varied or revoked by the court on an application by the child, a person in whose favour the adoption order was made or a person named in the order, and
(d) has effect until the child's 18th birthday, unless revoked.
(2) Subsection (3) applies to proceedings—
(a) on an application for an adoption order in which—
(i) an application is made for an order under section 51. A, or
(ii) the court indicates that it is considering making such an order on its own initiative;
(b) on an application for an order under section 51. A;
(c) on an application for such an order to be varied or revoked.
(3) The court must (in the light of any rules made by virtue of subsection (4))—

(a) draw up a timetable with a view to determining without delay whether to make, (or as the case may be) vary or revoke an order under section 51. A, and

(b) give directions for the purpose of ensuring, so far as is reasonably practicable, that that timetable is adhered to.

(4) Rules of court may—

(a) specify periods within which specified steps must be taken in relation to proceedings to which subsection (3) applies, and

(b) make other provision with respect to such proceedings for the purpose of ensuring, so far as is reasonably practicable, that the court makes determinations about orders under section 51. A without delay."

(2) In section 1 of the Adoption and Children Act 2002 (considerations applying to the exercise of powers relating to the adoption of a child), in subsection (7)(a) after "section 26" insert " or 51. A ".

(3) In section 26 of that Act (children placed, or authorised to be placed, for adoption: contact), omit subsection (5).

(4) In section 96. (3) of that Act (section 95 does not prohibit payment of legal or medical expenses in connection with applications under section 26 etc) after "26" insert " , 51. A ".

(5) In section 1. (1) of the Family Law Act 1986 (orders which are Part 1 orders) after paragraph (ab) insert—

"(ac)an order made under section 51. A of the Adoption and Children Act 2002 (post-adoption contact), other than an order varying or revoking such an order;".

(6) In section 2 of that Act (jurisdiction of courts in England and Wales to make Part 1 orders: pre-conditions) after subsection (2. B) insert—

"(2. C)A court in England and Wales shall not have jurisdiction to make an order under section 51. A of the Adoption and Children Act 2002 unless—

(a) it has jurisdiction under the Council Regulation or the Hague Convention, or

(b) neither the Council Regulation nor the Hague Convention applies but the condition in section 3 of this Act is satisfied."

(7) In section 9 of the Children Act 1989, in subsection (5)(a) (restrictions on making certain orders with respect to children) after "order" insert " or an order under section 51. A of the Adoption and Children Act 2002 (post-adoption contact) ".

(8) In section 17. (4) of the Armed Forces Act 1991 (persons to be given notice of application for service family child assessment order) before paragraph (e) insert—

"(db)any person in whose favour an order under section 51. A of the Adoption and Children Act 2002 (post-adoption contact) is in force with respect to the child;".

(9) In section 18. (7) of that Act (persons who may apply to vary or discharge a service family child assessment order) before paragraph (e) insert—

"(db)any person in whose favour an order under section 51. A of the Adoption and Children Act 2002 (post-adoption contact) is in force with respect to the child;".

(10) In section 20. (8) of that Act (persons who are to be allowed reasonable contact with a child subject to a protection order) before paragraph (d) insert—

"(cb)any person in whose favour an order under section 51. A of the Adoption and Children Act 2002 (post-adoption contact) is in force with respect to the child;".

(11) In section 22. A(7) of that Act (persons who are to be allowed reasonable contact with a child in service police protection) before paragraph (d) insert—

"(cb)any person in whose favour an order under section 51. A of the Adoption and Children Act 2002 (post-adoption contact) is in force with respect to the child,".

(12) In Part 1 of Schedule 1 to the Legal Aid, Sentencing and Punishment of Offenders Act 2012 (civil legal services)—

(a) in paragraph 12. (9) (victims of domestic violence and family matters), in the definition of "family enactment" after paragraph (o) insert—

"(xvi)section 51. A of the Adoption and Children Act 2002 (post-adoption contact orders).", and

(b) in paragraph 13. (1) (protection of children and family matters) after paragraph (f) insert—

"(g)orders under section 51. A of the Adoption and Children Act 2002 (post-adoption contact)."
Commencement Information
I9. S. 9 in force at 22.4.2014 by S.I. 2014/889, art. 4. (a) (with transitional provisions in S.I. 2014/1042, arts. 3, 4, 6-10)

PART 2. Family justice

PART 2 Family justice

10. Family mediation information and assessment meetings

(1) Before making a relevant family application, a person must attend a family mediation information and assessment meeting.
(2) Family Procedure Rules—
    (a) may provide for subsection (1) not to apply in circumstances specified in the Rules,
    (b) may make provision about convening a family mediation information and assessment meeting, or about the conduct of such a meeting,
    (c) may make provision for the court not to issue, or otherwise deal with, an application if, in contravention of subsection (1), the applicant has not attended a family mediation information and assessment meeting, and
    (d) may provide for a determination as to whether an applicant has contravened subsection (1) to be made after considering only evidence of a description specified in the Rules.
(3) In this section—
"the court" means the High Court or the family court;
"family mediation information and assessment meeting", in relation to a relevant family application, means a meeting held for the purpose of enabling information to be provided about—
    - mediation of disputes of the kinds to which relevant family applications relate,
    - ways in which disputes of those kinds may be resolved otherwise than by the court, and
    - the suitability of mediation, or of any such other way of resolving disputes, for trying to resolve any dispute to which the particular application relates;
"family proceedings" has the same meaning as in section 75 of the Courts Act 2003;
"relevant family application" means an application that—
    - is made to the court in, or to initiate, family proceedings, and
    - is of a description specified in Family Procedure Rules.
(4) This section is without prejudice to sections 75 and 76 of the Courts Act 2003 (power to make Family Procedure Rules).
Commencement Information
I1. S. 10 in force at 22.4.2014 by S.I. 2014/793, art. 2 (with transitional provisions in S.I. 2014/1042, arts. 5, 11)

11. Welfare of the child: parental involvement

(1) Section 1 of the Children Act 1989 (welfare of the child) is amended as follows.
(2) After subsection (2) insert—
"(2. A)A court, in the circumstances mentioned in subsection (4)(a) or (7), is as respects each parent within subsection (6)(a) to presume, unless the contrary is shown, that involvement of that parent in the life of the child concerned will further the child's welfare.
(2. B)In subsection (2. A) "involvement" means involvement of some kind, either direct or indirect, but not any particular division of a child's time."

(3) After subsection (5) insert—
"(6)In subsection (2. A) "parent" means parent of the child concerned; and, for the purposes of that subsection, a parent of the child concerned—
   (a) is within this paragraph if that parent can be involved in the child's life in a way that does not put the child at risk of suffering harm; and
   (b) is to be treated as being within paragraph (a) unless there is some evidence before the court in the particular proceedings to suggest that involvement of that parent in the child's life would put the child at risk of suffering harm whatever the form of the involvement.
(7) The circumstances referred to are that the court is considering whether to make an order under section 4. (1)(c) or (2. A) or 4. ZA(1)(c) or (5) (parental responsibility of parent other than mother)."
Modifications etc. (not altering text)
C1. S. 11 applied (N.I.) (10.7.2014) by The Police Rehabilitation and Retraining Trust Regulations (Northern Ireland) 2014 (S.R. 2014/163), regs. 1, 7. (1)
Commencement Information
I2. S. 11 in force at 22.10.2014 by S.I. 2014/2749, art. 3 (with art. 4)

12. Child arrangements orders

(1) Section 8. (1) of the Children Act 1989 is amended as follows.
(2) Omit the definitions of "contact order" and "residence order".
(3) After "In this Act—" insert—
""child arrangements order" means an order regulating arrangements relating to any of the following—
   (a) with whom a child is to live, spend time or otherwise have contact, and
   (b) when a child is to live, spend time or otherwise have contact with any person;".
(4) Schedule 2 (amendments relating to child arrangements orders) has effect.
Commencement Information
I3. S. 12 in force at 22.4.2014 by S.I. 2014/889, art. 4. (b) (with transitional provisions in S.I. 2014/1042, arts. 3, 4, 6-10)

13. Control of expert evidence, and of assessments, in children proceedings

(1) A person may not without the permission of the court instruct a person to provide expert evidence for use in children proceedings.
(2) Where in contravention of subsection (1) a person is instructed to provide expert evidence, evidence resulting from the instructions is inadmissible in children proceedings unless the court rules that it is admissible.
(3) A person may not without the permission of the court cause a child to be medically or psychiatrically examined or otherwise assessed for the purposes of the provision of expert evidence in children proceedings.
(4) Where in contravention of subsection (3) a child is medically or psychiatrically examined or otherwise assessed, evidence resulting from the examination or other assessment is inadmissible in children proceedings unless the court rules that it is admissible.
(5) In children proceedings, a person may not without the permission of the court put expert evidence (in any form) before the court.
(6) The court may give permission as mentioned in subsection (1), (3) or (5) only if the court is of the opinion that the expert evidence is necessary to assist the court to resolve the proceedings justly.
(7) When deciding whether to give permission as mentioned in subsection (1), (3) or (5) the court

is to have regard in particular to—
   (a) any impact which giving permission would be likely to have on the welfare of the children concerned, including in the case of permission as mentioned in subsection (3) any impact which any examination or other assessment would be likely to have on the welfare of the child who would be examined or otherwise assessed,
   (b) the issues to which the expert evidence would relate,
   (c) the questions which the court would require the expert to answer,
   (d) what other expert evidence is available (whether obtained before or after the start of proceedings),
   (e) whether evidence could be given by another person on the matters on which the expert would give evidence,
   (f) the impact which giving permission would be likely to have on the timetable for, and duration and conduct of, the proceedings,
   (g) the cost of the expert evidence, and
   (h) any matters prescribed by Family Procedure Rules.
(8) References in this section to providing expert evidence, or to putting expert evidence before a court, do not include references to—
   (a) the provision or giving of evidence—
(i) by a person who is a member of the staff of a local authority or of an authorised applicant,
(ii) in proceedings to which the authority or authorised applicant is a party, and
(iii) in the course of the person's work for the authority or authorised applicant,
   (b) the provision or giving of evidence—
(i) by a person within a description prescribed for the purposes of subsection (1) of section 94 of the Adoption and Children Act 2002 (suitability for adoption etc.), and
(ii) about the matters mentioned in that subsection,
   (c) the provision or giving of evidence by an officer of the Children and Family Court Advisory and Support Service when acting in that capacity, or
   (d) the provision or giving of evidence by a Welsh family proceedings officer (as defined by section 35. (4) of the Children Act 2004) when acting in that capacity.
(9) In this section—
"authorised applicant" means—
   - the National Society for the Prevention of Cruelty to Children, or
   - a person authorised by an order under section 31 of the Children Act 1989 to bring proceedings under that section;
"child" means a person under the age of 18;
"children proceedings" has such meaning as may be prescribed by Family Procedure Rules;
"the court", in relation to any children proceedings, means the court in which the proceedings are taking place;
"local authority"—
   - in relation to England means—
a county council,
a district council for an area for which there is no county council,
a London borough council,
the Common Council of the City of London, or
the Council of the Isles of Scilly, and
   - in relation to Wales means a county council or a county borough council.
(10) The preceding provisions of this section are without prejudice to sections 75 and 76 of the Courts Act 2003 (power to make Family Procedure Rules).
(11) In section 38 of the Children Act 1989 (court's power to make interim care and supervision orders, and to give directions as to medical examination etc. of children) after subsection (7) insert—
"(7. A)A direction under subsection (6) to the effect that there is to be a medical or psychiatric examination or other assessment of the child may be given only if the court is of the opinion that

the examination or other assessment is necessary to assist the court to resolve the proceedings justly.
(7. B)When deciding whether to give a direction under subsection (6) to that effect the court is to have regard in particular to—

(a) any impact which any examination or other assessment would be likely to have on the welfare of the child, and any other impact which giving the direction would be likely to have on the welfare of the child,
(b) the issues with which the examination or other assessment would assist the court,
(c) the questions which the examination or other assessment would enable the court to answer,
(d) the evidence otherwise available,
(e) the impact which the direction would be likely to have on the timetable, duration and conduct of the proceedings,
(f) the cost of the examination or other assessment, and
(g) any matters prescribed by Family Procedure Rules."

Commencement Information
I4. S. 13 in force at 22.4.2014 by S.I. 2014/793, art. 2 (with transitional provisions in S.I. 2014/1042, arts. 5, 11)

14. Care, supervision and other family proceedings: time limits and timetables

(1) The Children Act 1989 is amended as follows.
(2) In section 32. (1)(a) (timetable for dealing with application for care or supervision order) for "disposing of the application without delay; and" substitute "disposing of the application—
(i) without delay, and
(ii) in any event within twenty-six weeks beginning with the day on which the application was issued; and".
(3) In section 32 (care and supervision orders) after subsection (2) insert—
"(3)A court, when drawing up a timetable under subsection (1)(a), must in particular have regard to—
(a) the impact which the timetable would have on the welfare of the child to whom the application relates; and
(b) the impact which the timetable would have on the conduct of the proceedings.
(4) A court, when revising a timetable drawn up under subsection (1)(a) or when making any decision which may give rise to a need to revise such a timetable (which does not include a decision under subsection (5)), must in particular have regard to—
(a) the impact which any revision would have on the welfare of the child to whom the application relates; and
(b) the impact which any revision would have on the duration and conduct of the proceedings.
(5) A court in which an application under this Part is proceeding may extend the period that is for the time being allowed under subsection (1)(a)(ii) in the case of the application, but may do so only if the court considers that the extension is necessary to enable the court to resolve the proceedings justly.
(6) When deciding whether to grant an extension under subsection (5), a court must in particular have regard to—
(a) the impact which any ensuing timetable revision would have on the welfare of the child to whom the application relates, and
(b) the impact which any ensuing timetable revision would have on the duration and conduct of the proceedings;
and here "ensuing timetable revision" means any revision, of the timetable under subsection (1)(a) for the proceedings, which the court considers may ensue from the extension.
(7) When deciding whether to grant an extension under subsection (5), a court is to take account of

the following guidance: extensions are not to be granted routinely and are to be seen as requiring specific justification.
(8) Each separate extension under subsection (5) is to end no more than eight weeks after the later of—
    (a) the end of the period being extended; and
    (b) the end of the day on which the extension is granted.
(9) The Lord Chancellor may by regulations amend subsection (1)(a)(ii), or the opening words of subsection (8), for the purpose of varying the period for the time being specified in that provision.
(10) Rules of court may provide that a court—
    (a) when deciding whether to exercise the power under subsection (5), or
    (b) when deciding how to exercise that power,
must, or may or may not, have regard to matters specified in the rules, or must take account of any guidance set out in the rules."
(4) In section 38 (interim care and supervision orders)—
    (a) in subsection (4) (duration of interim order) omit—
(i) paragraph (a) (order may not last longer than 8 weeks), and
(ii) paragraph (b) (subsequent order generally may not last longer than 4 weeks),
    (b) in that subsection after paragraph (d) insert—
"(da)in a case which falls within subsection (1)(b) and in which—
(i) no direction has been given under section 37. (4), and
(ii) no application for a care order or supervision order has been made with respect to the child,
the expiry of the period of eight weeks beginning with the date on which the order is made;", and
    (c) omit subsection (5) (interpretation of subsection (4)(b)).
(5) In section 11. (1) (section 8 orders: court's duty, in the light of rules made by virtue of section 11. (2), to draw up timetable and give directions to implement it) for "rules made by virtue of subsection (2))" substitute " provision in rules of court that is of the kind mentioned in subsection (2)(a) or (b)) ".
(6) In section 14. E(1) (special guardianship orders: court's duty, in the light of rules made by virtue of subsection (3), to draw up timetable and give directions to implement it) for "rules made by virtue of subsection (3))" substitute " provision in rules of court that is of the kind mentioned in section 11. (2)(a) or (b)) ".
(7) In section 32. (1) (care and supervision orders: court's duty, in the light of rules made by virtue of section 32. (2), to draw up timetable and give directions to implement it)—
    (a) for "hearing an application for an order under this Part" substitute " in which an application for an order under this Part is proceeding ", and
    (b) for "rules made by virtue of subsection (2))" substitute " provision in rules of court that is of the kind mentioned in subsection (2)(a) or (b)) ".
(8) In section 109. (1) of the Adoption and Children Act 2002 (adoption and placement orders: court's duty, in the light of rules made by virtue of section 109. (2), to draw up timetable and give directions to implement it) for "rules made by virtue of subsection (2))" substitute " provision in rules of court that is of the kind mentioned in subsection (2)(a) or (b)) ".
Commencement Information
I5. S. 14 in force at 22.4.2014 by S.I. 2014/889, art. 4. (c) (with transitional provisions in S.I. 2014/1042, arts. 3, 4, 6-10)

15. Care plans

(1) For section 31. (3. A) of the Children Act 1989 (no care order to be made until court has considered section 31. A care plan) substitute—
"(3. A)A court deciding whether to make a care order—
    (a) is required to consider the permanence provisions of the section 31. A plan for the child concerned, but

(b) is not required to consider the remainder of the section 31. A plan, subject to section 34. (11).
(3. B)For the purposes of subsection (3. A), the permanence provisions of a section 31. A plan are such of the plan's provisions setting out the long-term plan for the upbringing of the child concerned as provide for any of the following—
    (a) the child to live with any parent of the child's or with any other member of, or any friend of, the child's family;
    (b) adoption;
    (c) long-term care not within paragraph (a) or (b).
(3. C)The Secretary of State may by regulations amend this section for the purpose of altering what for the purposes of subsection (3. A) are the permanence provisions of a section 31. A plan."
(2) In section 31. A of the Children Act 1989 (care plans)—
    (a) in subsection (1) (where application made for care order, care plan to be prepared within such time as the court may direct) for "the court may direct" substitute " may be prescribed ", and
    (b) after subsection (4) insert—
"(4. A)In this section "prescribed"—
    (a) in relation to a care plan whose preparation is the responsibility of a local authority for an area in England, means prescribed by the Secretary of State; and
    (b) in relation to a care plan whose preparation is the responsibility of a local authority in Wales, means prescribed by the Welsh Ministers."
(3) In consequence of subsection (1), section 121. (1) of the Adoption and Children Act 2002 is repealed.
Commencement Information
I6. S. 15. (1)(3) in force at 22.4.2014 by S.I. 2014/889, art. 4. (d) (with transitional provisions in S.I. 2014/1042, arts. 3, 4, 6-10)

16. Care proceedings and care plans: regulations: procedural requirements

(1) In section 104 of the Children Act 1989 (regulations and orders)—
    (a) in subsections (2) and (3. A) (regulations within subsection (3. B) or (3. C) not subject to annulment but to be approved in draft) after "(3. B)" insert " , (3. BA) ", and
    (b) after subsection (3. B) insert—
"(3. BA)Regulations fall within this subsection if they are regulations made in the exercise of the power conferred by section 31. (3. C) or 32. (9)."
F1. (2)..............................
Amendments (Textual)
F1. S. 16. (2) omitted (6.4.2016) by virtue of The Social Services and Well-being (Wales) Act 2014 (Consequential Amendments) Regulations 2016 (S.I. 2016/413), regs. 2. (1), 291
Commencement Information
I7. S. 16 in force at 22.4.2014 by S.I. 2014/889, art. 4. (e) (with transitional provisions in S.I. 2014/1042, arts. 3, 4, 6-10)

17. Repeal of restrictions on divorce and dissolution etc where there are children

(1) The following are repealed—
    (a) section 41 of the Matrimonial Causes Act 1973 (in proceedings for divorce etc. court is to consider whether to exercise powers under Children Act 1989);
    (b) section 63 of the Civil Partnership Act 2004 (in proceedings for dissolution etc. court is to consider whether to exercise powers under Children Act 1989).

(2) The following amendments and repeals are in consequence of the repeals made by subsection (1).
(3) In section 9. (1)(a) of the Matrimonial Causes Act 1973 (proceedings after decree of divorce: power to make decree absolute is subject to section 41)—
  (a) for "sections" substitute " section ", and
  (b) omit "and 41".
(4) In section 17. (2) of that Act (grant of decree of judicial separation is subject to section 41) omit ", subject to section 41 below,".
(5) Omit paragraph 31 of Schedule 12 to the Children Act 1989 (which substitutes section 41 of the Matrimonial Causes Act 1973).
(6) In section 40. (4)(b) of the Civil Partnership Act 2004 (proceedings after conditional order: power to make order final is subject to section 63) omit the words from "and section 63" to the end.
(7) In section 56. (3) of that Act (making of separation order is subject to section 63) omit ", subject to section 63,".
Commencement Information
I8. S. 17 in force at 22.4.2014 by S.I. 2014/793, art. 2 (with transitional provisions in S.I. 2014/1042, arts. 5, 11)

18. Repeal of uncommenced provisions of Part 2 of the Family Law Act 1996.

(1) Part 2 of the Family Law Act 1996 (divorce and separation), except section 22 (the only provision of Part 2 which is in force), is repealed.
(2) In consequence of subsection (1), the following provisions of the Family Law Act 1996 (which relate to provisions of Part 2) are repealed—
  (a) section 1. (c) and (d),
  (b) section 63. (2)(a),
  (c) section 64. (1)(a),
  (d) in section 65. (5) the words "to rules made under section 12 or",
  (e) Part 1 of Schedule 8, except—
(i) paragraph 16. (5)(a), (6)(b) and (7) (which have been brought into force), and
(ii) paragraphs 4 and 16. (1) (which relate to those provisions),
  (f) in Schedule 9, paragraphs 1 and 2 and, in paragraph 4, the definitions of "decree", "instrument" and "petition", and
  (j) in Schedule 10, the entries relating to—
(i) the Matrimonial Causes Act 1973,
(ii) the Domicile and Matrimonial Proceedings Act 1973,
(iii) sections 1, 7 and 63 of, and paragraph 38 of Schedule 2 to, the Domestic Proceedings and Magistrates' Courts Act 1978,
(iv) the Senior Courts Act 1981,
(v) the Administration of Justice Act 1982,
(vi) the Matrimonial and Family Proceedings Act 1984,
(vii) the Family Law Act 1986, and
(viii) Schedule 13 to the Children Act 1989.
(3) In consequence of subsections (1) and (2), the following provisions are repealed—
  (a) paragraphs 50 to 52 of Schedule 4 to the Access to Justice Act 1999,
  (b) the following provisions of the Welfare Reform and Pensions Act 1999—
(i) section 28. (1)(b) and (c), (2), (4) and (5),
(ii) section 48. (1)(b) and (c), (2), (4) and (5), and
(iii) in Schedule 12, paragraphs 64 to 66,
  (c) paragraphs 22 to 25 of Schedule 1 to the Constitutional Reform Act 2005,

(d) paragraph 12 of Schedule 2 to the Children and Adoption Act 2006, and
(e) the following provisions of Schedule 5 to the Legal Aid, Sentencing and Punishment of Offenders Act 2012—
(i) paragraphs 43 to 45, and
(ii) in the second column of the Table in Part 2, paragraph (l) of the entry relating to Schedule 4 to the Access to Justice Act 1999.
(4) In consequence of subsection (1), in section 1 of the Family Law Act 1996 (general principles underlying Part 2), in the words before paragraph (a) and in the title, for "Parts II and III" substitute " section 22 ".
(5) In consequence of subsection (3)(b)(i), in section 28. (11) of the Welfare Reform and Pensions Act 1999 (interpretation of subsections (4)(b), (5)(c) and (6)) for "subsections (4)(b), (5)(c) and" substitute " subsection ".
(6) The modifications set out in subsection (7), which were originally made by article 3. (2) of the No. 2 Order and article 4 of the No. 3 Order, are to continue to have effect but as amendments of the provisions concerned (rather than as modifications having effect until the coming into force of provisions of the Family Law Act 1996 repealed by this section without having come into force).
(7) The modifications are—
   (a) in section 22. (2) of the Matrimonial and Family Proceedings Act 1984 for the words from "if" to "granted" substitute " if a decree of divorce, a decree of nullity of marriage or a decree of judicial separation has been granted ", and
   (b) in section 31 of the Matrimonial Causes Act 1973—
(i) in subsection (7. D) for "Subsections (7) and (8) of section 22. A" substitute " Section 23. (6) ",
(ii) in subsection (7. D) for "section 22. A" substitute " section 23 ", and
(iii) in subsection (7. F) for "section 23. A" substitute " section 24 ".
(8) In section 31. (7. D) of the Matrimonial Causes Act 1973—
   (a) for "apply", in the first place, substitute " applies ", and
   (b) for "they apply where it" substitute " it applies where the court ".
(9) Articles 3. (2) and 4 of the No. 2 Order, and article 4 of the No. 3 Order, are revoked; and in subsection (6) and this subsection—
"the No. 2 Order" means the Family Law Act 1996 (Commencement No. 2) Order 1997 (S.I. 1997/1892), and
"the No. 3 Order" means the Family Law Act 1996 (Commencement No. 3) Order 1998 (S.I. 1998/2572).

Repeal of uncommenced provisions of Part 2. of the Family Law Act 1996

18. Repeal of uncommenced provisions of Part 2 of the Family Law Act 1996.

(1) Part 2 of the Family Law Act 1996 (divorce and separation), except section 22 (the only provision of Part 2 which is in force), is repealed.
(2) In consequence of subsection (1), the following provisions of the Family Law Act 1996 (which relate to provisions of Part 2) are repealed—
   (a) section 1. (c) and (d),
   (b) section 63. (2)(a),
   (c) section 64. (1)(a),
   (d) in section 65. (5) the words "to rules made under section 12 or",
   (e) Part 1 of Schedule 8, except—

(i) paragraph 16. (5)(a), (6)(b) and (7) (which have been brought into force), and
(ii) paragraphs 4 and 16. (1) (which relate to those provisions),
    (f) in Schedule 9, paragraphs 1 and 2 and, in paragraph 4, the definitions of "decree", "instrument" and "petition", and
    (j) in Schedule 10, the entries relating to—
(i) the Matrimonial Causes Act 1973,
(ii) the Domicile and Matrimonial Proceedings Act 1973,
(iii) sections 1, 7 and 63 of, and paragraph 38 of Schedule 2 to, the Domestic Proceedings and Magistrates' Courts Act 1978,
(iv) the Senior Courts Act 1981,
(v) the Administration of Justice Act 1982,
(vi) the Matrimonial and Family Proceedings Act 1984,
(vii) the Family Law Act 1986, and
(viii) Schedule 13 to the Children Act 1989.
(3) In consequence of subsections (1) and (2), the following provisions are repealed—
    (a) paragraphs 50 to 52 of Schedule 4 to the Access to Justice Act 1999,
    (b) the following provisions of the Welfare Reform and Pensions Act 1999—
(i) section 28. (1)(b) and (c), (2), (4) and (5),
(ii) section 48. (1)(b) and (c), (2), (4) and (5), and
(iii) in Schedule 12, paragraphs 64 to 66,
    (c) paragraphs 22 to 25 of Schedule 1 to the Constitutional Reform Act 2005,
    (d) paragraph 12 of Schedule 2 to the Children and Adoption Act 2006, and
    (e) the following provisions of Schedule 5 to the Legal Aid, Sentencing and Punishment of Offenders Act 2012—
(i) paragraphs 43 to 45, and
(ii) in the second column of the Table in Part 2, paragraph (l) of the entry relating to Schedule 4 to the Access to Justice Act 1999.
(4) In consequence of subsection (1), in section 1 of the Family Law Act 1996 (general principles underlying Part 2), in the words before paragraph (a) and in the title, for "Parts II and III" substitute " section 22 ".
(5) In consequence of subsection (3)(b)(i), in section 28. (11) of the Welfare Reform and Pensions Act 1999 (interpretation of subsections (4)(b), (5)(c) and (6)) for "subsections (4)(b), (5)(c) and" substitute " subsection ".
(6) The modifications set out in subsection (7), which were originally made by article 3. (2) of the No. 2 Order and article 4 of the No. 3 Order, are to continue to have effect but as amendments of the provisions concerned (rather than as modifications having effect until the coming into force of provisions of the Family Law Act 1996 repealed by this section without having come into force).
(7) The modifications are—
    (a) in section 22. (2) of the Matrimonial and Family Proceedings Act 1984 for the words from "if" to "granted" substitute " if a decree of divorce, a decree of nullity of marriage or a decree of judicial separation has been granted ", and
    (b) in section 31 of the Matrimonial Causes Act 1973—
(i) in subsection (7. D) for "Subsections (7) and (8) of section 22. A" substitute " Section 23. (6) ",
(ii) in subsection (7. D) for "section 22. A" substitute " section 23 ", and
(iii) in subsection (7. F) for "section 23. A" substitute " section 24 ".
(8) In section 31. (7. D) of the Matrimonial Causes Act 1973—
    (a) for "apply", in the first place, substitute " applies ", and
    (b) for "they apply where it" substitute " it applies where the court ".
(9) Articles 3. (2) and 4 of the No. 2 Order, and article 4 of the No. 3 Order, are revoked; and in subsection (6) and this subsection—
"the No. 2 Order" means the Family Law Act 1996 (Commencement No. 2) Order 1997 (S.I. 1997/1892), and
"the No. 3 Order" means the Family Law Act 1996 (Commencement No. 3) Order 1998 (S.I.

1998/2572).

PART 3. Children and young people in England with special educational needs or disabilities

PART 3 Children and young people in England with special educational needs or disabilities

Modifications etc. (not altering text)
C1. Pt. 3 modified (1.4.2015) by The Special Educational Needs and Disability (Detained Persons) Regulations 2015 (S.I. 2015/62), regs. 1, 31. (1), 32. (1)

19. Local authority functions: supporting and involving children and young people

In exercising a function under this Part in the case of a child or young person, a local authority in England must have regard to the following matters in particular—
　(a) the views, wishes and feelings of the child and his or her parent, or the young person;
　(b) the importance of the child and his or her parent, or the young person, participating as fully as possible in decisions relating to the exercise of the function concerned;
　(c) the importance of the child and his or her parent, or the young person, being provided with the information and support necessary to enable participation in those decisions;
　(d) the need to support the child and his or her parent, or the young person, in order to facilitate the development of the child or young person and to help him or her achieve the best possible educational and other outcomes.
Modifications etc. (not altering text)
C2. S. 19. (a)(b)(c)(d) modified (1.9.2014) by The Special Educational Needs and Disability Regulations 2014 (S.I. 2014/1530), regs. 1, 64. (1)(a), (2), Sch. 3 Pt. 1
Commencement Information
I1. S. 19 in force at 1.9.2014 by S.I. 2014/889, art. 7. (a) (with savings and transitional provisions in S.I. 2014/2270 (as amended (1.4.2015) by S.I. 2015/505 and (1.9.2015) by S.I. 2015/1619)

Special educational needs etc

20. When a child or young person has special educational needs

(1) A child or young person has special educational needs if he or she has a learning difficulty or disability which calls for special educational provision to be made for him or her.
(2) A child of compulsory school age or a young person has a learning difficulty or disability if he or she—
　(a) has a significantly greater difficulty in learning than the majority of others of the same age, or
　(b) has a disability which prevents or hinders him or her from making use of facilities of a kind generally provided for others of the same age in mainstream schools or mainstream post-16 institutions.
(3) A child under compulsory school age has a learning difficulty or disability if he or she is likely to be within subsection (2) when of compulsory school age (or would be likely, if no special

educational provision were made).

(4) A child or young person does not have a learning difficulty or disability solely because the language (or form of language) in which he or she is or will be taught is different from a language (or form of language) which is or has been spoken at home.

(5) This section applies for the purposes of this Part.

Commencement Information

I2. S. 20 in force at 1.9.2014 by S.I. 2014/889, art. 7. (a) (with savings and transitional provisions in S.I. 2014/2270 (as amended (1.4.2015) by S.I. 2015/505 and (1.9.2015) by S.I. 2015/1619)

21. Special educational provision, health care provision and social care provision

(1) "Special educational provision", for a child aged two or more or a young person, means educational or training provision that is additional to, or different from, that made generally for others of the same age in—
- (a) mainstream schools in England,
- (b) maintained nursery schools in England,
- (c) mainstream post-16 institutions in England, or
- (d) places in England at which relevant early years education is provided.

(2) "Special educational provision", for a child aged under two, means educational provision of any kind.

(3) "Health care provision" means the provision of health care services as part of the comprehensive health service in England continued under section 1. (1) of the National Health Service Act 2006.

(4) "Social care provision" means the provision made by a local authority in the exercise of its social services functions.

(5) Health care provision or social care provision which educates or trains a child or young person is to be treated as special educational provision (instead of health care provision or social care provision).

(6) This section applies for the purposes of this Part.

Commencement Information

I3. S. 21 in force at 1.9.2014 by S.I. 2014/889, art. 7. (a) (with savings and transitional provisions in S.I. 2014/2270 (as amended (1.4.2015) by S.I. 2015/505 and (1.9.2015) by S.I. 2015/1619)

Identifying children and young people with special educational needs and disabilities

22. Identifying children and young people with special educational needs and disabilities

A local authority in England must exercise its functions with a view to securing that it identifies—
- (a) all the children and young people in its area who have or may have special educational needs, and
- (b) all the children and young people in its area who have a disability.

Commencement Information

I4. S. 22 in force at 1.9.2014 by S.I. 2014/889, art. 7. (a) (with savings and transitional provisions in S.I. 2014/2270 (as amended (1.4.2015) by S.I. 2015/505 and (1.9.2015) by S.I. 2015/1619)

23. Duty of health bodies to bring certain children to local

authority's attention

(1) This section applies where, in the course of exercising functions in relation to a child who is under compulsory school age, a clinical commissioning group, NHS trust or NHS foundation trust form the opinion that the child has (or probably has) special educational needs or a disability.
(2) The group or trust must—
 (a) inform the child's parent of their opinion and of their duty under subsection (3), and
 (b) give the child's parent an opportunity to discuss their opinion with an officer of the group or trust.
(3) The group or trust must then bring their opinion to the attention of the appropriate local authority in England.
(4) If the group or trust think a particular voluntary organisation is likely to be able to give the parent advice or assistance in connection with any special educational needs or disability the child may have, they must inform the parent of that.
Commencement Information
I5. S. 23 in force at 1.9.2014 by S.I. 2014/889, art. 7. (a) (with savings and transitional provisions in S.I. 2014/2270 (as amended (1.4.2015) by S.I. 2015/505 and (1.9.2015) by S.I. 2015/1619)

Children and young people for whom a local authority is responsible

24. When a local authority is responsible for a child or young person

(1) A local authority in England is responsible for a child or young person if he or she is in the authority's area and has been—
 (a) identified by the authority as someone who has or may have special educational needs, or
 (b) brought to the authority's attention by any person as someone who has or may have special educational needs.
(2) This section applies for the purposes of this Part.
Commencement Information
I6. S. 24 in force at 1.9.2014 by S.I. 2014/889, art. 7. (a) (with savings and transitional provisions in S.I. 2014/2270 (as amended (1.4.2015) by S.I. 2015/505 and (1.9.2015) by S.I. 2015/1619)

Education, health and care provision: integration and joint commissioning

25. Promoting integration

(1) A local authority in England must exercise its functions under this Part with a view to ensuring the integration of educational provision and training provision with health care provision and social care provision, where it thinks that this would—
 (a) promote the well-being of children or young people in its area who have special educational needs or a disability, or
 (b) improve the quality of special educational provision—
(i) made in its area for children or young people who have special educational needs, or
(ii) made outside its area for children or young people for whom it is responsible who have special

educational needs.

(2) The reference in subsection (1) to the well-being of children and young people is to their well-being so far as relating to—

(a) physical and mental health and emotional well-being;
(b) protection from abuse and neglect;
(c) control by them over their day-to-day lives;
(d) participation in education, training or recreation;
(e) social and economic well-being;
(f) domestic, family and personal relationships;
(g) the contribution made by them to society.

Commencement Information

I7. S. 25 in force at 1.9.2014 by S.I. 2014/889, art. 7. (a) (with savings and transitional provisions in S.I. 2014/2270 (as amended (1.4.2015) by S.I. 2015/505 and (1.9.2015) by S.I. 2015/1619)

26. Joint commissioning arrangements

(1) A local authority in England and its partner commissioning bodies must make arrangements ("joint commissioning arrangements") about the education, health and care provision to be secured for—

(a) children and young people for whom the authority is responsible who have special educational needs, and
(b) children and young people in the authority's area who have a disability.

(2) In this Part "education, health and care provision" means—

(a) special educational provision;
(b) health care provision;
(c) social care provision.

(3) Joint commissioning arrangements must include arrangements for considering and agreeing—

(a) the education, health and care provision reasonably required by—
(i) the learning difficulties and disabilities which result in the children and young people within subsection (1)(a) having special educational needs, and
(ii) the disabilities of the children and young people within subsection (1)(b);
(b) what education, health and care provision is to be secured;
(c) by whom education, health and care provision is to be secured;
(d) what advice and information is to be provided about education, health and care provision;
(e) by whom, to whom and how such advice and information is to be provided;
(f) how complaints about education, health and care provision may be made and are to be dealt with;
(g) procedures for ensuring that disputes between the parties to the joint commissioning arrangements are resolved as quickly as possible.

(4) Joint commissioning arrangements about securing education, health and care provision must in particular include arrangements for—

(a) securing EHC needs assessments;
(b) securing the education, health and care provision specified in EHC plans;
(c) agreeing personal budgets under section 49.

(5) Joint commissioning arrangements may also include other provision.

(6) The parties to joint commissioning arrangements must—

(a) have regard to them in the exercise of their functions, and
(b) keep them under review.

(7) Section 116. B of the Local Government and Public Involvement in Health Act 2007 (duty to have regard to assessment of relevant needs and joint health and wellbeing strategy) applies in relation to functions exercisable under this section.

(8) A local authority's "partner commissioning bodies" are—

(a) the National Health Service Commissioning Board, to the extent that it is under a duty under section 3. B of the National Health Service Act 2006 to arrange for the provision of services or facilities for—
(i) any children and young people for whom the authority is responsible who have special educational needs, or
(ii) any children and young people in the authority's area who have a disability, and
(b) each clinical commissioning group that is under a duty under section 3 of that Act to arrange for the provision of services or facilities for any children and young people within paragraph (a).
(9) Regulations may prescribe circumstances in which a clinical commissioning group that would otherwise be a partner commissioning body of a local authority by virtue of subsection (8)(b) is to be treated as not being a partner commissioning body of the authority.
Commencement Information
I8. S. 26 in force at 1.9.2014 by S.I. 2014/889, art. 7. (a) (with savings and transitional provisions in S.I. 2014/2270 (as amended (1.4.2015) by S.I. 2015/505 and (1.9.2015) by S.I. 2015/1619)

Review of education and care provision

27. Duty to keep education and care provision under review

(1) A local authority in England must keep under review—
(a) the educational provision, training provision and social care provision made in its area for children and young people who have special educational needs or a disability, and
(b) the educational provision, training provision and social care provision made outside its area for—
(i) children and young people for whom it is responsible who have special educational needs, and
(ii) children and young people in its area who have a disability.
(2) The authority must consider the extent to which the provision referred to in subsection (1)(a) and (b) is sufficient to meet the educational needs, training needs and social care needs of the children and young people concerned.
(3) In exercising its functions under this section, the authority must consult—
(a) children and young people in its area with special educational needs, and the parents of children in its area with special educational needs;
(b) children and young people in its area who have a disability, and the parents of children in its area who have a disability;
(c) the governing bodies of maintained schools and maintained nursery schools in its area;
(d) the proprietors of Academies in its area;
(e) the governing bodies, proprietors or principals of post-16 institutions in its area;
(f) the governing bodies of non-maintained special schools in its area;
(g) the advisory boards of children's centres in its area;
(h) the providers of relevant early years education in its area;
(i) the governing bodies, proprietors or principals of other schools and post-16 institutions in England and Wales that the authority thinks are or are likely to be attended by—
(i) children or young people for whom it is responsible, or
(ii) children or young people in its area who have a disability;
(j) a youth offending team that the authority thinks has functions in relation to—
(i) children or young people for whom it is responsible, or
(ii) children or young people in its area who have a disability;
(k) such other persons as the authority thinks appropriate.
(4) Section 116. B of the Local Government and Public Involvement in Health Act 2007 (duty to have regard to assessment of relevant needs and joint health and wellbeing strategy) applies in relation to functions exercisable under this section.

(5) "Children's centre" has the meaning given by section 5. A(4) of the Childcare Act 2006.
Modifications etc. (not altering text)
C3. S. 27. (3)(a)(b) modified (1.9.2014) by The Special Educational Needs and Disability Regulations 2014 (S.I. 2014/1530), regs. 1, 64. (1)(a), 64. (2), Sch. 3 Pt. 1
Commencement Information
I9. S. 27 in force at 1.9.2014 by S.I. 2014/889, art. 7. (a) (with savings and transitional provisions in S.I. 2014/2270 (as amended (1.4.2015) by S.I. 2015/505 and (1.9.2015) by S.I. 2015/1619)

Co-operation and assistance

28. Co-operating generally: local authority functions

(1) A local authority in England must co-operate with each of its local partners, and each local partner must co-operate with the authority, in the exercise of the authority's functions under this Part.
(2) Each of the following is a local partner of a local authority in England for this purpose—
   (a) where the authority is a county council for an area for which there is also a district council, the district council;
   (b) the governing body of a maintained school or maintained nursery school that is maintained by the authority or provides education or training for children or young people for whom the authority is responsible;
   (c) the proprietor of an Academy that is in the authority's area or provides education or training for children or young people for whom the authority is responsible;
   (d) the proprietor of a non-maintained special school that is in the authority's area or provides education or training for children or young people for whom the authority is responsible;
   (e) the governing body of an institution within the further education sector that is in the authority's area, or is attended, or likely to be attended, by children or young people for whom the authority is responsible;
   (f) the management committee of a pupil referral unit that is in the authority's area, or is in England and is or is likely to be attended by children or young people for whom the authority is responsible;
   (g) the proprietor of an institution approved by the Secretary of State under section 41 (independent special schools and special post 16 institutions: approval) that is in the authority's area, or is attended, or likely to be attended, by children or young people for whom the authority is responsible;
   (h) any other person (other than a school or post-16 institution) that makes special educational provision for a child or young person for whom the authority is responsible;
   (i) a youth offending team that the authority thinks has functions in relation to children or young people for whom it is responsible;
   (j) a person in charge of relevant youth accommodation—
(i) in which there are detained persons aged 18 or under for whom the authority was responsible immediately before the beginning of their detention, or
(ii) that the authority thinks is accommodation in which such persons are likely to be detained;
   (k) the National Health Service Commissioning Board;
   (l) a clinical commissioning group—
(i) whose area coincides with, or falls wholly or partly within, the authority's area, or
(ii) which is under a duty under section 3 of the National Health Service Act 2006 to arrange for the provision of services or facilities for any children and young people for whom the authority is responsible;
   (m) an NHS trust or NHS foundation trust which provides services in the authority's area, or which exercises functions in relation to children or young people for whom the authority is

responsible;

(n) a Local Health Board which exercises functions in relation to children or young people for whom the authority is responsible.

(3) A local authority in England must make arrangements for ensuring co-operation between—

(a) the officers of the authority who exercise the authority's functions relating to education or training,

(b) the officers of the authority who exercise the authority's social services functions for children or young people with special educational needs, and

(c) the officers of the authority, so far as they are not officers within paragraph (a) or (b), who exercise the authority's functions relating to provision which is within section 30. (2)(e) (provision to assist in preparing children and young people for adulthood and independent living).

(4) Regulations may prescribe circumstances in which a clinical commissioning group that would otherwise be a local partner of a local authority by virtue of subsection (2)(l)(ii) is to be treated as not being a local partner of the authority.

Commencement Information

I10. S. 28 in force at 1.9.2014 by S.I. 2014/889, art. 7. (a) (with savings and transitional provisions in S.I. 2014/2270 (as amended (1.4.2015) by S.I. 2015/505 and (1.9.2015) by S.I. 2015/1619)

29. Co-operating generally: governing body functions

(1) This section applies where an appropriate authority for a school or post-16 institution mentioned in subsection (2) has functions under this Part.

(2) The schools and post-16 institutions referred to in subsection (1) are—

(a) mainstream schools;
(b) maintained nursery schools;
(c) 16 to 19 Academies;
(d) institutions within the further education sector;
(e) pupil referral units;
(f) alternative provision Academies.

(3) The appropriate authority must co-operate with each responsible local authority, and each responsible local authority must co-operate with the appropriate authority, in the exercise of those functions.

(4) A responsible local authority, in relation to an appropriate authority for a school or post-16 institution mentioned in subsection (2), is a local authority in England that is responsible for any child or young person who is a registered pupil or a student at the school or post-16 institution.

(5) The "appropriate authority" for a school or post-16 institution is—

(a) in the case of a maintained school, maintained nursery school, or institution within the further education sector, the governing body;

(b) in the case of an Academy, the proprietor;

(c) in the case of a pupil referral unit, the management committee.

Commencement Information

I11. S. 29 in force at 1.9.2014 by S.I. 2014/889, art. 7. (a) (with savings and transitional provisions in S.I. 2014/2270 (as amended (1.4.2015) by S.I. 2015/505 and (1.9.2015) by S.I. 2015/1619)

Information and advice

30. Local offer

(1) A local authority in England must publish information about—

(a) the provision within subsection (2) it expects to be available in its area at the time of publication for children and young people who have special educational needs or a disability, and

(b) the provision within subsection (2) it expects to be available outside its area at that time for—

(i) children and young people for whom it is responsible, and

(ii) children and young people in its area who have a disability.

(2) The provision for children and young people referred to in subsection (1) is—

(a) education, health and care provision;
(b) other educational provision;
(c) other training provision;
(d) arrangements for travel to and from schools and post-16 institutions and places at which relevant early years education is provided;
(e) provision to assist in preparing children and young people for adulthood and independent living.

(3) For the purposes of subsection (2)(e), provision to assist in preparation for adulthood and independent living includes provision relating to—

(a) finding employment;
(b) obtaining accommodation;
(c) participation in society.

(4) Information required to be published by an authority under this section is to be known as its "local offer".

(5) A local authority must keep its local offer under review and may from time to time revise it.

(6) A local authority must from time to time publish—

(a) comments about its local offer it has received from or on behalf of—

(i) children and young people with special educational needs, and the parents of children with special educational needs, and

(ii) children and young people who have a disability, and the parents of children who have a disability, and

(b) the authority's response to those comments (including details of any action the authority intends to take).

(7) Comments published under subsection (6)(a) must be published in a form that does not enable the person making them to be identified.

(8) Regulations may make provision about—

(a) the information to be included in an authority's local offer;
(b) how an authority's local offer is to be published;
(c) who is to be consulted by an authority in preparing and reviewing its local offer;
(d) how an authority is to involve—

(i) children and young people with special educational needs, and the parents of children with special educational needs, and

(ii) children and young people who have a disability, and the parents of children who have a disability,

in the preparation and review of its local offer;

(e) the publication of comments on the local offer, and the local authority's response, under subsection (6) (including circumstances in which comments are not required to be published).

(9) The regulations may in particular require an authority's local offer to include—

(a) information about how to obtain an EHC needs assessment;
(b) information about other sources of information, advice and support for—

(i) children and young people with special educational needs and those who care for them, and

(ii) children and young people who have a disability and those who care for them;

(c) information about gaining access to provision additional to, or different from, the provision mentioned in subsection (2);

(d) information about how to make a complaint about provision mentioned in subsection (2).

Modifications etc. (not altering text)

C4. S. 30. (6)(a)(i)(ii) modified (1.9.2014) by The Special Educational Needs and Disability

Regulations 2014 (S.I. 2014/1530), regs. 1, 64. (1)(a), 64. (2), Sch. 3 Pt. 1
C5. S. 30. (8)(d)(i)(ii) modified (1.9.2014) by The Special Educational Needs and Disability Regulations 2014 (S.I. 2014/1530), regs. 1, 64. (1)(a), 64. (2), Sch. 3 Pt. 1
Commencement Information
I12. S. 30 in force at 1.4.2014 for specified purposes by S.I. 2014/889, art. 3. (a)
I13. S. 30 in force at 1.9.2014 in so far as not already in force by S.I. 2014/889, art. 7. (a) (with savings and transitional provisions in S.I. 2014/2270 (as amended (1.4.2015) by S.I. 2015/505 and (1.9.2015) by S.I. 2015/1619)

31. Co-operating in specific cases: local authority functions

(1) This section applies where a local authority in England requests the co-operation of any of the following persons and bodies in the exercise of a function under this Part—
    (a) another local authority;
    (b) a youth offending team;
    (c) the person in charge of any relevant youth accommodation;
    (d) the National Health Service Commissioning Board;
    (e) a clinical commissioning group;
    (f) a Local Health Board;
    (g) an NHS trust or NHS foundation trust.
(2) The person or body must comply with the request, unless the person or body considers that doing so would—
    (a) be incompatible with the duties of the person or body, or
    (b) otherwise have an adverse effect on the exercise of the functions of the person or body.
(3) A person or body that decides not to comply with a request under subsection (1) must give the authority that made the request written reasons for the decision.
(4) Regulations may provide that, where a person or body is under a duty to comply with a request to co-operate with a local authority in securing an EHC needs assessment, a detained person's EHC needs assessment or the preparation of an EHC plan, the person or body must comply with the request within a prescribed period, unless a prescribed exception applies.
Commencement Information
I14. S. 31 in force at 1.4.2014 for specified purposes by S.I. 2014/889, art. 3. (a)
I15. S. 31 in force at 1.9.2014 in so far as not already in force by S.I. 2014/889, art. 7. (a) (with savings and transitional provisions in S.I. 2014/2270 (as amended (1.4.2015) by S.I. 2015/505 and (1.9.2015) by S.I. 2015/1619)

32. Advice and information

(1) A local authority in England must arrange for children and young people for whom it is responsible, and the parents of children for whom it is responsible, to be provided with advice and information about matters relating to the special educational needs of the children or young people concerned.
(2) A local authority in England must arrange for children and young people in its area with a disability, and the parents of children in its area with a disability, to be provided with advice and information about matters relating to the disabilities of the children or young people concerned.
(3) The authority must take such steps as it thinks appropriate for making the services provided under subsections (1) and (2) known to—
    (a) the parents of children in its area;
    (b) children in its area;
    (c) young people in its area;
    (d) the head teachers, proprietors and principals of schools and post-16 institutions in its area.
(4) The authority may also take such steps as it thinks appropriate for making the services

provided under subsections (1) and (2) known to such other persons as it thinks appropriate.
Modifications etc. (not altering text)
C6. S. 32. (1)(2) modified (1.9.2014) by The Special Educational Needs and Disability Regulations 2014 (S.I. 2014/1530), regs. 1, 64. (1)(a), 64. (2), Sch. 3 Pt. 1
C7. S. 32. (3)(c) modified (1.9.2014) by The Special Educational Needs and Disability Regulations 2014 (S.I. 2014/1530), regs. 1, 64. (1)(a), 64. (2), Sch. 3 Pt. 1
Commencement Information
I16. S. 32 in force at 1.9.2014 by S.I. 2014/889, art. 7. (a) (with savings and transitional provisions in S.I. 2014/2270 (as amended (1.4.2015) by S.I. 2015/505 and (1.9.2015) by S.I. 2015/1619)

Mainstream education

33. Children and young people with EHC plans

(1) This section applies where a local authority is securing the preparation of an EHC plan for a child or young person who is to be educated in a school or post-16 institution.
(2) In a case within section 39. (5) or 40. (2), the local authority must secure that the plan provides for the child or young person to be educated in a maintained nursery school, mainstream school or mainstream post-16 institution, unless that is incompatible with—
   (a) the wishes of the child's parent or the young person, or
   (b) the provision of efficient education for others.
(3) A local authority may rely on the exception in subsection (2)(b) in relation to maintained nursery schools, mainstream schools or mainstream post-16 institutions in its area taken as a whole only if it shows that there are no reasonable steps that it could take to prevent the incompatibility.
(4) A local authority may rely on the exception in subsection (2)(b) in relation to a particular maintained nursery school, mainstream school or mainstream post-16 institution only if it shows that there are no reasonable steps that it or the governing body, proprietor or principal could take to prevent the incompatibility.
(5) The governing body, proprietor or principal of a maintained nursery school, mainstream school or mainstream post-16 institution may rely on the exception in subsection (2)(b) only if they show that there are no reasonable steps that they or the local authority could take to prevent the incompatibility.
(6) Subsection (2) does not prevent the child or young person from being educated in an independent school, a non-maintained special school or a special post-16 institution, if the cost is not to be met by a local authority or the Secretary of State.
(7) This section does not affect the operation of section 63 (fees payable by local authority for special educational provision at non-maintained schools and post-16 institutions).
Modifications etc. (not altering text)
C8. S. 33. (2)(a) modified (1.9.2014) by The Special Educational Needs and Disability Regulations 2014 (S.I. 2014/1530), regs. 1, 64. (1)(b), 64. (2), Sch. 3 Pt. 2
Commencement Information
I17. S. 33 in force at 1.9.2014 by S.I. 2014/889, art. 7. (a) (with savings and transitional provisions in S.I. 2014/2270 (as amended (1.4.2015) by S.I. 2015/505 and (1.9.2015) by S.I. 2015/1619)

34. Children and young people with special educational needs but no EHC plan

(1) This section applies to a child or young person in England who has special educational needs but for whom no EHC plan is maintained, if he or she is to be educated in a school or post-16

institution.

(2) The child or young person must be educated in a maintained nursery school, mainstream school or mainstream post-16 institution, subject to subsections (3) and (4).

(3) The child or young person may be educated in an independent school, a non-maintained special school or a special post-16 institution, if the cost is not to be met by a local authority or the Secretary of State.

(4) The child or young person may be educated in a special school or special post-16 institution during any period in which any of subsections (5) to (9) applies.

(5) This subsection applies while the child or young person is admitted to a special school or special post-16 institution for the purposes of an EHC needs assessment, if all the following have agreed to his or her admission to the school or post-16 institution—

(a) the local authority which is responsible for him or her;
(b) the head teacher of the school or the principal of the Academy or post-16 institution;
(c) the child's parent or the young person;
(d) anyone else whose advice is required to be obtained in connection with the assessment by virtue of regulations under section 36. (11).

(6) This subsection applies while the child or young person remains admitted to a special school or special post-16 institution, in prescribed circumstances, following an EHC needs assessment at the school or post-16 institution.

(7) This subsection applies while the child or young person is admitted to a special school or special post-16 institution, following a change in his or her circumstances, if all the following have agreed to his or her admission to the school or post-16 institution—

(a) the local authority which is responsible for him or her;
(b) the head teacher of the school or the principal of the Academy or post-16 institution;
(c) the child's parent or the young person.

(8) This subsection applies while the child or young person is admitted to a special school which is established in a hospital and is—

(a) a community or foundation special school, or
(b) an Academy school.

(9) This subsection applies while the child is admitted to a special school or special post-16 institution that is an Academy, if the Academy arrangements made in respect of the school or post-16 institution permit it to admit children and young people with special educational needs for whom no EHC plan is maintained.

(10) This section does not affect the operation of section 63 (fees payable by local authority for special educational provision at non-maintained schools and post-16 institutions).

Modifications etc. (not altering text)

C9. S. 34. (5)(c)(7)(c) modified (1.9.2014) by The Special Educational Needs and Disability Regulations 2014 (S.I. 2014/1530), regs. 1, 64. (1)(b), 64. (2), Sch. 3 Pt. 2

Commencement Information

I18. S. 34 in force at 1.4.2014 for specified purposes by S.I. 2014/889, art. 3. (b)

I19. S. 34 in force at 1.9.2014 in so far as not already in force by S.I. 2014/889, art. 7. (a) (with savings and transitional provisions in S.I. 2014/2270 (as amended (1.4.2015) by S.I. 2015/505 and (1.9.2015) by S.I. 2015/1619)

35. Children with SEN in maintained nurseries and mainstream schools

(1) This section applies where a child with special educational needs is being educated in a maintained nursery school or a mainstream school.

(2) Those concerned with making special educational provision for the child must secure that the child engages in the activities of the school together with children who do not have special educational needs, subject to subsection (3).

(3) Subsection (2) applies only so far as is reasonably practicable and is compatible with—
    (a) the child receiving the special educational provision called for by his or her special educational needs,
    (b) the provision of efficient education for the children with whom he or she will be educated, and
    (c) the efficient use of resources.

Commencement Information

I20. S. 35 in force at 1.9.2014 by S.I. 2014/889, art. 7. (a) (with savings and transitional provisions in S.I. 2014/2270 (as amended (1.4.2015) by S.I. 2015/505 and (1.9.2015) by S.I. 2015/1619)

Assessment

36. Assessment of education, health and care needs

(1) A request for a local authority in England to secure an EHC needs assessment for a child or young person may be made to the authority by the child's parent, the young person or a person acting on behalf of a school or post-16 institution.

(2) An "EHC needs assessment" is an assessment of the educational, health care and social care needs of a child or young person.

(3) When a request is made to a local authority under subsection (1), or a local authority otherwise becomes responsible for a child or young person, the authority must determine whether it may be necessary for special educational provision to be made for the child or young person in accordance with an EHC plan.

(4) In making a determination under subsection (3), the local authority must consult the child's parent or the young person.

(5) Where the local authority determines that it is not necessary for special educational provision to be made for the child or young person in accordance with an EHC plan it must notify the child's parent or the young person—
    (a) of the reasons for that determination, and
    (b) that accordingly it has decided not to secure an EHC needs assessment for the child or young person.

(6) Subsection (7) applies where—
    (a) no EHC plan is maintained for the child or young person,
    (b) the child or young person has not been assessed under this section or section 71 during the previous six months, and
    (c) the local authority determines that it may be necessary for special educational provision to be made for the child or young person in accordance with an EHC plan.

(7) The authority must notify the child's parent or the young person—
    (a) that it is considering securing an EHC needs assessment for the child or young person, and
    (b) that the parent or young person has the right to—
(i) express views to the authority (orally or in writing), and
(ii) submit evidence to the authority.

(8) The local authority must secure an EHC needs assessment for the child or young person if, after having regard to any views expressed and evidence submitted under subsection (7), the authority is of the opinion that—
    (a) the child or young person has or may have special educational needs, and
    (b) it may be necessary for special educational provision to be made for the child or young person in accordance with an EHC plan.

(9) After an EHC needs assessment has been carried out, the local authority must notify the child's parent or the young person of—
    (a) the outcome of the assessment,

(b) whether it proposes to secure that an EHC plan is prepared for the child or young person, and

(c) the reasons for that decision.

(10) In making a determination or forming an opinion for the purposes of this section in relation to a young person aged over 18, a local authority must consider whether he or she requires additional time, in comparison to the majority of others of the same age who do not have special educational needs, to complete his or her education or training.

(11) Regulations may make provision about EHC needs assessments, in particular—

(a) about requests under subsection (1);

(b) imposing time limits in relation to consultation under subsection (4);

(c) about giving notice;

(d) about expressing views and submitting evidence under subsection (7);

(e) about how assessments are to be conducted;

(f) about advice to be obtained in connection with an assessment;

(g) about combining an EHC needs assessment with other assessments;

(h) about the use for the purposes of an EHC needs assessment of information obtained as a result of other assessments;

(i) about the use of information obtained as a result of an EHC needs assessment, including the use of that information for the purposes of other assessments;

(j) about the provision of information, advice and support in connection with an EHC needs assessment.

Modifications etc. (not altering text)

C10. S. 36 modified by 2002 c. 41, s. 36. (9)(aa) (as inserted (1.9.2014) by Children and Families Act 2014 (c. 6), s. 139. (6), Sch. 3 para. 79. (7); S.I. 2014/889, art. 7. (a))

C11. S. 36. (1)(4)(5)(7)(9) modified (1.9.2014) by The Special Educational Needs and Disability Regulations 2014 (S.I. 2014/1530), regs. 1, 64. (1)(b), 64. (2), Sch. 3 Pt. 2

Commencement Information

I21. S. 36 in force at 1.4.2014 for specified purposes by S.I. 2014/889, art. 3. (c)

I22. S. 36 in force at 1.9.2014 in so far as not already in force by S.I. 2014/889, art. 7. (a) (with savings and transitional provisions in S.I. 2014/2270 (as amended (1.4.2015) by S.I. 2015/505 and (1.9.2015) by S.I. 2015/1619)

Education, health and care plans

37. Education, health and care plans

(1) Where, in the light of an EHC needs assessment, it is necessary for special educational provision to be made for a child or young person in accordance with an EHC plan—

(a) the local authority must secure that an EHC plan is prepared for the child or young person, and

(b) once an EHC plan has been prepared, it must maintain the plan.

(2) For the purposes of this Part, an EHC plan is a plan specifying—

(a) the child's or young person's special educational needs;

(b) the outcomes sought for him or her;

(c) the special educational provision required by him or her;

(d) any health care provision reasonably required by the learning difficulties and disabilities which result in him or her having special educational needs;

(e) in the case of a child or a young person aged under 18, any social care provision which must be made for him or her by the local authority as a result of section 2 of the Chronically Sick and Disabled Persons Act 1970 F1...;

(f) any social care provision reasonably required by the learning difficulties and disabilities

which result in the child or young person having special educational needs, to the extent that the provision is not already specified in the plan under paragraph (e).
(3) An EHC plan may also specify other health care and social care provision reasonably required by the child or young person.
(4) Regulations may make provision about the preparation, content, maintenance, amendment and disclosure of EHC plans.
(5) Regulations under subsection (4) about amendments of EHC plans must include provision applying section 33 (mainstream education for children and young people with EHC plans) to a case where an EHC plan is to be amended under those regulations.
Amendments (Textual)
F1. Words in s. 37. (2)(e) omitted (1.4.2015) by virtue of The Care Act 2014 and Children and Families Act 2014 (Consequential Amendments) Order 2015 (S.I. 2015/914), art. 1. (2), Sch. para. 97 (with arts. 1. (3), 3)
Commencement Information
I23. S. 37 in force at 1.4.2014 for specified purposes by S.I. 2014/889, art. 3. (c)
I24. S. 37 in force at 1.9.2014 in so far as not already in force by S.I. 2014/889, art. 7. (a) (with savings and transitional provisions in S.I. 2014/2270 (as amended (1.4.2015) by S.I. 2015/505 and (1.9.2015) by S.I. 2015/1619)

38. Preparation of EHC plans: draft plan

(1) Where a local authority is required to secure that an EHC plan is prepared for a child or young person, it must consult the child's parent or the young person about the content of the plan during the preparation of a draft of the plan.
(2) The local authority must then—
    (a) send the draft plan to the child's parent or the young person, and
    (b) give the parent or young person notice of his or her right to—
(i) make representations about the content of the draft plan, and
(ii) request the authority to secure that a particular school or other institution within subsection (3) is named in the plan.
(3) A school or other institution is within this subsection if it is—
    (a) a maintained school;
    (b) a maintained nursery school;
    (c) an Academy;
    (d) an institution within the further education sector in England;
    (e) a non-maintained special school;
    (f) an institution approved by the Secretary of State under section 41 (independent special schools and special post-16 institutions: approval).
(4) A notice under subsection (2)(b) must specify a period before the end of which any representations or requests must be made.
(5) The draft EHC plan sent to the child's parent or the young person must not—
    (a) name a school or other institution, or
    (b) specify a type of school or other institution.
Modifications etc. (not altering text)
C12. S. 38. (1)(2)(a)(b)(5) modified (1.9.2014) by The Special Educational Needs and Disability Regulations 2014 (S.I. 2014/1530), regs. 1, 64. (1)(b), 64. (2), Sch. 3 Pt. 2
Commencement Information
I25. S. 38 in force at 1.9.2014 by S.I. 2014/889, art. 7. (a) (with savings and transitional provisions in S.I. 2014/2270 (as amended (1.4.2015) by S.I. 2015/505 and (1.9.2015) by S.I. 2015/1619)

39. Finalising EHC plans: request for particular school or other

institution

(1) This section applies where, before the end of the period specified in a notice under section 38. (2)(b), a request is made to a local authority to secure that a particular school or other institution is named in an EHC plan.

(2) The local authority must consult—

(a) the governing body, proprietor or principal of the school or other institution,

(b) the governing body, proprietor or principal of any other school or other institution the authority is considering having named in the plan, and

(c) if a school or other institution is within paragraph (a) or (b) and is maintained by another local authority, that authority.

(3) The local authority must secure that the EHC plan names the school or other institution specified in the request, unless subsection (4) applies.

(4) This subsection applies where—

(a) the school or other institution requested is unsuitable for the age, ability, aptitude or special educational needs of the child or young person concerned, or

(b) the attendance of the child or young person at the requested school or other institution would be incompatible with—

(i) the provision of efficient education for others, or

(ii) the efficient use of resources.

(5) Where subsection (4) applies, the local authority must secure that the plan—

(a) names a school or other institution which the local authority thinks would be appropriate for the child or young person, or

(b) specifies the type of school or other institution which the local authority thinks would be appropriate for the child or young person.

(6) Before securing that the plan names a school or other institution under subsection (5)(a), the local authority must (if it has not already done so) consult—

(a) the governing body, proprietor or principal of any school or other institution the authority is considering having named in the plan, and

(b) if that school or other institution is maintained by another local authority, that authority.

(7) The local authority must, at the end of the period specified in the notice under section 38. (2)(b), secure that any changes it thinks necessary are made to the draft EHC plan.

(8) The local authority must send a copy of the finalised EHC plan to—

(a) the child's parent or the young person, and

(b) the governing body, proprietor or principal of any school or other institution named in the plan.

Modifications etc. (not altering text)

C13. S. 39. (8)(a) modified (1.9.2014) by The Special Educational Needs and Disability Regulations 2014 (S.I. 2014/1530), regs. 1, 64. (1)(b), 64. (2), Sch. 3 Pt. 2

Commencement Information

I26. S. 39 in force at 1.9.2014 by S.I. 2014/889, art. 7. (a) (with savings and transitional provisions in S.I. 2014/2270 (as amended (1.4.2015) by S.I. 2015/505 and (1.9.2015) by S.I. 2015/1619)

40. Finalising EHC plans: no request for particular school or other institution

(1) This section applies where no request is made to a local authority before the end of the period specified in a notice under section 38. (2)(b) to secure that a particular school or other institution is named in an EHC plan.

(2) The local authority must secure that the plan—

(a) names a school or other institution which the local authority thinks would be appropriate for the child or young person concerned, or

(b) specifies the type of school or other institution which the local authority thinks would be appropriate for the child or young person.

(3) Before securing that the plan names a school or other institution under subsection (2)(a), the local authority must consult—

(a) the governing body, proprietor or principal of any school or other institution the authority is considering having named in the plan, and

(b) if that school or other institution is maintained by another local authority, that authority.

(4) The local authority must also secure that any changes it thinks necessary are made to the draft EHC plan.

(5) The local authority must send a copy of the finalised EHC plan to—

(a) the child's parent or the young person, and

(b) the governing body, proprietor or principal of any school or other institution named in the plan.

Modifications etc. (not altering text)

C14. S. 40. (5)(a) modified (1.9.2014) by The Special Educational Needs and Disability Regulations 2014 (S.I. 2014/1530), regs. 1, 64. (1)(b), 64. (2), Sch. 3 Pt. 2

Commencement Information

I27. S. 40 in force at 1.9.2014 by S.I. 2014/889, art. 7. (a) (with savings and transitional provisions in S.I. 2014/2270 (as amended (1.4.2015) by S.I. 2015/505 and (1.9.2015) by S.I. 2015/1619)

41. Independent special schools and special post-16 institutions: approval

(1) The Secretary of State may approve an institution within subsection (2) for the purpose of enabling the institution to be the subject of a request for it to be named in an EHC plan.

(2) An institution is within this subsection if it is—

(a) an independent educational institution (within the meaning of Chapter 1 of Part 4 of ESA 2008)—

(i) which has been entered on the register of independent educational institutions in England (kept under section 95 of that Act), and

(ii) which is specially organised to make special educational provision for students with special educational needs,

(b) an independent school—

(i) which has been entered on the register of independent schools in Wales (kept under section 158 of the Education Act 2002), and

(ii) which is specially organised to make special educational provision for pupils with special educational needs, or

(c) a special post-16 institution which is not an institution within the further education sector or a 16 to 19 Academy.

(3) The Secretary of State may approve an institution under subsection (1) only if its proprietor consents.

(4) The Secretary of State may withdraw approval given under subsection (1).

(5) Regulations may make provision about giving and withdrawing approval under this section, in particular—

(a) about the types of special post-16 institutions which may be approved under subsection (1);

(b) specifying criteria which an institution must meet before it can be approved under subsection (1);

(c) about the matters which may or must be taken into account in deciding to give or withdraw approval;

(d) about the publication of a list of all institutions who are approved under this section.

Commencement Information

I28. S. 41 in force at 1.4.2014 for specified purposes by S.I. 2014/889, art. 3. (d)
I29. S. 41 in force at 1.9.2014 in so far as not already in force by S.I. 2014/889, art. 7. (a) (with savings and transitional provisions in S.I. 2014/2270 (as amended (1.4.2015) by S.I. 2015/505 and (1.9.2015) by S.I. 2015/1619)

42. Duty to secure special educational provision and health care provision in accordance with EHC Plan

(1) This section applies where a local authority maintains an EHC plan for a child or young person.
(2) The local authority must secure the specified special educational provision for the child or young person.
(3) If the plan specifies health care provision, the responsible commissioning body must arrange the specified health care provision for the child or young person.
(4) "The responsible commissioning body", in relation to any specified health care provision, means the body (or each body) that is under a duty to arrange health care provision of that kind in respect of the child or young person.
(5) Subsections (2) and (3) do not apply if the child's parent or the young person has made suitable alternative arrangements.
(6) "Specified", in relation to an EHC plan, means specified in the plan.
Modifications etc. (not altering text)
C15. S. 42. (5) modified (1.9.2014) by The Special Educational Needs and Disability Regulations 2014 (S.I. 2014/1530), regs. 1, 64. (1)(b), 64. (2), Sch. 3 Pt. 2
Commencement Information
I30. S. 42 in force at 1.9.2014 by S.I. 2014/889, art. 7. (a) (with savings and transitional provisions in S.I. 2014/2270 (as amended (1.4.2015) by S.I. 2015/505 and (1.9.2015) by S.I. 2015/1619)

43. Schools and other institutions named in EHC plan: duty to admit

(1) Subsection (2) applies if one of the following is named in an EHC plan—
    (a) a maintained school;
    (b) a maintained nursery school;
    (c) an Academy;
    (d) an institution within the further education sector in England;
    (e) a non-maintained special school;
    (f) an institution approved by the Secretary of State under section 41.
(2) The governing body, proprietor or principal of the school or other institution must admit the child or young person for whom the plan is maintained.
(3) Subsection (2) has effect regardless of any duty imposed on the governing body of a school by section 1. (6) of SSFA 1998.
(4) Subsection (2) does not affect any power to exclude a pupil or student from a school or other institution.
Commencement Information
I31. S. 43 in force at 1.9.2014 by S.I. 2014/889, art. 7. (a) (with savings and transitional provisions in S.I. 2014/2270 (as amended (1.4.2015) by S.I. 2015/505 and (1.9.2015) by S.I. 2015/1619)

44. Reviews and re-assessments

(1) A local authority must review an EHC plan that it maintains—
    (a) in the period of 12 months starting with the date on which the plan was first made, and

(b) in each subsequent period of 12 months starting with the date on which the plan was last reviewed under this section.

(2) A local authority must secure a re-assessment of the educational, health care and social care needs of a child or young person for whom it maintains an EHC plan if a request is made to it by—

(a) the child's parent or the young person, or

(b) the governing body, proprietor or principal of the school, post-16 institution or other institution which the child or young person attends.

(3) A local authority may also secure a re-assessment of those needs at any other time if it thinks it necessary.

(4) Subsections (1) and (2) are subject to any contrary provision in regulations made under subsection (7)(b).

(5) In reviewing an EHC plan maintained for a young person aged over 18, or deciding whether to secure a re-assessment of the needs of such a young person, a local authority must have regard to whether the educational or training outcomes specified in the plan have been achieved.

(6) During a review or re-assessment, a local authority must consult the parent of the child, or the young person, for whom it maintains the EHC plan.

(7) Regulations may make provision about reviews and re-assessments, in particular—

(a) about other circumstances in which a local authority must or may review an EHC plan or secure a re-assessment (including before the end of a specified phase of a child's or young person's education);

(b) about circumstances in which it is not necessary for a local authority to review an EHC plan or secure a re-assessment;

(c) about amending or replacing an EHC plan following a review or re-assessment.

(8) Regulations under subsection (7) about re-assessments may in particular apply provisions of or made under this Part that are applicable to EHC needs assessments, with or without modifications.

(9) Regulations under subsection (7)(c) must include provision applying section 33 (mainstream education for children and young people with EHC plans) to a case where an EHC plan is to be amended following a review.

Modifications etc. (not altering text)

C16. S. 44. (2)(a)(6) modified (1.9.2014) by The Special Educational Needs and Disability Regulations 2014 (S.I. 2014/1530), regs. 1, 64. (1)(b), 64. (2), Sch. 3 Pt. 2

Commencement Information

I32. S. 44 in force at 1.4.2014 for specified purposes by S.I. 2014/889, art. 3. (e)

I33. S. 44 in force at 1.9.2014 in so far as not already in force by S.I. 2014/889, art. 7. (a) (with savings and transitional provisions in S.I. 2014/2270 (as amended (1.4.2015) by S.I. 2015/505 and (1.9.2015) by S.I. 2015/1619)

45. Ceasing to maintain an EHC plan

(1) A local authority may cease to maintain an EHC plan for a child or young person only if—

(a) the authority is no longer responsible for the child or young person, or

(b) the authority determines that it is no longer necessary for the plan to be maintained.

(2) The circumstances in which it is no longer necessary for an EHC plan to be maintained for a child or young person include where the child or young person no longer requires the special educational provision specified in the plan.

(3) When determining whether a young person aged over 18 no longer requires the special educational provision specified in his or her EHC plan, a local authority must have regard to whether the educational or training outcomes specified in the plan have been achieved.

(4) A local authority may not cease to maintain an EHC plan for a child or young person until—

(a) after the end of the period allowed for bringing an appeal under section 51 against its decision to cease to maintain the plan, where no such appeal is brought before the end of that period;

(b) after the appeal has been finally determined, where such an appeal is brought before the end of that period.

(5) Regulations may make provision about ceasing to maintain an EHC plan, in particular about—

(a) other circumstances in which it is no longer necessary for an EHC plan to be maintained;

(b) circumstances in which a local authority may not determine that it is no longer necessary for an EHC plan to be maintained;

(c) the procedure to be followed by a local authority when determining whether to cease to maintain an EHC plan.

Commencement Information

I34. S. 45 in force at 1.4.2014 for specified purposes by S.I. 2014/889, art. 3. (e)

I35. S. 45 in force at 1.9.2014 in so far as not already in force by S.I. 2014/889, art. 7. (a) (with savings and transitional provisions in S.I. 2014/2270 (as amended (1.4.2015) by S.I. 2015/505 and (1.9.2015) by S.I. 2015/1619)

46. Maintaining an EHC plan after young person's 25th birthday

(1) A local authority may continue to maintain an EHC plan for a young person until the end of the academic year during which the young person attains the age of 25.

(2) "Academic year" means the period of twelve months ending on the prescribed date.

Commencement Information

I36. S. 46 in force at 1.4.2014 for specified purposes by S.I. 2014/889, art. 3. (e)

I37. S. 46 in force at 1.9.2014 in so far as not already in force by S.I. 2014/889, art. 7. (a) (with savings and transitional provisions in S.I. 2014/2270 (as amended (1.4.2015) by S.I. 2015/505 and (1.9.2015) by S.I. 2015/1619)

47. Transfer of EHC plans

(1) Regulations may make provision for an EHC plan maintained for a child or young person by one local authority to be transferred to another local authority in England, where the other authority becomes responsible for the child or young person.

(2) The regulations may in particular—

(a) impose a duty on the other authority to maintain the plan;

(b) treat the plan as if originally prepared by the other authority;

(c) treat things done by the transferring authority in relation to the plan as done by the other authority.

Commencement Information

I38. S. 47 in force at 1.4.2014 for specified purposes by S.I. 2014/889, art. 3. (e)

I39. S. 47 in force at 1.9.2014 in so far as not already in force by S.I. 2014/889, art. 7. (a) (with savings and transitional provisions in S.I. 2014/2270 (as amended (1.4.2015) by S.I. 2015/505 and (1.9.2015) by S.I. 2015/1619)

48. Release of child or young person for whom EHC plan previously maintained

(1) This section applies where—

(a) a child or young person who has been subject to a detention order (within the meaning of section 562. (1. A)(a) of EA 1996) is released,

(b) on the release date, a local authority in England becomes responsible for him or her, and

(c) an EHC plan was—

(i) maintained for him or her immediately before the start of the detention, or

(ii) kept for him or her under section 74 during the detention.
(2) The local authority must—
    (a) maintain the plan, and
    (b) review the plan as soon as reasonably practicable after the release date.
(3) Subsection (2)(b) is subject to any contrary provision in regulations under section 44. (7)(b).
Commencement Information
140. S. 48 in force at 1.9.2014 by S.I. 2014/889, art. 7. (a) (with savings and transitional provisions in S.I. 2014/2270 (as amended (1.4.2015) by S.I. 2015/505 and (1.9.2015) by S.I. 2015/1619)

49. Personal budgets and direct payments

(1) A local authority that maintains an EHC plan, or is securing the preparation of an EHC plan, for a child or young person must prepare a personal budget for him or her if asked to do so by the child's parent or the young person.
(2) The authority prepares a "personal budget" for the child or young person if it identifies an amount as available to secure particular provision that is specified, or proposed to be specified, in the EHC plan, with a view to the child's parent or the young person being involved in securing the provision.
(3) Regulations may make provision about personal budgets, in particular—
    (a) about requests for personal budgets;
    (b) about the amount of a personal budget;
    (c) about the sources of the funds making up a personal budget;
    (d) for payments ("direct payments") representing all or part of a personal budget to be made to a child's parent or a young person, or a person of a prescribed description in prescribed circumstances, in order to secure provision to which the budget relates;
    (e) about the description of provision to which personal budgets and direct payments may (and may not) relate;
    (f) for a personal budget or direct payment to cover the agreed cost of the provision to which the budget or payment relates;
    (g) about when, how, to whom and on what conditions direct payments may (and may not) be made;
    (h) about when direct payments may be required to be repaid and the recovery of unpaid sums;
    (i) about conditions with which a person or body making direct payments must comply before, after or at the time of making a direct payment;
    (j) about arrangements for providing information, advice or support in connection with personal budgets and direct payments.
(4) If the regulations include provision authorising direct payments, they must—
    (a) require the consent of a child's parent or a young person, or a person of a prescribed description in prescribed circumstances, to be obtained before direct payments are made;
    (b) require the authority to stop making direct payments where the required consent is withdrawn.
(5) Special educational provision acquired by means of a direct payment made by a local authority is to be treated as having been secured by the authority in pursuance of its duty under section 42. (2), subject to any prescribed conditions or exceptions.
(6) Subsection (7) applies if—
    (a) an EHC plan is maintained for a child or young person, and
    (b) health care provision specified in the plan is acquired for him or her by means of a payment made by a commissioning body under section 12. A(1) of the National Health Service Act 2006 (direct payments for health care).
(7) The health care provision is to be treated as having been arranged by the commissioning body in pursuance of its duty under section 42. (3) of this Act, subject to any prescribed conditions or exceptions.

(8) "Commissioning body", in relation to any specified health care provision, means a body that is under a duty to arrange health care provision of that kind in respect of the child or young person.
Modifications etc. (not altering text)
C17. S. 49. (1)(2)(3)(d)(4)(a) modified (1.9.2014) by The Special Educational Needs and Disability Regulations 2014 (S.I. 2014/1530), regs. 1, 64. (1)(b), 64. (2), Sch. 3 Pt. 2
Commencement Information
I41. S. 49 in force at 1.4.2014 for specified purposes by S.I. 2014/889, art. 3. (f)
I42. S. 49 in force at 1.9.2014 in so far as not already in force by S.I. 2014/889, art. 7. (a) (with savings and transitional provisions in S.I. 2014/2270 (as amended (1.4.2015) by S.I. 2015/505 and (1.9.2015) by S.I. 2015/1619)

50. Continuation of services under section 17 of the Children Act 1989.

After section 17 of the Children Act 1989 (provision of services for children etc) insert—
"17. ZGSection 17 services: continued provision where EHC plan maintained
(1) This section applies where, immediately before a child in need reaches the age of 18—
    (a) a local authority in England is providing services for the child in the exercise of functions conferred by section 17, and
    (b) an EHC plan is maintained for the child.
(2) The local authority may continue to provide services for the child in the exercise of those functions after the child reaches the age of 18, but may not continue to do so after the EHC plan has ceased to be maintained.
(3) In this section "EHC plan" means a plan within section 37. (2) of the Children and Families Act 2014."
Commencement Information
I43. S. 50 in force at 1.9.2014 by S.I. 2014/889, art. 7. (a) (with savings and transitional provisions in S.I. 2014/2270 (as amended (1.4.2015) by S.I. 2015/505 and (1.9.2015) by S.I. 2015/1619)

Appeals, mediation and dispute resolution

51. Appeals

(1) A child's parent or a young person may appeal to the First-tier Tribunal against the matters set out in subsection (2), subject to section 55 (mediation).
(2) The matters are—
    (a) a decision of a local authority not to secure an EHC needs assessment for the child or young person;
    (b) a decision of a local authority, following an EHC needs assessment, that it is not necessary for special educational provision to be made for the child or young person in accordance with an EHC plan;
    (c) where an EHC plan is maintained for the child or young person—
(i) the child's or young person's special educational needs as specified in the plan;
(ii) the special educational provision specified in the plan;
(iii) the school or other institution named in the plan, or the type of school or other institution specified in the plan;
(iv) if no school or other institution is named in the plan, that fact;
    (d) a decision of a local authority not to secure a re-assessment of the needs of the child or young person under section 44 following a request to do so;
    (e) a decision of a local authority not to secure the amendment or replacement of an EHC plan it

maintains for the child or young person following a review or re-assessment under section 44;
    (f) a decision of a local authority under section 45 to cease to maintain an EHC plan for the child or young person.
(3) A child's parent or a young person may appeal to the First-tier Tribunal under subsection (2)(c)—
    (a) when an EHC plan is first finalised for the child or young person, and
    (b) following an amendment or replacement of the plan.
(4) Regulations may make provision about appeals to the First-tier Tribunal in respect of EHC needs assessments and EHC plans, in particular about—
    (a) other matters relating to EHC plans against which appeals may be brought;
    (b) making and determining appeals;
    (c) the powers of the First-tier Tribunal on determining an appeal;
    (d) unopposed appeals.
(5) Regulations under subsection (4)(c) may include provision conferring power on the First-tier Tribunal, on determining an appeal against a matter, to make recommendations in respect of other matters (including matters against which no appeal may be brought).
(6) A person commits an offence if without reasonable excuse that person fails to comply with any requirement—
    (a) in respect of the discovery or inspection of documents, or
    (b) to attend to give evidence and produce documents,
where that requirement is imposed by Tribunal Procedure Rules in relation to an appeal under this section or regulations under subsection (4)(a).
(7) A person guilty of an offence under subsection (6) is liable on summary conviction to a fine not exceeding level 3 on the standard scale.
Modifications etc. (not altering text)
C18. S. 51. (1)(3) modified (1.9.2014) by The Special Educational Needs and Disability Regulations 2014 (S.I. 2014/1530), regs. 1, 64. (1)(b), 64. (2), Sch. 3 Pt. 2
Commencement Information
I44. S. 51 in force at 1.4.2014 for specified purposes by S.I. 2014/889, art. 3. (g)
I45. S. 51 in force at 1.9.2014 in so far as not already in force by S.I. 2014/889, art. 7. (a) (with savings and transitional provisions in S.I. 2014/2270 (as amended (1.4.2015) by S.I. 2015/505 and (1.9.2015) by S.I. 2015/1619)

52. Right to mediation

(1) This section applies where—
    (a) a decision against which an appeal may be brought under section 51 is made in respect of a child or young person, or
    (b) an EHC plan for a child or young person is made, amended or replaced.
(2) Before the end of the prescribed period after the decision is made, or the plan is made, amended or replaced, the local authority must notify the child's parent or the young person of—
    (a) the right to mediation under section 53 or 54, and
    (b) the requirement to obtain a certificate under section 55 before making certain appeals.
(3) If the parent or young person wishes to pursue mediation under section 53 or 54, he or she must inform the local authority of—
    (a) that fact, and
    (b) the issues in respect of which he or she wishes to pursue mediation ("the mediation issues").
(4) If the mediation issues are, or include, the fact that no health care provision, or no health care provision of a particular kind, is specified in the plan, the parent or young person must also inform the local authority of the health care provision which he or she wishes to be specified in the plan.
Modifications etc. (not altering text)
C19. S. 52. (2)(3)(4) modified (1.9.2014) by The Special Educational Needs and Disability

Regulations 2014 (S.I. 2014/1530), regs. 1, 64. (1)(b), 64. (2), Sch. 3 Pt. 2
Commencement Information
I46. S. 52 in force at 1.4.2014 for specified purposes by S.I. 2014/889, art. 3. (g)
I47. S. 52 in force at 1.9.2014 in so far as not already in force by S.I. 2014/889, art. 7. (a) (with savings and transitional provisions in S.I. 2014/2270 (as amended (1.4.2015) by S.I. 2015/505 and (1.9.2015) by S.I. 2015/1619)

53. Mediation: health care issues

(1) This section applies where—
  (a) the parent or young person informs the local authority under section 52 that he or she wishes to pursue mediation, and
  (b) the mediation issues include health care provision specified in the plan or the fact that no health care provision, or no health care provision of a particular kind, is specified in the plan.
(2) The local authority must notify each relevant commissioning body of—
  (a) the mediation issues, and
  (b) anything of which it has been informed by the parent or young person under section 52. (4).
(3) If the mediation issues are limited to the health care provision specified in the plan or the fact that no health care provision, or no health care provision of a particular kind, is specified in the plan, the responsible commissioning body (or, where there is more than one, the responsible commissioning bodies acting jointly) must—
  (a) arrange for mediation between it (or them) and the parent or young person,
  (b) ensure that the mediation is conducted by an independent person, and
  (c) participate in the mediation.
(4) If the mediation issues include anything else—
  (a) the local authority must—
(i) arrange for mediation between it, each responsible commissioning body and the parent or young person,
(ii) ensure that the mediation is conducted by an independent person, and
(iii) participate in the mediation, and
  (b) each responsible commissioning body must also participate in the mediation.
(5) For the purposes of this section, a person is not independent if he or she is employed by any of the following—
  (a) a local authority in England;
  (b) a clinical commissioning group;
  (c) the National Health Service Commissioning Board.
(6) In this section "responsible commissioning body"—
  (a) if the mediation issues in question are or include the health care provision specified in an EHC plan, means a body that is under a duty to arrange health care provision of that kind in respect of the child or young person;
  (b) if the mediation issues in question are or include the fact that no health care provision, or no health care provision of a particular kind, is specified in an EHC plan, means a body that would be under a duty to arrange health care provision of the kind in question if it were specified in the plan.
Modifications etc. (not altering text)
C20. S. 53. (1)(a)(3)(a)(4)(a)(i) modified (1.9.2014) by The Special Educational Needs and Disability Regulations 2014 (S.I. 2014/1530), regs. 1, 64. (1)(b), 64. (2), Sch. 3 Pt. 2
Commencement Information
I48. S. 53 in force at 1.9.2014 by S.I. 2014/889, art. 7. (a) (with savings and transitional provisions in S.I. 2014/2270 (as amended (1.4.2015) by S.I. 2015/505 and (1.9.2015) by S.I. 2015/1619)

54. Mediation: educational and social care issues etc

(1) This section applies where—
    (a) the parent or young person informs the local authority under section 52 that he or she wishes to pursue mediation, and
    (b) the mediation issues do not include health care provision specified in the plan or the fact that no health care provision, or no health care provision of a particular kind, is specified in the plan.
(2) The local authority must—
    (a) arrange for mediation between it and the parent or young person,
    (b) ensure that the mediation is conducted by an independent person, and
    (c) participate in the mediation.
(3) For the purposes of this section, a person is not independent if he or she is employed by a local authority in England.

Modifications etc. (not altering text)
C21. S. 54. (1)(a)(2)(a) modified (1.9.2014) by The Special Educational Needs and Disability Regulations 2014 (S.I. 2014/1530), regs. 1, 64. (1)(b), 64. (2), Sch. 3 Pt. 2

Commencement Information
I49. S. 54 in force at 1.9.2014 by S.I. 2014/889, art. 7. (a) (with savings and transitional provisions in S.I. 2014/2270 (as amended (1.4.2015) by S.I. 2015/505 and (1.9.2015) by S.I. 2015/1619)

55. Mediation

(1) This section applies where a child's parent or young person intends to appeal to the First-tier Tribunal under section 51 or regulations made under that section in respect of—
    (a) a decision of a local authority, or
    (b) the content of an EHC plan maintained by a local authority.
(2) But this section does not apply in respect of an appeal concerning only—
    (a) the school or other institution named in an EHC plan;
    (b) the type of school or other institution specified in an EHC plan;
    (c) the fact that an EHC plan does not name a school or other institution.
(3) The parent or young person may make the appeal only if a mediation adviser has issued a certificate to him or her under subsection (4) or (5).
(4) A mediation adviser must issue a certificate under this subsection to the parent or young person if—
    (a) the adviser has provided him or her with information and advice about pursuing mediation under section 53 or 54, and
    (b) the parent or young person has informed the adviser that he or she does not wish to pursue mediation.
(5) A mediation adviser must issue a certificate under this subsection to the parent or young person if the adviser has provided him or her with information and advice about pursuing mediation under section 53 or 54, and the parent or young person has—
    (a) informed the adviser that he or she wishes to pursue mediation under the appropriate section, and
    (b) participated in such mediation.

Modifications etc. (not altering text)
C22. S. 55. (1)(3)(4)(5) modified (1.9.2014) by The Special Educational Needs and Disability Regulations 2014 (S.I. 2014/1530), regs. 1, 64. (1)(b), 64. (2), Sch. 3 Pt. 2

Commencement Information
I50. S. 55 in force at 1.9.2014 by S.I. 2014/889, art. 7. (a) (with savings and transitional provisions in S.I. 2014/2270 (as amended (1.4.2015) by S.I. 2015/505 and (1.9.2015) by S.I. 2015/1619)

56. Mediation: supplementary

(1) Regulations may make provision for the purposes of sections 52 to 55, in particular—

(a) about giving notice;
(b) imposing time limits;
(c) enabling a local authority or commissioning body to take prescribed steps following the conclusion of mediation;
(d) about who may attend mediation;
(e) where a child's parent is a party to mediation, requiring the mediator to take reasonable steps to ascertain the views of the child;
(f) about the provision of advocacy and other support services for the parent or young person;
(g) requiring a local authority or commissioning body to pay reasonable travel expenses and other expenses of a prescribed description, up to any prescribed limit;
(h) about exceptions to the requirement in section 55. (3);
(i) about the training, qualifications and experience of mediators and mediation advisers;
(j) conferring powers or imposing requirements on local authorities, commissioning bodies, mediators and mediation advisers.
(2) In section 55 and this section "mediation adviser" means an independent person who can provide information and advice about pursuing mediation.
(3) For the purposes of subsection (2), a person is not independent if he or she is employed by any of the following—
(a) a local authority in England;
(b) a clinical commissioning group;
(c) the National Health Service Commissioning Board.
(4) In this section "commissioning body" means a body that is under a duty to arrange health care provision of any kind.
Modifications etc. (not altering text)
C23. S. 56. (1)(f) modified (1.9.2014) by The Special Educational Needs and Disability Regulations 2014 (S.I. 2014/1530), regs. 1, 64. (1)(b), 64. (2), Sch. 3 Pt. 2
Commencement Information
I51. S. 56 in force at 1.4.2014 for specified purposes by S.I. 2014/889, art. 3. (h)
I52. S. 56 in force at 1.9.2014 in so far as not already in force by S.I. 2014/889, art. 7. (a) (with savings and transitional provisions in S.I. 2014/2270 (as amended (1.4.2015) by S.I. 2015/505 and (1.9.2015) by S.I. 2015/1619)

57. Resolution of disagreements

(1) A local authority in England must make arrangements with a view to avoiding or resolving disagreements within subsection (2) or (3).
(2) The disagreements within this subsection are those about the exercise by the local authority or relevant bodies of their functions under this Part, where the disagreement is between—
(a) the local authority or a relevant body, and
(b) the parents of children, and young people, in the authority's area.
(3) The disagreements within this subsection are those about the exercise by the local authority of its functions relating to EHC needs assessments, the preparation and review of EHC plans, and re-assessment of educational, health care and social care needs, where the disagreement is between—
(a) the local authority and a responsible commissioning body, or
(b) a responsible commissioning body and the parents of children, or young people, in the authority's area.
(4) A local authority in England must make arrangements with a view to avoiding or resolving, in each relevant school or post-16 institution, disagreements within subsection (5).
(5) The disagreements within this subsection are those about the special educational provision made for a child or young person with special educational needs who is a registered pupil or a student at the relevant school or post-16 institution concerned, where the disagreement is between—

(a) the child's parent, or the young person, and
(b) the appropriate authority for the school or post-16 institution.

(6) Arrangements within this section must provide for the appointment of independent persons with the function of facilitating the avoidance or resolution of the disagreements to which the arrangements apply.

(7) For the purposes of subsection (6) a person is not independent if he or she is employed by any of the following—
(a) a local authority in England;
(b) a clinical commissioning group;
(c) the National Health Service Commissioning Board.

(8) A local authority in England must take such steps as it thinks appropriate for making the arrangements under this section known to—
(a) the parents of children in its area with special educational needs,
(b) young people in its area with special educational needs, and
(c) the head teachers, governing bodies, proprietors and principals of schools and post-16 institutions in its area.

(9) A local authority in England may take such steps as it thinks appropriate for making the arrangements under this section known to such other persons as it thinks appropriate.

(10) In this section—
"relevant body" means—
- the governing body of a maintained school, maintained nursery school or institution within the further education sector;
- the proprietor of an Academy;
"relevant school or post-16 institution" means—
- a maintained school;
- a maintained nursery school;
- a post-16 institution;
- an Academy;
- an independent school;
- a non-maintained special school;
- a pupil referral unit;
- a place at which relevant early years education is provided;
"responsible commissioning body", in relation to any particular health care provision, means a body that is under a duty to arrange health care provision of that kind in respect of the child or young person concerned.

(11) For the purposes of this section, the "appropriate authority" for a relevant school or post-16 institution is—
(a) in the case of a maintained school, maintained nursery school or non-maintained special school, the governing body;
(b) in the case of a post-16 institution, the governing body, proprietor or principal;
(c) in the case of an Academy or independent school, the proprietor;
(d) in the case of a pupil referral unit, the management committee;
(e) in the case of a place at which relevant early years education is provided, the provider of the relevant early years education.

Modifications etc. (not altering text)
C24. S. 57. (2)(b)(3)(b)(5)(a)(8)(b) modified (1.9.2014) by The Special Educational Needs and Disability Regulations 2014 (S.I. 2014/1530), regs. 1, 64. (1)(b), 64. (2), Sch. 3 Pt. 2
Commencement Information
I53. S. 57 in force at 1.9.2014 by S.I. 2014/889, art. 7. (a) (with savings and transitional provisions in S.I. 2014/2270 (as amended (1.4.2015) by S.I. 2015/505 and (1.9.2015) by S.I. 2015/1619)

[F258. Appeals and claims by children: pilot schemes

(1) The Secretary of State may by order make pilot schemes enabling children in England to—
  (a) appeal to the First-tier Tribunal under section 51;
  (b) make a claim to the First-tier Tribunal under Schedule 17 to the Equality Act 2010 (disabled pupils: enforcement) that a responsible body in England has contravened Chapter 1 of Part 6 of that Act because of the child's disability.
(2) An order under subsection (1) may, in particular, make provision—
  (a) about the age from which children may appeal or make a claim;
  (b) in respect of appeals under section 51, about mediation and the application of section 55;
  (c) about the bringing of appeals or making of claims by a child and by his or her parent concurrently;
  (d) about determining whether a child is capable of bringing an appeal or making a claim, and the assistance and support a child may require to be able to do so;
  (e) enabling a person to exercise a child's rights under an order under subsection (1) on behalf of the child;
  (f) enabling children to have access to advice and information which is available to a parent or young person in respect of an appeal or claim of a kind mentioned in subsection (1);
  (g) about the provision of advocacy and other support services to children;
  (h) requiring notices to be given to a child (as well as to his or her parent);
  (i) requiring documents to be served on a child (as well as on his or her parent).
(3) An order under subsection (1) may apply a statutory provision, with or without modifications.
(4) In subsection (3). " statutory provision " means a provision made by or under this or any other Act, whenever passed or made.
(5) This section is repealed at the end of five years beginning with the day on which this Act is passed.]
Amendments (Textual)
F2. S. 58 repealed at the end of five years beginning with the day on which this Act is passed by Children and Families Act 2014 (c. 6), s. 58. (5); S.I. 2014/889, art. 7. (a) (with savings and transitional provisions in S.I. 2014/2270 (as amended (1.4.2015) by S.I. 2015/505)
Commencement Information
I54. S. 58 in force at 1.9.2014 by S.I. 2014/889, art. 7. (a) (with savings and transitional provisions in S.I. 2014/2270 (as amended (1.4.2015) by S.I. 2015/505 and (1.9.2015) by S.I. 2015/1619)

59. Appeals and claims by children: follow-up provision

(1) The Secretary of State may by order provide that children in England may—
  (a) appeal to the First-tier Tribunal under section 51;
  (b) make a claim to the First-tier Tribunal under Schedule 17 to the Equality Act 2010 (disabled pupils: enforcement) that a responsible body in England has contravened Chapter 1 of Part 6 of that Act because of the child's disability.
(2) The Secretary of State may not make an order under subsection (1) until the end of two years beginning with the day on which the first order is made under section 58. (1).
(3) An order under subsection (1) may, in particular, make provision—
  (a) about the age from which children may appeal or make a claim;
  (b) in respect of appeals under section 51, about mediation and the application of section 55;
  (c) about the bringing of appeals or making of claims by a child and by his or her parent concurrently;
  (d) about determining whether a child is capable of bringing an appeal or making a claim, and the assistance and support a child may require to be able to do so;
  (e) enabling a person to exercise a child's rights under an order under subsection (1) on behalf of the child;
  (f) enabling children to have access to advice and information which is available to a parent or

young person in respect of an appeal or claim of a kind mentioned in subsection (1);
(g) about the provision of advocacy and other support services to children;
(h) requiring notices to be given to a child (as well as to his or her parent);
(i) requiring documents to be served on a child (as well as on his or her parent).
(4) An order under subsection (1) may—
(a) amend, repeal or revoke a statutory provision, or
(b) apply a statutory provision, with or without modifications.
(5) In subsection (4), "statutory provision" means a provision made by or under this or any other Act, whenever passed or made.
Commencement Information
I55. S. 59 in force at 1.9.2014 by S.I. 2014/889, art. 7. (a) (with savings and transitional provisions in S.I. 2014/2270 (as amended (1.4.2015) by S.I. 2015/505 and (1.9.2015) by S.I. 2015/1619)

60. Equality Act 2010: claims against schools by disabled young people

In Part 2 of Schedule 17 to the Equality Act 2010 (disabled pupils: enforcement in tribunals in England and Wales), in paragraph 3 (who may make a claim that a school has contravened Chapter 1 of Part 6 of that Act because of a person's disability) for "to the Tribunal by the person's parent" substitute "—
(a) to the English Tribunal by the person's parent or, if the person is over compulsory school age, the person;
(b) to the Welsh Tribunal by the person's parent."
Commencement Information
I56. S. 60 in force at 1.9.2014 by S.I. 2014/889, art. 7. (a) (with savings and transitional provisions in S.I. 2014/2270 (as amended (1.4.2015) by S.I. 2015/505 and (1.9.2015) by S.I. 2015/1619)

Special educational provision: functions of local authorities

61. Special educational provision otherwise than in schools, post-16 institutions etc

(1) A local authority in England may arrange for any special educational provision that it has decided is necessary for a child or young person for whom it is responsible to be made otherwise than in a school or post-16 institution or a place at which relevant early years education is provided.
(2) An authority may do so only if satisfied that it would be inappropriate for the provision to be made in a school or post-16 institution or at such a place.
(3) Before doing so, the authority must consult the child's parent or the young person.
Modifications etc. (not altering text)
C25. S. 61. (3) modified (1.9.2014) by The Special Educational Needs and Disability Regulations 2014 (S.I. 2014/1530), regs. 1, 64. (1)(b), 64. (2), Sch. 3 Pt. 2
Commencement Information
I57. S. 61 in force at 1.9.2014 by S.I. 2014/889, art. 7. (a) (with savings and transitional provisions in S.I. 2014/2270 (as amended (1.4.2015) by S.I. 2015/505 and (1.9.2015) by S.I. 2015/1619)

62. Special educational provision outside England and Wales

(1) This section applies where a local authority in England makes arrangements for a child or

young person for whom it maintains an EHC plan to attend an institution outside England and Wales which specialises in providing for children or young people with special educational needs.
(2) The arrangements may (in particular) include contributing to or paying—
(a) fees charged by the institution;
(b) the child's or young person's travelling expenses;
(c) expenses reasonably incurred in maintaining the child or young person while at the institution or travelling to or from it;
(d) expenses reasonably incurred by someone accompanying the child or young person while travelling to or from the institution or staying there.
Commencement Information
I58. S. 62 in force at 1.9.2014 by S.I. 2014/889, art. 7. (a) (with savings and transitional provisions in S.I. 2014/2270 (as amended (1.4.2015) by S.I. 2015/505 and (1.9.2015) by S.I. 2015/1619)

63. Fees for special educational provision at non-maintained schools and post-16 institutions

(1) Subsection (2) applies where—
(a) a local authority maintains an EHC plan for a child or young person,
(b) special educational provision in respect of the child or young person is made at a school, post-16 institution or place at which relevant early years education is provided, and
(c) that school, institution or place is named in the EHC plan.
(2) The local authority must pay any fees payable in respect of education or training provided for the child or young person at that school, institution or place in accordance with the EHC plan.
(3) Subsection (4) applies where—
(a) a local authority is responsible for a child or young person for whom no EHC plan is maintained,
(b) special educational provision in respect of the child or young person is made at a school, post-16 institution or place at which relevant early years education is provided, and
(c) the local authority is satisfied that—
(i) the interests of the child or young person require special educational provision to be made, and
(ii) it is appropriate for education or training to be provided to the child or young person at the school, institution or place in question.
(4) The local authority must pay any fees payable in respect of the special educational provision made at the school, institution or place in question which is required to meet the special educational needs of the child or young person.
(5) Where board and lodging are provided for the child or young person at the school, post-16 institution or place mentioned in subsection (2) or (4), the authority must also pay any fees in respect of the board and lodging, if satisfied that special educational provision cannot be provided at the school, post-16 institution or place unless the board and lodging are also provided.
Commencement Information
I59. S. 63 in force at 1.9.2014 by S.I. 2014/889, art. 7. (a) (with savings and transitional provisions in S.I. 2014/2270 (as amended (1.4.2015) by S.I. 2015/505 and (1.9.2015) by S.I. 2015/1619)

64. Supply of goods and services

(1) A local authority in England may supply goods and services to—
(a) the governing body of a maintained school or maintained nursery school in England;
(b) the proprietor of an Academy;
(c) the governing body of an institution within the further education sector that the authority thinks is or is to be attended by a young person for whom the authority maintains an EHC plan, but only for the purpose set out in subsection (2).

(2) The purpose is that of assisting the governing body or proprietor in the performance of—
   (a) any duty imposed on the body under section 66. (2) (duty to use best endeavours to secure special educational provision called for by special educational needs);
   (b) in the case of a governing body of a community or foundation special school, any duty imposed on the body.
(3) The goods and services may be supplied on the terms and conditions that the authority thinks fit, including terms as to payment.
(4) A local authority in England may supply goods and services to any authority or other person (other than a governing body or proprietor within subsection (1)), but only for the purpose set out in subsection (5).
(5) The purpose is that of assisting the authority or other person in making special educational provision for a child who is receiving relevant early years education, in a case where the authority has decided that the special educational provision is necessary for the child.
Commencement Information
I60. S. 64 in force at 1.9.2014 by S.I. 2014/889, art. 7. (a) (with savings and transitional provisions in S.I. 2014/2270 (as amended (1.4.2015) by S.I. 2015/505 and (1.9.2015) by S.I. 2015/1619)

65. Access to schools, post-16 institutions and other institutions

(1) This section applies where a local authority in England maintains an EHC plan for a child or young person.
(2) A person authorised by the authority is entitled to have access at any reasonable time to the premises of a school, post-16 institution or other institution at which education or training is provided in pursuance of the plan, for the purpose of monitoring the education or training.
(3) Subsection (2) does not apply to the premises of a mainstream post-16 institution in Wales.
Commencement Information
I61. S. 65 in force at 1.9.2014 by S.I. 2014/889, art. 7. (a) (with savings and transitional provisions in S.I. 2014/2270 (as amended (1.4.2015) by S.I. 2015/505 and (1.9.2015) by S.I. 2015/1619)

Special educational provision: functions of governing bodies and others

66. Using best endeavours to secure special educational provision

(1) This section imposes duties on the appropriate authorities for the following schools and other institutions in England—
   (a) mainstream schools;
   (b) maintained nursery schools;
   (c) 16 to 19 Academies;
   (d) alternative provision Academies;
   (e) institutions within the further education sector;
   (f) pupil referral units.
(2) If a registered pupil or a student at a school or other institution has special educational needs, the appropriate authority must, in exercising its functions in relation to the school or other institution, use its best endeavours to secure that the special educational provision called for by the pupil's or student's special educational needs is made.
(3) The "appropriate authority" for a school or other institution is—
   (a) in the case of a maintained school, maintained nursery school or institution within the further education sector, the governing body;
   (b) in the case of an Academy, the proprietor;

(c) in the case of a pupil referral unit, the management committee.
Commencement Information
I62. S. 66 in force at 1.9.2014 by S.I. 2014/889, art. 7. (a) (with savings and transitional provisions in S.I. 2014/2270 (as amended (1.4.2015) by S.I. 2015/505 and (1.9.2015) by S.I. 2015/1619)

67. SEN co-ordinators

(1) This section imposes duties on the appropriate authorities of the following schools in England—
    (a) mainstream schools;
    (b) maintained nursery schools.
(2) The appropriate authority must designate a member of staff at the school (to be known as the "SEN co-ordinator") as having responsibility for co-ordinating the provision for pupils with special educational needs.
(3) Regulations may—
    (a) require appropriate authorities which are subject to the duty imposed by subsection (2) to ensure that SEN co-ordinators have prescribed qualifications or prescribed experience (or both);
    (b) confer other functions relating to SEN co-ordinators on appropriate authorities which are subject to the duty imposed by subsection (2).
(4) The "appropriate authority" for a school is—
    (a) in the case of a maintained school or maintained nursery school, the governing body;
    (b) in the case of an Academy, the proprietor.
Commencement Information
I63. S. 67 in force at 1.4.2014 for specified purposes by S.I. 2014/889, art. 3. (i)
I64. S. 67 in force at 1.9.2014 in so far as not already in force by S.I. 2014/889, art. 7. (a) (with savings and transitional provisions in S.I. 2014/2270 (as amended (1.4.2015) by S.I. 2015/505 and (1.9.2015) by S.I. 2015/1619)

68. Informing parents and young people

(1) This section applies if—
    (a) special educational provision is made for a child or young person at a maintained school, a maintained nursery school, an Academy school, an alternative provision Academy or a pupil referral unit, and
    (b) no EHC plan is maintained for the child or young person.
(2) The appropriate authority for the school must inform the child's parent or the young person that special educational provision is being made for the child or young person.
(3) The "appropriate authority" for a school is—
    (a) in the case of a maintained school or maintained nursery school, the governing body;
    (b) in the case of an Academy school or an alternative provision Academy, the proprietor;
    (c) in the case of a pupil referral unit, the management committee.
Modifications etc. (not altering text)
C26. S. 68. (2) modified (1.9.2014) by The Special Educational Needs and Disability Regulations 2014 (S.I. 2014/1530), regs. 1, 64. (1)(b), 64. (2), Sch. 3 Pt. 2
Commencement Information
I65. S. 68 in force at 1.9.2014 by S.I. 2014/889, art. 7. (a) (with savings and transitional provisions in S.I. 2014/2270 (as amended (1.4.2015) by S.I. 2015/505 and (1.9.2015) by S.I. 2015/1619)

69. SEN information report

(1) This section imposes a duty on—

(a) the governing bodies of maintained schools and maintained nursery schools in England, and
(b) the proprietors of Academy schools.
(2) A governing body or proprietor must prepare a report containing SEN information.
(3) "SEN information" is—
(a) such information as may be prescribed about the implementation of the governing body's or proprietor's policy for pupils at the school with special educational needs;
(b) information as to—
(i) the arrangements for the admission of disabled persons as pupils at the school;
(ii) the steps taken to prevent disabled pupils from being treated less favourably than other pupils;
(iii) the facilities provided to assist access to the school by disabled pupils;
(iv) the plan prepared by the governing body or proprietor under paragraph 3 of Schedule 10 to the Equality Act 2010 (accessibility plan).
(4) In this section—
"disabled person" means a person who is a disabled person for the purposes of the Equality Act 2010;
"disabled pupil" includes a disabled person who may be admitted to a school as a pupil.
Commencement Information
I66. S. 69 in force at 1.4.2014 for specified purposes by S.I. 2014/889, art. 3. (j)
I67. S. 69 in force at 1.9.2014 in so far as not already in force by S.I. 2014/889, art. 7. (a) (with savings and transitional provisions in S.I. 2014/2270 (as amended (1.4.2015) by S.I. 2015/505 and (1.9.2015) by S.I. 2015/1619)

Detained persons

70. Application of Part to detained persons

(1) Subject to this section and sections 71 to 75, nothing in or made under this Part applies to, or in relation to, a child or young person detained in pursuance of—
(a) an order made by a court, or
(b) an order of recall made by the Secretary of State.
(2) Subsection (1) does not apply to—
(a) section 28;
(b) section 31;
(c) section 77;
(d) section 80;
(e) section 83;
(f) any amendment made by this Part of a provision which applies to, or in relation to, a child or young person detained in pursuance of—
(i) an order made by a court, or
(ii) an order of recall made by the Secretary of State.
(3) Regulations may apply any provision of this Part, with or without modifications, to or in relation to a child or young person detained in pursuance of—
(a) an order made by a court, or
(b) an order of recall made by the Secretary of State.
(4) The Secretary of State must consult the Welsh Ministers before making regulations under subsection (3) which will apply any provision of this Part to, or in relation to, a child or young person who is detained in Wales.
(5) For the purposes of this Part—
"appropriate person", in relation to a detained person, means—
- where the detained person is a child, the detained person's parent, or
- where the detained person is a young person, the detained person;

"detained person" means a child or young person who is—
- 18 or under,
- subject to a detention order (within the meaning of section 562. (1. A)(a) of EA 1996), and
- detained in relevant youth accommodation,

and in provisions applying on a person's release, includes a person who, immediately before release, was a detained person;

"detained person's EHC needs assessment" means an assessment of what the education, health care and social care needs of a detained person will be on his or her release from detention;

"relevant youth accommodation" has the same meaning as in section 562. (1. A)(b) of EA 1996, save that it does not include relevant youth accommodation which is not in England.

(6) For the purposes of this Part—
    (a) "beginning of the detention" has the same meaning as in Chapter 5. A of Part 10 of EA 1996 (persons detained in youth accommodation), and
    (b) "the home authority" has the same meaning as in that Chapter, subject to regulations under subsection (7) (and regulations under section 562. J(4) of EA 1996 made by the Secretary of State may also make provision in relation to the definition of "the home authority" for the purposes of this Part).

(7) For the purposes of this Part, regulations may provide for paragraph (a) of the definition of "the home authority" in section 562. J(1) of EA 1996 (the home authority of a looked after child) to apply with modifications in relation to such provisions of this Part as may be specified in the regulations.

Modifications etc. (not altering text)
C27. S. 70. (5) modified (1.9.2014) by The Special Educational Needs and Disability Regulations 2014 (S.I. 2014/1530), regs. 1, 64. (1)(b), 64. (2), Sch. 3 Pt. 2

Commencement Information
I68. S. 70. (1) in force at 1.9.2014 for specified purposes by S.I. 2014/889, art. 7. (a) (with savings and transitional provisions in S.I. 2014/2270 (as amended (1.4.2015) by S.I. 2015/505 and (1.9.2015) by S.I. 2015/1619))
I69. S. 70. (1) in force at 1.4.2015 in so far as not already in force by S.I. 2015/375, art. 2. (a)
I70. S. 70. (2)-(7) in force at 1.4.2015 by S.I. 2015/375, art. 2. (b)

71. Assessment of post-detention education, health and care needs of detained persons

(1) This section applies in relation to a detained person for whom—
    (a) the home authority is a local authority in England, and
    (b) no EHC plan is being kept by a local authority.

(2) A request to the home authority to secure a detained person's EHC needs assessment for the detained person may be made by—
    (a) the appropriate person, or
    (b) the person in charge of the relevant youth accommodation where the detained person is detained.

(3) Where this subsection applies, the home authority must determine whether it may be necessary for special educational provision to be made for the detained person in accordance with an EHC plan on release from detention.

(4) Subsection (3) applies where—
    (a) a request is made under subsection (2),
    (b) the detained person has been brought to the home authority's attention by any person as someone who has or may have special educational needs, or
    (c) the detained person has otherwise come to the home authority's attention as someone who has or may have special educational needs.

(5) In making a determination under subsection (3), the home authority must consult—

(a) the appropriate person, and
(b) the person in charge of the relevant youth accommodation where the detained person is detained.
(6) Where the home authority determines that it will not be necessary for special educational provision to be made for the detained person in accordance with an EHC plan on release from detention, it must notify the appropriate person and the person in charge of the relevant youth accommodation where the detained person is detained—
(a) of the reasons for that determination, and
(b) that accordingly it has decided not to secure a detained person's EHC needs assessment for the detained person.
(7) Subsection (8) applies where—
(a) the detained person has not been assessed under this section or section 36 during the previous six months, and
(b) the home authority determines that it may be necessary for special educational provision to be made for the detained person in accordance with an EHC plan on release from detention.
(8) The home authority must notify the appropriate person and the person in charge of the relevant youth accommodation where the detained person is detained—
(a) that it is considering securing a detained person's EHC needs assessment for the detained person, and
(b) that the appropriate person and the person in charge of the relevant youth accommodation where the detained person is detained each have the right to—
(i) express views to the authority (orally or in writing), and
(ii) submit evidence to the authority.
(9) The home authority must secure a detained person's EHC needs assessment if, after having regard to any views expressed and evidence submitted under subsection (8), the authority is of the opinion that—
(a) the detained person has or may have special educational needs, and
(b) it may be necessary for special educational provision to be made for the detained person in accordance with an EHC plan on release from detention.
(10) After a detained person's EHC needs assessment has been carried out, the local authority must notify the appropriate person and the person in charge of the relevant youth accommodation where the detained person is detained of—
(a) the outcome of the assessment,
(b) whether it proposes to secure that an EHC plan is prepared for the detained person, and
(c) the reasons for that decision.
(11) Regulations may make provision about detained persons' EHC needs assessments, in particular—
(a) about requests under subsection (2);
(b) imposing time limits in relation to consultation under subsection (5);
(c) about giving notice;
(d) about expressing views and submitting evidence under subsection (8);
(e) about how detained persons' EHC needs assessments are to be conducted;
(f) about advice to be obtained in connection with a detained person's EHC needs assessment;
(g) about combining a detained person's EHC needs assessment with other assessments;
(h) about the use for the purposes of a detained person's EHC needs assessment of information obtained as a result of other assessments;
(i) about the use of information obtained as a result of a detained person's EHC needs assessment, including the use of that information for the purposes of other assessments;
(j) about the provision of information, advice and support in connection with a detained person's EHC needs assessment.
Commencement Information
I71. S. 71 in force at 1.4.2015 by S.I. 2015/375, art. 2. (b)

72. Securing EHC plans for certain detained persons

(1) Where, in the light of a detained person's EHC needs assessment it is necessary for special education provision to be made for the detained person in accordance with an EHC plan on release from detention, the home authority must secure that an EHC plan is prepared for him or her.
(2) Sections 37. (2) to (5) and 38 to 40 apply in relation to an EHC plan secured under subsection (1) as they apply to an EHC plan secured under section 37. (1), with the following modifications—
    (a) references to "the child or young person" are to be read as references to the detained person,
    (b) references to the local authority are to be read as references to the home authority, and
    (c) references to the child's parent or the young person are to be read as references to the appropriate person.
(3) Section 33. (2) to (7) apply where a home authority is securing the preparation of an EHC plan under this section as they apply where a local authority is securing a plan under section 37, with the following modifications—
    (a) references to "the child or young person" are to be read as references to the detained person,
    (b) references to the local authority are to be read as references to the home authority,
    (c) references to the child's parent or the young person are to be read as references to the appropriate person, and
    (d) the reference in subsection (2) to section 39. (5) and 40. (2) is to be read as a reference to those provisions as applied by subsection (2) of this section.
Commencement Information
I72. S. 72 in force at 1.4.2015 by S.I. 2015/375, art. 2. (b)

73. EHC plans for certain detained persons: appeals and mediation

(1) An appropriate person in relation to a detained person may appeal to the First-tier Tribunal against the matters set out in subsection (2), subject to section 55 (as applied by this section).
(2) The matters are—
    (a) a decision of the home authority not to secure a detained person's EHC needs assessment for the detained person;
    (b) a decision of the home authority, following a detained person's EHC needs assessment, that it is not necessary for special educational provision to be made for the detained person in accordance with an EHC plan on release from detention;
    (c) where an EHC plan is secured for the detained person—
(i) the school or other institution named in the plan, or the type of school or other institution named in the plan;
(ii) if no school or other institution is named in the plan, that fact.
(3) The appropriate person may appeal to the First-tier Tribunal under subsection (2)(c) only when an EHC plan is first finalised for the detained person in accordance with section 72.
(4) Regulations may make provision about appeals to the First-tier Tribunal in respect of detained persons' EHC needs assessments and EHC plans secured under section 72, in particular about—
    (a) making and determining appeals;
    (b) the powers of the First-tier Tribunal on determining an appeal;
    (c) unopposed appeals.
(5) A person commits an offence if without reasonable excuse that person fails to comply with any requirement—
    (a) in respect of the discovery or inspection of documents, or
    (b) to attend to give evidence and produce documents,
where that requirement is imposed by Tribunal Procedure Rules in relation to an appeal under this

section.

(6) A person guilty of an offence under subsection (5) is liable on summary conviction to a fine not exceeding level 3 on the standard scale.

(7) Section 55. (2) to (5) apply where an appropriate person intends to appeal to the First-tier Tribunal under this section as they apply where a child's parent or young person intends to appeal under section 51, with the following modifications—

   (a) references to the child's parent or young person are to be read as references to the appropriate person, and

   (b) references to mediation under section 53 or 54 are to be read as references to mediation with the home authority.

(8) Where, by virtue of subsection (7), the appropriate person has informed the mediation adviser that he or she wishes to pursue mediation with the home authority—

   (a) the adviser must notify the authority, and

   (b) the authority must—

(i) arrange for mediation between it and the appropriate person,

(ii) ensure that the mediation is conducted by an independent person, and

(iii) participate in the mediation.

For this purpose a person is not independent if he or she is employed by a local authority in England.

(9) Regulations under section 56 may make provision for the purposes of subsections (7) and (8) of this section, and accordingly section 56 has effect for those purposes with the following modifications—

   (a) the references in subsection (1) to commissioning bodies are to be ignored;

   (b) the reference in subsection (1)(e) to a child's parent is to be read as a reference to the parent of a detained person who is a child;

   (c) the reference in subsection (1)(f) to the child's parent or young person is to be read as a reference to the appropriate person;

   (d) in subsection (3), paragraphs (b) and (c) are to be ignored;

   (e) subsection (4) is to be ignored.

Commencement Information

I73. S. 73 in force at 1.4.2015 by S.I. 2015/375, art. 2. (b)

74. Duty to keep EHC plans for detained persons

(1) This section applies in relation to a detained person—

   (a) for whom a local authority in England was maintaining an EHC plan immediately before the beginning of his or her detention, or

   (b) for whom the home authority has secured the preparation of an EHC plan under section 72.

(2) The home authority must keep the EHC plan while the person is detained in relevant youth accommodation.

(3) Regulations may make provision about the keeping of EHC plans under subsection (2), and the disclosure of such plans.

(4) The home authority must arrange appropriate special educational provision for the detained person while he or she is detained in relevant youth accommodation.

(5) If the EHC plan specifies health care provision, the detained person's health services commissioner must arrange appropriate health care provision for the detained person while he or she is detained in relevant youth accommodation.

(6) For the purposes of subsection (4), appropriate special educational provision is—

   (a) the special educational provision specified in the EHC plan, or

   (b) if it appears to the home authority that it is not practicable for that special educational provision to be provided, educational provision corresponding as closely as possible to that special educational provision, or

(c) if it appears to the home authority that the special educational provision specified in the plan is no longer appropriate for the person, such special educational provision as reasonably appears to the home authority to be appropriate.

(7) For the purposes of subsection (5), appropriate health care provision is—

(a) the health care provision specified in the EHC plan, or

(b) if it appears to the detained person's health services commissioner that it is not practicable for that health care provision to be provided, health care provision corresponding as closely as possible to that health care provision, or

(c) if it appears to the detained person's health services commissioner that the health care provision specified in the plan is no longer appropriate for the person, such health care provision as reasonably appears to the detained person's health services commissioner to be appropriate.

(8) In this section, "detained person's health services commissioner", in relation to a detained person, means the body that is under a duty under the National Health Service Act 2006 to arrange for the provision of services or facilities in respect of the detained person during his or her detention.

Commencement Information

I74. S. 74 in force at 1.4.2015 by S.I. 2015/375, art. 2. (b)

75. Supply of goods and services: detained persons

(1) A local authority in England may supply goods and services to any authority or other person making special educational provision for a detained person, but only for the purpose set out in subsection (2).

(2) The purpose is that of assisting the local authority in the performance of a duty under section 74.

(3) The goods and services may be supplied on the terms and conditions that the authority thinks fit, including terms as to payment.

Commencement Information

I75. S. 75 in force at 1.4.2015 by S.I. 2015/375, art. 2. (b)

Information to improve well-being of children and young people with SEN

76. Provision and publication of special needs information

(1) The Secretary of State must exercise the powers listed in subsection (2) with a view to securing, in particular, the provision of special needs information which the Secretary of State thinks would be likely to assist the Secretary of State or others in improving the well-being of—

(a) children in England with special educational needs, and

(b) young people aged under 19 in England with special educational needs.

(2) The powers are those of the Secretary of State under the following provisions of EA 1996 (so far as relating to England)—

(a) section 29 (information from local authorities for purposes of Secretary of State's functions);

(b) section 408 (information in relation to maintained schools);

(c) section 537 (information about schools);

(d) section 537. A (information about individual pupils);

(e) section 537. B (information about children receiving funded education outside school);

(f) section 538 (information from governing bodies for purposes of Secretary of State's education functions).

(3) In each calendar year, the Secretary of State must publish, or arrange to be published, special

needs information which has been obtained under EA 1996, where the Secretary of State thinks the publication of the information would be likely to assist the Secretary of State or others in improving the well-being of—
 (a) children in England with special educational needs, and
 (b) young people aged under 19 in England with special educational needs.
(4) Information published under subsection (3) must be published in the form and manner that the Secretary of State thinks fit, except that the names of the children and young people to whom the information relates must not be included.
(5) The Secretary of State may make a charge, or arrange for a charge to be made, for documents supplied by virtue of this section.
(6) A charge under subsection (5) must not exceed the cost of supply.
(7) "Special needs information" means—
 (a) information about children, and young people, in England with special educational needs, and
 (b) information about special educational provision made for those children and young people.
(8) References in this section to the well-being of children and young people with special educational needs are to their well-being so far as relating to—
 (a) physical and mental health and emotional well-being;
 (b) protection from abuse and neglect;
 (c) control by them over their day-to-day lives;
 (d) participation in education, training or recreation;
 (e) social and economic well-being;
 (f) domestic, family and personal relationships;
 (g) the contribution made by them to society.

Commencement Information
I76. S. 76 in force at 1.9.2014 by S.I. 2014/889, art. 7. (a) (with savings and transitional provisions in S.I. 2014/2270 (as amended (1.4.2015) by S.I. 2015/505 and (1.9.2015) by S.I. 2015/1619)

Code of practice

77. Code of practice

(1) The Secretary of State must issue a code of practice giving guidance about the exercise of their functions under this Part to—
 (a) local authorities in England;
 (b) the governing bodies of schools;
 (c) the governing bodies of institutions within the further education sector;
 (d) the proprietors of Academies;
 (e) the management committees of pupil referral units;
 (f) the proprietors of institutions approved by the Secretary of State under section 41 (independent special schools and special post-16 institutions: approval);
 (g) providers of relevant early years education;
 (h) youth offending teams;
 (i) persons in charge of relevant youth accommodation;
 (j) the National Health Service Commissioning Board;
 (k) clinical commissioning groups;
 (l) NHS trusts;
 (m) NHS foundation trusts;
 (n) Local Health Boards.
(2) The Secretary of State may revise the code from time to time.
(3) The Secretary of State must publish the current version of the code.

(4) The persons listed in subsection (1) must have regard to the code in exercising their functions under this Part.
(5) Those who exercise functions for the purpose of the exercise by those persons of functions under this Part must also have regard to the code.
(6) The First-tier Tribunal must have regard to any provision of the code that appears to it to be relevant to a question arising on an appeal under this Part.
Commencement Information
I77. S. 77 in force at 1.9.2014 by S.I. 2014/889, art. 7. (a) (with savings and transitional provisions in S.I. 2014/2270 (as amended (1.4.2015) by S.I. 2015/505 and (1.9.2015) by S.I. 2015/1619)

78. Making and approval of code

(1) Where the Secretary of State proposes to issue or revise a code under section 77, the Secretary of State must prepare a draft of the code (or revised code).
(2) The Secretary of State must consult such persons as the Secretary of State thinks fit about the draft and must consider any representations made by them.
(3) If the Secretary of State decides to proceed with the draft (in its original form or with modifications), the Secretary of State must lay a copy of the draft before each House of Parliament.
(4) The Secretary of State may not take any further steps in relation to—
   (a) a proposed code unless the draft is approved by a resolution of each House, or
   (b) a proposed revised code if, within the 40-day period, either House resolves not to approve the draft.
(5) Subsection (6) applies if—
   (a) both Houses resolve to approve the draft, as mentioned in subsection (4)(a), or
   (b) neither House resolves not to approve the draft, as mentioned in subsection (4)(b).
(6) The Secretary of State must issue the code or revised code in the form of the draft, and it comes into force on such date as the Secretary of State may by order appoint.
(7) Subsection (4) does not prevent a new draft of a proposed code (or proposed revised code) from being laid before Parliament.
(8) In this section "40-day period", in relation to the draft of a proposed revised code, means—
   (a) if the draft is laid before one House on a later day than the day on which it is laid before the other, the period of 40 days beginning with the later of the two days, and
   (b) in any other case, the period of 40 days beginning with the day on which the draft is laid before each House.
(9) For the purposes of subsection (8), no account is to be taken of any period during which Parliament is dissolved or prorogued or during which both Houses are adjourned for more than four days.
Commencement Information
I78. S. 78 in force at 1.5.2014 by S.I. 2014/889, art. 4. A (as inserted (30.4.2014) by S.I. 2014/1134, art. 2. (2))

79. Review of resolution of disagreements

(1) The Secretary of State and the Lord Chancellor must carry out a review of how effectively disagreements about the exercise of functions under this Part are being resolved.
(2) The Secretary of State and the Lord Chancellor must prepare a report on the outcome of the review.
(3) The Secretary of State and the Lord Chancellor must lay the report before Parliament before the end of the period of three years beginning with the earliest date on which any provision of this Part comes into force.
Commencement Information

I79. S. 79 in force at 1.9.2014 by S.I. 2014/889, art. 7. (a) (with savings and transitional provisions in S.I. 2014/2270 (as amended (1.4.2015) by S.I. 2015/505 and (1.9.2015) by S.I. 2015/1619)

Supplementary

80. Parents and young people lacking capacity

(1) Regulations may apply any statutory provision with modifications, for the purpose of giving effect to this Part in a case where the parent of a child, or a young person, lacks capacity at the relevant time.
(2) Regulations under subsection (1) may in particular include provision for—
 (a) references to a child's parent to be read as references to, or as including references to, a representative of the parent;
 (b) references to a young person to be read as references to, or as including references to, a representative of the young person, the young person's parent, or a representative of the young person's parent;
 (c) modifications to have effect in spite of section 27. (1)(g) of the Mental Capacity Act 2005 (Act does not permit decisions on discharging parental responsibilities in matters not relating to a child's property to be made on a person's behalf).
(3) "Statutory provision" means a provision made by or under this or any other Act, whenever passed or made.
(4) "The relevant time" means the time at which, under the statutory provision in question, something is required or permitted to be done by or in relation to the parent or young person.
(5) The reference in subsection (1) to lacking capacity is to lacking capacity within the meaning of the Mental Capacity Act 2005.
(6) "Representative", in relation to a parent or young person, means—
 (a) a deputy appointed by the Court of Protection under section 16. (2)(b) of the Mental Capacity Act 2005 to make decisions on the parent's or young person's behalf in relation to matters within this Part;
 (b) the donee of a lasting power of attorney (within the meaning of section 9 of that Act) appointed by the parent or young person to make decisions on his or her behalf in relation to matters within this Part;
 (c) an attorney in whom an enduring power of attorney (within the meaning of Schedule 4 to that Act) created by the parent or young person is vested, where the power of attorney is registered in accordance with paragraphs 4 and 13 of that Schedule or an application for registration of the power of attorney has been made.
Commencement Information
I80. S. 80 in force at 1.4.2014 for specified purposes by S.I. 2014/889, art. 3. (k)
I81. S. 80 in force at 1.9.2014 in so far as not already in force by S.I. 2014/889, art. 7. (a) (with savings and transitional provisions in S.I. 2014/2270 (as amended (1.4.2015) by S.I. 2015/505 and (1.9.2015) by S.I. 2015/1619)

81. Disapplication of Chapter 1 of Part 4 of EA 1996 in relation to children in England

Chapter 1 of Part 4 of EA 1996 (children with special educational needs) ceases to apply in relation to children in the area of a local authority in England.
Commencement Information
I82. S. 81 in force at 1.9.2014 by S.I. 2014/889, art. 7. (a) (with savings and transitional provisions in S.I. 2014/2270 (as amended (1.4.2015) by S.I. 2015/505 and (1.9.2015) by S.I. 2015/1619)

82. Consequential amendments

Schedule 3 (amendments consequential on this Part) has effect.
Commencement Information
I83. S. 82 in force at 1.9.2014 by S.I. 2014/889, art. 7. (a) (with savings and transitional provisions in S.I. 2014/2270 (as amended (1.4.2015) by S.I. 2015/505 and (1.9.2015) by S.I. 2015/1619)

83. Interpretation of Part 3.

(1) In this Part—
"EA 1996" means the Education Act 1996;
"ESA 2008" means the Education and Skills Act 2008;
"SSFA 1998" means the School Standards and Framework Act 1998.
(2) In this Part—
"appropriate person" has the meaning given by section 70. (5);
"beginning of the detention" has the meaning given by section 70. (6);
"detained person" has the meaning given by section 70. (5);
"detained person's EHC needs assessment" has the meaning given by section 70. (5);
"education, health and care provision" has the meaning given by section 26. (2);
"EHC needs assessment" has the meaning given by section 36. (2);
"EHC plan" means a plan within section 37. (2);
"health care provision" has the meaning given by section 21. (3);
"the home authority" has the meaning given by section 70. (6) (subject to subsection (7) of that section);
"mainstream post-16 institution" means a post-16 institution that is not a special post-16 institution;
"mainstream school" means—
  - a maintained school that is not a special school, or
  - an Academy school that is not a special school;
"maintained school" means—
  - a community, foundation or voluntary school, or
  - a community or foundation special school not established in a hospital;
"post-16 institution" means an institution which—
  - provides education or training for those over compulsory school age, but
  - is not a school or other institution which is within the higher education sector or which provides only higher education;
"proprietor", in relation to an institution that is not a school, means the person or body of persons responsible for the management of the institution;
"relevant early years education" has the meaning given by section 123 of SSFA 1998;
"relevant youth accommodation" has the meaning given by section 70. (5);
"social care provision" has the meaning given by section 21. (4);
"social services functions" in relation to a local authority has the same meaning as in the Local Authority Social Services Act 1970;
"special educational needs" has the meaning given by section 20. (1);
"special educational provision" has the meaning given by section 21. (1) and (2);
"special post-16 institution" means a post-16 institution that is specially organised to make special educational provision for students with special educational needs;
"training" has the same meaning as in section 15. ZA of EA 1996;
"young person" means a person over compulsory school age but under 25.
(3) A child or young person has a disability for the purposes of this Part if he or she has a disability for the purposes of the Equality Act 2010.

(4) A reference in this Part to "education"—
   (a) includes a reference to full-time and part-time education, but
   (b) does not include a reference to higher education,
and "educational" and "educate" (and other related terms) are to be read accordingly.
(5) A reference in this Part to—
   (a) a community, foundation or voluntary school, or
   (b) a community or foundation special school,
is to such a school within the meaning of SSFA 1998.
(6) A reference in this Part to a child or young person who is "in the area" of a local authority in England does not include a child or young person who is wholly or mainly resident in the area of a local authority in Wales.
(7) EA 1996 and the preceding provisions of this Part (except so far as they amend other Acts) are to be read as if those provisions were contained in EA 1996.
Commencement Information
I84. S. 83 in force at 1.9.2014 by S.I. 2014/889, art. 7. (a) (with savings and transitional provisions in S.I. 2014/2270 (as amended (1.4.2015) by S.I. 2015/505 and (1.9.2015) by S.I. 2015/1619)

Application of Part to detained persons

70. Application of Part to detained persons

(1) Subject to this section and sections 71 to 75, nothing in or made under this Part applies to, or in relation to, a child or young person detained in pursuance of—
   (a) an order made by a court, or
   (b) an order of recall made by the Secretary of State.
(2) Subsection (1) does not apply to—
   (a) section 28;
   (b) section 31;
   (c) section 77;
   (d) section 80;
   (e) section 83;
   (f) any amendment made by this Part of a provision which applies to, or in relation to, a child or young person detained in pursuance of—
(i) an order made by a court, or
(ii) an order of recall made by the Secretary of State.
(3) Regulations may apply any provision of this Part, with or without modifications, to or in relation to a child or young person detained in pursuance of—
   (a) an order made by a court, or
   (b) an order of recall made by the Secretary of State.
(4) The Secretary of State must consult the Welsh Ministers before making regulations under subsection (3) which will apply any provision of this Part to, or in relation to, a child or young person who is detained in Wales.
(5) For the purposes of this Part—
"appropriate person", in relation to a detained person, means—
   - where the detained person is a child, the detained person's parent, or
   - where the detained person is a young person, the detained person;
"detained person" means a child or young person who is—
   - 18 or under,
   - subject to a detention order (within the meaning of section 562. (1. A)(a) of EA 1996), and
   - detained in relevant youth accommodation,

and in provisions applying on a person's release, includes a person who, immediately before release, was a detained person;

"detained person's EHC needs assessment" means an assessment of what the education, health care and social care needs of a detained person will be on his or her release from detention;

"relevant youth accommodation" has the same meaning as in section 562. (1. A)(b) of EA 1996, save that it does not include relevant youth accommodation which is not in England.

(6) For the purposes of this Part—

(a) "beginning of the detention" has the same meaning as in Chapter 5. A of Part 10 of EA 1996 (persons detained in youth accommodation), and

(b) "the home authority" has the same meaning as in that Chapter, subject to regulations under subsection (7) (and regulations under section 562. J(4) of EA 1996 made by the Secretary of State may also make provision in relation to the definition of "the home authority" for the purposes of this Part).

(7) For the purposes of this Part, regulations may provide for paragraph (a) of the definition of "the home authority" in section 562. J(1) of EA 1996 (the home authority of a looked after child) to apply with modifications in relation to such provisions of this Part as may be specified in the regulations.

Modifications etc. (not altering text)

C1. S. 70. (5) modified (1.9.2014) by The Special Educational Needs and Disability Regulations 2014 (S.I. 2014/1530), regs. 1, 64. (1)(b), 64. (2), Sch. 3 Pt. 2

Commencement Information

I1. S. 70. (1) in force at 1.9.2014 for specified purposes by S.I. 2014/889, art. 7. (a) (with savings and transitional provisions in S.I. 2014/2270 (as amended (1.4.2015) by S.I. 2015/505 and (1.9.2015) by S.I. 2015/1619))

I2. S. 70. (1) in force at 1.4.2015 in so far as not already in force by S.I. 2015/375, art. 2. (a)

I3. S. 70. (2)-(7) in force at 1.4.2015 by S.I. 2015/375, art. 2. (b)

Disapplication of Chapter 1. of Part 4. of EA 1996. in relation to children in England

81. Disapplication of Chapter 1 of Part 4 of EA 1996 in relation to children in England

Chapter 1 of Part 4 of EA 1996 (children with special educational needs) ceases to apply in relation to children in the area of a local authority in England.

Commencement Information

I1. S. 81 in force at 1.9.2014 by S.I. 2014/889, art. 7. (a) (with savings and transitional provisions in S.I. 2014/2270 (as amended (1.4.2015) by S.I. 2015/505 and (1.9.2015) by S.I. 2015/1619)

Interpretation of Part 3

83. Interpretation of Part 3.

(1) In this Part—

"EA 1996" means the Education Act 1996;

"ESA 2008" means the Education and Skills Act 2008;

"SSFA 1998" means the School Standards and Framework Act 1998.

(2) In this Part—

"appropriate person" has the meaning given by section 70. (5);

"beginning of the detention" has the meaning given by section 70. (6);

"detained person" has the meaning given by section 70. (5);

"detained person's EHC needs assessment" has the meaning given by section 70. (5);

"education, health and care provision" has the meaning given by section 26. (2);

"EHC needs assessment" has the meaning given by section 36. (2);

"EHC plan" means a plan within section 37. (2);

"health care provision" has the meaning given by section 21. (3);

"the home authority" has the meaning given by section 70. (6) (subject to subsection (7) of that section);

"mainstream post-16 institution" means a post-16 institution that is not a special post-16 institution;

"mainstream school" means—
  - a maintained school that is not a special school, or
  - an Academy school that is not a special school;

"maintained school" means—
  - a community, foundation or voluntary school, or
  - a community or foundation special school not established in a hospital;

"post-16 institution" means an institution which—
  - provides education or training for those over compulsory school age, but
  - is not a school or other institution which is within the higher education sector or which provides only higher education;

"proprietor", in relation to an institution that is not a school, means the person or body of persons responsible for the management of the institution;

"relevant early years education" has the meaning given by section 123 of SSFA 1998;

"relevant youth accommodation" has the meaning given by section 70. (5);

"social care provision" has the meaning given by section 21. (4);

"social services functions" in relation to a local authority has the same meaning as in the Local Authority Social Services Act 1970;

"special educational needs" has the meaning given by section 20. (1);

"special educational provision" has the meaning given by section 21. (1) and (2);

"special post-16 institution" means a post-16 institution that is specially organised to make special educational provision for students with special educational needs;

"training" has the same meaning as in section 15. ZA of EA 1996;

"young person" means a person over compulsory school age but under 25.

(3) A child or young person has a disability for the purposes of this Part if he or she has a disability for the purposes of the Equality Act 2010.

(4) A reference in this Part to "education"—
  (a) includes a reference to full-time and part-time education, but
  (b) does not include a reference to higher education,
and "educational" and "educate" (and other related terms) are to be read accordingly.

(5) A reference in this Part to—
  (a) a community, foundation or voluntary school, or
  (b) a community or foundation special school,
is to such a school within the meaning of SSFA 1998.

(6) A reference in this Part to a child or young person who is "in the area" of a local authority in England does not include a child or young person who is wholly or mainly resident in the area of a local authority in Wales.

(7) EA 1996 and the preceding provisions of this Part (except so far as they amend other Acts) are to be read as if those provisions were contained in EA 1996.

Commencement Information

I1. S. 83 in force at 1.9.2014 by S.I. 2014/889, art. 7. (a) (with savings and transitional provisions in S.I. 2014/2270 (as amended (1.4.2015) by S.I. 2015/505 and (1.9.2015) by S.I. 2015/1619)

PART 4. Childcare etc

PART 4 Childcare etc

84. Childminder agencies

Schedule 4 (amendments to the Childcare Act 2006 to provide for the registration of childminder agencies on the childcare registers and the registration of certain childcare providers with those agencies, and other related amendments) has effect.
Commencement Information
I1. S. 84 in force at 1.4.2014 for specified purposes by S.I. 2014/889, art. 3. (l)
I2. S. 84 in force at 1.9.2014 in so far as not already in force by S.I. 2014/889, art. 7. (b)

85. Inspections at request of providers of childcare to young children

In section 49 of the Childcare Act 2006 (inspections of early years provision), after subsection (5) insert—
"(5. A)The Chief Inspector may charge a prescribed fee for conducting an inspection of early years provision where—
   (a) the inspection is conducted at the request of a registered person who provides that early years provision, and
   (b) the Chief Inspector is required by the Secretary of State under subsection (2)(b) to conduct that inspection."
Commencement Information
I3. S. 85 in force at 13.5.2014 by S.I. 2014/889, art. 5. (d)

86. Repeal of local authority's duty to assess sufficiency of childcare provision

Section 11 of the Childcare Act 2006 (duty of local authority in England to assess sufficiency of childcare provision) is repealed.
Commencement Information
I4. S. 86 in force at 13.5.2014 by S.I. 2014/889, art. 5. (d)

87. Discharge of authority's duty to secure free early years provision

(1) Part 1 of the Childcare Act 2006 (general functions of local authorities in England in relation to childcare) is amended as follows.
(2) After section 7 (duty to secure early years provision free of charge in accordance with regulations) insert—

"7. ADischarge of duty under section 7

(1) Regulations may require an English local authority to discharge its duty to a young child under section 7 by making arrangements which secure that an early years provider chosen by a parent of the child provides the early years provision to which the child is entitled in cases where—
   (a) the early years provider is willing to provide it, and
   (b) the early years provider is also willing to accept—
(i) any terms as to the payments which would be made to him or her in respect of the provision, and
(ii) any requirements which would be imposed in respect of it.
(2) Arrangements made by an authority to satisfy any requirement imposed under subsection (1) may be made with an early years provider or with an early years childminder agency or any other person who is able to arrange for an early years provider to provide early years provision.
(3) The regulations may provide that such a requirement—
   (a) applies only if the early years provider is of a prescribed description;
   (b) applies only if the early years provision provided by the early years provider is of a prescribed description;
   (c) does not apply in prescribed circumstances.
(4) The regulations may provide that arrangements made by an authority for the purpose of complying with such a requirement must include provision allowing the local authority to terminate the arrangements in prescribed circumstances.
(5) In this section—
"early years childminder agency" and "early years provider" have the same meanings as in Part 3;
"parent" has the same meaning as in section 2."
(3) After section 9 (arrangements between local authority and childcare providers) insert—

"9. AArrangements made by local authorities for the purposes of section 7

Regulations may provide that arrangements made by an English local authority for the purpose of discharging its duty under section 7—
   (a) may impose requirements on the person with whom the arrangements are made only if the requirements are of a prescribed description;
   (b) may not impose requirements of a prescribed description on the person with whom the arrangements are made."
Commencement Information
I5. S. 87 in force at 13.5.2014 by S.I. 2014/889, art. 5. (d)

88. Governing bodies: provision of community facilities

(1) Section 28 of the Education Act 2002 (limits on the powers of governing bodies of maintained schools to provide community facilities etc under section 27) is amended as follows.
(2) In subsection (4), for "a governing body" substitute " the governing body of a maintained school in Wales ".
(3) Omit subsection (4. C).
(4) In subsection (5)—
   (a) for "a governing body" substitute " the governing body of a maintained school in Wales ", and
   (b) in paragraph (a) omit "(in relation to England) by the Secretary of State or (in relation to Wales)".
Commencement Information
I6. S. 88 in force at 13.5.2014 by S.I. 2014/889, art. 5. (d)

89. Childcare costs scheme: preparatory expenditure

The Commissioners for Her Majesty's Revenue and Customs may incur expenditure in preparing for the introduction of a scheme for providing assistance in respect of the costs of childcare.
Commencement Information
I7. S. 89 in force at 13.5.2014 by S.I. 2014/889, art. 5. (d)

PART 5. Welfare of children

PART 5 Welfare of children

90. Extension of licensing of child performances to children under 14.

Section 38 of the Children and Young Persons Act 1963 (licences for performances by children under 14 not to be granted except for certain dramatic or musical performances) is repealed.

Tobacco, nicotine products and smoking

91. Purchase of tobacco[F1, nicotine products] etc. on behalf of persons under 18.

(1) A person aged 18 or over who buys or attempts to buy tobacco [F2, cigarette papers or a relevant nicotine product] on behalf of an individual aged under 18 commits an offence.
(2) Where a person is charged with an offence under this section it is a defence—
    (a) that the person had no reason to suspect that the individual concerned was aged under 18, or
    (b) in a case where the person has bought or attempted to buy cigarette papers, that the person had no reason to suspect that the individual concerned intended to use the papers for smoking.
(3) A person guilty of an offence under this section is liable on summary conviction to a fine not exceeding level 4 on the standard scale.
(4) A local weights and measures authority in England and Wales must enforce the provisions of this section in its area.
(5) Section 9 of, and Schedule 1 to, the Health Act 2006 (issue of fixed penalty notices in relation to certain smoking related offences) apply in relation to an offence under this section as they apply in relation to an offence under section 6. (5) or 7. (2) of that Act but with the following modifications—
    (a) references to an enforcement authority are to be read as references to a local weights and measures authority;
    (b) references to an authorised officer of an enforcement authority are to be read as references to any person authorised by a local weights and measures authority (whether or not an officer of the authority) in writing, either generally or specially, to act in matters arising under this section.
(6) Section 11 of, and Schedule 2 to, the Health Act 2006 (offence of obstruction of enforcement officers and powers of entry etc) apply for the purposes of this section as they apply for the purposes of Chapter 1 of Part 1 of that Act but with the following modifications—
    (a) references to an enforcement authority are to be read as references to a local weights and

measures authority;

(b) references to an authorised officer of an enforcement authority are to be read as references to any person (whether or not an officer of the authority) authorised by a local weights and measures authority in writing, either generally or specially, to act in matters arising under this section;

(c) references to Chapter 1 of Part 1 of the Act of 2006 are to be read as references to this section;

(d) section 11. (5) is to be ignored;

(e) paragraph 10 of Schedule 2 is to be ignored.

(7) "Tobacco" has the same meaning in this section as in section 7 of the Children and Young Persons Act 1933 (offence of selling tobacco to children).

[F3. (8)In this section "relevant nicotine product" means a nicotine product within the meaning of section 92 the sale of which at the same time and in the same circumstances to the individual aged under 18 would be prohibited by regulations for the time being in force under subsection (1) of that section.]

Amendments (Textual)

F1. Words in s. 91 heading inserted (26.3.2015) by The Nicotine Inhaling Products (Age of Sale and Proxy Purchasing) Regulations 2015 (S.I. 2015/895), regs. 1. (2), 2. (2)

F2. Words in s. 91. (1) substituted (26.3.2015) by The Nicotine Inhaling Products (Age of Sale and Proxy Purchasing) Regulations 2015 (S.I. 2015/895), regs. 1. (2), 2. (3)

F3. S. 91. (8) added (26.3.2015) by The Nicotine Inhaling Products (Age of Sale and Proxy Purchasing) Regulations 2015 (S.I. 2015/895), regs. 1. (2), 2. (4)

Commencement Information

I1. S. 91 in force at 1.10.2014 for specified purposes by S.I. 2014/2609, art. 2

I2. S. 91 in force at 1.10.2015 in so far as not already in force by S.I. 2015/375, art. 3

92. Prohibition of sale of nicotine products to persons under 18.

(1) The Secretary of State may by regulations make provision prohibiting the sale of nicotine products to persons aged under 18.

(2) A person who breaches a prohibition in regulations under subsection (1) commits an offence.

(3) Subsection (2) does not apply if—

(a) at the time of the sale, the person to whom the nicotine product is sold is employed by a manufacturer of nicotine products to which regulations under subsection (1) apply or by a dealer in such products (whether wholesale or retail), and

(b) the purchase of the product is for the purposes of the manufacturer's or dealer's business.

(4) Where a person is charged with an offence under this section it is a defence that the person took all reasonable precautions and exercised all due diligence to avoid committing the offence.

(5) A person guilty of an offence under this section is liable on summary conviction to a fine not exceeding level 4 on the standard scale.

(6) The Secretary of State may by regulations—

(a) amend section 91 (purchase of tobacco etc on behalf of persons under 18) so as to apply it (with or without modifications) in relation to nicotine products, or

(b) provide for that section to apply (with or without modifications) in relation to nicotine products.

(7) Regulations under this section may make provision in relation to—

(a) all nicotine products,

(b) nicotine products of a specified kind, or

(c) nicotine products subject to specified exceptions.

(8) The Secretary of State must obtain the consent of the Welsh Ministers before making regulations under this section which would (if contained in an Act of the National Assembly for Wales) be within the legislative competence of that Assembly.

(9) For the purposes of this section "nicotine product" means—

(a) a device which is intended to enable nicotine to be consumed by an individual or otherwise to be delivered into the human body,

(b) an item which is intended to form part of a device within paragraph (a), or

(c) a substance or item which consists of or contains nicotine and which is intended for human consumption or otherwise to be delivered into the human body.

(10) It does not matter for the purposes of subsection (9)(a) whether the device is also intended to enable any other substance to be consumed by an individual or otherwise to be delivered into the human body.

(11) The following are not nicotine products for the purposes of this section—

(a) tobacco;

(b) cigarette papers;

(c) any device which is intended to be used for the consumption of lit tobacco.

(12) In this section—

"specified" means specified in regulations under this section;

"tobacco" has the same meaning as in section 7 of the Children and Young Persons Act 1933 (offence of selling tobacco to children).

Commencement Information

I3. S. 92 in force at 1.10.2014 for specified purposes by S.I. 2014/2609, art. 2

I4. S. 92 in force at 1.10.2015 in so far as not already in force by S.I. 2015/375, art. 3

93. Amendments consequential on section 92.

(1) The Children and Young Persons Act 1933 is amended in accordance with subsections (2) to (6).

(2) In the italic heading before section 12. A, after "tobacco" insert " or nicotine products ".

(3) In section 12. A (restricted premises orders)—

(a) in subsection (1), after "tobacco" insert " or nicotine ",

(b) in subsection (3), for "or cigarette papers" substitute " , cigarette papers or nicotine product ", and

(c) in subsection (7)(a), after "tobacco" insert " or nicotine ".

(4) In section 12. B (restricted sale orders)—

(a) in subsection (1), after "tobacco" insert " or nicotine ",

(b) in subsection (3)—

(i) in paragraph (a), for "or cigarette papers" substitute " , cigarette papers or nicotine product ",

(ii) in paragraph (b), for "or cigarette papers" substitute " , cigarette papers or nicotine products ",

(iii) in each of paragraphs (c) and (d) omit "cigarette" in each place, and

(iv) in each of those paragraphs, after "tobacco" insert " or nicotine products ",

(c) in subsection (5), after "tobacco" insert " or nicotine ", and

(d) in subsection (6)—

(i) omit "cigarette", and

(ii) after "tobacco" insert " or nicotine products ".

(5) In section 12. C(1)(a) (enforcement), for "or cigarette papers" substitute " , cigarette papers or nicotine product ".

(6) In section 12. D (interpretation)—

(a) in subsection (1), in the opening words, for " "tobacco offence"" substitute " "tobacco or nicotine offence" ",

(b) in that subsection omit the "or" at the end of paragraph (b) and at the end of paragraph (c) insert ", or

(d) an offence committed under section 92 of the Children and Families Act 2014 on any premises (which are accordingly "the premises in relation to which the offence is committed").", and

(c) after subsection (2) insert—

"(2. A)In sections 12. A to 12. C "nicotine product" means a nicotine product within the meaning of section 92 of the Children and Families Act 2014 the sale of which to persons aged under 18 is for the time being prohibited by regulations under subsection (1) of that section."
(7) In section 5 of the Children and Young Persons (Protection from Tobacco) Act 1991 (enforcement action by local authorities in England and Wales)—
　(a) in subsection (1)(a), for "and sections 3 and 4 above" substitute " , sections 3 and 4 above and section 92 of the Children and Families Act 2014 (prohibition of sale of nicotine products to persons under 18) ", and
　(b) after subsection (1) insert—
"(1. A)Subsection (1) applies in relation to section 92 of the Children and Families Act 2014 only if regulations under subsection (1) of that section are for the time being in force."
(8) The Secretary of State may by regulations make provision amending, repealing, revoking or otherwise modifying any provision made by or under an enactment (whenever passed or made) in connection with provision made by or under section 92.
(9) In subsection (8) "enactment" includes a Measure or Act of the National Assembly for Wales.
Commencement Information
I5. S. 93 in force at 1.10.2014 for specified purposes by S.I. 2014/2609, art. 2
I6. S. 93 in force at 1.10.2015 in so far as not already in force by S.I. 2015/375, art. 3

94. Regulation of retail packaging etc of tobacco products

(1) The Secretary of State may make regulations under subsection (6) or (8) if the Secretary of State considers that the regulations may contribute at any time to reducing the risk of harm to, or promoting, the health or welfare of people under the age of 18.
(2) Subsection (1) does not prevent the Secretary of State, in making regulations under subsection (6) or (8), from considering whether the regulations may contribute at any time to reducing the risk of harm to, or promoting, the health or welfare of people aged 18 or over.
(3) The Secretary of State may treat regulations under subsection (6) or (8) as capable of contributing to reducing the risk of harm to, or promoting, the health or welfare of people under the age of 18 if the Secretary of State considers that—
　(a) at least some of the provisions of the regulations are capable of having that effect, or
　(b) the regulations are capable of having that effect when taken together with other regulations that were previously made under subsection (6) or (8) and are in force.
(4) Regulations under subsection (6) or (8) are to be treated for the purposes of subsection (1) or (2) as capable of contributing to reducing the risk of harm to, or promoting, people's health or welfare if (for example) they may contribute to any of the following—
　(a) discouraging people from starting to use tobacco products;
　(b) encouraging people to give up using tobacco products;
　(c) helping people who have given up, or are trying to give up, using tobacco products not to start using them again;
　(d) reducing the appeal or attractiveness of tobacco products;
　(e) reducing the potential for elements of the packaging of tobacco products other than health warnings to detract from the effectiveness of those warnings;
　(f) reducing opportunities for the packaging of tobacco products to mislead consumers about the effects of using them;
　(g) reducing opportunities for the packaging of tobacco products to create false perceptions about the nature of such products;
　(h) having an effect on attitudes, beliefs, intentions and behaviours relating to the reduction in use of tobacco products.
(5) Regulations under subsection (6) or (8) are to be treated for the purposes of subsection (1) as capable of contributing to reducing the risk of harm to, or promoting, the health or welfare of people under the age of 18 if—

(a) they may contribute to reducing activities by such people which risk harming their health or welfare after they reach the age of 18, or

(b) they may benefit such people by reducing the use of tobacco products among people aged 18 or over.

(6) The Secretary of State may by regulations make provision about the retail packaging of tobacco products.

(7) Regulations under subsection (6) may in particular impose prohibitions, requirements or limitations relating to—

(a) the markings on the retail packaging of tobacco products (including the use of branding, trademarks or logos);

(b) the appearance of such packaging;

(c) the materials used for such packaging;

(d) the texture of such packaging;

(e) the size of such packaging;

(f) the shape of such packaging;

(g) the means by which such packaging is opened;

(h) any other features of the retail packaging of tobacco products which could be used to distinguish between different brands of tobacco product;

(i) the number of individual tobacco products contained in an individual packet;

(j) the quantity of a tobacco product contained in an individual packet.

(8) The Secretary of State may by regulations make provision imposing prohibitions, requirements or limitations relating to—

(a) the markings on tobacco products (including the use of branding, trademarks or logos);

(b) the appearance of such products;

(c) the size of such products;

(d) the shape of such products;

(e) the flavour of such products;

(f) any other features of tobacco products which could be used to distinguish between different brands of tobacco product.

(9) The Secretary of State may by regulations—

(a) create offences which may be committed by persons who produce or supply tobacco products the retail packaging of which breaches prohibitions, requirements or limitations imposed by regulations under subsection (6);

(b) create offences which may be committed by persons who produce or supply tobacco products which breach prohibitions, requirements or limitations imposed by regulations under subsection (8);

(c) provide for exceptions and defences to such offences;

(d) make provision about the liability of others to be convicted of such offences if committed by a body corporate or a Scottish partnership.

(10) The Secretary of State may by regulations—

(a) provide that regulations under subsection (6) or (8) are to be treated for the purposes specified in regulations under this subsection as safety regulations within the meaning of the Consumer Protection Act 1987;

(b) make provision for the appropriate minister to direct, in relation to cases of a particular description or a particular case, that any duty imposed on a local weights and measures authority in Great Britain or a district council in Northern Ireland by virtue of provision under paragraph (a) is to be discharged instead by the appropriate minister.

(11) The Secretary of State may by regulations make provision amending, repealing, revoking or otherwise modifying any provision made by or under an enactment (whenever passed or made) in connection with provision made by regulations under any of subsections (6), (8), (9) or (10).

(12) The Secretary of State must—

(a) obtain the consent of the Scottish Ministers before making regulations under any of subsections (6), (8), (9) or (10) containing provision which would (if contained in an Act of the

Scottish Parliament) be within the legislative competence of that Parliament;

(b) obtain the consent of the Welsh Ministers before making regulations under any of those subsections containing provision which would (if contained in an Act of the National Assembly for Wales) be within the legislative competence of that Assembly;

(c) obtain the consent of the Office of the First Minister and deputy First Minister in Northern Ireland before making regulations under any of those subsections containing provision which would (if contained in an Act of the Northern Ireland Assembly) be within the legislative competence of that Assembly.

(13) For the purposes of this section a person produces a tobacco product if, in the course of a business and with a view to the product being supplied for consumption in the United Kingdom or through the travel retail sector, the person—

(a) manufactures the product,

(b) puts a name, trademark or other distinguishing mark on it by which the person is held out to be its manufacturer or originator, or

(c) imports it into the United Kingdom.

(14) For the purposes of this section a person supplies a tobacco product if in the course of a business the person—

(a) supplies the product,

(b) offers or agrees to supply it, or

(c) exposes or possesses it for supply.

(15) In this section—

"appropriate minister"—

- in relation to England, means the Secretary of State,
- in relation to Wales, means the Welsh Ministers,
- in relation to Northern Ireland, means the Department of Health, Social Services and Public Safety, and
- in relation to Scotland, means the Scottish Ministers;

"enactment" includes—

- an Act of the Scottish Parliament,
- a Measure or Act of the National Assembly for Wales, or
- Northern Ireland legislation;

"external packaging", "internal packaging" and "wrapper" have the meanings given by regulations under subsection (6);

"packaging", in relation to a tobacco product, means—

- the external packaging of that product,
- any internal packaging of that product,
- any wrapper of that product, or
- any other material attached to or included with that product or anything within paragraphs (a) to (c);

"retail packaging", in relation to a tobacco product, means the packaging in which it is, or is intended to be, presented for retail sale;

"retail sale" means sale otherwise than to a person who is acting in the course of a business which is part of the tobacco trade;

"tobacco product" means a product consisting wholly or partly of tobacco and intended to be smoked, sniffed, sucked or chewed;

"travel retail sector" means retail outlets in the United Kingdom at which tobacco products may be purchased only by people travelling on journeys to destinations outside the United Kingdom.

Commencement Information

I7. S. 94 in force at 1.10.2014 for specified purposes by S.I. 2014/2609, art. 2

I8. S. 94 in force at 1.10.2015 in so far as not already in force by S.I. 2015/375, art. 3

95. Smoking in a private vehicle

(1) The Health Act 2006 is amended as follows.
(2) In section 5 (smoke-free vehicles)—
  (a) after subsection (1) insert—
"(1. A)Regulations under this section may in particular provide for a private vehicle to be smoke-free where a person under the age of 18 is present in the vehicle.", and
  (b) in subsection (2), for "The regulations" substitute " Regulations under this section ".
(3) In section 9 (fixed penalties), after subsection (1) insert—
"(1. A)The appropriate national authority may by regulations provide that, in the circumstances specified in the regulations, an authorised officer of an enforcement authority (see section 10) who has reason to believe that a person has committed an offence under section 8. (4) in relation to a vehicle in relation to which the authorised officer has functions may give the person a penalty notice in respect of the offence."
(4) In section 10. (1) (power to designate bodies or descriptions of body as enforcement authorities)—
  (a) after "designating the" insert " persons or ", and
  (b) after "descriptions of" insert " person or ".
(5) In section 79 (orders and regulations)—
  (a) in subsection (4) (powers to which affirmative procedure applies), in paragraph (a) (powers in Part 1), for "or 8. (7)" substitute " , 8. (7) or 9. (1. A) ",
  (b) in that subsection, in paragraph (f) (powers in Schedule 1), for "or 8" substitute " , 8 or 17 ", and
  (c) after that subsection insert—
"(4. A)No statutory instrument containing regulations under section 9. (1. A) or paragraph 17 of Schedule 1 may be made by the Welsh Ministers unless a draft of the instrument has been laid before, and approved by a resolution of, the National Assembly for Wales."
(6) In Schedule 1 (fixed penalties), after paragraph 16 insert—
17. The appropriate national authority may by regulations—
(a) amend this Schedule so as to modify its application in relation to penalty notices issued by an authorised officer of an enforcement authority of a particular kind, or
(b) provide for this Schedule to apply with modifications in relation to such notices."
Commencement Information
I9. S. 95 in force at 1.10.2014 for specified purposes by S.I. 2014/2609, art. 2
I10. S. 95 in force at 1.10.2015 in so far as not already in force by S.I. 2015/375, art. 3

Young carers and parent carers

96. Young carers

(1) In the Children Act 1989, after section 17 insert—
"17. ZAYoung carers' needs assessments: England
(1) A local authority in England must assess whether a young carer within their area has needs for support and, if so, what those needs are, if—
  (a) it appears to the authority that the young carer may have needs for support, or
  (b) the authority receive a request from the young carer or a parent of the young carer to assess the young carer's needs for support.
(2) An assessment under subsection (1) is referred to in this Part as a "young carer's needs assessment".
(3) In this Part "young carer" means a person under 18 who provides or intends to provide care for another person (but this is qualified by section 17. ZB(3)).
(4) Subsection (1) does not apply in relation to a young carer if the local authority have previously

carried out a care-related assessment of the young carer in relation to the same person cared for.
(5) But subsection (1) does apply (and so a young carer's needs assessment must be carried out) if it appears to the authority that the needs or circumstances of the young carer or the person cared for have changed since the last care-related assessment.
(6) "Care-related assessment" means—
   (a) a young carer's needs assessment;
   (b) an assessment under any of the following—
(i) section 1 of the Carers (Recognition and Services) Act 1995;
(ii) section 1 of the Carers and Disabled Children Act 2000;
(iii) section 4. (3) of the Community Care (Delayed Discharges) Act 2003.
(7) A young carer's needs assessment must include an assessment of whether it is appropriate for the young carer to provide, or continue to provide, care for the person in question, in the light of the young carer's needs for support, other needs and wishes.
(8) A local authority, in carrying out a young carer's needs assessment, must have regard to—
   (a) the extent to which the young carer is participating in or wishes to participate in education, training or recreation, and
   (b) the extent to which the young carer works or wishes to work.
(9) A local authority, in carrying out a young carer's needs assessment, must involve—
   (a) the young carer,
   (b) the young carer's parents, and
   (c) any person who the young carer or a parent of the young carer requests the authority to involve.
(10) A local authority that have carried out a young carer's needs assessment must give a written record of the assessment to—
   (a) the young carer,
   (b) the young carer's parents, and
   (c) any person to whom the young carer or a parent of the young carer requests the authority to give a copy.
(11) Where the person cared for is under 18, the written record must state whether the local authority consider him or her to be a child in need.
(12) A local authority in England must take reasonable steps to identify the extent to which there are young carers within their area who have needs for support.
17. ZBYoung carers' needs assessments: supplementary
(1) This section applies for the purposes of section 17. ZA.
(2) "Parent", in relation to a young carer, includes—
   (a) a parent of the young carer who does not have parental responsibility for the young carer, and
   (b) a person who is not a parent of the young carer but who has parental responsibility for the young carer.
(3) A person is not a young carer if the person provides or intends to provide care—
   (a) under or by virtue of a contract, or
   (b) as voluntary work.
(4) But in a case where the local authority consider that the relationship between the person cared for and the person under 18 providing or intending to provide care is such that it would be appropriate for the person under 18 to be regarded as a young carer, that person is to be regarded as such (and subsection (3) is therefore to be ignored in that case).
(5) The references in section 17. ZA and this section to providing care include a reference to providing practical or emotional support.
(6) Where a local authority—
   (a) are required to carry out a young carer's needs assessment, and
   (b) are required or have decided to carry out some other assessment of the young carer or of the person cared for;
the local authority may, subject to subsection (7), combine the assessments.

(7) A young carer's needs assessment may be combined with an assessment of the person cared for only if the young carer and the person cared for agree.
(8) The Secretary of State may by regulations make further provision about carrying out a young carer's needs assessment; the regulations may, in particular—
    (a) specify matters to which a local authority is to have regard in carrying out a young carer's needs assessment;
    (b) specify matters which a local authority is to determine in carrying out a young carer's needs assessment;
    (c) make provision about the manner in which a young carer's needs assessment is to be carried out;
    (d) make provision about the form a young carer's needs assessment is to take.
(9) The Secretary of State may by regulations amend the list in section 17. ZA(6)(b) so as to—
    (a) add an entry,
    (b) remove an entry, or
    (c) vary an entry.
17. ZCConsideration of young carers' needs assessments
A local authority that carry out a young carer's needs assessment must consider the assessment and decide—
    (a) whether the young carer has needs for support in relation to the care which he or she provides or intends to provide;
    (b) if so, whether those needs could be satisfied (wholly or partly) by services which the authority may provide under section 17; and
    (c) if they could be so satisfied, whether or not to provide any such services in relation to the young carer."
(2) In section 104 of the Children Act 1989 (regulations and orders)—
    (a) in subsections (2) and (3. A) (regulations within subsection (3. B) or (3. C) not subject to annulment but to be approved in draft) before "(3. B)" insert " (3. AA), ", and
    (b) after subsection (3. A) insert—
"(3. AA)Regulations fall within this subsection if they are regulations made in the exercise of the power conferred by section 17. ZB(9)."
Commencement Information
I11. S. 96 in force at 1.4.2015 by S.I. 2015/375, art. 2. (c)

97. Parent carers

(1) In the Children Act 1989, after section 17. ZC (as inserted by section 96) insert—
"17. ZDParent carers' needs assessments: England
(1) A local authority in England must, if the conditions in subsections (3) and (4) are met, assess whether a parent carer within their area has needs for support and, if so, what those needs are.
(2) In this Part "parent carer" means a person aged 18 or over who provides or intends to provide care for a disabled child for whom the person has parental responsibility.
(3) The first condition is that—
    (a) it appears to the authority that the parent carer may have needs for support, or
    (b) the authority receive a request from the parent carer to assess the parent carer's needs for support.
(4) The second condition is that the local authority are satisfied that the disabled child cared for and the disabled child's family are persons for whom they may provide or arrange for the provision of services under section 17.
(5) An assessment under subsection (1) is referred to in this Part as a "parent carer's needs assessment".
(6) Subsection (1) does not apply in relation to a parent carer if the local authority have previously carried out a care-related assessment of the parent carer in relation to the same disabled child cared

for.

(7) But subsection (1) does apply (and so a parent carer's needs assessment must be carried out) if it appears to the authority that the needs or circumstances of the parent carer or the disabled child cared for have changed since the last care-related assessment.

(8) "Care-related assessment" means—

(a) a parent carer's needs assessment;

(b) an assessment under any of the following—

(i) section 1 of the Carers (Recognition and Services) Act 1995;

(ii) section 6 of the Carers and Disabled Children Act 2000;

(iii) section 4. (3) of the Community Care (Delayed Discharges) Act 2003.

(9) A parent carer's needs assessment must include an assessment of whether it is appropriate for the parent carer to provide, or continue to provide, care for the disabled child, in the light of the parent carer's needs for support, other needs and wishes.

(10) A local authority in carrying out a parent carer's needs assessment must have regard to—

(a) the well-being of the parent carer, and

(b) the need to safeguard and promote the welfare of the disabled child cared for and any other child for whom the parent carer has parental responsibility.

(11) In subsection (10) "well-being" has the same meaning as in Part 1 of the Care Act 2014.

(12) A local authority, in carrying out a parent carer's needs assessment, must involve—

(a) the parent carer,

(b) any child for whom the parent carer has parental responsibility, and

(c) any person who the parent carer requests the authority to involve.

(13) A local authority that have carried out a parent carer's needs assessment must give a written record of the assessment to—

(a) the parent carer, and

(b) any person to whom the parent carer requests the authority to give a copy.

(14) A local authority in England must take reasonable steps to identify the extent to which there are parent carers within their area who have needs for support.

17. ZEParent carers' needs assessments: supplementary

(1) This section applies for the purposes of section 17. ZD.

(2) The references in section 17. ZD to providing care include a reference to providing practical or emotional support.

(3) Where a local authority—

(a) are required to carry out a parent carer's needs assessment, and

(b) are required or have decided to carry out some other assessment of the parent carer or of the disabled child cared for,

the local authority may combine the assessments.

(4) The Secretary of State may by regulations make further provision about carrying out a parent carer's needs assessment; the regulations may, in particular—

(a) specify matters to which a local authority is to have regard in carrying out a parent carer's needs assessment;

(b) specify matters which a local authority is to determine in carrying out a parent carer's needs assessment;

(c) make provision about the manner in which a parent carer's needs assessment is to be carried out;

(d) make provision about the form a parent carer's needs assessment is to take.

(5) The Secretary of State may by regulations amend the list in section 17. ZD(8)(b) so as to—

(a) add an entry,

(b) remove an entry, or

(c) vary an entry.

17. ZFConsideration of parent carers' needs assessments

A local authority that carry out a parent carer's needs assessment must consider the assessment and decide—

(a) whether the parent carer has needs for support in relation to the care which he or she provides or intends to provide;

(b) whether the disabled child cared for has needs for support;

(c) if paragraph (a) or (b) applies, whether those needs could be satisfied (wholly or partly) by services which the authority may provide under section 17; and

(d) if they could be so satisfied, whether or not to provide any such services in relation to the parent carer or the disabled child cared for."

(2) In section 104 of the Children Act 1989 (regulations and orders)—

(a) in subsections (2) and (3. A) (regulations within subsection (3. B) or (3. C) not subject to annulment but to be approved in draft) after "(3. AA)," insert " (3. AB), ", and

(b) after subsection (3. AA) insert—

"(3. AB)Regulations fall within this subsection if they are regulations made in the exercise of the power conferred by section 17. ZE(5)."

Commencement Information

I12. S. 97 in force at 1.4.2015 by S.I. 2015/375, art. 2. (c)

Staying put arrangements

98. Arrangements for living with former foster parents after reaching adulthood

(1) The Children Act 1989 is amended as follows.

(2) After section 23. C (continuing functions in respect of former relevant children) insert—

"23. CZAArrangements for certain former relevant children to continue to live with former foster parents

(1) Each local authority in England have the duties provided for in subsection (3) in relation to a staying put arrangement.

(2) A "staying put arrangement" is an arrangement under which—

(a) a person who is a former relevant child by virtue of section 23. C(1)(b), and

(b) a person (a "former foster parent") who was the former relevant child's local authority foster parent immediately before the former relevant child ceased to be looked after by the local authority,

continue to live together after the former relevant child has ceased to be looked after.

(3) It is the duty of the local authority (in discharging the duties in section 23. C(3) and by other means)—

(a) to monitor the staying put arrangement, and

(b) to provide advice, assistance and support to the former relevant child and the former foster parent with a view to maintaining the staying put arrangement.

(4) Support provided to the former foster parent under subsection (3)(b) must include financial support.

(5) Subsection (3)(b) does not apply if the local authority consider that the staying put arrangement is not consistent with the welfare of the former relevant child.

(6) The duties set out in subsection (3) subsist until the former relevant child reaches the age of 21."

(3) In Part 2 of Schedule 2 (local authority support for looked after children) after paragraph 19. B (preparation for ceasing to be looked after) insert—

19. BA(1)This paragraph applies in relation to an eligible child (within the meaning of paragraph 19. B) who has been placed by a local authority in England with a local authority foster parent.

(2) When carrying out the assessment of the child's needs in accordance with paragraph 19. B(4), the local authority must determine whether it would be appropriate to provide advice, assistance

and support under this Act in order to facilitate a staying put arrangement, and with a view to maintaining such an arrangement, after the local authority cease to look after him or her.
(3) The local authority must provide advice, assistance and support under this Act in order to facilitate a staying put arrangement if—
(a) the local authority determine under sub-paragraph (2) that it would be appropriate to do so, and
(b) the eligible child and the local authority foster parent wish to make a staying put arrangement.
(4) In this paragraph, "staying put arrangement" has the meaning given by section 23. CZA."
Commencement Information
I13. S. 98 in force at 13.5.2014 by S.I. 2014/889, art. 5. (e)

Educational achievement of looked after children

99. Promotion of educational achievement of children looked after by local authorities

In the Children Act 1989, in section 22 after subsection (3. A) (duty of local authorities to promote the educational achievement of looked after children) insert—
"(3. B)A local authority in England must appoint at least one person for the purpose of discharging the duty imposed by virtue of subsection (3. A).
(3. C)A person appointed by a local authority under subsection (3. B) must be an officer employed by that authority or another local authority in England."
Commencement Information
I14. S. 99 in force at 13.5.2014 by S.I. 2014/889, art. 5. (e)

Pupils with medical conditions

100. Duty to support pupils with medical conditions

(1) The appropriate authority for a school to which this section applies must make arrangements for supporting pupils at the school with medical conditions.
(2) In meeting the duty in subsection (1) the appropriate authority must have regard to guidance issued by the Secretary of State.
(3) The duty in subsection (1) does not apply in relation to a pupil who is a young child for the purposes of Part 3 of the Childcare Act 2006 (regulation of provision of childcare in England).
(4) This section applies to the following schools in England—
    (a) a maintained school;
    (b) an Academy school;
    (c) an alternative provision Academy;
    (d) a pupil referral unit.
(5) In this section—
"the appropriate authority for a school" means—
    - in the case of a maintained school, the governing body,
    - in the case of an Academy, the proprietor, and
    - in the case of a pupil referral unit, the management committee;
"maintained school" means—
    - a community, foundation or voluntary school, within the meaning of the School Standards and Framework Act 1998, or
    - a community or foundation special school, within the meaning of that Act.
(6) The Education Act 1996 and this section are to be read as if this section were included in that

Act.
Commencement Information
I15. S. 100 in force at 1.9.2014 by S.I. 2014/889, art. 7. (c)

Local authority functions: intervention

101. Local authority functions relating to children etc: intervention

(1) Section 497. A of the Education Act 1996 (which confers power on the Secretary of State to secure the proper performance of local authority education functions, and is applied to social services functions relating to children by section 50 of the Children Act 2004 and to functions relating to childcare by section 15 of the Childcare Act 2006) is amended in accordance with subsection (2).
(2) After subsection (4. A) insert—
"(4. AA)So far as is appropriate in consequence of a direction given under subsection (4. A), a reference (however expressed) in an enactment, instrument or other document to a local authority is to be read as a reference to the person by whom the function is exercisable.
(4. AB)Subsection (4. AC) applies if a direction given under subsection (4. A) expires or is revoked without being replaced.
(4. AC)So far as is appropriate in consequence of the expiry or revocation, a reference (however expressed) in an instrument or other document to the person by whom the function was exercisable is to be read as a reference to the local authority to which the direction was given."
(3) In section 15 of the Local Government Act 1999 (Secretary of State's power to secure compliance with requirements of Part 1 of that Act) after subsection (6) insert—
"(6. A)So far as is appropriate in consequence of a direction given under subsection (6)(a), a reference (however expressed) in an enactment, instrument or other document to a best value authority is to be read as a reference to the person by whom the function is exercisable.
(6. B)Subsection (6. C) applies if a direction given under subsection (6)(a) expires or is revoked without being replaced.
(6. C)So far as is appropriate in consequence of the expiry or revocation, a reference (however expressed) in an instrument or other document to the person by whom the function was exercisable is to be read as a reference to the best value authority to which the direction was given."

Regulation of children's homes etc

102. Application of suspension etc powers to establishments and agencies in England

(1) In section 14. A of the Care Standards Act 2000 (power of Welsh Ministers to suspend registration of person in respect of establishment or agency), in subsection (1)—
   (a) for "Welsh Ministers" substitute " registration authority ", and
   (b) omit "for which the Welsh Ministers are the registration authority".
(2) In subsection (2) of that section, for "Welsh Ministers give" substitute " registration authority gives ".
(3) In section 15. (4. A) of that Act (duty of Welsh Ministers to give notice of decision to grant application for cancellation or variation of suspension)—

(a) for "Welsh Ministers decide" substitute " registration authority decides ",
(b) for "they" substitute " it ", and
(c) for "their" substitute " its ".

(4) In section 20. B of that Act (urgent procedure for suspension or variation etc: Wales), in the heading omit ": Wales".

(5) In subsection (1) of that section—
(a) in paragraph (a) omit "for which the Welsh Ministers are the registration authority", and
(b) in paragraph (b)—
(i) for "Welsh Ministers have" substitute " registration authority has ", and
(ii) for "they act" substitute " it acts ".

(6) In subsection (2) of that section, for "Welsh Ministers" in both places substitute " registration authority ".

(7) In subsection (4)(b) of that section, for "Welsh Ministers'" substitute "registration authority's".

103. Objectives and standards for establishments and agencies in England

(1) In section 22 of the Care Standards Act 2000 (regulation of establishments and agencies), in subsection (1), for the words from "may in particular" to the end substitute "—
(a) regulations made by the Secretary of State may in particular make any provision such as is mentioned in subsection (1. A), (2), (7) or (8), and
(b) regulations made by the Welsh Ministers may in particular make any provision such as is mentioned in subsection (2), (7) or (8)."

(2) In that section, after subsection (1) insert—
"(1. A)Regulations made by the Secretary of State may prescribe objectives and standards which must be met in relation to an establishment or agency for which the CIECSS is the registration authority."

104. National minimum standards for establishments and agencies in England

In section 23 of the Care Standards Act 2000 (national minimum standards), after subsection (1) insert—
"(1. A)The standards applicable to an establishment or agency for which the CIECSS is the registration authority may, in particular, explain or supplement requirements imposed in relation to that establishment or agency by regulations under section 22."

105. Disqualification from carrying on, or being employed in, a children's home

(1) Section 65 of the Children Act 1989 (person disqualified from fostering a child privately to be disqualified from carrying on etc children's home) is amended as follows.
(2) Before subsection (1) insert—
"(A1)A person ("P") who is disqualified (under section 68) from fostering a child privately must not carry on, or be otherwise concerned in the management of, or have any financial interest in, a children's home in England unless—
(a) P has, within the period of 28 days beginning with the day on which P became aware of P's disqualification, disclosed to the appropriate authority the fact that P is so disqualified, and
(b) P has obtained the appropriate authority's written consent.
(A2) A person ("E") must not employ a person ("P") who is so disqualified in a children's home in

England unless—
 (a) E has, within the period of 28 days beginning with the day on which E became aware of P's disqualification, disclosed to the appropriate authority the fact that P is so disqualified, and
 (b) E has obtained the appropriate authority's written consent."
(3) In subsection (1), after "children's home" insert " in Wales ".
(4) In subsection (2), after "children's home" insert " in Wales ".
(5) In subsection (4), after "subsection" insert " (A1), (A2), ".
(6) In subsection (5), after "subsection" insert " (A2) or ".
Commencement Information
I16. S. 105 in force at 1.4.2015 by S.I. 2015/375, art. 2. (d)

Free school lunches

106. Provision of free school lunches

(1) The Education Act 1996 is amended as follows.
(2) In section 512. ZB (provision of free school lunches and milk at maintained schools)—
 (a) in subsection (2)(a) after "subsection (4)" insert " or (4. A) (or both) ",
 (b) after subsection (4) insert—
"(4. A)A person is within this subsection if the person—
 (a) is a registered pupil at a maintained school or pupil referral unit in England, and
 (b) is in reception, year 1, year 2 or any other prescribed year group at the school.
(4. B)The Secretary of State may by order provide for the following to be treated as persons within subsection (4. A)—
 (a) registered pupils, or any description of registered pupils, at a maintained nursery school in England;
 (b) children, or any description of children, who receive relevant funded early years education, or any description of such education, in England.
(4. C)In subsection (4. A)—
"maintained school" means—
 - a community, foundation or voluntary school, or
 - a community or foundation special school;
"reception" means a year group in which the majority of children will, in the school year, attain the age of 5;
"year 1" means a year group in which the majority of children will, in the school year, attain the age of 6;
"year 2" means a year group in which the majority of children will, in the school year, attain the age of 7;
"year group" means a group of children at a school the majority of whom will, in a particular school year, attain the same age.", and
 (c) in subsection (5), after " "prescribed"" insert " , "relevant funded early years education" ".
(3) After section 512. A insert—
"512. BProvision of school lunches: Academies
(1) Academy arrangements in relation to an Academy school or an alternative provision Academy must include provision imposing obligations on the proprietor that are equivalent to the school lunches obligations.
(2) "The school lunches obligations" are the obligations imposed in relation to maintained schools and pupil referral units in England by—
 (a) section 512. (3) (provision of school lunches on request), and
 (b) section 512. ZB(1) (provision of free school lunches to eligible persons).
(3) Academy arrangements in relation to an Academy (other than a 16 to 19 Academy) that are

entered into before the date on which section 106. (3) of the Children and Families Act 2014 comes into force are to be treated as if they included the provision required by subsection (1), to the extent that they do not otherwise include such provision."
Commencement Information
I17. S. 106 in force at 1.9.2014 by S.I. 2014/889, art. 7. (d)

PART 6. The Children's Commissioner

PART 6 The Children's Commissioner

107. Primary function of the Children's Commissioner

For section 2 of the Children Act 2004 (general function of the Children's Commissioner) substitute—

"2. Primary function: children's rights, views and interests

(1) The Children's Commissioner's primary function is promoting and protecting the rights of children in England.
(2) The primary function includes promoting awareness of the views and interests of children in England.
(3) In the discharge of the primary function the Children's Commissioner may, in particular—
    (a) advise persons exercising functions or engaged in activities affecting children on how to act compatibly with the rights of children;
    (b) encourage such persons to take account of the views and interests of children;
    (c) advise the Secretary of State on the rights, views and interests of children;
    (d) consider the potential effect on the rights of children of government policy proposals and government proposals for legislation;
    (e) bring any matter to the attention of either House of Parliament;
    (f) investigate the availability and effectiveness of complaints procedures so far as relating to children;
    (g) investigate the availability and effectiveness of advocacy services for children;
    (h) investigate any other matter relating to the rights or interests of children;
    (i) monitor the implementation in England of the United Nations Convention on the Rights of the Child;
    (j) publish a report on any matter considered or investigated under this section.
(4) In the discharge of the primary function, the Children's Commissioner must have particular regard to the rights of children who are within section 8. A (children living away from home or receiving social care) and other groups of children who the Commissioner considers to be at particular risk of having their rights infringed.
(5) The Children's Commissioner may not conduct an investigation of the case of an individual child in the discharge of the primary function.

2. AUnited Nations Convention on the Rights of the Child

(1) The Children's Commissioner must, in particular, have regard to the United Nations Convention on the Rights of the Child in considering for the purposes of the primary function what constitute the rights and interests of children (generally or so far as relating to a particular

matter).

(2) The references in section 2. (3)(i) and this section to the United Nations Convention on the Rights of the Child are to the Convention on the Rights of the Child adopted by the General Assembly of the United Nations on 20th November 1989 (including any Protocols to that Convention which are in force in relation to the United Kingdom), subject to any reservations, objections or interpretative declarations by the United Kingdom for the time being in force.

2. BInvolving children in the discharge of the primary function

(1) The Children's Commissioner must take reasonable steps to involve children in the discharge of the primary function.
(2) The Commissioner must in particular take reasonable steps to—
    (a) ensure that children are aware of the Commissioner's primary function and how they may communicate with him or her, and
    (b) consult children, and organisations working with children, on the matters the Commissioner proposes to consider or investigate in the discharge of the primary function.
(3) The Children's Commissioner must for the purposes of this section have particular regard to children who are within section 8. A (children living away from home or receiving social care) and other groups of children who the Commissioner considers do not have adequate means by which they can make their views known.

2. CPrimary function: reports

(1) This section applies where the Children's Commissioner publishes a report in the discharge of the primary function.
(2) The Commissioner must, if and to the extent he or she considers it appropriate, also publish the report in a version which is suitable for children (or, if the report relates to a particular group of children, for those children).
(3) Where the report contains recommendations about the exercise by a person of functions of a public nature, the Commissioner may require that person to state in writing, within such period as the Commissioner may reasonably require, what action the person has taken or proposes to take in response to the recommendations."

108. Provision by Commissioner of advice and assistance to certain children

After section 2. C of the Children Act 2004 (as inserted by section 107) insert—

"2. DProvision of advice and assistance to certain children in England

(1) The Children's Commissioner may provide advice and assistance to any child who is within section 8. A (children living away from home or receiving social care).
(2) The Children's Commissioner may in particular under this section make representations on behalf of a child who is within section 8. A to a person in England who is—
    (a) providing the child with accommodation or services, or
    (b) otherwise exercising functions in relation to the child."

109. Commissioner's powers to enter premises

After section 2.D of the Children Act 2004 (as inserted by section 108) insert—

"2.E Powers to enter premises to conduct interviews or observe standards

(1) This section applies for the purposes of the Children's Commissioner's primary function and the function under section 2.D.
(2) The Children's Commissioner, or a person authorised by the Commissioner, may at any reasonable time enter any premises, other than a private dwelling—
    (a) for the purpose of interviewing a child, or
    (b) for the purpose of observing the standard of care provided to children accommodated or otherwise cared for there.
(3) An interview of a child under subsection (2)(a) may be conducted in private, if the child consents.
(4) A person who enters premises under subsection (1) may interview any person present on the premises who works there.
(5) It is immaterial for the purposes of subsection (4) whether a person's work is paid, or under a contract of employment."

110. Provision of information to Commissioner

After section 2.E of the Children Act 2004 (as inserted by section 109) insert—

"2.F Provision of information to Commissioner

(1) Any person exercising functions of a public nature must supply the Children's Commissioner with such information in that person's possession relating to those functions as the Commissioner may reasonably request for the purposes of the primary function or the function under section 2.D.
(2) The information must be information which that person would, apart from subsection (1), lawfully be able to disclose to the Commissioner."

111. Advisory board

After section 7 of the Children Act 2004 insert—

"7.A Advisory board

(1) The Children's Commissioner must appoint an advisory board to provide the Commissioner with advice and assistance relating to the discharge of his or her functions.
(2) The advisory board must consist of persons who (taken together) represent a broad range of interests which are relevant to the Children's Commissioner's functions.
(3) The Children's Commissioner must from time to time publish a report on the procedure followed and the criteria used when making appointments to the advisory board."

112. Business plans

After section 7.A of the Children Act 2004 (as inserted by section 111) insert—

"7. BBusiness plans

(1) The Children's Commissioner must publish a business plan which sets out, in relation to the discharge of the Commissioner's functions—
    (a) the Commissioner's proposed main activities for the period covered by the plan (including the matters he or she intends to consider or investigate), and
    (b) the Commissioner's proposed strategic priorities for that period.
(2) A business plan must cover a period of at least 12 months beginning with the date of publication.
(3) The Commissioner must publish a new business plan before the end of the period covered by the preceding business plan.
(4) Before publishing a business plan under this section, the Children's Commissioner must—
    (a) take reasonable steps to consult children,
    (b) consult persons who (taken together) represent a broad range of interests which are relevant to the Children's Commissioner's functions, and
    (c) consult such other persons as the Commissioner thinks appropriate.
(5) The Children's Commissioner must for the purposes of subsection (4)(a) have particular regard to children who are within section 8. A (children living away from home or receiving social care) and other groups of children who the Commissioner considers do not have adequate means by which they can make their views known."

113. Annual reports

(1) Section 8 of the Children Act 2004 (annual reports) is amended as follows.
(2) In subsection (1)—
    (a) in paragraph (a) omit "under this Part, other than functions of holding inquiries",
    (b) after paragraph (a) insert " and ", and
    (c) omit paragraph (c) and the "and" which precedes it.
(3) In subsection (2) for the words from "an account" to the end substitute "—
    (a) a summary of the Commissioner's activities and an analysis of the effectiveness of those activities in promoting and protecting the rights of children,
    (b) an account of what the Commissioner has done in the discharge of his or her functions in relation to children who are within section 8. A (children living away from home or receiving social care),
    (c) an account of the steps taken by the Commissioner to consult children or otherwise involve them in the discharge of his or her functions, and
    (d) a summary of how the Commissioner has taken into account the results of any such consultation and anything else resulting from involving children in the discharge of his or her functions."
(4) In subsection (3)(b) for "the Secretary of State" substitute " the Commissioner ".
(5) In subsection (4) for "the Secretary of State has laid" substitute " laying ".
(6) For subsection (5) substitute—
"(5)If the Children's Commissioner does not consider a report made under this section to be suitable for children, the Commissioner must publish a version of the report which is suitable for children."

114. Children living away from home or receiving social care

After section 8 of the Children Act 2004 insert—

"8. AChildren in England living away from home or receiving

social care

(1) For the purposes of this Part, a child is within this section if he or she is within any of subsections (2) to (5).
(2) A child is within this subsection if he or she is provided with accommodation by a school or college in England to which section 87. (1) of the Children Act 1989 applies.
(3) A child is within this subsection if he or she is accommodated in an establishment (within the meaning of the Care Standards Act 2000) in respect of which Her Majesty's Chief Inspector of Education, Children's Services and Skills is the registration authority under section 5 of that Act.
(4) A child is within this subsection if functions are being exercised in relation to him or her by an agency (within the meaning of the Care Standards Act 2000) in respect of which Her Majesty's Chief Inspector of Education, Children's Services and Skills is the registration authority under section 5 of that Act.
(5) A child is within this subsection if a local authority in England exercises social services functions (within the meaning of the Local Authority Social Services Act 1970) in relation to him or her.
(6) For the purposes of this Part, a person who is not a child is to be treated as a child who is within this section if—
   (a) he or she is aged 18 or over and under 25, and
   (b) a local authority in England has provided services to him or her under any of sections 23. C to 24. D of the Children Act 1989 at any time after he or she reached the age of 16."

115. Children's Commissioner: minor and consequential amendments

Schedule 5 (minor and consequential amendments to Part 1 of the Children Act 2004 and to other Acts) has effect.

116. Repeal of requirement to appoint Children's Rights Director

(1) Section 120 of the Education and Inspections Act 2006 (requirement to appoint Children's Rights Director) is repealed.
(2) In that Act—
   (a) in section 117 (performance of functions of the Office for Standards in Education, Children's Services and Skills), in subsection (2) after paragraph (a) insert—
   "(aa)any matters raised by the Children's Commissioner with the Office or the Chief Inspector;", and
   (b) in section 119 (performance of the functions of the Chief Inspector of Education, Children's Services and Skills), in subsection (3) after paragraph (a) (and before the "and" which follows it) insert—
   "(aa)any matters raised by the Children's Commissioner with the Chief Inspector;".
(3) Schedule 6 (transfers of staff and property in consequence of the repeal of the requirement to appoint a Children's Rights Director) has effect.

PART 7. Statutory rights to leave and pay

PART 7 Statutory rights to leave and pay

117. Shared parental leave

(1) In Part 8 of the Employment Rights Act 1996, after section 75. D there is inserted—
"CHAPTER 1. BShared parental leave
75. EEntitlement to shared parental leave: birth
(1) The Secretary of State may make regulations entitling an employee who satisfies specified conditions—
    (a) as to duration of employment,
    (b) as to being, or expecting to be, the mother of a child,
    (c) as to caring or intending to care, with another person ("P"), for the child,
    (d) as to entitlement to maternity leave,
    (e) as to the exercise of that entitlement and the extent of any such exercise,
    (f) as to giving notice of an intention to exercise an entitlement to leave under this subsection, and
    (g) as to the consent of P to the amount of leave under this subsection that the employee intends to take,
to be absent from work on leave under this subsection for the purpose of caring for the child.
(2) Regulations under subsection (1) may provide that the employee's entitlement is subject to the satisfaction by P of specified conditions—
    (a) as to employment or self-employment,
    (b) as to having earnings of a specified amount for a specified period,
    (c) as to caring or intending to care, with the employee, for the child, and
    (d) as to relationship with the child or the employee.
(3) Provision under subsection (1)(f) may require the employee to give notice to the employer about—
    (a) the amount of leave to which the employee would be entitled if the entitlement were fully exercised (disregarding for these purposes any intention of P to exercise an entitlement to leave under subsection (4) or to statutory shared parental pay);
    (b) how much of the entitlement to leave the employee intends to exercise;
    (c) the extent to which P intends to exercise an entitlement to leave under subsection (4) or to statutory shared parental pay.
(4) The Secretary of State may make regulations entitling an employee who satisfies specified conditions—
    (a) as to duration of employment,
    (b) as to relationship with a child or expected child or with the child's mother,
    (c) as to caring or intending to care, with the child's mother, for the child,
    (d) as to giving notice of an intention to exercise an entitlement to leave under this subsection, and
    (e) as to the consent of the child's mother to the amount of leave under this subsection that the employee intends to take,
to be absent from work on leave under this subsection for the purpose of caring for the child.
(5) Regulations under subsection (4) may provide that the employee's entitlement is subject to the satisfaction by the child's mother of specified conditions—
    (a) as to employment or self-employment,
    (b) as to having earnings of a specified amount for a specified period,
    (c) as to caring or intending to care, with the employee, for the child,
    (d) as to entitlement (or lack of entitlement) to maternity leave, statutory maternity pay or maternity allowance, and
    (e) as to the exercise of any such entitlement and the extent of any such exercise.
(6) Provision under subsection (4)(d) may require the employee to give notice to the employer about—
    (a) the amount of leave to which the employee would be entitled if the entitlement were fully

exercised (disregarding for these purposes any intention of the child's mother to exercise an entitlement to leave under subsection (1) or to statutory shared parental pay);

(b) how much of the entitlement to leave the employee intends to exercise;

(c) the extent to which the child's mother intends to exercise an entitlement to leave under subsection (1) or to statutory shared parental pay.

75. FEntitlement to leave under section 75. E: further provision

(1) Regulations under section 75. E are to include provision for determining—

(a) the amount of leave under section 75. E(1) or (4) to which an employee is entitled in respect of a child;

(b) when leave under section 75. E(1) or (4) may be taken.

(2) Provision under subsection (1)(a) is to secure that the amount of leave to which an employee is entitled in respect of a child does not exceed—

(a) in a case where the child's mother became entitled to maternity leave, the relevant amount of time reduced by—

(i) where her maternity leave ends without her ordinary or additional maternity leave period having been curtailed by virtue of section 71. (3)(ba) or 73. (3)(a), the amount of maternity leave taken by the child's mother, or

(ii) except where sub-paragraph (i) applies, the amount of time between the beginning of her maternity leave and the time when her ordinary or additional maternity leave period, as curtailed by virtue of section 71. (3)(ba) or 73. (3)(a), comes to an end;

(b) in a case where the child's mother became entitled to statutory maternity pay or maternity allowance but not maternity leave, the relevant amount of time reduced by an amount determined in accordance with paragraph (a) or, as the case may be, paragraph (b) of section 171. ZU(6) of the Social Security Contributions and Benefits Act 1992.

(3) In subsection (2) "the relevant amount of time" means an amount of time specified in or determined in accordance with regulations under section 75. E.

(4) Provision under subsection (1)(a) is to secure that the amount of leave that an employee is entitled to take in respect of a child takes into account—

(a) in a case where another person is entitled to leave under section 75. E in respect of the child, the amount of such leave taken by the other person;

(b) in a case where another person is entitled to statutory shared parental pay in respect of the child but not leave under section 75. E, the number of weeks in respect of which such pay is payable to the other person.

(5) In reckoning for the purposes of subsection (2) the amount of maternity leave taken, a part of a week is to be treated as a full week.

(6) In reckoning for the purposes of subsection (4) the amount of leave under section 75. E taken during a period of such leave, a part of a week is to be treated as a full week.

(7) Provision under subsection (1)(b) is to secure that leave under section 75. E must be taken before the end of such period as may be specified by the regulations.

(8) Regulations under section 75. E are to provide for the taking of leave under section 75. E in a single period or in non-consecutive periods.

(9) Regulations under section 75. E may—

(a) provide for an employer, subject to such restrictions as may be specified, to require an employee who proposes to take non-consecutive periods of leave under section 75. E to take that amount of leave as a single period of leave;

(b) provide for a single period of leave that is so imposed on an employee to start with a day proposed by the employee or, if no day is proposed, with the first day of the first period of leave proposed by the employee.

(10) Regulations under section 75. E may provide for the variation, subject to such restrictions as may be specified, of—

(a) the period or periods during which an amount of leave under section 75. E may be taken;

(b) the amount of leave under section 75. E that the employee previously specified in accordance with provision under section 75. E(3)(b) or (6)(b) or subsection (13)(b) of this section.

(11) Provision under subsection (10)(a) may provide for variation to be subject to the consent of an employer in circumstances specified by the regulations.

(12) Provision under subsection (10)(b) may require an employee to satisfy specified conditions—

(a) as to giving notice of an intention to vary the amount of leave under section 75. E to be taken by the employee;

(b) if the employee proposes to vary the amount of leave under section 75. E(1) to be taken by the employee, as to the consent of P to that variation;

(c) if the employee proposes to vary the amount of leave under section 75. E(4) to be taken by the employee, as to the consent of the child's mother to that variation.

(13) Provision under subsection (12)(a) may require an employee to give notice to the employer about—

(a) the extent to which the employee has exercised an entitlement to leave under section 75. E(1) or (4) in respect of the child;

(b) how much of the entitlement to leave the employee intends to exercise;

(c) the extent to which a person other than the employee has exercised an entitlement to leave under section 75. E or to statutory shared parental pay in respect of the child;

(d) the extent to which a person other than the employee intends to exercise such an entitlement.

(14) Regulations under section 75. E may—

(a) specify things which are, or are not, to be taken as done for the purpose of caring for a child;

(b) make provision excluding the right to be absent on leave under section 75. E in respect of a child where more than one child is born as a result of the same pregnancy;

(c) specify a minimum amount of leave under section 75. E which may be taken;

(d) make provision about how leave under section 75. E may be taken;

(e) specify circumstances in which an employee may work for the employer during a period of leave under section 75. E without bringing the particular period of leave, or the employee's entitlement to leave under section 75. E, to an end;

(f) specify circumstances in which an employee may be absent on leave under section 75. E otherwise than for the purpose of caring for a child without bringing the person's entitlement to leave under section 75. E to an end.

(15) In this section "week" means any period of seven days.

(16) The Secretary of State may by regulations provide that the following do not have effect, or have effect with modifications specified by the regulations, in a case where the mother of a child dies before another person has become entitled to leave under section 75. E in respect of the child—

(a) section 75. E(4)(b), (c) and (e);

(b) section 75. E(5);

(c) section 75. E(6)(c);

(d) subsection (12)(c);

(e) subsection (13)(c) and (d).

75. GEntitlement to shared parental leave: adoption

(1) The Secretary of State may make regulations entitling an employee who satisfies specified conditions—

(a) as to duration of employment,

(b) as to being a person with whom a child is, or is expected to be, placed for adoption under the law of any part of the United Kingdom,

(c) as to caring or intending to care, with another person ("P"), for the child,

(d) as to entitlement to adoption leave,

(e) as to the exercise of that entitlement and the extent of any such exercise,

(f) as to giving notice of an intention to exercise an entitlement to leave under this subsection, and

(g) as to the consent of P to the amount of leave under this subsection that the employee intends to take,

to be absent from work on leave under this subsection for the purpose of caring for the child.

(2) Regulations under subsection (1) may provide that the employee's entitlement is subject to the satisfaction by P of specified conditions—
    (a) as to employment or self-employment,
    (b) as to having earnings of a specified amount for a specified period,
    (c) as to caring or intending to care, with the employee, for the child, and
    (d) as to relationship with the child or the employee.
(3) Provision under subsection (1)(f) may require the employee to give notice to the employer about—
    (a) the amount of leave to which the employee would be entitled if the entitlement were fully exercised (disregarding for these purposes any intention of P to exercise an entitlement to leave under subsection (4) or to statutory shared parental pay);
    (b) how much of the entitlement to leave the employee intends to exercise;
    (c) the extent to which P intends to exercise an entitlement to leave under subsection (4) or to statutory shared parental pay.
(4) The Secretary of State may make regulations entitling an employee who satisfies specified conditions—
    (a) as to duration of employment,
    (b) as to relationship with a child placed, or expected to be placed, for adoption under the law of any part of the United Kingdom or with a person ("A") with whom the child is, or is expected to be, so placed,
    (c) as to caring or intending to care, with A, for the child,
    (d) as to giving notice of an intention to exercise an entitlement to leave under this subsection, and
    (e) as to the consent of A to the amount of leave under this subsection that the employee intends to take,
to be absent from work on leave under this subsection for the purpose of caring for the child.
(5) Regulations under subsection (4) may provide that the employee's entitlement is subject to the satisfaction by A of specified conditions—
    (a) as to employment or self-employment,
    (b) as to having earnings of a specified amount for a specified period,
    (c) as to caring or intending to care, with the employee, for the child,
    (d) as to entitlement (or lack of entitlement) to adoption leave or statutory adoption pay, and
    (e) as to the exercise of any such entitlement and the extent of any such exercise.
(6) Provision under subsection (4)(d) may require the employee to give notice to the employer about—
    (a) the amount of leave to which the employee would be entitled if the entitlement were fully exercised (disregarding for these purposes any intention of A to exercise an entitlement to leave under subsection (1) or to statutory shared parental pay);
    (b) how much of the entitlement to leave the employee intends to exercise;
    (c) the extent to which A intends to exercise an entitlement to leave under subsection (1) or to statutory shared parental pay.
(7) Regulations under subsections (1) and (4) are to provide for leave in respect of a child placed, or expected to be placed, under section 22. C of the Children Act 1989 by a local authority in England with a local authority foster parent who has been approved as a prospective adopter.
(8) This section and section 75. H have effect in relation to regulations made by virtue of subsection (7) as if references to a child being placed for adoption under the law of any part of the United Kingdom were references to being placed under section 22. C of the Children Act 1989 with a local authority foster parent who has been approved as a prospective adopter.
75. HEntitlement to leave under section 75. G: further provision
(1) Regulations under section 75. G are to include provision for determining—
    (a) the amount of leave under section 75. G(1) or (4) to which an employee is entitled in respect of a child;
    (b) when leave under section 75. G(1) or (4) may be taken.

(2) Provision under subsection (1)(a) is to secure that the amount of leave to which an employee is entitled in respect of a child does not exceed—
    (a) in a case where a person with whom the child is, or is expected to be, placed for adoption became entitled to adoption leave, the relevant amount of time reduced by—
(i) where the person's adoption leave ends without the person's ordinary or additional adoption leave period having been curtailed by virtue of section 75. A(2. A)(a) or 75. B(3)(a), the amount of adoption leave taken by that person, or
(ii) except where sub-paragraph (i) applies, the amount of time between the beginning of the person's adoption leave and the time when the person's ordinary or additional adoption leave period, as curtailed by virtue of section 75. A(2. A)(a) or 75. B(3)(a), comes to an end;
    (b) in a case where a person with whom the child is, or is expected to be, placed for adoption became entitled to statutory adoption pay but not adoption leave, the relevant amount of time reduced by an amount determined in accordance with paragraph (a) or, as the case may be, paragraph (b) of section 171. ZV(6) of the Social Security Contributions and Benefits Act 1992.
(3) In subsection (2) "the relevant amount of time" means an amount of time specified in or determined in accordance with regulations under section 75. G.
(4) Provision under subsection (1)(a) is to secure that the amount of leave that an employee is entitled to take in respect of a child takes into account—
    (a) in a case where another person is entitled to leave under section 75. G in respect of the child, the amount of such leave taken by the other person;
    (b) in a case where another person is entitled to statutory shared parental pay in respect of the child but not leave under section 75. G, the number of weeks in respect of which such pay is payable to the other person.
(5) In reckoning for the purposes of subsection (2) the amount of adoption leave taken, a part of a week is to be treated as a full week.
(6) In reckoning for the purposes of subsection (4) the amount of leave under section 75. G taken during a period of such leave, a part of a week is to be treated as a full week.
(7) Provision under subsection (1)(b) is to secure that leave under section 75. G must be taken before the end of such period as may be prescribed by the regulations.
(8) Regulations under section 75. G are to provide for the taking of leave under section 75. G in a single period or in non-consecutive periods.
(9) Regulations under section 75. G may—
    (a) provide for an employer, subject to such restrictions as may be specified, to require an employee who proposes to take non-consecutive periods of leave under section 75. G to take that amount of leave as a single period of leave, and
    (b) provide for a single period of leave that is so imposed on an employee to start with a day proposed by the employee or, if no day is proposed, with the first day of the first period of leave proposed by the employee.
(10) Regulations under section 75. G may provide for the variation, subject to such restrictions as may be specified, of—
    (a) the period or periods during which an amount of leave under section 75. G is to be taken;
    (b) the amount of leave under section 75. G that the employee previously specified in accordance with provision under section 75. G(3)(b) or (6)(b) or subsection (13)(b) of this section.
(11) Provision under subsection (10)(a) may provide for variation to be subject to the consent of an employer in circumstances specified by the regulations.
(12) Provision under subsection (10)(b) may require an employee to satisfy specified conditions—
    (a) as to giving notice of an intention to vary the amount of leave under section 75. G to be taken by the employee;
    (b) if the employee proposes to vary the amount of leave under section 75. G(1) to be taken by the employee, as to the consent of P to that variation;
    (c) if the employee proposes to vary the amount of leave under section 75. G(4) to be taken by the employee, as to the consent of A to that variation.
(13) Provision under subsection (12)(a) may require an employee to give notice to the employer

about—
   (a) the extent to which the employee has exercised an entitlement to leave under section 75. G(1) or (4) in respect of the child;
   (b) how much of the entitlement to leave the employee intends to exercise;
   (c) the extent to which a person other than the employee has exercised an entitlement to leave under section 75. G or to statutory shared parental pay in respect of the child;
   (d) the extent to which a person other than the employee intends to exercise such an entitlement.
(14) Regulations under section 75. G may—
   (a) specify things which are, or are not, to be taken as done for the purpose of caring for a child;
   (b) make provision excluding the right to be absent on leave under section 75. G in respect of a child where more than one child is placed for adoption as part of the same arrangement;
   (c) specify a minimum amount of leave under section 75. G which may be taken;
   (d) make provision about how leave under section 75. G may be taken;
   (e) specify circumstances in which an employee may work for the employer during a period of leave under section 75. G without bringing the particular period of leave, or the employee's entitlement to leave under section 75. G, to an end;
   (f) specify circumstances in which an employee may be absent on leave under section 75. G otherwise than for the purpose of caring for a child without bringing the person's entitlement to leave under section 75. G to an end.
(15) In this section "week" means any period of seven days.
(16) The Secretary of State may by regulations provide that the following do not have effect, or have effect with modifications specified by the regulations, in a case where a person who is taking adoption leave or is entitled to be paid statutory adoption pay in respect of a child dies before another person has become entitled to leave under section 75. G in respect of the child—
   (a) section 75. G(4)(b), (c) and (e);
   (b) section 75. G(5);
   (c) section 75. G(6)(c);
   (d) subsection (12)(c);
   (e) subsection (13)(c) and (d).
(17) The Secretary of State may by regulations provide for section 75. G and this section to have effect in relation to cases which involve adoption, but not the placement of a child for adoption under the law of any part of the United Kingdom, with such modifications as the regulations may prescribe.
(18) The Secretary of State may by regulations provide for section 75. G and this section to have effect in relation to cases which involve an employee who has applied, or intends to apply, with another person for a parental order under section 54 of the Human Fertilisation and Embryology Act 2008 and a child who is, or will be, the subject of the order, with such modifications as the regulations may prescribe.
75. IRights during and after shared parental leave
(1) Regulations under section 75. E or 75. G are to provide—
   (a) that an employee who is absent on leave under that section is entitled, for such purposes and to such extent as the regulations may prescribe, to the benefit of the terms and conditions of employment which would have applied if the employee had not been absent;
   (b) that an employee who is absent on leave under that section is bound, for such purposes and to such extent as the regulations may prescribe, by obligations arising under those terms and conditions, except in so far as they are inconsistent with section 75. E(1) or (4) or 75. G(1) or (4), as the case may be; and
   (c) that an employee who is absent on leave under that section is entitled to return from leave to a job of a kind prescribed by the regulations, subject to section 75. J(1).
(2) In subsection (1)(a) "terms and conditions of employment"—
   (a) includes matters connected with an employee's employment whether or not they arise under the employee's contract of employment, but
   (b) does not include terms and conditions about remuneration.

(3) The reference in subsection (1)(c) to absence on leave under section 75. E or 75. G includes, where appropriate, a reference to a continuous period of absence attributable partly to leave under one of those sections and partly to any one or more of the following—
    (a) leave under the other of those sections,
    (b) maternity leave,
    (c) paternity leave,
    (d) adoption leave, and
    (e) parental leave.
(4) Regulations under section 75. E or 75. G may specify matters which are, or are not, to be treated as remuneration for the purposes of this section.
(5) Regulations under section 75. E or 75. G may make provision, in relation to the right to return mentioned in subsection (1)(c), about—
    (a) seniority, pension rights and similar rights;
    (b) terms and conditions of employment on return.
75. JRedundancy and dismissal
(1) Regulations under section 75. E or 75. G may make provision about—
    (a) redundancy, or
    (b) dismissal (other than by reason of redundancy),
during a period of leave under that section.
(2) Provision made by virtue of subsection (1) may include—
    (a) provision requiring an employer to offer alternative employment;
    (b) provision for the consequences of failure to comply with the regulations (which may include provision for a dismissal to be treated as unfair for the purposes of Part 10).
75. KChapter 1. B: supplemental
(1) Regulations under section 75. E or 75. G may—
    (a) make provision about notices to be given, evidence to be produced and other procedures to be followed by—
(i) employees,
(ii) employers, and
(iii) relevant persons;
    (b) make provision requiring such persons to keep records;
    (c) make provision for the consequences of failure to give notices, to produce evidence, to keep records or to comply with other procedural requirements;
    (d) make provision for the consequences of failure to act in accordance with a notice given by virtue of paragraph (a);
    (e) make special provision for cases where an employee has a right which corresponds to a right under section 75. E or 75. G and which arises under the employee's contract of employment or otherwise;
    (f) make provision modifying the effect of Chapter 2 of Part 14 (calculation of a week's pay) in relation to an employee who is or has been absent from work on leave under section 75. E or 75. G;
    (g) make provision applying, modifying or excluding an enactment, in such circumstances as may be specified and subject to any conditions which may be specified, in relation to a person entitled to take leave under section 75. E or 75. G.
(2) In subsection (1) "relevant person" means—
    (a) a person who, in connection with an employee's claim to be entitled to leave under section 75. E or 75. G, is required to satisfy conditions specified in provision under section 75. E(2) or (5) or 75. G(2) or (5), or
    (b) a person who is an employer or former employer of such a person.
(3) In subsection (2)(b) "employer", in relation to a person falling within subsection (2)(a) who is an employed earner, includes a person who is a secondary contributor as regards that employed earner.
(4) The conditions as to employment or self-employment that may be specified in provision under

section 75. E(2) or (5) or 75. G(2) or (5) include conditions as to being in employed or self-employed earner's employment.
(5) In subsections (3) and (4)—
"employed earner" and "self-employed earner" have the meaning given by section 2 of the Social Security Contributions and Benefits Act 1992, subject for these purposes to the effect of regulations made under section 2. (2)(b) of that Act (persons who are to be treated as employed or self-employed earners);
"employment", in the case of employment as an employed or self-employed earner, has the meaning given by section 122 of that Act;
"secondary contributor", as regards an employed earner, means a person who—
   - is indicated by section 7. (1) of that Act, as that subsection has effect subject to section 7. (2) of that Act, as being a secondary contributor as regards the earner, or
   - is indicated by regulations under section 7. (2) of that Act as being a person to be treated as a secondary contributor as regards the earner.
(6) Regulations under any of sections 75. E to 75. H may make different provision for different cases or circumstances.
(7) Where sections 75. G and 75. H have effect in relation to such cases as are described in section 75. H(18), regulations under section 75. G about evidence to be produced may require statutory declarations as to—
   (a) eligibility to apply for a parental order;
   (b) intention to apply for such an order."
(2) In section 236 of the Employment Rights Act 1996 (orders and regulations), in subsection (3) (affirmative procedure required), after "75. A, 75. B," there is inserted " 75. E, 75. F(16), 75. G, 75. H(16), (17) or (18) ".
Commencement Information
I1. S. 117 in force at 30.6.2014 by S.I. 2014/1640, art. 3. (1)(a)

118. Exclusion or curtailment of other statutory rights to leave

(1) The Employment Rights Act 1996 is amended as follows.
(2) In section 71 (ordinary maternity leave)—
   (a) in subsection (3), after paragraph (b) there is inserted—
"(ba)may allow an employee to bring forward the date on which an ordinary maternity leave period ends, subject to prescribed restrictions and subject to satisfying prescribed conditions;
   (bb) may allow an employee in prescribed circumstances to revoke, or to be treated as revoking, the bringing forward of that date;";
   (b) after subsection (3) there is inserted—
"(3. A)Provision under subsection (3)(ba) is to secure that an employee may bring forward the date on which an ordinary maternity leave period ends only if the employee or another person has taken, or is taking, prescribed steps as regards leave under section 75. E or statutory shared parental pay in respect of the child."
(3) In section 73 (additional maternity leave)—
   (a) in subsection (3)(a), for the words from "to choose" to the end there is substituted " to bring forward the date on which an additional maternity leave period ends, subject to prescribed restrictions and subject to satisfying prescribed conditions; ";
   (b) after subsection (3)(a) there is inserted—
"(aa)may allow an employee in prescribed circumstances to revoke, or to be treated as revoking, the bringing forward of that date;";
   (c) after subsection (3) there is inserted—
"(3. A)Provision under subsection (3)(a) is to secure that an employee may bring forward the date on which an additional maternity leave period ends only if the employee or another person has taken, or is taking, prescribed steps as regards leave under section 75. E or statutory shared

parental pay in respect of the child."

(4) In section 75. A (ordinary adoption leave)—

(a) in subsection (2. A), after "subsection (2)" there is inserted "—

(a) may allow an employee to bring forward the date on which an ordinary adoption leave period ends, subject to prescribed restrictions and subject to satisfying prescribed conditions;

(b) may allow an employee in prescribed circumstances to revoke, or to be treated as revoking, the bringing forward of that date;";

(b) in subsection (2. A), the words from "may specify circumstances" to the end become paragraph (c);

(c) after subsection (2. A) there is inserted—

"(2. B)Provision under subsection (2. A)(a) is to secure that an employee may bring forward the date on which an ordinary adoption leave period ends only if the employee or another person has taken, or is taking, prescribed steps as regards leave under section 75. G or statutory shared parental pay in respect of the child."

(5) In section 75. B (additional adoption leave)—

(a) in subsection (3)(a), for the words from "to choose" to the end there is substituted " to bring forward the date on which an additional adoption leave period ends, subject to prescribed restrictions and subject to satisfying prescribed conditions; ";

(b) after subsection (3)(a) there is inserted—

"(aa)may allow an employee in prescribed circumstances to revoke, or to be treated as revoking, the bringing forward of that date;";

(c) after subsection (3) there is inserted—

"(3. A)Provision under subsection (3)(a) is to secure that an employee may bring forward the date on which an additional adoption leave period ends only if the employee or another person has taken, or is taking, prescribed steps as regards leave under section 75. G or statutory shared parental pay in respect of the child."

(6) In section 80. A (entitlement to ordinary paternity leave: birth), after subsection (4) there is inserted—

"(4. A)Provision under subsection (2)(b) must secure that, once an employee takes leave under section 75. E in respect of a child, the employee may not take leave under this section in respect of the child."

(7) In section 80. B (entitlement to ordinary paternity leave: adoption), after subsection (4) there is inserted—

"(4. A)Provision under subsection (2)(b) must secure that, once an employee takes leave under section 75. G in respect of a child, the employee may not take leave under this section in respect of the child."

Commencement Information

I2. S. 118 in force at 30.6.2014 by S.I. 2014/1640, art. 3. (1)(b)

Statutory shared parental pay

119. Statutory shared parental pay

(1) In the Social Security Contributions and Benefits Act 1992, after section 171. ZT there is inserted—

"PART 12. ZC Statutory shared parental pay

171. ZUEntitlement: birth

(1) Regulations may provide that, where all the conditions in subsection (2) are satisfied in relation to a person who is the mother of a child ("the claimant mother"), the claimant mother is to be entitled in accordance with the following provisions of this Part to payments to be known as "statutory shared parental pay".

(2) The conditions are—
(a) that the claimant mother and another person ("P") satisfy prescribed conditions as to caring or intending to care for the child;
(b) that P satisfies prescribed conditions—
(i) as to employment or self-employment,
(ii) as to having earnings of a prescribed amount for a prescribed period, and
(iii) as to relationship either with the child or with the claimant mother;
(c) that the claimant mother has been in employed earner's employment with an employer for a continuous period of at least the prescribed length ending with a prescribed week;
(d) that at the end of that prescribed week the claimant mother was entitled to be in that employment;
(e) that the claimant mother's normal weekly earnings for a prescribed period ending with a prescribed week are not less than the lower earnings limit in force under section 5.(1)(a) at the end of that week;
(f) if regulations so provide, that the claimant mother continues in employed earner's employment (whether or not with the employer by reference to whom the condition in paragraph (c) is satisfied) until a prescribed time;
(g) that the claimant mother became entitled to statutory maternity pay by reference to the birth of the child;
(h) that the claimant mother satisfies prescribed conditions as to the reduction of the duration of the maternity pay period;
(i) that the claimant mother has given the person who will be liable to pay statutory shared parental pay to her notice of—
(i) the number of weeks in respect of which she would be entitled to claim statutory shared parental pay in respect of the child if the entitlement were fully exercised (disregarding for these purposes any intention of P to claim statutory shared parental pay in respect of the child),
(ii) the number of weeks in respect of which she intends to claim statutory shared parental pay, and
(iii) the number of weeks in respect of which P intends to claim statutory shared parental pay;
(j) that the claimant mother has given the person who will be liable to pay statutory shared parental pay to her notice of the period or periods during which she intends to claim statutory shared parental pay in respect of the child;
(k) that a notice under paragraph (i) or (j)—
(i) is given by such time as may be prescribed, and
(ii) satisfies prescribed conditions as to form and content;
(l) that P consents to the extent of the claimant mother's intended claim for statutory shared parental pay;
(m) that it is the claimant mother's intention to care for the child during each week in respect of which statutory shared parental pay is paid to her;
(n) that the claimant mother is absent from work during each week in respect of which statutory shared parental pay is paid to her;
(o) that, where she is an employee within the meaning of the Employment Rights Act 1996, the claimant mother's absence from work during each such week is absence on shared parental leave.
(3) Regulations may provide that, where all the conditions in subsection (4) are satisfied in relation to a person ("the claimant"), the claimant is to be entitled in accordance with the following provisions of this Part to payments to be known as "statutory shared parental pay".
(4) The conditions are—
(a) that the claimant and another person ("M") who is the mother of a child satisfy prescribed conditions as to caring or intending to care for the child;
(b) that the claimant satisfies—
(i) prescribed conditions as to relationship with the child, or
(ii) prescribed conditions as to relationship with M;
(c) that M satisfies prescribed conditions—

(i) as to employment or self-employment, and

(ii) as to having earnings of a prescribed amount for a prescribed period;

(d) that the claimant has been in employed earner's employment with an employer for a continuous period of at least the prescribed length ending with a prescribed week;

(e) that at the end of that prescribed week the claimant was entitled to be in that employment;

(f) that the claimant's normal weekly earnings for a prescribed period ending with a prescribed week are not less than the lower earnings limit in force under section 5. (1)(a) at the end of that week;

(g) if regulations so provide, that the claimant continues in employed earner's employment (whether or not with the employer by reference to whom the condition in paragraph (d) is satisfied) until a prescribed time;

(h) that M became entitled, by reference to the birth of the child, to—

(i) a maternity allowance, or

(ii) statutory maternity pay;

(i) that M satisfies prescribed conditions as to—

(i) the reduction of the duration of the maternity allowance period, or

(ii) the reduction of the duration of the maternity pay period, as the case may be;

(j) that the claimant has given the person who will be liable to pay statutory shared parental pay to the claimant notice of—

(i) the number of weeks in respect of which the claimant would be entitled to claim statutory shared parental pay in respect of the child if the entitlement were fully exercised (disregarding for these purposes any intention of M to claim statutory shared parental pay in respect of the child),

(ii) the number of weeks in respect of which the claimant intends to claim statutory shared parental pay, and

(iii) the number of weeks in respect of which M intends to claim statutory shared parental pay;

(k) that the claimant has given the person who will be liable to pay statutory shared parental pay to the claimant notice of the period or periods during which the claimant intends to claim statutory shared parental pay in respect of the child;

(l) that a notice under paragraph (j) or (k)—

(i) is given by such time as may be prescribed, and

(ii) satisfies prescribed conditions as to form and content;

(m) that M consents to the extent of the claimant's intended claim for statutory shared parental pay;

(n) that it is the claimant's intention to care for the child during each week in respect of which statutory shared parental pay is paid to the claimant;

(o) that the claimant is absent from work during each week in respect of which statutory shared parental pay is paid to the claimant;

(p) that, where the claimant is an employee within the meaning of the Employment Rights Act 1996, the claimant's absence from work during each such week is absence on shared parental leave.

(5) Regulations may provide for—

(a) the determination of the extent of a person's entitlement to statutory shared parental pay in respect of a child;

(b) when statutory shared parental pay is to be payable.

(6) Provision under subsection (5)(a) is to secure that the number of weeks in respect of which a person is entitled to payments of statutory shared parental pay in respect of a child does not exceed the number of weeks of the maternity pay period reduced by—

(a) where the mother of the child takes action that is treated by regulations as constituting for the purposes of this section her return to work without satisfying conditions prescribed under subsection (2)(h) or, as the case may be, subsection (4)(i)—

(i) the number of relevant weeks in respect of which maternity allowance or statutory maternity pay is payable to the mother, or

(ii) if that number of relevant weeks is less than a number prescribed by regulations, that prescribed number of weeks, or

(b) except where paragraph (a) applies, the number of weeks to which the maternity allowance period is reduced by virtue of section 35. (3. A) or, as the case may be, the maternity pay period is reduced by virtue of section 165. (3. A).

(7) In subsection (6)(a) "relevant week" means—

(a) where maternity allowance is payable to a mother, a week or part of a week falling before the time at which the mother takes action that is treated by regulations as constituting for the purposes of this section her return to work;

(b) where statutory maternity pay is payable to a mother, a week falling before the week in which the mother takes action that is so treated.

For these purposes "week" has the meaning given by section 122. (1), in relation to maternity allowance, or the meaning given by section 165. (8), in relation to statutory maternity pay.

(8) In determining the number of weeks for the purposes of subsection (6)(b)—

(a) "week" has the same meaning as in subsection (7), and

(b) a part of a week is to be treated as a week.

(9) Provision under subsection (5)(a) is to secure that, where two persons are entitled to payments of statutory shared parental pay in respect of a child, the extent of one's entitlement and the extent of the other's entitlement do not, taken together, exceed what would be available to one person (see subsection (6)).

(10) Provision under subsection (5)(b) is to secure that no payment of statutory shared parental pay may be made to a person in respect of a child after the end of such period as may be prescribed.

(11) Provision under subsection (5)(b) is to secure that no payment of statutory shared parental pay in respect of a child may be made to a person who is the mother of the child before the end of the mother's maternity pay period.

(12) Regulations may provide that, where the conditions in subsection (13) are satisfied in relation to a person who is entitled to statutory shared parental pay under subsection (1) or (3) ("V"), V may vary the period or periods during which V intends to claim statutory shared parental pay in respect of the child in question, subject to complying with provision under subsection (14) where that is relevant.

(13) The conditions are—

(a) that V has given the person who will be liable to pay statutory shared parental pay to V notice of an intention to vary the period or periods during which V intends to claim statutory shared parental pay;

(b) that a notice under paragraph (a)—

(i) is given by such time as may be prescribed, and

(ii) satisfies prescribed conditions as to form and content.

(14) Regulations may provide that, where the conditions in subsection (15) are satisfied in relation to a person who is entitled to statutory shared parental pay under subsection (1) or (3) ("V"), V may vary the number of weeks in respect of which V intends to claim statutory shared parental pay.

(15) The conditions are—

(a) that V has given the person who will be liable to pay statutory shared parental pay to V notice of—

(i) the extent to which V has exercised an entitlement to statutory shared parental pay in respect of the child,

(ii) the extent to which V intends to claim statutory shared parental pay in respect of the child,

(iii) the extent to which another person has exercised an entitlement to statutory shared parental pay in respect of the child, and

(iv) the extent to which another person intends to claim statutory shared parental pay in respect of the child;

(b) that a notice under paragraph (a)—

(i) is given by such time as may be prescribed, and

(ii) satisfies prescribed conditions as to form and content;

(c) that the person who is P or, as the case may be, M in relation to V consents to that variation.

(16) A person's entitlement to statutory shared parental pay under this section is not affected by the birth of more than one child as a result of the same pregnancy.

171. ZV Entitlement: adoption

(1) Regulations may provide that, where all the conditions in subsection (2) are satisfied in relation to a person with whom a child is, or is expected to be, placed for adoption under the law of any part of the United Kingdom ("claimant A"), claimant A is to be entitled in accordance with the following provisions of this Part to payments to be known as "statutory shared parental pay".

(2) The conditions are—

(a) that claimant A and another person ("X") satisfy prescribed conditions as to caring or intending to care for the child;

(b) that X satisfies prescribed conditions—
(i) as to employment or self-employment,
(ii) as to having earnings of a prescribed amount for a prescribed period, and
(iii) as to relationship either with the child or with claimant A;

(c) that claimant A has been in employed earner's employment with an employer for a continuous period of at least the prescribed length ending with a prescribed week;

(d) that at the end of that prescribed week claimant A was entitled to be in that employment;

(e) that claimant A's normal weekly earnings for a prescribed period ending with a prescribed week are not less than the lower earnings limit in force under section 5. (1)(a) at the end of that week;

(f) if regulations so provide, that claimant A continues in employed earner's employment (whether or not with the employer by reference to whom the condition in paragraph (c) is satisfied) until a prescribed time;

(g) that claimant A became entitled to statutory adoption pay by reference to the placement for adoption of the child;

(h) that claimant A satisfies prescribed conditions as to the reduction of the duration of the adoption pay period;

(i) that claimant A has given the person who will be liable to pay statutory shared parental pay to claimant A notice of—
(i) the number of weeks in respect of which claimant A would be entitled to claim statutory shared parental pay in respect of the child if the entitlement were fully exercised (disregarding for these purposes any intention of X to claim statutory shared parental pay in respect of the child),
(ii) the number of weeks in respect of which claimant A intends to claim statutory shared parental pay, and
(iii) the number of weeks in respect of which X intends to claim statutory shared parental pay;

(j) that claimant A has given the person who will be liable to pay statutory shared parental pay to claimant A notice of the period or periods during which claimant A intends to claim statutory shared parental pay in respect of the child;

(k) that a notice under paragraph (i) or (j)—
(i) is given by such time as may be prescribed, and
(ii) satisfies prescribed conditions as to form and content;

(l) that X consents to the extent of claimant A's intended claim for statutory shared parental pay;

(m) that it is claimant A's intention to care for the child during each week in respect of which statutory shared parental pay is paid to claimant A;

(n) that claimant A is absent from work during each week in respect of which statutory shared parental pay is paid to claimant A;

(o) that, where claimant A is an employee within the meaning of the Employment Rights Act 1996, claimant A's absence from work during each such week is absence on shared parental leave.

(3) Regulations may provide that, where all the conditions in subsection (4) are satisfied in relation to a person ("claimant B"), claimant B is to be entitled in accordance with the following provisions of this Part to payments to be known as "statutory shared parental pay".

(4) The conditions are—

(a) that claimant B and another person ("Y") who is a person with whom a child is, or is expected to be, placed for adoption under the law of any part of the United Kingdom satisfy prescribed conditions as to caring or intending to care for the child;

(b) that claimant B satisfies—
(i) prescribed conditions as to relationship with the child, or
(ii) prescribed conditions as to relationship with Y;

(c) that Y satisfies prescribed conditions—
(i) as to employment or self-employment, and
(ii) as to having earnings of a prescribed amount for a prescribed period;

(d) that claimant B has been in employed earner's employment with an employer for a continuous period of at least the prescribed length ending with a prescribed week;

(e) that at the end of that prescribed week claimant B was entitled to be in that employment;

(f) that claimant B's normal weekly earnings for a prescribed period ending with a prescribed week are not less than the lower earnings limit in force under section 5.(1)(a) at the end of that week;

(g) if regulations so provide, that claimant B continues in employed earner's employment (whether or not with the employer by reference to whom the condition in paragraph (d) is satisfied) until a prescribed time;

(h) that Y became entitled to statutory adoption pay by reference to the placement for adoption of the child;

(i) that Y satisfies prescribed conditions as to the reduction of the duration of the adoption pay period;

(j) that claimant B has given the person who will be liable to pay statutory shared parental pay to claimant B notice of—
(i) the number of weeks in respect of which claimant B would be entitled to claim statutory shared parental pay in respect of the child if the entitlement were fully exercised (disregarding for these purposes any intention of Y to claim statutory shared parental pay in respect of the child),
(ii) the number of weeks in respect of which claimant B intends to claim statutory shared parental pay, and
(iii) the number of weeks in respect of which Y intends to claim statutory shared parental pay;

(k) that claimant B has given the person who will be liable to pay statutory shared parental pay to claimant B notice of the period or periods during which claimant B intends to claim statutory shared parental pay in respect of the child;

(l) that a notice under paragraph (j) or (k)—
(i) is given by such time as may be prescribed, and
(ii) satisfies prescribed conditions as to form and content;

(m) that Y consents to the extent of claimant B's intended claim for statutory shared parental pay;

(n) that it is claimant B's intention to care for the child during each week in respect of which statutory shared parental pay is paid to claimant B;

(o) that claimant B is absent from work during each week in respect of which statutory shared parental pay is paid to claimant B;

(p) that, where claimant B is an employee within the meaning of the Employment Rights Act 1996, claimant B's absence from work during each such week is absence on shared parental leave.

(5) Regulations may provide for—
(a) the determination of the extent of a person's entitlement to statutory shared parental pay in respect of a child;
(b) when statutory shared parental pay is to be payable.

(6) Provision under subsection (5)(a) is to secure that the number of weeks in respect of which a person is entitled to payments of statutory shared parental pay in respect of a child does not exceed the number of weeks of the adoption pay period reduced by—

(a) where the person who became entitled to receive statutory adoption pay takes action that is

treated by regulations as constituting for the purposes of this section the person's return to work without satisfying conditions prescribed under subsection (2)(h) or, as the case may be, subsection (4)(i)—
(i) the number of relevant weeks in respect of which statutory adoption pay is payable to the person, or
(ii) if that number of relevant weeks is less than a number prescribed by regulations, that prescribed number of weeks, or
   (b) except where paragraph (a) applies, the number of weeks to which the adoption pay period has been reduced by virtue of section 171. ZN(2. A).
(7) In subsection (6)(a) "relevant week" means a week falling before the week in which a person takes action that is treated by regulations as constituting for the purposes of this section the person's return to work, and for these purposes "week" has the meaning given by section 171. ZN(8).
(8) In determining the number of weeks for the purposes of subsection (6)(b)—
   (a) "week" has the same meaning as in subsection (7), and
   (b) a part of a week is to be treated as a week.
(9) Provision under subsection (5)(a) is to secure that, where two persons are entitled to payments of statutory shared parental pay in respect of a child, the extent of one's entitlement and the extent of the other's entitlement do not, taken together, exceed what would be available to one person (see subsection (6)).
(10) Provision under subsection (5)(b) is to secure that no payment of statutory shared parental pay may be made to a person in respect of a child after the end of such period as may be prescribed.
(11) Provision under subsection (5)(b) is to secure that no payment of statutory shared parental pay in respect of a child may be made to a person who became entitled to receive statutory adoption pay in respect of the child before the end of the person's adoption pay period.
(12) Regulations may provide that, where the conditions in subsection (13) are satisfied in relation to a person who is entitled to statutory shared parental pay under subsection (1) or (3) ("V"), V may vary the period or periods during which V intends to claim statutory shared parental pay in respect of the child in question, subject to complying with provision under subsection (14) where that is relevant.
(13) The conditions are—
   (a) that V has given the person who will be liable to pay statutory shared parental pay to V notice of an intention to vary the period or periods during which V intends to claim statutory shared parental pay;
   (b) that a notice under paragraph (a)—
(i) is given by such time as may be prescribed, and
(ii) satisfies prescribed conditions as to form and content.
(14) Regulations may provide that, where the conditions in subsection (15) are satisfied in relation to a person who is entitled to statutory shared parental pay under subsection (1) or (3) ("V"), V may vary the number of weeks in respect of which V intends to claim statutory shared parental pay.
(15) The conditions are—
   (a) that V has given the person who will be liable to pay statutory shared parental pay to V notice of—
(i) the extent to which V has exercised an entitlement to statutory shared parental pay in respect of the child,
(ii) the extent to which V intends to claim statutory shared parental pay in respect of the child,
(iii) the extent to which another person has exercised an entitlement to statutory shared parental pay in respect of the child, and
(iv) the extent to which another person intends to claim statutory shared parental pay in respect of the child;
   (b) that a notice under paragraph (a)—

(i) is given by such time as may be prescribed, and
(ii) satisfies prescribed conditions as to form and content;
   (c) that the person who is X or, as the case may be, Y in relation to V consents to that variation.
(16) A person's entitlement to statutory shared parental pay under this section is not affected by the placement for adoption of more than one child as part of the same arrangement.
(17) Regulations are to provide for entitlement to statutory shared parental pay in respect of a child placed, or expected to be placed, under section 22. C of the Children Act 1989 by a local authority in England with a local authority foster parent who has been approved as a prospective adopter.
(18) This section has effect in relation to regulations made by virtue of subsection (17) as if—
   (a) references to a child being placed for adoption under the law of any part of the United Kingdom were references to being placed under section 22. C of the Children Act 1989 with a local authority foster parent who has been approved as a prospective adopter;
   (b) references to placement for adoption were references to placement under section 22. C with such a person.

171. ZWEntitlement: general
(1) Regulations may—
   (a) provide that the following do not have effect, or have effect subject to prescribed modifications, in such cases as may be prescribed—
(i) section 171. ZU(2)(a) to (o),
(ii) section 171. ZU(4)(a) to (p),
(iii) section 171. ZU(13)(a) and (b),
(iv) section 171. ZU(15)(a) to (c),
(v) section 171. ZV(2)(a) to (o),
(vi) section 171. ZV(4)(a) to (p),
(vii) section 171. ZV(13)(a) and (b), and
(viii) section 171. ZV(15)(a) to (c);
   (b) impose requirements about evidence of entitlement and procedures to be followed;
   (c) specify in what circumstances employment is to be treated as continuous for the purposes of section 171. ZU or 171. ZV;
   (d) provide that a person is to be treated for the purposes of section 171. ZU or 171. ZV as being employed for a continuous period of at least the prescribed period where—
(i) the person has been employed by the same employer for at least the prescribed period under two or more separate contracts of service, and
(ii) those contracts were not continuous;
   (e) provide for amounts earned by a person under separate contracts of service with the same employer to be aggregated for the purposes of section 171. ZU or 171. ZV;
   (f) provide that—
(i) the amount of a person's earnings for any period, or
(ii) the amount of the person's earnings to be treated as comprised in any payment made to the person or for the person's benefit,
are to be calculated or estimated for the purposes of section 171. ZU or 171. ZV in such manner and on such basis as may be prescribed and that for that purpose payments of a particular class or description made or falling to be made to or by a person are, to such extent as may be prescribed, to be disregarded or, as the case may be, to be deducted from the amount of the person's earnings.
(2) The persons upon whom requirements may be imposed by virtue of subsection (1)(b) include—
   (a) a person who, in connection with another person's claim to be paid statutory shared parental pay, is required to satisfy conditions prescribed under section 171. ZU(2)(b) or (4)(c) or 171. ZV(2)(b) or (4)(c);
   (b) an employer or former employer of such a person.
(3) In subsection (1)(d) "the prescribed period" means the period of the length prescribed by regulations under section 171. ZU(2)(c) or (4)(d) or 171. ZV(2)(c) or (4)(d), as the case may be.

171. ZXLiability to make payments

(1) The liability to make payments of statutory shared parental pay under section 171. ZU or 171. ZV is a liability of any person of whom the person entitled to the payments has been an employee as mentioned in section 171. ZU(2)(c) or (4)(d) or 171. ZV(2)(c) or (4)(d), as the case may be.
(2) Regulations must make provision as to a former employer's liability to pay statutory shared parental pay to a person in any case where the former employee's contract of service with the person has been brought to an end by the former employer solely, or mainly, for the purpose of avoiding liability for statutory shared parental pay.
(3) The Secretary of State may, with the concurrence of the Commissioners for Her Majesty's Revenue and Customs, by regulations specify circumstances in which, notwithstanding this section, liability to make payments of statutory shared parental pay is to be a liability of the Commissioners.

171. ZYRate and period of pay
(1) Statutory shared parental pay is payable at such fixed or earnings-related weekly rate as may be prescribed by regulations, which may prescribe different kinds of rate for different cases.
(2) Subject to the following provisions of this section, statutory shared parental pay is payable to a person in respect of each week falling within a relevant period, up to the number of weeks determined in the case of that person in accordance with regulations under section 171. ZU(5) or 171. ZV(5).
(3) Except in such cases as may be prescribed, statutory shared parental pay is not payable to a person in respect of a week falling within a relevant period if it is not the person's intention at the beginning of the week to care for the child by reference to whom the person satisfies—
    (a) the condition in section 171. ZU(2)(a) or (4)(a), or
    (b) the condition in section 171. ZV(2)(a) or (4)(a).
(4) Except in such cases as may be prescribed, statutory shared parental pay is not payable to a person in respect of a week falling within a relevant period during any part of which week the person works for any employer.
(5) The Secretary of State may by regulations specify circumstances in which there is to be no liability to pay statutory shared parental pay in respect of a week falling within a relevant period.
(6) Where for any purpose of this Part or of regulations it is necessary to calculate the daily rate of statutory shared parental pay, the amount payable by way of statutory shared parental pay for any day shall be taken as one seventh of the weekly rate.
(7) For the purposes of this section a week falls within a relevant period if it falls within a period specified in a notice under—
    (a) section 171. ZU(2)(j), (4)(k) or (13)(a), or
    (b) section 171. ZV(2)(j), (4)(k) or (13)(a),
and is not afterwards excluded from such a period by a variation of the period or periods during which the person in question intends to claim statutory shared parental pay.
(8) In this section "week", in relation to a relevant period, means a period of seven days beginning with the day of the week on which the relevant period starts.

171. ZZRestrictions on contracting out
(1) An agreement is void to the extent that it purports—
    (a) to exclude, limit or otherwise modify any provision of this Part, or
    (b) to require a person to contribute (whether directly or indirectly) towards any costs incurred by that person's employer or former employer under this Part.
(2) For the avoidance of doubt, an agreement between an employer and an employee, authorising deductions from statutory shared parental pay which the employer is liable to pay to the employee in respect of any period, is not void by virtue of subsection (1)(a) if the employer—
    (a) is authorised by that or another agreement to make the same deductions from any contractual remuneration which the employer is liable to pay in respect of the same period, or
    (b) would be so authorised if the employer were liable to pay contractual remuneration in respect of that period.

171. ZZ1. Relationship with contractual remuneration
(1) Subject to subsections (2) and (3), any entitlement to statutory shared parental pay is not to

affect any right of a person in relation to remuneration under any contract of service ("contractual remuneration").

(2) Subject to subsection (3)—

(a) any contractual remuneration paid to a person by an employer of that person in respect of any period is to go towards discharging any liability of that employer to pay statutory shared parental pay to that person in respect of that period; and

(b) any statutory shared parental pay paid by an employer to a person who is an employee of that employer in respect of any period is to go towards discharging any liability of that employer to pay contractual remuneration to that person in respect of that period.

(3) Regulations may make provision as to payments which are, and those which are not, to be treated as contractual remuneration for the purposes of subsections (1) and (2).

171. ZZ2. Crown employment

The provisions of this Part apply in relation to persons employed by or under the Crown as they apply in relation to persons employed otherwise than by or under the Crown.

171. ZZ3. Special classes of person

(1) The Secretary of State may with the concurrence of the Treasury make regulations modifying any provision of this Part in such manner as the Secretary of State thinks proper in its application to any person who is, has been or is to be—

(a) employed on board any ship, vessel, hovercraft or aircraft;

(b) outside Great Britain at any prescribed time or in any prescribed circumstances; or

(c) in prescribed employment in connection with continental shelf operations, as defined in section 120. (2).

(2) Regulations under subsection (1) may, in particular, provide—

(a) for any provision of this Part to apply to any such person, notwithstanding that it would not otherwise apply;

(b) for any such provision not to apply to any such person, notwithstanding that it would otherwise apply;

(c) for excepting any such person from the application of any such provision where the person neither is domiciled nor has a place of residence in any part of Great Britain;

(d) for the taking of evidence, for the purposes of the determination of any question arising under any such provision, in a country or territory outside Great Britain, by a British consular official or such other person as may be determined in accordance with the regulations.

171. ZZ4. Part 12. ZC: supplementary

(1) In this Part—

"adoption pay period" has the meaning given in section 171. ZN(2);

"employer", in relation to a person who is an employee, means a person who—

- under section 6 is liable to pay secondary Class 1 contributions in relation to any of the earnings of the person who is an employee, or

- would be liable to pay such contributions but for—

the condition in section 6. (1)(b), or

the employee being under the age of 16;

"local authority" has the same meaning as in the Children Act 1989 (see section 105. (1) of that Act);

"local authority foster parent" has the same meaning as in the Children Act 1989 (see section 22. C(12) of that Act);

"maternity allowance period" has the meaning given in section 35. (2);

"maternity pay period" has the meaning given in section 165. (1);

"modifications" includes additions, omissions and amendments, and related expressions are to be read accordingly;

"prescribed" means prescribed by regulations.

(2) In this Part "employee" means a person who is gainfully employed in Great Britain either under a contract of service or in an office (including elective office) with general earnings (as defined by section 7 of the Income Tax (Earnings and Pensions) Act 2003).

(3) Regulations may provide—

(a) for cases where a person who falls within the definition in subsection (2) is not to be treated as an employee for the purposes of this Part, and

(b) for cases where a person who would not otherwise be an employee for the purposes of this Part is to be treated as an employee for those purposes.

(4) Without prejudice to any other power to make regulations under this Part, regulations may specify cases in which, for the purposes of this Part or of such provisions of this Part as may be prescribed—

(a) two or more employers are to be treated as one;

(b) two or more contracts of service in respect of which the same person is an employee are to be treated as one.

(5) In this Part, except where otherwise provided, "week" means a period of seven days beginning with Sunday or such other period as may be prescribed in relation to any particular case or class of cases.

(6) For the purposes of this Part, a person's normal weekly earnings are, subject to subsection (8), to be taken to be the average weekly earnings which in the relevant period have been paid to the person or paid for the person's benefit under the contract of service with the employer in question.

(7) For the purposes of subsection (6) "earnings" and "relevant period" have the meanings given to them by regulations.

(8) In such cases as may be prescribed, a person's normal weekly earnings are to be calculated in accordance with regulations.

(9) Where—

(a) in consequence of the establishment of one or more National Health Service trusts under the National Health Service Act 2006, the National Health Service (Wales) Act 2006 or the National Health Service (Scotland) Act 1978, a person's contract of employment is treated by a scheme under any of those Acts as divided so as to constitute two or more contracts, or

(b) an order under paragraph 26. (1) of Schedule 3 to the National Health Service Act 2006 provides that a person's contract of employment is so divided,

regulations may make provision enabling the person to elect for all of those contracts to be treated as one contract for the purposes of this Part or such provisions of this Part as may be prescribed.

(10) Regulations under subsection (9) may prescribe—

(a) the conditions that must be satisfied if a person is to be entitled to make such an election;

(b) the manner in which, and the time within which, such an election is to be made;

(c) the persons to whom, and the manner in which, notice of such an election is to be given;

(d) the information which a person who makes such an election is to provide, and the persons to whom, and the time within which, the person is to provide it;

(e) the time for which such an election is to have effect;

(f) which one of the person's employers under two or more contracts is to be regarded for the purposes of statutory shared parental pay as the person's employer under the contract.

(11) The powers under subsections (9) and (10) are without prejudice to any other power to make regulations under this Part.

(12) Regulations under any of subsections (4) to (10) must be made with the concurrence of the Commissioners for Her Majesty's Revenue and Customs.

171. ZZ5. Power to apply Part 12. ZC

(1) The Secretary of State may by regulations provide for this Part to have effect in relation to cases which involve adoption, but not the placement of a child for adoption under the law of any part of the United Kingdom, with such modifications as the regulations may prescribe.

(2) The Secretary of State may by regulations provide for this Part to have effect in relation to cases which involve a person who has applied, or intends to apply, with another person for a parental order under section 54 of the Human Fertilisation and Embryology Act 2008 and a child who is, or will be, the subject of the order, with such modifications as the regulations may prescribe.

(3) Where section 171. ZW(1)(b) has effect in relation to such cases as are described in subsection

(2), regulations under section 171. ZW(1)(b) may impose requirements to make statutory declarations as to—
   (a) eligibility to apply for a parental order;
   (b) intention to apply for such an order."
(2) In section 176 of the Social Security Contributions and Benefits Act 1992 (Parliamentary control of subordinate legislation), in subsection (1) (affirmative procedure), in paragraph (a), at the appropriate place there is inserted— " any of sections 171. ZU to 171. ZY; ".
Commencement Information
I3. S. 119 in force at 30.6.2014 by S.I. 2014/1640, art. 3. (1)(c)

120. Exclusion or curtailment of other statutory rights to pay

(1) The Social Security Contributions and Benefits Act 1992 is amended as follows.
(2) In section 35 (entitlement to maternity allowance), after subsection (3) there is inserted—
"(3. A)Regulations may provide for the duration of the maternity allowance period as it applies to a woman to be reduced, subject to prescribed restrictions and conditions.
(3. B)Regulations under subsection (3. A) are to secure that the reduced period ends at a time—
   (a) after a prescribed period beginning with the day on which the woman is confined, and
   (b) when at least a prescribed part of the maternity allowance period remains unexpired.
(3. C)Regulations under subsection (3. A) may, in particular, prescribe restrictions and conditions relating to—
   (a) the end of the woman's entitlement to maternity leave;
   (b) the doing of work by the woman;
   (c) the taking of prescribed steps by the woman or another person as regards leave under section 75. E of the Employment Rights Act 1996 in respect of the child;
   (d) the taking of prescribed steps by a person other than the woman as regards statutory shared parental pay in respect of the child.
(3. D)Regulations may provide for a reduction in the duration of the maternity allowance period as it applies to a woman to be revoked, or to be treated as revoked, subject to prescribed restrictions and conditions."
(3) In section 35, after subsection (3. D) (as inserted by subsection (2)) there is inserted—
"(3. E)A woman who would, but for the reduction in duration of a maternity pay period by virtue of section 165. (3. A), be entitled to statutory maternity pay for a week is not entitled to a maternity allowance for that week."
(4) In section 165 (the maternity pay period), after subsection (3) there is inserted—
"(3. A)Regulations may provide for the duration of the maternity pay period as it applies to a woman to be reduced, subject to prescribed restrictions and conditions.
(3. B)Regulations under subsection (3. A) are to secure that the reduced period ends at a time—
   (a) after a prescribed period beginning with the day on which the woman is confined, and
   (b) when at least a prescribed part of the maternity pay period remains unexpired.
(3. C)Regulations under subsection (3. A) may, in particular, prescribe restrictions and conditions relating to—
   (a) the end of the woman's entitlement to maternity leave;
   (b) the doing of work by the woman;
   (c) the taking of prescribed steps by the woman or another person as regards leave under section 75. E of the Employment Rights Act 1996 in respect of the child;
   (d) the taking of prescribed steps by the woman or another person as regards statutory shared parental pay in respect of the child.
(3. D)Regulations may provide for a reduction in the duration of the maternity pay period as it applies to a woman to be revoked, or to be treated as revoked, subject to prescribed restrictions and conditions."
(5) In section 171. ZE (rate and period of statutory paternity pay), after subsection (3) there is

inserted—

"(3. A)Statutory paternity pay is not payable to a person in respect of a statutory pay week if—

(a) statutory shared parental pay is payable to that person in respect of any part of that week or that person takes shared parental leave in any part of that week, or

(b) statutory shared parental pay was payable to that person or that person has taken shared parental leave in respect of the child before that week."

(6) In section 171. ZN (rate and period of statutory adoption pay), after subsection (2) there is inserted—

"(2. A)Regulations may provide for the duration of the adoption pay period as it applies to a person ("A") to be reduced, subject to prescribed restrictions and conditions.

(2. B)Regulations under subsection (2. A) are to secure that the reduced period ends at a time—

(a) after a prescribed part of the adoption pay period has expired, and

(b) when at least a prescribed part of the adoption pay period remains unexpired.

(2. C)Regulations under subsection (2. A) may, in particular, prescribe restrictions and conditions relating to—

(a) the end of A's entitlement to adoption leave;

(b) the doing of work by A;

(c) the taking of prescribed steps by A or another person as regards leave under section 75. G of the Employment Rights Act 1996 in respect of the child;

(d) the taking of prescribed steps by A or another person as regards statutory shared parental pay in respect of the child.

(2. D)Regulations may provide for a reduction in the duration of the adoption pay period as it applies to a person to be revoked, or to be treated as revoked, subject to prescribed restrictions and conditions."

Commencement Information

I4. S. 120 in force at 30.6.2014 by S.I. 2014/1640, art. 3. (1)(d)

Other statutory rights

121. Statutory rights to leave and pay of prospective adopters with whom looked after children are placed

(1) In section 75. A of the Employment Rights Act 1996 (ordinary adoption leave), after subsection (1) there is inserted—

"(1. A)The conditions that may be prescribed under subsection (1) include conditions as to—

(a) being a local authority foster parent;

(b) being approved as a prospective adopter;

(c) being notified by a local authority in England that a child is to be, or is expected to be, placed with the employee under section 22. C of the Children Act 1989."

(2) In section 80. B of the Employment Rights Act 1996 (entitlement to ordinary paternity leave: adoption)—

(a) in subsection (5), after paragraph (a) there is inserted—

"(aa)make provision excluding the right to be absent on leave under this section in the case of an employee who, by virtue of provision under subsection (6. A), has already exercised a right to be absent on leave under this section in connection with the same child;";

(b) after subsection (6) there is inserted—

"(6. A)Regulations under subsection (1) shall include provision for leave in respect of a child placed, or expected to be placed, under section 22. C of the Children Act 1989 by a local authority in England with a local authority foster parent who has been approved as a prospective adopter.

(6. B)This section has effect in relation to regulations made by virtue of subsection (6. A) as if—

(a) references to being placed for adoption were references to being placed under section 22. C of the Children Act 1989 with a local authority foster parent who has been approved as a prospective adopter;

(b) references to placement for adoption were references to placement under section 22. C with such a person;

(c) paragraph (aa) of subsection (5) were omitted."

(3) In section 171. ZB of the Social Security Contributions and Benefits Act 1992 (entitlement to ordinary statutory paternity pay: adoption), after subsection (7) there is inserted—

"(8)This section has effect in a case involving a child placed under section 22. C of the Children Act 1989 by a local authority in England with a local authority foster parent who has been approved as a prospective adopter with the following modifications—

(a) the references in subsection (2) to a child being placed for adoption under the law of any part of the United Kingdom are to be treated as references to a child being placed under section 22. C in that manner;

(b) the reference in subsection (3) to the week in which the adopter is notified of being matched with the child for the purposes of adoption is to be treated as a reference to the week in which the prospective adopter is notified that the child is to be, or is expected to be, placed with the prospective adopter under section 22. C;

(c) the reference in subsection (6) to placement for adoption is to be treated as a reference to placement under section 22. C;

(d) the definition in subsection (7) is to be treated as if it were a definition of "prospective adopter".

(9) Where, by virtue of subsection (8), a person becomes entitled to statutory paternity pay in connection with the placement of a child under section 22. C of the Children Act 1989, the person may not become entitled to payments of statutory paternity pay in connection with the placement of the child for adoption."

(4) In section 171. ZE of the Social Security Contributions and Benefits Act 1992 (rate and period of pay), after subsection (11) there is inserted—

"(12)Where statutory paternity pay is payable to a person by virtue of section 171. ZB(8), this section has effect as if—

(a) the references in subsections (3)(b) and (10) to placement for adoption were references to placement under section 22. C of the Children Act 1989;

(b) the references in subsection (10) to being placed for adoption were references to being placed under section 22. C."

(5) In section 171. ZL of the Social Security Contributions and Benefits Act 1992 (entitlement to statutory adoption pay), after subsection (8) there is inserted—

"(9)This section has effect in a case involving a child who is, or is expected to be, placed under section 22. C of the Children Act 1989 by a local authority in England with a local authority foster parent who has been approved as a prospective adopter with the following modifications—

(a) the references in subsections (2)(a) and (4. A)(a) to a child being placed for adoption under the law of any part of the United Kingdom are to be treated as references to a child being placed under section 22. C in that manner;

(b) the reference in subsection (3) to the week in which the person is notified that he has been matched with the child for the purposes of adoption is to be treated as a reference to the week in which the person is notified that the child is to be, or is expected to be, placed with him under section 22. C;

(c) the references in subsection (4. B)(a) to adoption are to be treated as references to placement under section 22. C;

(d) the reference in subsection (5) to placement, or expected placement, for adoption is to be treated as a reference to placement, or expected placement, under section 22. C.

(10) Where, by virtue of subsection (9), a person becomes entitled to statutory adoption pay in respect of a child who is, or is expected to be, placed under section 22. C of the Children Act 1989, the person may not become entitled to payments of statutory adoption pay as a result of the

child being, or being expected to be, placed for adoption."

(6) In section 171. ZN of the Social Security Contributions and Benefits Act 1992 (rate and period of pay), after subsection (8) there is inserted—

"(9)Where statutory adoption pay is payable to a person by virtue of section 171. ZL(9), this section has effect as if the reference in subsection (2. F) to the week in which the person is notified that he has been matched with a child for the purposes of adoption were a reference to the week in which the person is notified that a child is to be, or is expected to be, placed with him under section 22. C of the Children Act 1989."

(7) In the Social Security Contributions and Benefits Act 1992—

(a) in section 171. ZJ(1), at the appropriate place there is inserted—

""local authority" has the same meaning as in the Children Act 1989 (see section 105. (1) of that Act);";

""local authority foster parent" has the same meaning as in the Children Act 1989 (see section 22. C(12) of that Act);";

(b) in section 171. ZS(1), at the appropriate place there is inserted—

""local authority" has the same meaning as in the Children Act 1989 (see section 105. (1) of that Act);";

""local authority foster parent" has the same meaning as in the Children Act 1989 (see section 22. C(12) of that Act);".

Commencement Information

I5. S. 121 in force at 30.6.2014 by S.I. 2014/1640, art. 3. (1)(e)

122. Statutory rights to leave and pay of applicants for parental orders

(1) In section 75. A of the Employment Rights Act 1996 (ordinary adoption leave), after subsection (7) there is inserted—

"(8)The Secretary of State may by regulations provide for this section to have effect in relation to cases which involve an employee who has applied, or intends to apply, with another person for a parental order under section 54 of the Human Fertilisation and Embryology Act 2008 and a child who is, or will be, the subject of the order, with such modifications as the regulations may prescribe."

(2) In section 75. B of the Employment Rights Act 1996 (additional adoption leave), after subsection (8) there is inserted—

"(9)The Secretary of State may by regulations provide for this section to have effect in relation to cases which involve an employee who has applied, or intends to apply, with another person for a parental order under section 54 of the Human Fertilisation and Embryology Act 2008 and a child who is, or will be, the subject of the order, with such modifications as the regulations may prescribe."

(3) In section 75. D of the Employment Rights Act 1996 (supplemental provision about adoption leave), after subsection (1) there is inserted—

"(1. A)Where section 75. A or 75. B has effect in relation to such cases as are described in section 75. A(8) or 75. B(9), regulations under section 75. A or 75. B about evidence to be produced may require statutory declarations as to—

(a) eligibility to apply for a parental order;

(b) intention to apply for such an order."

(4) In section 80. B of the Employment Rights Act 1996 (entitlement to ordinary paternity leave: adoption), after subsection (8) there is inserted—

"(9)The Secretary of State may by regulations provide for this section to have effect in relation to cases which involve an employee who has applied, or intends to apply, with another person for a parental order under section 54 of the Human Fertilisation and Embryology Act 2008 and a child who is, or will be, the subject of the order, with such modifications as the regulations may

prescribe."
(5) In section 171. ZK of the Social Security Contributions and Benefits Act 1992 (power to apply Part 12. ZA, statutory paternity pay, to adoption cases not involving placement)—
    (a) in the title, the words "to adoption cases not involving placement" are repealed;
    (b) the existing text becomes subsection (1);
    (c) after that subsection there is inserted—
"(2)The Secretary of State may by regulations provide for this Part to have effect in relation to cases which involve a person who has applied, or intends to apply, with another person for a parental order under section 54 of the Human Fertilisation and Embryology Act 2008 and a child who is, or will be, the subject of the order, with such modifications as the regulations may prescribe."
(6) In section 171. ZT of the Social Security Contributions and Benefits Act 1992 (power to apply Part 12. ZB, statutory adoption pay, to adoption cases not involving placement)—
    (a) in the title, the words "to adoption cases not involving placement" are repealed;
    (b) the existing text becomes subsection (1);
    (c) after that subsection there is inserted—
"(2)The Secretary of State may by regulations provide for this Part to have effect in relation to cases which involve a person who has applied, or intends to apply, with another person for a parental order under section 54 of the Human Fertilisation and Embryology Act 2008 and a child who is, or will be, the subject of the order, with such modifications as the regulations may prescribe."
(3) Regulations under subsection (2) may modify section 171. ZL(8)(c) so as to enable regulations to impose requirements to make statutory declarations as to—
    (a) eligibility to apply for a parental order;
    (b) intention to apply for such an order."
Commencement Information
I6. S. 122 in force at 30.6.2014 by S.I. 2014/1640, art. 3. (1)(f)

123. Statutory paternity pay: notice requirement and period of payment

(1) The Social Security Contributions and Benefits Act 1992 is amended as follows.
(2) In section 171. ZC (further provision as to entitlement to statutory paternity pay)—
    (a) in subsection (1) (requirement to give notice), for the words from "only if" to the end there is substituted " only if he gives the person who will be liable to pay it notice of the week or weeks in respect of which he expects there to be liability to pay him statutory paternity pay. ";
    (b) after subsection (1) there is inserted—
"(1. A)Regulations may provide for the time by which notice under subsection (1) is to be given."
(3) In section 171. ZE (rate and period of statutory paternity pay)—
    (a) in subsection (2) (period of pay), for the words from "be payable" to the end there is substituted "be payable in respect of—
"(a)such week within the qualifying period, or
    (b) such number of weeks, not exceeding the prescribed number of weeks, within the qualifying period,
as he may choose in accordance with regulations. ";
    (b) after subsection (2) there is inserted—
"(2. A)Provision under subsection (2)(b) is to secure that the prescribed number of weeks is not less than two.";
    (c) after subsection (2. A) (as inserted by paragraph (b)) there is inserted—
"(2. B)Regulations under subsection (2) may permit a person entitled to receive statutory paternity pay to choose to receive such pay in respect of non-consecutive periods each of which is a week or a number of weeks."

(4) In section 176 (Parliamentary control of subordinate legislation), in subsection (1) (affirmative procedure), in paragraph (a), after "section 171. ZE(1)" there is inserted " or (2)(b) ".
Commencement Information
I7. S. 123. (1)(2) in force at 30.6.2014 by S.I. 2014/1640, art. 3. (1)(g) (with art. 9)

124. Rate of statutory adoption pay

(1) In section 171. ZN of the Social Security Contributions and Benefits Act 1992 (rate and period of statutory adoption pay)—
 (a) subsection (1) is repealed;
 (b) after subsection (2. D) (as inserted by section 120. (6)) there is inserted—
"(2. E)Statutory adoption pay shall be payable to a person—
 (a) at the earnings-related rate, in respect of the first 6 weeks in respect of which it is payable; and
 (b) at whichever is the lower of the earnings-related rate and such weekly rate as may be prescribed, in respect of the remaining portion of the adoption pay period.
(2. F)The earnings-related rate is a weekly rate equivalent to 90 per cent of a person's normal weekly earnings for the period of 8 weeks ending with the week in which the person is notified that the person has been matched with a child for the purposes of adoption.
(2. G)The weekly rate prescribed under subsection (2. E)(b) must not be less than the weekly rate of statutory sick pay for the time being specified in section 157. (1) or, if two or more such rates are for the time being so specified, the higher or highest of those rates.";
 (c) in subsection (7), for "subsection (2)" there is substituted " subsections (2) and (2. E) ".
(2) In section 176 of the Social Security Contributions and Benefits Act 1992 (Parliamentary control of subordinate legislation), in subsection (1) (affirmative procedure), in paragraph (a), the entry for section 171. ZN(1) is repealed.
Commencement Information
I8. S. 124 in force at 5.4.2015 by S.I. 2014/1640, art. 6. (a) (with art. 13)

125. Abolition of additional paternity leave and additional statutory paternity pay

(1) In Part 8 of the Employment Rights Act 1996, sections 80. AA and 80. BB (entitlement to additional paternity leave: birth and adoption) are repealed.
(2) In Part 12. ZA of the Social Security Contributions and Benefits Act 1992, sections 171. ZEA to 171. ZEE (additional statutory paternity pay: birth and adoption) are repealed.
Commencement Information
I9. S. 125 in force at 5.4.2015 by S.I. 2014/1640, art. 6. (b) (with art. 14)

Further amendments

126. Further amendments

(1) Schedule 7 (which contains further amendments relating to statutory rights to leave and pay) has effect.
(2) A reference to ordinary statutory paternity pay in an instrument or document made before the commencement of paragraphs 12 and 13 of Schedule 7 is to be read, in relation to any time after that commencement, as a reference to statutory paternity pay.
(3) A reference to statutory paternity pay in an enactment (including an enactment amended by this Act) or in an instrument or document is to be read, in relation to any time that falls—

(a) after the commencement of paragraphs 12 and 13 of Schedule 1 to the Work and Families Act 2006, and
(b) before the commencement of paragraphs 12 and 13 of Schedule 7,
as a reference to ordinary statutory paternity pay.
(4) Subsection (3) does not apply to the extent that a reference to statutory paternity pay is a reference to additional statutory paternity pay.
Commencement Information
I10. S. 126. (1) in force at 30.6.2014 for specified purposes by S.I. 2014/1640, art. 3. (1)(h)
I11. S. 126. (1) in force at 1.12.2014 for specified purposes by S.I. 2014/1640, art. 5. (1)
I12. S. 126. (1) in force at 15.3.2015 for specified purposes, that being the date on which 1992 c. 7, Pt. 12. ZC comes into force by virtue of S.R. 2015/86, art. 3. (1)(d) by S.I. 2014/1640, art. 8
I13. S. 126. (1) in force at 5.4.2015 for specified purposes by S.I. 2014/1640, art. 6. (c)
I14. S. 126. (2)-(4) in force at 5.4.2015 by S.I. 2014/1640, art. 6. (c) (with art. 15)

PART 8. Time off work: ante-natal care etc

PART 8 Time off work: ante-natal care etc

127. Time off work to accompany to ante-natal appointments

(1) After section 57. ZD of the Employment Rights Act 1996 there is inserted—
57. ZERight to time off to accompany to ante-natal appointment
(1) An employee who has a qualifying relationship with a pregnant woman or her expected child is entitled to be permitted by his or her employer to take time off during the employee's working hours in order that he or she may accompany the woman when she attends by appointment at any place for the purpose of receiving ante-natal care.
(2) In relation to any particular pregnancy, an employee is not entitled to take time off for the purpose specified in subsection (1) on more than two occasions.
(3) On each of those occasions, the maximum time off during working hours to which the employee is entitled is six and a half hours.
(4) An employee is not entitled to take time off for the purpose specified in subsection (1) unless the appointment is made on the advice of a registered medical practitioner, registered midwife or registered nurse.
(5) Where the employer requests the employee to give the employer a declaration signed by the employee, the employee is not entitled to take time off for the purpose specified in subsection (1) unless the employee gives that declaration (which may be given in electronic form).
(6) The employee must state in the declaration—
(a) that the employee has a qualifying relationship with a pregnant woman or her expected child,
(b) that the employee's purpose in taking time off is the purpose specified in subsection (1),
(c) that the appointment in question is made on the advice of a registered medical practitioner, registered midwife or registered nurse, and
(d) the date and time of the appointment.
(7) A person has a qualifying relationship with a pregnant woman or her expected child if—
(a) the person is the husband or civil partner of the pregnant woman,
(b) the person, being of a different sex or the same sex, lives with the woman in an enduring family relationship but is not a relative of the woman,
(c) the person is the father of the expected child,
(d) the person is a parent of the expected child by virtue of section 42 or 43 of the Human

Fertilisation and Embryology Act 2008, or

(e) the person is a potential applicant for a parental order under section 54 of the Human Fertilisation and Embryology Act 2008 in respect of the expected child.

(8) For the purposes of subsection (7) a relative of a person is the person's parent, grandparent, sister, brother, aunt or uncle.

(9) The references to relationships in subsection (8)—

(a) are to relationships of the full blood or half blood or, in the case of an adopted person, such of those relationships as would exist but for the adoption, and

(b) include the relationship of a child with the child's adoptive, or former adoptive, parents, but do not include any other adoptive relationships.

(10) For the purposes of subsection (7)(e) a person ("A") is a potential applicant for a parental order under section 54 of the Human Fertilisation and Embryology Act 2008 in respect of an expected child only if—

(a) A intends to apply, jointly with another person ("B"), for such an order in respect of the expected child within the time allowed by section 54. (3),

(b) the expected child is being carried by the pregnant woman as a result of such procedure as is described in section 54. (1)(a),

(c) the requirement in section 54. (1)(b) is satisfied by reference to A or B,

(d) A and B would satisfy section 54. (2) if they made an application under section 54 at the time that A seeks to exercise the right under this section, and

(e) A expects that A and B will satisfy the conditions in section 54. (2), (4), (5) and (8) as regards the intended application.

(11) The references in this section to a registered nurse are references to a registered nurse—

(a) who is also registered in the Specialist Community Public Health Nurses Part of the register maintained under article 5 of the Nursing and Midwifery Order 2001 (S.I. 2002/253), and

(b) whose entry in that Part of the register is annotated to show that the nurse holds a qualification in health visiting.

(12) For the purposes of this section the working hours of an employee are to be taken to be any time when, in accordance with the employee's contract of employment, the employee is required to be at work.

57. ZFComplaint to employment tribunal

(1) An employee may present a complaint to an employment tribunal that his or her employer has unreasonably refused to let him or her take time off as required by section 57. ZE.

(2) An employment tribunal may not consider a complaint under this section unless it is presented—

(a) before the end of the period of three months beginning with the day of the appointment in question, or

(b) within such further period as the tribunal considers reasonable in a case where it is satisfied that it was not reasonably practicable for the complaint to be presented before the end of that period of three months.

(3) Sections 207. A(3) and 207. B apply for the purposes of subsection (2)(a).

(4) Where an employment tribunal finds a complaint under subsection (1) well-founded, it—

(a) must make a declaration to that effect, and

(b) must order the employer to pay to the employee an amount determined in accordance with subsection (5).

(5) The amount payable to the employee is—

where—

A is the appropriate hourly rate for the employee, and

B is the number of working hours for which the employee would have been entitled under section 57. ZE to be absent if the time off had not been refused.

(6) The appropriate hourly rate, in relation to an employee, is the amount of one week's pay divided by the number of normal working hours in a week for that employee when employed under the contract of employment in force on the day when the time off would have been taken.

(7) But where the number of normal working hours differs from week to week or over a longer period, the amount of one week's pay shall be divided instead by—
   (a) the average number of normal working hours calculated by dividing by twelve the total number of the employee's normal working hours during the period of twelve weeks ending with the last complete week before the day on which the time off would have been taken, or
   (b) where the employee has not been employed for a sufficient period to enable the calculation to be made under paragraph (a), a number which fairly represents the number of normal working hours in a week having regard to such of the considerations specified in subsection (8) as are appropriate in the circumstances.
(8) The considerations referred to in subsection (7)(b) are—
   (a) the average number of normal working hours in a week which the employee could expect in accordance with the terms of the employee's contract, and
   (b) the average number of normal working hours of other employees engaged in relevant comparable employment with the same employer.

Accompanying to ante-natal appointments: agency workers

57. ZGRight to time off to accompany to ante-natal appointment: agency workers
(1) An agency worker who has a qualifying relationship with a pregnant woman or her expected child is entitled to be permitted, by the temporary work agency and the hirer, to take time off during the agency worker's working hours in order that he or she may accompany the woman when she attends by appointment at any place for the purpose of receiving ante-natal care.
(2) In relation to any particular pregnancy, an agency worker is not entitled to take time off for the purpose specified in subsection (1) on more than two occasions.
(3) On each of those occasions, the maximum time off during working hours to which the agency worker is entitled is six and a half hours.
(4) An agency worker is not entitled to take time off for the purpose specified in subsection (1) unless the appointment is made on the advice of a registered medical practitioner, registered midwife or registered nurse.
(5) Where the temporary work agency or the hirer requests the agency worker to give that person a declaration signed by the agency worker, the agency worker is not entitled to take time off for the purpose specified in subsection (1) unless the agency worker gives that declaration (which may be given in electronic form).
(6) The agency worker must state in the declaration—
   (a) that the agency worker has a qualifying relationship with a pregnant woman or her expected child,
   (b) that the agency worker's purpose in taking time off is the purpose specified in subsection (1),
   (c) that the appointment in question is made on the advice of a registered medical practitioner, registered midwife or registered nurse, and
   (d) the date and time of the appointment.
(7) A person has a qualifying relationship with a pregnant woman or her expected child if—
   (a) the person is the husband or civil partner of the pregnant woman,
   (b) the person, being of a different sex or the same sex, lives with the woman in an enduring family relationship but is not a relative of the woman,
   (c) the person is the father of the expected child,
   (d) the person is a parent of the expected child by virtue of section 42 or 43 of the Human Fertilisation and Embryology Act 2008, or
   (e) the person is a potential applicant for a parental order under section 54 of the Human Fertilisation and Embryology Act 2008 in respect of the expected child.
(8) For the purposes of subsection (7) a relative of a person is the person's parent, grandparent, sister, brother, aunt or uncle.
(9) The references to relationships in subsection (8)—

(a) are to relationships of the full blood or half blood or, in the case of an adopted person, such of those relationships as would exist but for the adoption, and

(b) include the relationship of a child with the child's adoptive, or former adoptive, parents, but do not include any other adoptive relationships.

(10) For the purposes of subsection (7)(e) a person ("A") is a potential applicant for a parental order under section 54 of the Human Fertilisation and Embryology Act 2008 in respect of an expected child only if—

(a) A intends to apply, jointly with another person ("B"), for such an order in respect of the expected child within the time allowed by section 54. (3),

(b) the expected child is being carried by the pregnant woman as a result of such procedure as is described in section 54. (1)(a),

(c) the requirement in section 54. (1)(b) is satisfied by reference to A or B,

(d) A and B would satisfy section 54. (2) if they made an application under section 54 at the time that A seeks to exercise the right under this section, and

(e) A expects that A and B will satisfy the conditions in section 54. (2), (4), (5) and (8) as regards the intended application.

(11) The references in this section to a registered nurse are references to a registered nurse—

(a) who is also registered in the Specialist Community Public Health Nurses Part of the register maintained under article 5 of the Nursing and Midwifery Order 2001 (S.I. 2002/253), and

(b) whose entry in that Part of the register is annotated to show that the nurse holds a qualification in health visiting.

(12) For the purposes of this section the working hours of an agency worker are to be taken to be any time when, in accordance with the terms under which the agency worker works temporarily for and under the supervision and direction of the hirer, the agency worker is required to be at work.

57. ZHComplaint to employment tribunal: agency workers

(1) An agency worker may present a complaint to an employment tribunal that the temporary work agency has unreasonably refused to let him or her take time off as required by section 57. ZG.

(2) An agency worker may present a complaint to an employment tribunal that the hirer has unreasonably refused to let him or her take time off as required by section 57. ZG.

(3) An employment tribunal may not consider a complaint under subsection (1) or (2) unless it is presented—

(a) before the end of the period of three months beginning with the day of the appointment in question, or

(b) within such further period as the tribunal considers reasonable in a case where it is satisfied that it was not reasonably practicable for the complaint to be presented before the end of that period of three months.

(4) Sections 207. A(3) and 207. B apply for the purposes of subsection (3)(a).

(5) Where an employment tribunal finds a complaint under subsection (1) or (2) well-founded, it—

(a) must make a declaration to that effect, and

(b) must order the payment to the agency worker of an amount determined in accordance with subsection (7).

(6) Where the tribunal orders that payment under subsection (5) be made by the temporary work agency and the hirer, the proportion of that amount payable by each respondent is to be such as may be found by the tribunal to be just and equitable having regard to the extent of each respondent's responsibility for the infringement to which the complaint relates.

(7) The amount payable to the agency worker is—

where—

A is the appropriate hourly rate for the agency worker, and

B is the number of working hours for which the agency worker would have been entitled under section 57. ZG to be absent if the time off had not been refused.

(8) The appropriate hourly rate, in relation to an agency worker, is the amount of one week's pay

divided by the number of normal working hours in a week for that agency worker in accordance with the terms under which the agency worker works temporarily for and under the supervision and direction of the hirer that are in force on the day when the time off would have been taken.
(9) But where the number of normal working hours during the assignment differs from week to week or over a longer period, the amount of one week's pay shall be divided instead by the average number of normal working hours calculated by dividing by twelve the total number of the agency worker's normal working hours during the period of twelve weeks ending with the last complete week before the day on which the time off would have been taken.
57. ZIAgency workers: supplementary
(1) Without prejudice to any other duties of the hirer or temporary work agency under any enactment or rule of law, sections 57. ZG and 57. ZH do not apply where the agency worker—
    (a) has not completed the qualifying period, or
    (b) pursuant to regulation 8. (a) or (b) of the Agency Workers Regulations 2010 (S.I. 2010/93), is no longer entitled to the rights conferred by regulation 5 of those Regulations.
(2) Nothing in sections 57. ZG and 57. ZH imposes a duty on the hirer or temporary work agency beyond the original intended duration, or likely duration, of the assignment, whichever is the longer.
(3) Sections 57. ZG and 57. ZH do not apply where sections 57. ZE and 57. ZF apply.
(4) In this section and sections 57. ZG and 57. ZH the following have the same meaning as in the Agency Workers Regulations 2010—
"agency worker";
"assignment";
"hirer";
"qualifying period";
"temporary work agency"."
(2) In the Employment Rights Act 1996—
    (a) in section 47. C (right not to be subject to detriment: leave for family reasons), in subsection (2) (prescribed reasons), after paragraph (a) there is inserted—
    "(aa)time off under section 57. ZE,";
    (b) in section 99 (being regarded as unfairly dismissed: leave for family reasons), in subsection (3) (prescribed kinds of reasons), after paragraph (a) there is inserted—
    "(aa)time off under section 57. ZE,";
    (c) in section 225 (the calculation date in finding a week's pay), after subsection (3) there is inserted—
"(3. A)Where the calculation is for the purposes of section 57. ZF, the calculation date is the day of the appointment."
Commencement Information
I1. S. 127. (1)(2)(c) in force at 1.10.2014 by S.I. 2014/1640, art. 4. (a)
I2. S. 127. (2)(a)(b) in force at 30.6.2014 by S.I. 2014/1640, art. 3. (1)(i)

128. Time off work to attend adoption appointments

(1) After section 57. ZI of the Employment Rights Act 1996 (as inserted by section 127) there is inserted—
57. ZJRight to paid time off to attend adoption appointments
(1) An employee who has been notified by an adoption agency that a child is to be, or is expected to be, placed for adoption with the employee alone is entitled to be permitted by his or her employer to take time off during the employee's working hours in order that he or she may attend by appointment at any place for the purpose of having contact with the child or for any other purpose connected with the adoption.
(2) An employee who—
    (a) has been notified by an adoption agency that a child is to be, or is expected to be, placed for

adoption with the employee and another person jointly, and

(b) has elected to exercise the right to take time off under this section in connection with the adoption,

is entitled to be permitted by his or her employer to take time off during the employee's working hours in order that he or she may attend by appointment at any place for the purpose of having contact with the child or for any other purpose connected with the adoption.

(3) An employee may not make an election for the purposes of subsection (2)(b) if—

(a) the employee has made an election for the purposes of section 57. ZL(1)(b) in connection with the adoption, or

(b) the other person with whom the child is to be, or is expected to be, placed for adoption has made an election for the purposes of subsection (2)(b) or section 57. ZN(2)(b) in connection with the adoption.

(4) An employee is not entitled to take time off under this section on or after the date of the child's placement for adoption with the employee.

(5) In relation to any particular adoption, an employee is not entitled to take time off under this section on more than five occasions.

(6) On each of those occasions, the maximum time off during working hours to which the employee is entitled is six and a half hours.

(7) An employee is not entitled to take time off under this section unless the appointment has been arranged by or at the request of the adoption agency which made the notification described in subsection (1) or (2)(a).

(8) An employee is not entitled to take time off under subsection (1) unless, if the employer requests it, the employee gives the employer a document showing the date and time of the appointment in question and that it has been arranged as described in subsection (7).

(9) An employee is not entitled to take time off under subsection (2) unless, if the employer requests it, the employee gives the employer—

(a) a declaration signed by the employee stating that the employee has made an election for the purposes of subsection (2)(b) in connection with the adoption, and

(b) a document showing the date and time of the appointment in question and that it has been arranged as described in subsection (7).

(10) A document or declaration requested under subsection (8) or (9) may be given in electronic form.

(11) In cases where more than one child is to be, or is expected to be, placed for adoption with an employee as part of the same arrangement, this section has effect as if—

(a) the purposes specified in subsections (1) and (2) were the purpose of having contact with any one or more of the children and any other purpose connected with any of the adoptions that are part of the arrangement;

(b) the references in subsections (2)(b) and (9)(a) to the adoption were references to all of the adoptions that are part of the arrangement;

(c) the references in subsection (3) to the adoption were references to any of the adoptions that are part of the arrangement;

(d) the reference in subsection (4) to the date of the child's placement for adoption were a reference to the date of placement of the first child to be placed as part of the arrangement;

(e) the reference in subsection (5) to a particular adoption were a reference to the adoptions that are part of a particular arrangement.

(12) For the purposes of this section the working hours of an employee are to be taken to be any time when, in accordance with the employee's contract of employment, the employee is required to be at work.

(13) In this section "adoption agency" means an adoption agency within the meaning of section 2 of the Adoption and Children Act 2002 or as defined in section 119. (1)(a) of the Adoption and Children (Scotland) Act 2007.

57. ZKRight to remuneration for time off under section 57. ZJ

(1) An employee who is permitted to take time off under section 57. ZJ is entitled to be paid

remuneration by his or her employer for the number of working hours for which the employee is entitled to be absent at the appropriate hourly rate.

(2) The appropriate hourly rate, in relation to an employee, is the amount of one week's pay divided by the number of normal working hours in a week for that employee when employed under the contract of employment in force on the day when the time off is taken.

(3) But where the number of normal working hours differs from week to week or over a longer period, the amount of one week's pay shall be divided instead by—

(a) the average number of normal working hours calculated by dividing by twelve the total number of the employee's normal working hours during the period of twelve weeks ending with the last complete week before the day on which the time off is taken, or

(b) where the employee has not been employed for a sufficient period to enable the calculation to be made under paragraph (a), a number which fairly represents the number of normal working hours in a week having regard to such of the considerations specified in subsection (4) as are appropriate in the circumstances.

(4) The considerations referred to in subsection (3)(b) are—

(a) the average number of normal working hours in a week which the employee could expect in accordance with the terms of the employee's contract, and

(b) the average number of normal working hours of other employees engaged in relevant comparable employment with the same employer.

(5) A right to any amount under subsection (1) does not affect any right of an employee in relation to remuneration under the employee's contract of employment ("contractual remuneration").

(6) Any contractual remuneration paid to an employee in respect of a period of time off under section 57. ZJ goes towards discharging any liability of the employer to pay remuneration under subsection (1) in respect of that period.

(7) Any payment of remuneration under subsection (1) in respect of a period of time off under section 57. ZJ goes towards discharging any liability of the employer to pay contractual remuneration in respect of that period.

57. ZLRight to unpaid time off to attend adoption appointments

(1) An employee who—

(a) has been notified by an adoption agency that a child is to be, or is expected to be, placed for adoption with the employee and another person jointly, and

(b) has elected to exercise the right to take time off under this section in connection with the adoption,

is entitled to be permitted by his or her employer to take time off during the employee's working hours in order that he or she may attend by appointment at any place for the purpose of having contact with the child or for any other purpose connected with the adoption.

(2) An employee may not make an election for the purposes of subsection (1)(b) if—

(a) the employee has made an election for the purposes of section 57. ZJ(2)(b) in connection with the adoption, or

(b) the other person with whom the child is to be, or is expected to be, placed for adoption has made an election for the purposes of subsection (1)(b) or section 57. ZP(1)(b) in connection with the adoption.

(3) An employee is not entitled to take time off under this section on or after the date of the child's placement for adoption with the employee.

(4) In relation to any particular adoption, an employee is not entitled to take time off under this section on more than two occasions.

(5) On each of those occasions, the maximum time off during working hours to which the employee is entitled is six and a half hours.

(6) An employee is not entitled to take time off under this section unless the appointment has been arranged by or at the request of the adoption agency which made the notification described in subsection (1)(a).

(7) An employee is not entitled to take time off under this section unless, if the employer requests it, the employee gives the employer—

(a) a declaration signed by the employee stating that the employee has made an election for the purposes of subsection (1)(b) in connection with the adoption, and

(b) a document showing the date and time of the appointment in question and that it has been arranged as described in subsection (6).

(8) A declaration or document requested under subsection (7) may be given in electronic form.

(9) In cases where more than one child is to be, or is expected to be, placed for adoption with an employee and another person jointly as part of the same arrangement, this section has effect as if—

(a) the purposes specified in subsection (1) were the purpose of having contact with any one or more of the children and any other purpose connected with any of the adoptions that are part of the arrangement;

(b) the references in subsections (1)(b) and (7)(a) to the adoption were references to all of the adoptions that are part of the arrangement;

(c) the references in subsection (2) to the adoption were references to any of the adoptions that are part of the arrangement;

(d) the reference in subsection (3) to the date of the child's placement for adoption were a reference to the date of placement of the first child to be placed as part of the arrangement;

(e) the reference in subsection (4) to a particular adoption were a reference to the adoptions that are part of a particular arrangement.

(10) For the purposes of this section the working hours of an employee are to be taken to be any time when, in accordance with the employee's contract of employment, the employee is required to be at work.

(11) In this section "adoption agency" means an adoption agency within the meaning of section 2 of the Adoption and Children Act 2002 or as defined in section 119. (1)(a) of the Adoption and Children (Scotland) Act 2007.

57. ZMComplaint to employment tribunal

(1) An employee may present a complaint to an employment tribunal that his or her employer—

(a) has unreasonably refused to let him or her take time off as required by section 57. ZJ or 57. ZL, or

(b) has failed to pay the whole or any part of any amount to which the employee is entitled under section 57. ZK.

(2) An employment tribunal may not consider a complaint under this section unless it is presented—

(a) before the end of the period of three months beginning with the day of the appointment in question, or

(b) within such further period as the tribunal considers reasonable in a case where it is satisfied that it was not reasonably practicable for the complaint to be presented before the end of that period of three months.

(3) Sections 207. A(3) and 207. B apply for the purposes of subsection (2)(a).

(4) Where an employment tribunal finds a complaint under subsection (1) well-founded, it must make a declaration to that effect.

(5) If the complaint is that the employer has unreasonably refused to let the employee take time off as required by section 57. ZJ, the tribunal must also order the employer to pay to the employee an amount that is twice the amount of the remuneration to which the employee would have been entitled under section 57. ZK if the employer had not refused.

(6) If the complaint is that the employer has failed to pay the employee the whole or part of any amount to which the employee is entitled under section 57. ZK, the tribunal must also order the employer to pay to the employee the amount which it finds due to the employee.

(7) If the complaint is that the employer has unreasonably refused to let the employee take time off as required by section 57. ZL, the tribunal must also order the employer to pay to the employee an amount determined in accordance with subsection (8).

(8) The amount payable to the employee is—

where—

A is the appropriate hourly rate for the employee determined in accordance with section 57. ZK(2) to (4), and
B is the number of working hours for which the employee would have been entitled under section 57. ZL to be absent if the time off had not been refused.

Adoption appointments: agency workers

57. ZNRight to paid time off to attend adoption appointments: agency workers
(1) An agency worker who has been notified by an adoption agency that a child is to be, or is expected to be, placed for adoption with the agency worker alone is entitled to be permitted by the temporary work agency and the hirer to take time off during the agency worker's working hours in order that he or she may attend by appointment at any place for the purpose of having contact with the child or for any other purpose connected with the adoption.
(2) An agency worker who—
    (a) has been notified by an adoption agency that a child is to be, or is expected to be, placed for adoption with the agency worker and another person jointly, and
    (b) has elected to exercise the right to take time off under this section in connection with the adoption,
is entitled to be permitted by the temporary work agency and the hirer to take time off during the agency worker's working hours in order that he or she may attend by appointment at any place for the purpose of having contact with the child or for any other purpose connected with the adoption.
(3) An agency worker may not make an election for the purposes of subsection (2)(b) if—
    (a) the agency worker has made an election for the purposes of section 57. ZP(1)(b) in connection with the adoption, or
    (b) the other person with whom the child is to be, or is expected to be, placed for adoption has made an election for the purposes of subsection (2)(b) or section 57. ZJ(2)(b) in connection with the adoption.
(4) An agency worker is not entitled to take time off under this section on or after the date of the child's placement for adoption with the agency worker.
(5) In relation to any particular adoption, an agency worker is not entitled to take time off under this section on more than five occasions.
(6) On each of those occasions, the maximum time off during working hours to which the agency worker is entitled is six and a half hours.
(7) An agency worker is not entitled to take time off under this section unless the appointment has been arranged by or at the request of the adoption agency which made the notification described in subsection (1) or (2)(a).
(8) An agency worker is not entitled to take time off under subsection (1) unless, if the temporary work agency or the hirer requests it, the agency worker gives that person a document showing the date and time of the appointment in question and that it has been arranged as described in subsection (7).
(9) An agency worker is not entitled to take time off under subsection (2) unless, if the temporary work agency or the hirer requests it, the agency worker gives that person—
    (a) a declaration signed by the agency worker stating that the agency worker has made an election for the purposes of subsection (2)(b) in connection with the adoption, and
    (b) a document showing the date and time of the appointment in question and that it has been arranged as described in subsection (7).
(10) A document or declaration requested under subsection (8) or (9) may be given in electronic form.
(11) In cases where more than one child is to be, or is expected to be, placed for adoption with an agency worker as part of the same arrangement, this section has effect as if—
    (a) the purposes specified in subsections (1) and (2) were the purpose of having contact with any one or more of the children and any other purpose connected with any of the adoptions that

are part of the arrangement;

(b) the references in subsections (2)(b) and (9)(a) to the adoption were references to all of the adoptions that are part of the arrangement;

(c) the references in subsection (3) to the adoption were references to any of the adoptions that are part of the arrangement;

(d) the reference in subsection (4) to the date of the child's placement for adoption were a reference to the date of placement of the first child to be placed as part of the arrangement;

(e) the reference in subsection (5) to a particular adoption were a reference to the adoptions that are part of a particular arrangement.

(12) For the purposes of this section the working hours of an agency worker are to be taken to be any time when, in accordance with the terms under which the agency worker works temporarily for and under the supervision and direction of the hirer, the agency worker is required to be at work.

(13) In this section "adoption agency" means an adoption agency within the meaning of section 2 of the Adoption and Children Act 2002 or as defined in section 119. (1)(a) of the Adoption and Children (Scotland) Act 2007.

57. ZORight to remuneration for time off under section 57. ZN

(1) An agency worker who is permitted to take time off under section 57. ZN is entitled to be paid remuneration by the temporary work agency for the number of working hours for which the agency worker is entitled to be absent at the appropriate hourly rate.

(2) The appropriate hourly rate, in relation to an agency worker, is the amount of one week's pay divided by the number of normal working hours in a week for that agency worker in accordance with the terms under which the agency worker works temporarily for and under the supervision and direction of the hirer that are in force on the day when the time off is taken.

(3) But where the number of normal working hours during the assignment differs from week to week or over a longer period, the amount of one week's pay shall be divided instead by the average number of normal working hours calculated by dividing by twelve the total number of the agency worker's normal working hours during the period of twelve weeks ending with the last complete week before the day on which the time off is taken.

(4) A right to any amount under subsection (1) does not affect any right of an agency worker in relation to remuneration under the agency worker's contract with the temporary work agency ("contractual remuneration").

(5) Any contractual remuneration paid to an agency worker in respect of a period of time off under section 57. ZN goes towards discharging any liability of the temporary work agency to pay remuneration under subsection (1) in respect of that period.

(6) Any payment of remuneration under subsection (1) in respect of a period of time off under section 57. ZN goes towards discharging any liability of the temporary work agency to pay contractual remuneration in respect of that period.

57. ZPRight to unpaid time off to attend adoption meetings: agency workers

(1) An agency worker who—

(a) has been notified by an adoption agency that a child is to be, or is expected to be, placed for adoption with the agency worker and another person jointly, and

(b) has elected to exercise the right to take time off under this section in connection with the adoption,

is entitled to be permitted by the temporary work agency and the hirer to take time off during the agency worker's working hours in order that he or she may attend by appointment at any place for the purpose of having contact with the child or for any other purpose connected with the adoption.

(2) An agency worker may not make an election for the purposes of subsection (1)(b) if—

(a) the agency worker has made an election for the purposes of section 57. ZN(2)(b) in connection with the adoption, or

(b) the other person with whom the child is to be, or is expected to be, placed for adoption has made an election for the purposes of subsection (1)(b) or section 57. ZL(1)(b) in connection with the adoption.

(3) An agency worker is not entitled to take time off under this section on or after the date of the child's placement for adoption with the agency worker.
(4) In relation to any particular adoption, an agency worker is not entitled to take time off under this section on more than two occasions.
(5) On each of those occasions, the maximum time off during working hours to which the agency worker is entitled is six and a half hours.
(6) An agency worker is not entitled to take time off under this section unless the appointment has been arranged by or at the request of the adoption agency which made the notification described in subsection (1)(a).
(7) An agency worker is not entitled to take time off under this section unless, if the temporary work agency or the hirer requests it, the agency worker gives that person—

(a) a declaration signed by the agency worker stating that the agency worker has made an election for the purposes of subsection (1)(b) in connection with the adoption, and

(b) a document showing the date and time of the appointment in question and that it has been arranged as described in subsection (6).

(8) A declaration or document requested under subsection (7) may be given in electronic form.
(9) In cases where more than one child is to be, or is expected to be, placed for adoption with an agency worker and another person jointly as part of the same arrangement, this section has effect as if—

(a) the purposes specified in subsection (1) were the purpose of having contact with any one or more of the children and any other purpose connected with any of the adoptions that are part of the arrangement;

(b) the references in subsections (1)(b) and (7)(a) to the adoption were references to all of the adoptions that are part of the arrangement;

(c) the references in subsection (2) to the adoption were references to any of the adoptions that are part of the arrangement;

(d) the reference in subsection (3) to the date of the child's placement for adoption were a reference to the date of placement of the first child to be placed as part of the arrangement;

(e) the reference in subsection (4) to a particular adoption were a reference to the adoptions that are part of a particular arrangement.

(10) For the purposes of this section the working hours of an agency worker are to be taken to be any time when, in accordance with the terms under which the agency worker works temporarily for and under the supervision and direction of the hirer, the agency worker is required to be at work.
(11) In this section "adoption agency" means an adoption agency within the meaning of section 2 of the Adoption and Children Act 2002 or as defined by section 119. (1)(a) of the Adoption and Children (Scotland) Act 2007.
57. ZQComplaint to employment tribunal: agency workers
(1) An agency worker may present a complaint to an employment tribunal that the temporary work agency—

(a) has unreasonably refused to let him or her take time off as required by section 57. ZN or 57. ZP, or

(b) has failed to pay the whole or any part of any amount to which the agency worker is entitled under section 57. ZO.

(2) An agency worker may present a complaint to an employment tribunal that the hirer has unreasonably refused to let him or her take time off as required by section 57. ZN or 57. ZP.
(3) An employment tribunal may not consider a complaint under subsection (1) or (2) unless it is presented—

(a) before the end of the period of three months beginning with the day of the appointment in question, or

(b) within such further period as the tribunal considers reasonable in a case where it is satisfied that it was not reasonably practicable for the complaint to be presented before the end of that period of three months.

(4) Sections 207. A(3) and 207. B apply for the purposes of subsection (3)(a).
(5) Where an employment tribunal finds a complaint under subsection (1) or (2) well-founded, it must make a declaration to that effect.
(6) If the complaint is that the temporary work agency or hirer has unreasonably refused to let the agency worker take time off as required by section 57. ZN, the tribunal must also order payment to the agency worker of an amount that is twice the amount of the remuneration to which the agency worker would have been entitled under section 57. ZO if the agency worker had not been refused the time off.
(7) If the complaint is that the temporary work agency has failed to pay the agency worker the whole or part of any amount to which the agency worker is entitled under section 57. ZO, the tribunal must also order the temporary work agency to pay to the agency worker the amount which it finds due to the agency worker.
(8) If the complaint is that the temporary work agency or hirer has unreasonably refused to let the agency worker take time off as required by section 57. ZP, the tribunal must also order payment to the agency worker of an amount determined in accordance with subsection (9).
(9) The amount payable to the agency worker under subsection (8) is—
where—
A is the appropriate hourly rate for the agency worker determined in accordance with section 57. ZO(2) and (3), and
B is the number of working hours for which the agency worker would have been entitled under section 57. ZP to be absent if the time off had not been refused.
(10) Where the tribunal orders that payment under subsection (6) or (8) be made by the temporary work agency and the hirer, the proportion of that amount payable by each respondent is to be such as may be found by the tribunal to be just and equitable having regard to the extent of each respondent's responsibility for the infringement to which the complaint relates.

57. ZRAgency workers: supplementary
(1) Without prejudice to any other duties of the hirer or temporary work agency under any enactment or rule of law, sections 57. ZN to 57. ZQ do not apply where the agency worker—
    (a) has not completed the qualifying period, or
    (b) pursuant to regulation 8. (a) or (b) of the Agency Workers Regulations 2010 (S.I. 2010/93), is no longer entitled to the rights conferred by regulation 5 of those Regulations.
(2) Nothing in sections 57. ZN to 57. ZQ imposes a duty on the hirer or temporary work agency beyond the original intended duration, or likely duration, of the assignment, whichever is the longer.
(3) Sections 57. ZN to 57. ZQ do not apply where sections 57. ZJ to 57. ZM apply.
(4) In this section and sections 57. ZN to 57. ZQ the following have the same meaning as in the Agency Workers Regulations 2010—
"agency worker";
"assignment";
"hirer";
"qualifying period";
"temporary work agency".

57. ZSPlacement of looked after children with prospective adopters
(1) Subsection (2) applies where a local authority in England notifies a person—
    (a) who is a local authority foster parent, and
    (b) who has been approved as a prospective adopter,
that a child is to be, or is expected to be, placed with that person under section 22. C of the Children Act 1989.
(2) Where this subsection applies, sections 57. ZJ, 57. ZL, 57. ZN and 57. ZP have effect as if—
    (a) references to adoption or placement for adoption were references to placement of a child under section 22. C of the Children Act 1989 with a local authority foster parent who has been approved as a prospective adopter;
    (b) references to placing for adoption were references to placing a child under section 22. C of

that Act with a local authority foster parent who has been approved as a prospective adopter;

(c) references to an adoption agency were references to a local authority in England.

(3) Where a child is placed under section 22. C of the Children Act 1989 with a local authority foster parent who has been approved as a prospective adopter, notification of that person by an adoption agency during that placement that the child is to be, or is expected to be, placed with that person for adoption is not to give rise to a right to time off under section 57. ZJ, 57. ZL, 57. ZN or 57. ZP for that person or another person."

(2) In the Employment Rights Act 1996—

(a) in section 47. C (right not to be subject to detriment: leave for family reasons), in subsection (2) (prescribed reasons), after paragraph (aa) (as inserted by section 127. (2)(a)) there is inserted—

"(ab)time off under section 57. ZJ or 57. ZL,";

(b) in section 80. B (entitlement to ordinary paternity leave: adoption), in subsection (5) (provision that may be made in regulations under subsection (1)), after paragraph (b) there is inserted—

"(ba)make provision excluding the right to be absent on leave under this section in the case of an employee who has exercised a right to take time off under section 57. ZJ;";

(c) in section 99 (being regarded as unfairly dismissed: leave for family reasons), in subsection (3) (prescribed reasons), after paragraph (aa) (as inserted by section 127. (2)(b)) there is inserted—

"(ab)time off under section 57. ZJ or 57. ZL,";

(d) in section 225 (the calculation date in finding a week's pay), after subsection (3. A) (as inserted by section 127. (2)(c)) there is inserted—

"(3. B)Where the calculation is for the purposes of section 57. ZK or 57. ZM, the calculation date is the day of the appointment.";

(e) in section 235 (other definitions), in subsection (1), at the appropriate place there is inserted—

""local authority", in relation to the placement of children under section 22. C of the Children Act 1989, has the same meaning as in that Act (see section 105. (1) of that Act);";

" "local authority foster parent" has the same meaning as in the Children Act 1989 (see section 22. C(12) of that Act);".

Commencement Information

I3. S. 128. (1)(2)(d)(e) in force at 5.4.2015 by S.I. 2014/1640, art. 6. (d)

I4. S. 128. (2)(a)-(c) in force at 30.6.2014 by S.I. 2014/1640, art. 3. (1)(j)

129. Right not to be subjected to detriment: agency workers

(1) In section 47. C of the Employment Rights Act 1996 (right not to be subjected to detriment for taking leave for family and domestic reasons), after subsection (4) there is inserted—

"(5)An agency worker has the right not to be subjected to any detriment by any act, or any deliberate failure to act, by the temporary work agency or the hirer done on the ground that—

(a) being a person entitled to—

(i) time off under section 57. ZA, and

(ii) remuneration under section 57. ZB in respect of that time off,

the agency worker exercised (or proposed to exercise) that right or received (or sought to receive) that remuneration,

(b) being a person entitled to time off under section 57. ZG, the agency worker exercised (or proposed to exercise) that right,

(c) being a person entitled to—

(i) time off under section 57. ZN, and

(ii) remuneration under section 57. ZO in respect of that time off,

the agency worker exercised (or proposed to exercise) that right or received (or sought to receive) that remuneration, or

(d) being a person entitled to time off under section 57. ZP, the agency worker exercised (or proposed to exercise) that right.

(6) Subsection (5) does not apply where the agency worker is an employee.

(7) In this section the following have the same meaning as in the Agency Workers Regulations 2010 (S.I. 2010/93)—

"agency worker";

"hirer";

"temporary work agency"."

(2) In section 48 of that Act (complaints to employment tribunals)—

    (a) in subsection (1), for "47. C" there is substituted " 47. C(1) ";

    (b) after subsection (1. A) there is inserted—

"(1. AA)An agency worker may present a complaint to an employment tribunal that the agency worker has been subjected to a detriment in contravention of section 47. C(5) by the temporary work agency or the hirer.";

    (c) in subsection (2), for "such a complaint" there is substituted " a complaint under subsection (1), (1. ZA), (1. A) or (1. B) ";

    (d) after subsection (2) there is inserted—

"(2. A)On a complaint under subsection (1. AA) it is for the temporary work agency or (as the case may be) the hirer to show the ground on which any act, or deliberate failure to act, was done.";

    (e) in subsection (4), after "an employer" there is inserted " , a temporary work agency or a hirer ";

    (f) after subsection (5) there is inserted—

"(6)In this section and section 49 the following have the same meaning as in the Agency Workers Regulations 2010 (S.I. 2010/93)—

"agency worker";

"hirer";

"temporary work agency"."

(3) In section 49 of that Act (remedies in the case of complaints to an employment tribunal)—

    (a) in subsection (1), for "under section 48" there is substituted " under section 48. (1), (1. ZA), (1. A) or (1. B) ";

    (b) after subsection (1), there is inserted—

"(1. A)Where an employment tribunal finds a complaint under section 48. (1. AA) well-founded, the tribunal—

    (a) shall make a declaration to that effect, and

    (b) may make an award of compensation to be paid by the temporary work agency or (as the case may be) the hirer to the complainant in respect of the act or failure to act to which the complaint relates."

Commencement Information

I5. S. 129. (1) in force at 1.10.2014 for specified purposes by S.I. 2014/1640, art. 4. (b)

I6. S. 129. (1) in force at 5.4.2015 for specified purposes by S.I. 2014/1640, art. 6. (e)

I7. S. 129. (2)(3) in force at 1.10.2014 by S.I. 2014/1640, art. 4. (b)

130. Time off work for ante-natal care: increased amount of award

(1) In section 57 of the Employment Rights Act 1996 (complaints to employment tribunals where time off work for ante-natal care refused to employee), in subsection (4) (amount of award for unreasonable refusal), for "an amount equal to" there is substituted " an amount that is twice the amount of ".

(2) In section 57. ZC of the Employment Rights Act 1996 (complaints to employment tribunals where time off work for ante-natal care refused to agency worker), in subsection (5) (amount of award for unreasonable refusal), for "an amount equal to" there is substituted " an amount that is

twice the amount of ".
Commencement Information
I8. S. 130 in force at 1.10.2014 by S.I. 2014/1640, art. 4. (c) (with art. 11)

PART 9. Right to request flexible working

PART 9 Right to request flexible working

131. Removal of requirement to be a carer

(1) In section 80. F(1) of the Employment Rights Act 1996 (conditions for exercising right to request flexible working), paragraph (b) (condition that employee's purpose be to enable caring for a child or adult) is repealed.
(2) Section 80. F is further amended as follows—
   (a) in subsection (1), the "and" following paragraph (a) is repealed;
   (b) in subsection (2), after paragraph (b) there is inserted "and";
   (c) in subsection (2), paragraph (d) and the "and" preceding it are repealed;
   (d) subsection (10) is repealed.
Commencement Information
I1. S. 131 in force at 30.6.2014 by S.I. 2014/1640, art. 3. (1)(k) (with art. 10)

132. Dealing with applications

(1) Section 80. G of the Employment Rights Act 1996 (employer's duties in relation to an application for flexible working) is amended as follows.
(2) In subsection (1), for paragraph (a) (requirement to deal with application in accordance with regulations) there is substituted—
   "(a)shall deal with the application in a reasonable manner,
   (aa) shall notify the employee of the decision on the application within the decision period, and".
(3) After subsection (1) there is inserted—
"(1. A)If an employer allows an employee to appeal a decision to reject an application, the reference in subsection (1)(aa) to the decision on the application is a reference to—
   (a) the decision on the appeal, or
   (b) if more than one appeal is allowed, the decision on the final appeal.
(1. B)For the purposes of subsection (1)(aa) the decision period applicable to an employee's application under section 80. F is—
   (a) the period of three months beginning with the date on which the application is made, or
   (b) such longer period as may be agreed by the employer and the employee.
(1. C)An agreement to extend the decision period in a particular case may be made—
   (a) before it ends, or
   (b) with retrospective effect, before the end of a period of three months beginning with the day after that on which the decision period that is being extended came to an end."
(4) After subsection (1. C) (as inserted by subsection (3)) there is inserted—
"(1. D)An application under section 80. F is to be treated as having been withdrawn by the employee if—
   (a) the employee without good reason has failed to attend both the first meeting arranged by the employer to discuss the application and the next meeting arranged for that purpose, or
   (b) where the employer allows the employee to appeal a decision to reject an application or to

make a further appeal, the employee without good reason has failed to attend both the first meeting arranged by the employer to discuss the appeal and the next meeting arranged for that purpose,
and the employer has notified the employee that the employer has decided to treat that conduct of the employee as a withdrawal of the application."
(5) In the Employment Rights Act 1996, the following are repealed—
- (a) section 47. E(1)(b);
- (b) section 80. G(2) to (4);
- (c) section 80. H(4);
- (d) in section 80. I(4), the words ", and the regulations under that section,";
- (e) section 104. C(1)(b).

Commencement Information

I2. S. 132 in force at 30.6.2014 by S.I. 2014/1640, art. 3. (1)(l) (with art. 10)

133. Complaints to employment tribunals

(1) Section 80. H of the Employment Rights Act 1996 (complaints to employment tribunals) is amended as follows.
(2) In subsection (1) (grounds of complaint)—
- (a) the "or" after paragraph (a) is repealed;
- (b) after paragraph (b) there is inserted ", or
- (c) that the employer's notification under section 80. G(1. D) was given in circumstances that did not satisfy one of the requirements in section 80. G(1. D)(a) and (b)."

(3) In subsection (2) (no complaints under section 80. H in respect of an application disposed of by agreement or withdrawn), for "under this section" there is substituted " under subsection (1)(a) or (b) ".
(4) For subsection (3) (no complaints to be made until the employer rejects an application on appeal or contravenes specified regulations under section 80. G(1)(a)) there is substituted—
"(3)In the case of an application which has not been disposed of by agreement or withdrawn, no complaint under subsection (1)(a) or (b) may be made until—
- (a) the employer notifies the employee of the employer's decision on the application, or
- (b) if the decision period applicable to the application (see section 80. G(1. B)) comes to an end without the employer notifying the employee of the employer's decision on the application, the end of the decision period.

(3. A)If an employer allows an employee to appeal a decision to reject an application, a reference in other subsections of this section to the decision on the application is a reference to the decision on the appeal or, if more than one appeal is allowed, the decision on the final appeal.
(3. B)If an agreement to extend the decision period is made as described in section 80. G(1. C)(b), subsection (3)(b) is to be treated as not allowing a complaint until the end of the extended period."
(5) After subsection (3. B) (as inserted by subsection (4)) there is inserted—
"(3. C)A complaint under subsection (1)(c) may be made as soon as the notification under section 80. G(1. D) complained of is given to the employee."
(6) In subsection (6) (meaning of the relevant date), from "relevant date" to the end there is substituted " relevant date is a reference to the first date on which the employee may make a complaint under subsection (1)(a), (b) or (c), as the case may be. "

Commencement Information

I3. S. 133 in force at 30.6.2014 by S.I. 2014/1640, art. 3. (1)(m) (with art. 10)

134. Review of sections 131 to 133.

(1) The Secretary of State must from time to time—
- (a) carry out a review of sections 131 to 133,

(b) set out the conclusions of the review in a report, and

(c) publish the report.

(2) The report must in particular—

(a) set out the objectives intended to be achieved by the amendments of the Employment Rights Act 1996 made by sections 131 to 133,

(b) assess the extent to which those objectives are achieved, and

(c) assess whether those objectives remain appropriate and, if so, the extent to which they could be achieved in a way that imposes less regulation.

(3) The first report to be published under this section must be published before the end of the period of seven years beginning with the day on which sections 131 to 133 come into force.

(4) Reports under this section are afterwards to be published at intervals not exceeding seven years.

Commencement Information

I4. S. 134 in force at 30.6.2014 by S.I. 2014/1640, art. 3. (1)(n) (with art. 10)

PART 10. General provisions

PART 10 General provisions

135. Orders and regulations

(1) A power to make an order or regulations under this Act is exercisable by statutory instrument.

(2) A power to make an order or regulations under this Act includes power—

(a) to make different provision for different purposes (including different areas);

(b) to make provision generally or in relation to specific cases.

(3) A power to make an order or regulations under this Act (except a power conferred by section 78. (6), 137 or 139) includes power to make incidental, supplementary, consequential, transitional or transitory provision or savings.

(4) Subject to subsection (5), a statutory instrument that contains an order or regulations made under this Act by the Secretary of State or the Lord Chancellor is subject to annulment in pursuance of a resolution of either House of Parliament.

(5) Subsection (4) does not apply to—

(a) a statutory instrument containing an order under section 78. (6), 137 or 139, or

(b) a statutory instrument to which subsection (6) applies.

(6) A statutory instrument containing (whether alone or with other provision)—

(a) the first regulations to be made under section 49,

(b) an order under section 58. (1) or 59. (1),

(c) regulations under section 70. (3),

(d) regulations under section 92 or 93,

(e) regulations under subsection (6), (8), (9) or (10) of section 94,

(f) regulations under subsection (11) of that section which amend, repeal or revoke any provision of an enactment within the meaning of that section, or

(g) an order under section 136 which amends or repeals any provision of primary legislation,

is not to be made unless a draft of the instrument has been laid before, and approved by a resolution of, each House of Parliament.

(7) "Primary legislation" means—

(a) an Act of Parliament;

(b) a Measure or Act of the National Assembly for Wales.

136. Consequential amendments, repeals and revocations

(1) The Secretary of State or the Lord Chancellor may by order make provision in consequence of any provision of this Act.
(2) The power conferred by subsection (1) includes power to amend, repeal, revoke or otherwise modify any provision made by or under an enactment (including any enactment passed or made in the same Session as this Act).
(3) "Enactment" includes a Measure or Act of the National Assembly for Wales.

137. Transitional, transitory or saving provision

(1) The Secretary of State or the Lord Chancellor may by order make transitional, transitory or saving provision in connection with the coming into force of any provision of this Act.
(2) Subsections (3) to (5) apply if section 85. (1) of the Legal Aid, Sentencing and Punishment of Offenders Act 2012 ("the 2012 Act") comes into force on or before the day on which this Act is passed.
(3) Section 85 of the 2012 Act (removal of £5,000 limit on certain fines on conviction by magistrates' court) applies in relation to the following offences as if the offences were relevant offences (as defined in section 85. (3) of that Act)—
　(a) the offence contained in the new section 51. C(4) to be inserted into the Childcare Act 2006 by paragraph 13 of Schedule 4 to this Act;
　(b) the offence contained in the new section 51. F(1) to be inserted into that Act by paragraph 13 of that Schedule;
　(c) the offence contained in the new section 61. D(4) to be inserted into that Act by paragraph 26 of that Schedule;
　(d) the offence contained in the new section 61. G(1) to be inserted into that Act by paragraph 26 of that Schedule;
　(e) the offence contained in the new section 69. C(6) to be inserted into that Act by paragraph 36 of that Schedule;
　(f) the offence contained in the new section 76. B(3) to be inserted into that Act by paragraph 46 of that Schedule.
(4) Section 85 of the 2012 Act (removal of £5,000 limit on certain fines on conviction by magistrates' court) applies in relation to the power in the new section 69. A(1)(b) to be inserted into the Childcare Act 2006 by paragraph 35 of Schedule 4 to this Act as if the power were a relevant power (as defined in section 85. (3) of the 2012 Act).
(5) Regulations described in section 85. (11) of the 2012 Act may amend, repeal or otherwise modify a provision of this Act or the Childcare Act 2006.

138. Financial provision

(1) There is to be paid out of money provided by Parliament—
　(a) any expenses incurred by a Minister of the Crown or a government department under this Act, and
　(b) any increase attributable to this Act in the sums payable under any other Act out of money so provided.
(2) There is to be paid into the Consolidated Fund any increase attributable to this Act in the sums payable into that Fund under any other Act.

139. Commencement

(1) This Part comes into force on the day on which this Act is passed.

(2) Section 1—

(a) so far as it relates to England, comes into force on such day as the Secretary of State appoints by order, and

(b) so far as it relates to Wales, comes into force on such day as the Welsh Ministers appoint by order.

(3) Sections 10, 13 and 17 come into force on such day as the Lord Chancellor appoints by order.

(4) Sections 18, 90, 101, 102, 103 and 104 come into force at the end of the period of two months beginning with the day on which this Act is passed.

(5) Part 6 comes into force on 1 April 2014.

(6) The remaining provisions of this Act come into force on such day as the Secretary of State appoints by order.

(7) An order under subsection (2), (3) or (6) may appoint different days for different purposes.

140. Short title and extent

(1) This Act may be cited as the Children and Families Act 2014.

(2) Part 3 of this Act (children and young people in England with special educational needs or disabilities) and section 100 (duty to support pupils with medical conditions) are to be included in the list of Education Acts set out in section 578 of the Education Act 1996.

(3) This Act extends to England and Wales only, subject to the following subsections.

(4) Section 94 extends to the whole of the United Kingdom.

(5) Sections 126. (2) to (4) and 134 extend to England and Wales and Scotland.

(6) Section 126. (3) and (4), so far as relating to paragraphs 5, 56 to 62 and 64 of Schedule 7, extends to Northern Ireland.

(7) This Part extends to the whole of the United Kingdom.

(8) An amendment or repeal made by this Act has the same extent as the provision to which it relates (ignoring extent by virtue of an Order in Council), subject to subsection (9).

(9) Subsection (8) does not apply to the repeal made by section 90, which extends to England and Wales only.

Schedules

Schedule 1. The Adoption and Children Act Register

Section 7

1. The Adoption and Children Act 2002 is amended as follows.
Commencement Information
I1. Sch. 1 para. 1 in force at 13.5.2014 by S.I. 2014/889, art. 5. (f)
2. (1)Section 125 (Adoption and Children Act Register) is amended as follows.

(2) In subsection (1) for "Her Majesty may by Order in Council make provision for the Secretary of State to" substitute " The Secretary of State may ".

(3) After subsection (1) insert—

"(1. A)Regulations may provide that the register may contain—

(a) prescribed information about children who a Welsh, Scottish or Northern Irish adoption agency is satisfied are suitable for adoption,

(b) prescribed information about prospective adopters who a Welsh, Scottish or Northern Irish adoption agency is satisfied are suitable to adopt a child,

(c) prescribed information about persons included in the register in pursuance of paragraph (a) or (b) in respect of things occurring after their inclusion."
(4) In subsection (2) for "an Order under this section" substitute " regulations ".
(5) In subsection (4) for "An Order under this section" substitute " Regulations ".
Commencement Information
I2. Sch. 1 para. 2 in force at 13.5.2014 by S.I. 2014/889, art. 5. (f)
3. (1)Section 126 (use of an organisation to establish the register) is amended as follows.
(2) In subsection (1) omit "under an Order under section 125".
(3) In subsection (3) omit "(or general application in any part of Great Britain)".
(4) Omit subsection (4).
Commencement Information
I3. Sch. 1 para. 3 in force at 13.5.2014 by S.I. 2014/889, art. 5. (f)
4. (1)Section 127 (use of an organisation as agency for payments) is amended as follows.
(2) In subsection (1) for "An Order under section 125" substitute " Regulations ".
(3) In subsection (2) omit "(or general application in any part of Great Britain)".
(4) Omit subsection (3).
Commencement Information
I4. Sch. 1 para. 4 in force at 13.5.2014 by S.I. 2014/889, art. 5. (f)
5. (1)Section 128 (supply of information for the register) is amended as follows.
(2) In subsection (1) for "An Order under section 125" substitute " Regulations ".
(3) In subsection (2) for "the Order" substitute " regulations ".
(4) In subsection (3) for "An Order under section 125" substitute " Regulations ".
Commencement Information
I5. Sch. 1 para. 5 in force at 13.5.2014 by S.I. 2014/889, art. 5. (f)
6. (1)Section 129 (disclosure of information) is amended as follows.
(2) In subsection (1) for "or (3)" substitute " , (2. A) or (3) or section 128. A ".
(3) After subsection (2) insert—
"(2. A)Regulations may make provision permitting the disclosure of prescribed information entered in the register, or compiled from information entered in the register—
(a) to an adoption agency or to a Welsh, Scottish or Northern Irish adoption agency for any prescribed purpose, or
(b) for the purpose of enabling the information to be entered in a register which is maintained in respect of Wales, Scotland or Northern Ireland and which contains information about children who are suitable for adoption or prospective adopters who are suitable to adopt a child."
(4) In subsection (4)—
(a) for "An Order under section 125" substitute " Regulations ", and
(b) after "(2)" insert " or (2. A) ".
(5) In subsection (5) omit paragraph (b) (and the "or" which precedes it).
(6) In subsection (6) after "(2)" insert " , (2. A) ".
(7) In subsection (7)—
(a) for "An Order under section 125" substitute " Regulations ",
(b) in paragraph (a) after "(2)" insert " or (2. A) ",
(c) after paragraph (a) (and before the "or" which follows it) insert—
"(aa)by a prescribed Welsh, Scottish or Northern Irish adoption agency in respect of information disclosed under subsection (2. A),", and
(d) in paragraph (b) for "to whom information is disclosed under subsection (3)" substitute " in respect of information disclosed under subsection (2. A) or (3) ".
Commencement Information
I6. Sch. 1 para. 6 in force at 13.5.2014 by S.I. 2014/889, art. 5. (f)
7. Section 130 (territorial application) is repealed.
Commencement Information
I7. Sch. 1 para. 7 in force at 13.5.2014 by S.I. 2014/889, art. 5. (f)
8. (1)Section 131 (supplementary) is amended as follows.

(2) In subsection (1)—
(a) before paragraph (a) insert—
"(za)adoption agency" means—
(i) a local authority in England,
(ii) a registered adoption society whose principal office is in England,",
(b) in paragraph (b) for "an Order under section 125" substitute " regulations ",
(c) after paragraph (c) insert—
"(ca)Welsh adoption agency" means—
(i) a local authority in Wales,
(ii) a registered adoption society whose principal office is in Wales.", and
(d) omit paragraphs (d) and (e).
(3) In subsection (2) after "sections" insert " (except sections 125. (1. A) and 129. (2. A)) ".
(4) After subsection (2) insert—
"(2. A)For the purposes of sections 125. (1. A) and 129. (2. A)—
(a) a child is suitable for adoption if a Welsh, Scottish or Northern Irish adoption agency is satisfied that the child ought to be placed for adoption,
(b) prospective adopters are suitable to adopt a child if a Welsh, Scottish or Northern Irish adoption agency is satisfied that they are suitable to have a child placed with them for adoption."
(5) Omit subsections (4) to (7).
Commencement Information
I8. Sch. 1 para. 8 in force at 13.5.2014 by S.I. 2014/889, art. 5. (f)
9. In section 142 (supplementary and consequential provision), in subsection (4) omit the words from "or of Her Majesty" to the end.
Commencement Information
I9. Sch. 1 para. 9 in force at 13.5.2014 by S.I. 2014/889, art. 5. (f)
10. In section 144 (general interpretation etc), in subsection (2)—
(a) omit "Order in Council or", and
(b) in paragraph (b) omit "Order or, as the case may be,".
Commencement Information
I10. Sch. 1 para. 10 in force at 13.5.2014 by S.I. 2014/889, art. 5. (f)
11. (1)Sections 125 to 131 cease to have effect in relation to Scotland.
(2) Accordingly, in section 149 (extent), in subsection (4) omit paragraph (b).
Commencement Information
I11. Sch. 1 para. 11 in force at 13.5.2014 by S.I. 2014/889, art. 5. (f)

Schedule 2. Child arrangements orders: amendments

Section 12

PART 1 Amendments of the Children Act 1989

1. The Children Act 1989 is amended as follows.
Commencement Information
I1. Sch. 2 para. 1 in force at 22.4.2014 by S.I. 2014/889, art. 4. (f) (with transitional provisions in S.I. 2014/1042, arts. 3, 4, 6-10)
2. (1)Section 5 (appointment of guardians) is amended as follows.
(2) In subsection (1)(b) (application to court for appointment of guardian may be made following death of person with whom child was to live) for "residence order has been made with respect to the child in favour of a parent, guardian or special guardian of his who" substitute " parent,

guardian or special guardian of the child's was named in a child arrangements order as a person with whom the child was to live and ".

(3) In subsection (7)(b) (when non-court appointment of guardian under subsection (3) or (4) takes effect) for "residence order in his favour was in force with respect to the child or he" substitute " child arrangements order was in force in which the person was named as a person with whom the child was to live or the person ".

(4) In subsection (9)—

(a) for "residence" substitute " child arrangements ",

(b) for "was also made in favour of" substitute " also named ", and

(c) after "child" insert " as a person with whom the child was to live ".

Commencement Information

I2. Sch. 2 para. 2 in force at 22.4.2014 by S.I. 2014/889, art. 4. (f) (with transitional provisions in S.I. 2014/1042, arts. 3, 4. 6-10)

3. In the title of section 8 for "Residence, contact" substitute " Child arrangements orders ".

Commencement Information

I3. Sch. 2 para. 3 in force at 22.4.2014 by S.I. 2014/889, art. 4. (f) (with transitional provisions in S.I. 2014/1042, arts. 3, 4. 6-10)

4. (1)Section 9 (restrictions on making section 8 orders) is amended as follows.

(2) In subsection (1) (no section 8 order other than a residence order to be made if child is in care) for "residence order" substitute " child arrangements order to which subsection (6. B) applies ".

(3) In subsection (2) (local authorities cannot obtain residence or contact orders) for "residence order or contact" substitute " child arrangements ".

(4) In subsection (5)(a) (specific issue order or prohibited steps order not to be made where result could be achieved by a residence or contact order) for "residence or contact" substitute " child arrangements ".

(5) In subsection (6) (section 8 orders other than residence orders are only exceptionally to have effect once child is 16) for "specific issue order, contact order or prohibited steps" substitute " section 8 ".

(6) After subsection (6) insert—

"(6. A)Subsection (6) does not apply to a child arrangements order to which subsection (6. B) applies.

(6. B)This subsection applies to a child arrangements order if the arrangements regulated by the order relate only to either or both of the following—

(a) with whom the child concerned is to live, and

(b) when the child is to live with any person."

Commencement Information

I4. Sch. 2 para. 4 in force at 22.4.2014 by S.I. 2014/889, art. 4. (f) (with transitional provisions in S.I. 2014/1042, arts. 3, 4, 6-10)

5. (1)Section 10 (power of court to make section 8 orders) is amended as follows.

(2) For subsection (4)(b) (person may apply for section 8 order if residence order is in force in favour of the person) substitute—

"(b)any person who is named, in a child arrangements order that is in force with respect to the child, as a person with whom the child is to live."

(3) In subsection (5) (persons entitled to apply for a residence or contact order)—

(a) in the words before paragraph (a) for "residence or contact" substitute " child arrangements ",

(b) for paragraph (c)(i) substitute—

"(i)in any case where a child arrangements order in force with respect to the child regulates arrangements relating to with whom the child is to live or when the child is to live with any person, has the consent of each of the persons named in the order as a person with whom the child is to live;", and

(c) after paragraph (c) insert—

"(d)any person who has parental responsibility for the child by virtue of provision made under section 12. (2. A)."

(4) In each of subsections (5. A) and (5. B) (foster parent, or relative, may apply for residence order if child has lived with applicant for at least a year) for "residence order" substitute " child arrangements order to which subsection (5. C) applies ".
(5) After subsection (5. B) insert—
"(5. C)This subsection applies to a child arrangements order if the arrangements regulated by the order relate only to either or both of the following—
(a) with whom the child concerned is to live, and
(b) when the child is to live with any person."
(6) In subsection (6)(b) (person may apply for variation or discharge of a contact order if named in the order)—
(a) for "contact" substitute " child arrangements ", and
(b) for "the order." substitute "provisions of the order regulating arrangements relating to—
(i) with whom the child concerned is to spend time or otherwise have contact, or
(ii) when the child is to spend time or otherwise have contact with any person."
(7) In subsection (7. A) (if special guardianship order in force, application for residence order may be made only with leave of the court) for "residence order" substitute " child arrangements order to which subsection (7. B) applies ".
(8) After subsection (7. A) insert—
"(7. B)This subsection applies to a child arrangements order if the arrangements regulated by the order consist of, or include, arrangements which relate to either or both of the following—
(a) with whom the child concerned is to live, and
(b) when the child is to live with any person."
Commencement Information
I5. Sch. 2 para. 5 in force at 22.4.2014 by S.I. 2014/889, art. 4. (f) (with transitional provisions in S.I. 2014/1042, arts. 3, 4, 6-10)
6. (1)Section 11 (section 8 orders: general principles and supplementary provisions) is amended as follows.
(2) Omit subsection (4) (residence order may make provision about when a child is to live with persons who do not live together).
(3) In subsection (5) (residence order ceases to have effect where parents resume cohabitation for at least 6 months)—
(a) in paragraph (a) for "residence" substitute " child arrangements ",
(b) in paragraph (b) for the words before "two" substitute " the child has ", and
(c) in the words after paragraph (b) for "residence order" substitute " order, so far as it has the result that there are times when the child lives or is to live with one of the parents, ".
(4) In subsection (6) (contact order ceases to have effect where parents resume cohabitation for at least 6 months) for the words before "shall cease" substitute " A child arrangements order made with respect to a child, so far as it provides for the child to spend time or otherwise have contact with one of the child's parents at times when the child is living with the child's other parent, ".
(5) In subsection (7)(b) (persons on whom conditions may be imposed by a section 8 order)—
(a) for sub-paragraph (i) (person in whose favour the order is made) substitute—
"(i)who is named in the order as a person with whom the child concerned is to live, spend time or otherwise have contact;", and
(b) in sub-paragraph (ii) omit "concerned".
Commencement Information
I6. Sch. 2 para. 6 in force at 22.4.2014 by S.I. 2014/889, art. 4. (f) (with transitional provisions in S.I. 2014/1042, arts. 3, 4, 6-10)
7. (1)Section 11. A (contact activity directions) is amended as follows.
(2) For subsections (1) to (3) (power to make directions) substitute—
"(1)Subsection (2) applies in proceedings in which the court is considering whether to make provision about one or more of the matters mentioned in subsection (1. A) by making—
(a) a child arrangements order with respect to the child concerned, or
(b) an order varying or discharging a child arrangements order with respect to the child

concerned.
(1. A)The matters mentioned in this subsection are—
(a) with whom a child is to live,
(b) when a child is to live with any person,
(c) with whom a child is to spend time or otherwise have contact, and
(d) when a child is to spend time or otherwise have contact with any person.
(2) The court may make an activity direction in connection with the provision that the court is considering whether to make.
(2. A)Subsection (2. B) applies in proceedings in which subsection (2) does not apply and in which the court is considering—
(a) whether a person has failed to comply with a provision of a child arrangements order, or
(b) what steps to take in consequence of a person's failure to comply with a provision of a child arrangements order.
(2. B)The court may make an activity direction in connection with that provision of the child arrangements order.
(3) An activity direction is a direction requiring an individual who is a party to the proceedings concerned to take part in an activity that would, in the court's opinion, help to establish, maintain or improve the involvement in the life of the child concerned of—
(a) that individual, or
(b) another individual who is a party to the proceedings."
(3) In subsection (5) (particular activities that may be required), in paragraph (a)(i) and (ii) and in paragraph (b), for "contact with a child" substitute " involvement in a child's life ".
(4) In subsection (6) (activities which may not be required) for "a contact" substitute " an ".
(5) In subsection (7) (court may not make contact activity direction on same occasion as disposing of proceedings as they relate to contact)—
(a) in paragraph (a) for "a contact activity direction" substitute " an activity direction under subsection (2) ", and
(b) in paragraph (b) for "contact with the child concerned" substitute " the matters mentioned in subsection (1. A) in connection with which the activity direction is made ".
(6) After subsection (7) insert—
"(7. A)A court may not on the same occasion—
(a) make an activity direction under subsection (2. B), and
(b) dispose finally of the proceedings as they relate to failure to comply with the provision in connection with which the activity direction is made."
(7) In subsection (8) (limitations on power to make direction under subsection (2)) for "Subsection (2)" substitute " Each of subsections (2) and (2. B) ".
(8) In subsection (9) (welfare of child is paramount consideration in considering whether to make contact activity direction) for "a contact" substitute " an ".
(9) In the title omit "Contact".
Commencement Information
I7. Sch. 2 para. 7 in force at 22.4.2014 by S.I. 2014/889, art. 4. (f) (with transitional provisions in S.I. 2014/1042, arts. 3, 4, 6-10)
8. (1)Section 11. B (further provision about contact activity directions) is amended as follows.
(2) In subsection (1) (court may not make contact activity direction in proceedings unless there is a dispute about contact)—
(a) for "a contact activity direction in any proceedings" substitute " an activity direction under section 11. A(2) in connection with any matter mentioned in section 11. A(1. A) ", and
(b) for "about contact" substitute " about that matter ".
(3) In subsection (2) (contact activity direction may not require a child to take part in an activity unless child is a parent of the child in relation to whom court is considering contact)—
(a) for "a contact" substitute " an ", and
(b) for "about contact" substitute " about a matter mentioned in section 11. A(1. A) ".
(4) In subsection (3) (no contact activity direction to be made in connection with contact order

which is excepted order)—
(a) for "a contact activity" substitute " an activity ", and
(b) for "contact order", in both places, substitute " child arrangements order ".
(5) In subsection (4) (excepted orders) for "contact order" substitute " child arrangements order ".
(6) In subsection (7) (no contact activity direction to be made unless individual concerned is habitually resident in England and Wales) for "a contact" substitute " an ".
(7) In the title omit "Contact".
Commencement Information
I8. Sch. 2 para. 8 in force at 22.4.2014 by S.I. 2014/889, art. 4. (f) (with transitional provisions in S.I. 2014/1042, arts. 3, 4, 6-10)
9. (1)Section 11. C (contact activity conditions) is amended as follows.
(2) In subsection (1) (section applies if court makes certain orders) for paragraphs (a) and (b) substitute—
  "(a)a child arrangements order containing—
(i) provision for a child to live with different persons at different times,
(ii) provision regulating arrangements relating to with whom a child is to spend time or otherwise have contact, or
(iii) provision regulating arrangements relating to when a child is to spend time or otherwise have contact with any person; or
  (b) an order varying a child arrangements order so as to add, vary or omit provision of a kind mentioned in paragraph (a)(i), (ii) or (iii)."
(3) In subsection (2) (court may impose contact activity condition)—
(a) for "contact order", in both places, substitute " child arrangements order ",
(b) for "(a "contact activity condition")" substitute " (an "activity condition") ", and
(c) for "promotes contact with the child concerned." substitute "would, in the court's opinion, help to establish, maintain or improve the involvement in the life of the child concerned of—
  (a) that individual, or
  (b) another individual who is a party to the proceedings."
(4) In subsection (3) (persons who may be required to take part in activities)—
(a) in paragraph (a)—
(i) for "contact order" substitute " child arrangements order ", and
(ii) for "the person" substitute " a person ", and
(b) in paragraph (b) for "the person" substitute " a person ".
(5) In subsection (5) (particular activities that may be required) for "a contact", in both places, substitute " an ".
(6) In the title omit "Contact".
Commencement Information
I9. Sch. 2 para. 9 in force at 22.4.2014 by S.I. 2014/889, art. 4. (f) (with transitional provisions in S.I. 2014/1042, arts. 3, 4, 6-10)
10. (1)Section 11. D (further provision about contact activity conditions) is amended as follows.
(2) In subsection (1) (contact activity condition may not be imposed on child unless child is a parent of the child concerned)—
(a) for "contact order" substitute " child arrangements order ", and
(b) for "a contact activity" substitute " an activity ".
(3) In subsection (2) (excepted order may not impose contact activity condition)—
(a) for "contact order" substitute " child arrangements order ", and
(b) for "a contact activity" substitute " an activity ".
(4) In subsection (3) (no contact activity condition to be imposed unless individual concerned is habitually resident in England and Wales)—
(a) for "contact order" substitute " child arrangements order ", and
(b) for "a contact activity" substitute " an activity ".
(5) In the title omit "Contact".
Commencement Information

I10. Sch. 2 para. 10 in force at 22.4.2014 by S.I. 2014/889, art. 4. (f) (with transitional provisions in S.I. 2014/1042, arts. 3, 4, 6-10)

11. (1)Section 11. E (making of contact activity directions and conditions) is amended as follows.
(2) In subsection (1) (court to satisfy itself of matters within subsections (2) to (4))—
(a) for "a contact activity", in both places, substitute " an activity ", and
(b) for "contact order" substitute " child arrangements order ".
(3) In subsection (8) (meaning of "specified") for "a contact", in both places, substitute " an ".
(4) In the title omit "Contact".
Commencement Information
I11. Sch. 2 para. 11 in force at 22.4.2014 by S.I. 2014/889, art. 4. (f) (with transitional provisions in S.I. 2014/1042, arts. 3, 4, 6-10)

12. (1)Section 11. F (contact activity: financial assistance) is amended as follows.
(2) For "a contact activity", in each place, substitute " an activity ".
(3) In subsections (2) and (4) (fee-assistance may be given in respect of persons required to take part in activity that promotes contact) for "promotes contact with" substitute " is expected to help to establish, maintain or improve the involvement of that or another individual in the life of ".
(4) In the title omit "Contact".
Commencement Information
I12. Sch. 2 para. 12 in force at 22.4.2014 by S.I. 2014/889, art. 4. (f) (with transitional provisions in S.I. 2014/1042, arts. 3, 4, 6-10)

13. (1)Section 11. G (contact activity: monitoring) is amended as follows.
(2) In subsection (1) for "a contact activity", in each place, substitute " an activity ".
(3) In subsections (1) and (2) for "contact order", in each place, substitute " child arrangements order ".
(4) In the title omit "Contact".
Commencement Information
I13. Sch. 2 para. 13 in force at 22.4.2014 by S.I. 2014/889, art. 4. (f) (with transitional provisions in S.I. 2014/1042, arts. 3, 4, 6-10)

14. (1)Section 11. H (monitoring contact) is amended as follows.
(2) In subsection (1) (section applies if court makes or varies a contact order) for paragraphs (a) and (b) substitute—
"(a)a child arrangements order containing provision of a kind mentioned in section 11. C(1)(a)(i), (ii) or (iii), or
(b) an order varying a child arrangements order so as to add, vary or omit provision of any of those kinds."
(3) In subsection (2)(a) (court may ask officer to monitor compliance) for "the contact order (or the contact order as varied);" substitute " each provision of any of those kinds that is contained in the child arrangements order (or in the child arrangements order as varied); ".
(4) In subsection (3) (individuals whose compliance may be monitored)—
(a) for "contact order", in both places, substitute " child arrangements order ", and
(b) for paragraphs (a) and (b) (including the "or" at the end of paragraph (b)) substitute—
"(za)provides for the child concerned to live with different persons at different times and names the individual as one of those persons;
(a) imposes requirements on the individual with regard to the child concerned spending time or otherwise having contact with some other person;
(b) names the individual as a person with whom the child concerned is to spend time or otherwise have contact; or".
(5) In subsection (4) (requests under subsection (2) not to relate to contact activity conditions)—
(a) for "contact order", in both places, substitute " child arrangements order ",
(b) for "a contact activity" substitute " an activity ", and
(c) for "the contact activity" substitute " the activity ".
(6) In subsection (5) (when court may make request under subsection (2))—
(a) in paragraph (a) for "contact order", in both places, substitute " child arrangements order ", and

(b) in paragraph (b) after "the child concerned" insert " or to the child's living arrangements ".
(7) In subsection (10) (request not to be made under subsection (2) if contact order is an excepted order) for "contact" substitute " child arrangements ".
(8) In the title after "contact" insert " and shared residence ".
Commencement Information
I14. Sch. 2 para. 14 in force at 22.4.2014 by S.I. 2014/889, art. 4. (f) (with transitional provisions in S.I. 2014/1042, arts. 3, 4, 6-10)
15. In section 11.I (warning notices to be attached to contact orders and to orders varying contact orders)—
(a) for "contact", in each place, substitute " child arrangements ", and
(b) in the title for "Contact" substitute " Child arrangements ".
Commencement Information
I15. Sch. 2 para. 15 in force at 22.4.2014 by S.I. 2014/889, art. 4. (f) (with transitional provisions in S.I. 2014/1042, arts. 3, 4, 6-10)
16. (1)Section 11.J (enforcement orders where contact order not complied with) is amended as follows.
(2) In subsection (1) for "contact" substitute " child arrangements ".
(3) In subsection (2) for "the contact" substitute " a provision of the child arrangements ".
(4) In subsection (3) for "contact order" substitute " provision ".
(5) In subsection (5)—
(a) for "contact order", in each place, substitute " child arrangements order ",
(b) in paragraphs (a) and (b) for "the person", in each place, substitute " a person ", and
(c) in paragraph (c) for "a contact activity" substitute " an activity ".
(6) In subsection (6) for "contact" substitute " child arrangements ".
Commencement Information
I16. Sch. 2 para. 16 in force at 22.4.2014 by S.I. 2014/889, art. 4. (f) (with transitional provisions in S.I. 2014/1042, arts. 3, 4, 6-10)
17. (1)Section 11.K (enforcement orders: further provisions) is amended as follows.
(2) In subsection (1) (enforcement order not to be made where notice not given under section 11.I)—
(a) in the words before paragraph (a), for "contact order" substitute " provision of a child arrangements order ",
(b) in paragraph (a)—
(i) for "a contact order that" substitute " a provision of a child arrangements order where the order ", and
(ii) for "the contact" substitute " the child arrangements ", and
(c) in paragraph (b) for "contact" substitute " child arrangements ".
(3) In subsection (2) (enforcement order not to be made where person failed to comply with contact order when under 18) for "contact" substitute " provision of a child arrangements ".
(4) In subsection (3) (enforcement order not to be made where contact order is an excepted order) for "contact order that" substitute " provision of a child arrangements order where the child arrangements order ".
Commencement Information
I17. Sch. 2 para. 17 in force at 22.4.2014 by S.I. 2014/889, art. 4. (f) (with transitional provisions in S.I. 2014/1042, arts. 3, 4, 6-10)
18. (1)Section 11.L (making of enforcement orders) is amended as follows.
(2) In subsection (1) (order must be necessary and its likely effect proportionate)—
(a) for "a contact" substitute " a provision of a child arrangements ",
(b) in paragraph (a) for "contact", in each place, substitute " child arrangements ", and
(c) in paragraph (b) omit "of the contact order".
(3) In subsection (3) for "contact" substitute " provision of a child arrangements ".
(4) In subsection (7) for "contact", in both places, substitute " child arrangements ".
Commencement Information

I18. Sch. 2 para. 18 in force at 22.4.2014 by S.I. 2014/889, art. 4. (f) (with transitional provisions in S.I. 2014/1042, arts. 3, 4, 6-10)

19. (1)Section 11. O (compensation for financial loss arising from breach of contact order) is amended as follows.

(2) In subsection (1) for "contact" substitute " child arrangements ".

(3) In subsection (2)(a) for "the contact" substitute " a provision of the child arrangements ".

(4) In subsection (3) for "contact" substitute " particular provision of the child arrangements ".

(5) In subsection (6)—

(a) for "contact order", in each place, substitute " child arrangements order ",

(b) in paragraphs (a) and (b) for "the person", in each place, substitute " a person ", and

(c) in paragraph (c) for "a contact activity" substitute " an activity ".

Commencement Information

I19. Sch. 2 para. 19 in force at 22.4.2014 by S.I. 2014/889, art. 4. (f) (with transitional provisions in S.I. 2014/1042, arts. 3, 4, 6-10)

20. (1)Section 11. P (compensation orders under section 11. O(2): further provision) is amended as follows.

(2) In subsection (1) (compensation not to be ordered where notice not given under section 11. I)—

(a) in the words before paragraph (a), for "contact order" substitute " provision of a child arrangements order ",

(b) in paragraph (a)—

(i) for "a contact order that" substitute " a provision of a child arrangements order where the order ", and

(ii) for "the contact" substitute " the child arrangements ", and

(c) in paragraph (b) for "contact" substitute " child arrangements ".

(3) In subsection (2) (compensation not to be ordered where person failed to comply with contact order when under 18) for "contact" substitute " provision of a child arrangements ".

(4) In subsection (3) (compensation not to be ordered where contact order is an excepted order) for "contact order that" substitute " provision of a child arrangements order where the child arrangements order ".

Commencement Information

I20. Sch. 2 para. 20 in force at 22.4.2014 by S.I. 2014/889, art. 4. (f) (with transitional provisions in S.I. 2014/1042, arts. 3, 4, 6-10)

21. (1)Section 12 (residence orders and parental responsibility) is amended as follows.

(2) For subsections (1) and (1. A) (court making residence order in favour of father without parental responsibility is also to make order giving parental responsibility to the father) substitute—

"(1)Where—

(a) the court makes a child arrangements order with respect to a child,

(b) the father of the child, or a woman who is a parent of the child by virtue of section 43 of the Human Fertilisation and Embryology Act 2008, is named in the order as a person with whom the child is to live, and

(c) the father, or the woman, would not otherwise have parental responsibility for the child,

the court must also make an order under section 4 giving the father, or under section 4. ZA giving the woman, that responsibility.

(1. A)Where—

(a) the court makes a child arrangements order with respect to a child,

(b) the father of the child, or a woman who is a parent of the child by virtue of section 43 of the Human Fertilisation and Embryology Act 2008, is named in the order as a person with whom the child is to spend time or otherwise have contact but is not named in the order as a person with whom the child is to live, and

(c) the father, or the woman, would not otherwise have parental responsibility for the child,

the court must decide whether it would be appropriate, in view of the provision made in the order with respect to the father or the woman, for him or her to have parental responsibility for the child and, if it decides that it would be appropriate for the father or the woman to have that responsibility, must also make an order under section 4 giving him, or under section 4. ZA giving her, that responsibility."

(3) In subsection (2) (residence order in favour of person other than parent or guardian)—
(a) for "residence order in favour of any person who is not the" substitute " child arrangements order and a person who is not a ",
(b) after "concerned" insert " is named in the order as a person with whom the child is to live, ", and
(c) for "residence order remains in force" substitute " order remains in force so far as providing for the child to live with that person ".

(4) After subsection (2) insert—
"(2. A)Where the court makes a child arrangements order and—
  (a) a person who is not the parent or guardian of the child concerned is named in the order as a person with whom the child is to spend time or otherwise have contact, but
  (b) the person is not named in the order as a person with whom the child is to live,
the court may provide in the order for the person to have parental responsibility for the child while paragraphs (a) and (b) continue to be met in the person's case."

(5) In subsection (3) (limits on parental responsibility given by subsection (2)) after "subsection (2)" insert " or (2. A) ".

(6) In subsection (4) (where order giving parental responsibility was made in compliance with subsection (1) or (1. A), order not to be revoked while residence order remains in force)—
(a) omit "or (1. A)",
(b) for "in respect of the" substitute " in respect of a ", and
(c) for "residence order concerned remains in force" substitute " child arrangements order concerned remains in force so far as providing for the child to live with that parent ".

(7) In the title for "Residence" substitute " Child arrangements ".

Commencement Information

I21. Sch. 2 para. 21 in force at 22.4.2014 by S.I. 2014/889, art. 4. (f) (with transitional provisions in S.I. 2014/1042, arts. 3, 4, 6-10)

22. (1)Section 13 (effect of residence order on change of child's name or removal from jurisdiction) is amended as follows.

(2) In subsection (1) (new surname or removal from UK requires consent of all with parental responsibility or leave of court) for "residence order" substitute " child arrangements order to which subsection (4) applies ".

(3) In subsection (2) (child may be removed from UK for up to 1 month by person in whose favour residence order is made) for "the person in whose favour the residence order is made" substitute " a person named in the child arrangements order as a person with whom the child is to live ".

(4) In subsection (3) (court's leave may be given in making a residence order) for "residence order with respect to a child" substitute " child arrangements order to which subsection (4) applies, ".

(5) After subsection (3) insert—
"(4)This subsection applies to a child arrangements order if the arrangements regulated by the order consist of, or include, arrangements which relate to either or both of the following—
  (a) with whom the child concerned is to live, and
  (b) when the child is to live with any person."

Commencement Information

I22. Sch. 2 para. 22 in force at 22.4.2014 by S.I. 2014/889, art. 4. (f) (with transitional provisions in S.I. 2014/1042, arts. 3, 4, 6-10)

23. Omit section 14 (enforcement of residence orders in magistrates' courts).

Commencement Information

I23. Sch. 2 para. 23 in force at 22.4.2014 by S.I. 2014/889, art. 4. (f) (with transitional provisions in S.I. 2014/1042, arts. 3, 4, 6-10)

24. In section 14. A(5) (persons eligible to apply for special guardianship order), in paragraph (b) for the words after "individual" substitute " who is named in a child arrangements order as a person with whom the child is to live; ".
Commencement Information
I24. Sch. 2 para. 24 in force at 22.4.2014 by S.I. 2014/889, art. 4. (f) (with transitional provisions in S.I. 2014/1042, arts. 3, 4, 6-10)
25. (1)Section 14. B (making of special guardianship orders) is amended as follows.
(2) In subsection (1) (matters for court to consider before making special guardianship order)—
(a) in paragraph (a) for "contact order" substitute " child arrangements order containing contact provision ",
(b) in paragraph (c)—
(i) for "a contact order" substitute " provision contained in a child arrangements order ", and
(ii) for "that contact order" substitute " that provision ", and
(c) for paragraph (d) (whether contact activity direction should be discharged) substitute—
"(d)where an activity direction has been made—
(i) in proceedings for the making, variation or discharge of a child arrangements order with respect to the child, or
(ii) in other proceedings that relate to such an order,
that direction should be discharged."
(3) After subsection (1) insert—
"(1. A)In subsection (1) "contact provision" means provision which regulates arrangements relating to—
(a) with whom a child is to spend time or otherwise have contact, or
(b) when a child is to spend time or otherwise have contact with any person;
but in paragraphs (a) and (b) a reference to spending time or otherwise having contact with a person is to doing that otherwise than as a result of living with the person."
Commencement Information
I25. Sch. 2 para. 25 in force at 22.4.2014 by S.I. 2014/889, art. 4. (f) (with transitional provisions in S.I. 2014/1042, arts. 3, 4, 6-10)
26. In section 14. D(1) (persons eligible to apply for variation or discharge of special guardianship order), in paragraph (c) for the words after "individual" substitute " who is named in a child arrangements order as a person with whom the child is to live; ".
Commencement Information
I26. Sch. 2 para. 26 in force at 22.4.2014 by S.I. 2014/889, art. 4. (f) (with transitional provisions in S.I. 2014/1042, arts. 3, 4, 6-10)
27. (1)Section 16 (family assistance orders) is amended as follows.
(2) In subsection (2)(b) (persons may be named in order if child lives with them or if contact order in their favour is in force) for the words after "living or" substitute " who is named in a child arrangements order as a person with whom the child is to live, spend time or otherwise have contact ".
(3) In subsection (4. A) (family assistance order may direct officer to give advice and assistance as to contact where contact order in force) for "a contact order" substitute " contact provision contained in a child arrangements order ".
(4) After subsection (4. A) insert—
"(4. B)In subsection (4. A) "contact provision" means provision which regulates arrangements relating to—
(a) with whom a child is to spend time or otherwise have contact, or
(b) when a child is to spend time or otherwise have contact with any person."
Commencement Information
I27. Sch. 2 para. 27 in force at 22.4.2014 by S.I. 2014/889, art. 4. (f) (with transitional provisions in S.I. 2014/1042, arts. 3, 4, 6-10)
28. For section 20. (9)(a) (if accommodation under section 20 provided for child with agreement of person in whose favour a residence order has been made, that agreement overrides objections of

a person with parental responsibility) substitute—

"(a)who is named in a child arrangements order as a person with whom the child is to live;".

Commencement Information

I28. Sch. 2 para. 28 in force at 22.4.2014 by S.I. 2014/889, art. 4. (f) (with transitional provisions in S.I. 2014/1042, arts. 3, 4, 6-10)

29. In section 22. C(3)(c) (where residence order in favour of a person was in force before care order was made, local authority may arrange for the child to live with that person)—
(a) for "a residence order" substitute " a child arrangements order ", and
(b) for "in whose favour the residence order was made" substitute " named in the child arrangements order as a person with whom C was to live ".

Commencement Information

I29. Sch. 2 para. 29 in force at 22.4.2014 by S.I. 2014/889, art. 4. (f) (with transitional provisions in S.I. 2014/1042, arts. 3, 4, 6-10)

30. In section 23. (4) (persons not referred to as local authority foster parents), in paragraph (c) for the words from "a residence order" to the end substitute " a child arrangements order in force with respect to the child immediately before the care order was made, a person named in the child arrangements order as a person with whom the child was to live. "

Commencement Information

I30. Sch. 2 para. 30 in force at 22.4.2014 by S.I. 2014/889, art. 4. (f) (with transitional provisions in S.I. 2014/1042, arts. 3, 4, 6-10)

31. In section 34. (1)(c) (child in care to be allowed reasonable contact with person in whose favour residence order was in force before care order was made)—
(a) for "residence" substitute " child arrangements ", and
(b) for "the person in whose favour the order was made" substitute " any person named in the child arrangements order as a person with whom the child was to live ".

Commencement Information

I31. Sch. 2 para. 31 in force at 22.4.2014 by S.I. 2014/889, art. 4. (f) (with transitional provisions in S.I. 2014/1042, arts. 3, 4, 6-10)

32. (1)Section 38 (interim care or supervision orders) is amended as follows.
(2) In subsection (3) (interim supervision order to be made in certain cases where residence order made in proceedings for a care or supervision order) for "residence order with respect to" substitute " child arrangements order with respect to the living arrangements of ".
(3) After subsection (3) insert—

"(3. A)For the purposes of subsection (3), a child arrangements order is one made with respect to the living arrangements of the child concerned if the arrangements regulated by the order consist of, or include, arrangements which relate to either or both of the following—
   (a) with whom the child is to live, and
   (b) when the child is to live with any person."

Commencement Information

I32. Sch. 2 para. 32 in force at 22.4.2014 by S.I. 2014/889, art. 4. (f) (with transitional provisions in S.I. 2014/1042, arts. 3, 4, 6-10)

33. (1)Section 41 (representation of child: meaning of "specified proceedings") is amended as follows.
(2) In subsection (6)(e) and (h)(ii) (which refer to the making of a residence order) for "residence order with respect to" substitute " child arrangements order with respect to the living arrangements of ".
(3) After subsection (6. A) insert—

"(6. B)For the purposes of subsection (6), a child arrangements order is one made with respect to the living arrangements of a child if the arrangements regulated by the order consist of, or include, arrangements which relate to either or both of the following—
   (a) with whom the child is to live, and
   (b) when the child is to live with any person."

Commencement Information

133. Sch. 2 para. 33 in force at 22.4.2014 by S.I. 2014/889, art. 4. (f) (with transitional provisions in S.I. 2014/1042, arts. 3, 4, 6-10)

34. In section 43. (11) (persons to be given notice of application for child assessment order) for paragraph (d) substitute—

"(d)any person named in a child arrangements order as a person with whom the child is to spend time or otherwise have contact;".

Commencement Information

134. Sch. 2 para. 34 in force at 22.4.2014 by S.I. 2014/889, art. 4. (f) (with transitional provisions in S.I. 2014/1042, arts. 3, 4, 6-10)

35. In section 44. (13) (persons to be allowed reasonable contact with child where emergency protection order made) for paragraph (d) substitute—

"(d)any person named in a child arrangements order as a person with whom the child is to spend time or otherwise have contact;".

Commencement Information

135. Sch. 2 para. 35 in force at 22.4.2014 by S.I. 2014/889, art. 4. (f) (with transitional provisions in S.I. 2014/1042, arts. 3, 4, 6-10)

36. In section 46. (10) (persons to be allowed reasonable contact with child in police protection where that is in child's best interests) for paragraph (d) substitute—

"(d)any person named in a child arrangements order as a person with whom the child is to spend time or otherwise have contact;".

Commencement Information

136. Sch. 2 para. 36 in force at 22.4.2014 by S.I. 2014/889, art. 4. (f) (with transitional provisions in S.I. 2014/1042, arts. 3, 4, 6-10)

37. (1)Section 91 (effect and duration of orders etc.) is amended as follows.

(2) In subsection (1) (making of residence order discharges care order) for "residence order with respect to" substitute " child arrangements order with respect to the living arrangements of ".

(3) After subsection (1) insert—

"(1. A)For the purposes of subsection (1), a child arrangements order is one made with respect to the living arrangements of a child if the arrangements regulated by the order consist of, or include, arrangements which relate to either or both of the following—

(a) with whom the child is to live, and

(b) when the child is to live with any person."

(4) In subsection (2. A) (making of care order discharges contact activity direction)—

(a) for "a contact" substitute " an ", and

(b) for "as regards contact with" substitute " with respect to ".

(5) In subsection (10) (section 8 order other than residence order ceases to have effect when child turns 16 unless it is to have effect beyond that age by virtue of section 9. (6)) omit "other than a residence order".

(6) After subsection (10) insert—

"(10. A)Subsection (10) does not apply to provision in a child arrangements order which regulates arrangements relating to—

(a) with whom a child is to live, or

(b) when a child is to live with any person."

Commencement Information

137. Sch. 2 para. 37 in force at 22.4.2014 by S.I. 2014/889, art. 4. (f) (with transitional provisions in S.I. 2014/1042, arts. 3, 4, 6-10)

38. (1)Section 105 (interpretation) is amended as follows.

(2) In subsection (1) (definitions)—

(a) before the definition of "adoption agency" insert—

""activity condition" has the meaning given by section 11. C;

"activity direction" has the meaning given by section 11. A;",

(b) at the appropriate place insert—

"child arrangements order" has the meaning given by section 8. (1);", and

(c) omit the definition of "contact activity condition", the definition of "contact activity direction", the definition of "contact order" and the definition of "residence order".
(3) Omit subsection (3) (interpretation of certain references relating to residence orders).
Commencement Information
I38. Sch. 2 para. 38 in force at 22.4.2014 by S.I. 2014/889, art. 4. (f) (with transitional provisions in S.I. 2014/1042, arts. 3, 4, 6-10)
39. (1)Schedule A1 (enforcement orders) is amended as follows.
(2) In paragraphs 4. (1), 5. (1), 6. (1), 7. (1), 8. (1) and 9. (1) and (11)(a) for "contact" substitute " provision of a child arrangements ".
(3) In paragraphs 4. (2)(c), (4)(b) and (5), 6. (3) and 9. (6) and (10)(a) for "contact", in each place, substitute " child arrangements ".
(4) In paragraph 9. (5) for "the contact" substitute " a provision of the child arrangements ".
(5) In paragraph 9. (10)(b) for "contact order and" substitute " provisions of the child arrangements order and with ".
Commencement Information
I39. Sch. 2 para. 39 in force at 22.4.2014 by S.I. 2014/889, art. 4. (f) (with transitional provisions in S.I. 2014/1042, arts. 3, 4, 6-10)
40. (1)Schedule 1 (financial provision for children) is amended as follows.
(2) In paragraph 1 (power of court to make orders on application of parent, guardian, special guardian or person in whose favour residence order in force)—
(a) in sub-paragraph (1) for the words from "in whose favour" to "to a child" substitute " who is named in a child arrangements order as a person with whom a child is to live ",
(b) in sub-paragraph (6)—
(i) omit "a residence order or", and
(ii) after "special guardianship order" insert " , or on making, varying or discharging provision in a child arrangements order with respect to the living arrangements of a child, " and
(c) after sub-paragraph (6) insert—
"(6. A)For the purposes of sub-paragraph (6) provision in a child arrangements order is with respect to the living arrangements of a child if it regulates arrangements relating to—
   (a) with whom the child is to live, or
   (b) when the child is to live with any person."
(3) In paragraph 8 (circumstances in which court may revoke financial relief order under other enactment)—
(a) in sub-paragraph (1) for "residence order" substitute " child arrangements order to which sub-paragraph (1. A) applies ", and
(b) after sub-paragraph (1) insert—
"(1. A)This sub-paragraph applies to a child arrangements order if the arrangements regulated by the order consist of, or include, arrangements which relate to either or both of the following—
   (a) with whom the child concerned is to live, and
   (b) when the child is to live with any person.", and
(c) in sub-paragraph (2)(b)—
(i) after "any person" insert " who is named in a child arrangements order as a person with whom the child is to live or ", and
(ii) omit "a residence order or".
(4) In paragraph 15 (local authority may contribute to maintenance of child living with person as a result of residence order) for "residence order" substitute " child arrangements order ".
Commencement Information
I40. Sch. 2 para. 40 in force at 22.4.2014 by S.I. 2014/889, art. 4. (f) (with transitional provisions in S.I. 2014/1042, arts. 3, 4, 6-10)
41. In Schedule 14, omit paragraph 10 (certain orders made under legislation repealed by the Children Act 1989 to be enforceable under section 14 of that Act).
Commencement Information
I41. Sch. 2 para. 41 in force at 22.4.2014 by S.I. 2014/889, art. 4. (f) (with transitional provisions

in S.I. 2014/1042, arts. 3, 4, 6-10)

PART 2 Amendments in other legislation

Marriage Act 1949 (c. 76)

42. (1)Section 3 of the Marriage Act 1949 (marriage of persons under 18) is amended as follows.
(2) In subsection (1. A) (persons whose consent is required), in each of paragraphs (d) and (h), for "residence order" substitute " child arrangements order to which subsection (1. C) applies ".
(3) In subsection (1. B) (interpretation) for " "residence order"," substitute " "child arrangements order", ".
(4) After that subsection insert—
"(1. C)A child arrangements order is one to which this subsection applies if the order regulates arrangements that consist of, or include, arrangements which relate to either or both of the following—
   (a) with whom the child is to live, and
   (b) when the child is to live with any person."
Commencement Information
I42. Sch. 2 para. 42 in force at 22.4.2014 by S.I. 2014/889, art. 4. (f) (with transitional provisions in S.I. 2014/1042, arts. 3, 4, 6-10)

Children and Young Persons Act 1969 (c. 54)

43. (1)Section 70 of the Children and Young Persons Act 1969 (interpretation) is amended as follows.
(2) In subsection (1. A) ("father" includes father not married at child's birth to child's mother if there is residence order in father's favour) for paragraph (b) substitute—
   "(b)whose father is named in a child arrangements order as a person with whom the child or young person is to live,".
(3) In subsection (1. B) for " "residence" substitute " "child arrangements".
Commencement Information
I43. Sch. 2 para. 43 in force at 22.4.2014 by S.I. 2014/889, art. 4. (f) (with transitional provisions in S.I. 2014/1042, arts. 3, 4, 6-10)

Local Authority Social Services Act 1970 (c. 42)

44. In Schedule 1 to the Local Authority Social Services Act 1970 (social services functions), in the second column of the entry for the Children Act 1989, for "residence" substitute " child arrangements ".
Commencement Information
I44. Sch. 2 para. 44 in force at 22.4.2014 by S.I. 2014/889, art. 4. (f) (with transitional provisions in S.I. 2014/1042, arts. 3, 4, 6-10)

Domicile and Matrimonial Proceedings Act 1973 (c. 45)

45. (1)Paragraph 11 of Schedule 1 to the Domicile and Matrimonial Proceedings Act 1973 (restrictions on court's powers while matrimonial proceedings are stayed) is amended as follows.
(2) In sub-paragraph (4. A)(b) (contact order in force when proceedings stayed) for "contact" substitute " child arrangements ".
(3) In sub-paragraph (4. B) (enforcement of the contact order while the proceedings are stayed) for

"contact", in both places, substitute " child arrangements ".
Commencement Information
I45. Sch. 2 para. 45 in force at 22.4.2014 by S.I. 2014/889, art. 4. (f) (with transitional provisions in S.I. 2014/1042, arts. 3, 4, 6-10)

Mental Health Act 1983 (c. 20)

46. In section 28. (1) of the Mental Health Act 1983 ("nearest relative" of child in respect of whom residence order is in force etc)—
(a) in paragraph (b)—
(i) for "residence" substitute " person is named in a child arrangements ", and
(ii) for "is in force with respect to such a person" substitute " as a person with whom a person who has not attained the age of eighteen years is to live ", and
(b) in the words after paragraph (b), for "named in the residence order" substitute " so named (or the persons so named, where there is more than one) ".
Commencement Information
I46. Sch. 2 para. 46 in force at 22.4.2014 by S.I. 2014/889, art. 4. (f) (with transitional provisions in S.I. 2014/1042, arts. 3, 4, 6-10)

Child Abduction Act 1984 (c. 37)

47. (1)Section 1 of the Child Abduction Act 1984 (offence of abduction of child by connected person without appropriate consent) is amended as follows.
(2) In subsection (2)(d) (person in whose favour residence order is in force is connected person) for the words after "person" substitute " named in a child arrangements order as a person with whom the child is to live; or ".
(3) In subsection (3)(a) ("appropriate consent" includes consent of every person listed) for sub-paragraph (iv) (person in whose favour residence order is in force) substitute—
"(iv)any person named in a child arrangements order as a person with whom the child is to live;".
(4) In subsection (4)(a) (exception for short foreign trip organised by person in whose favour residence order made) for "in whose favour there is a residence order in force with respect to the child," substitute " named in a child arrangements order as a person with whom the child is to live ".
(5) For subsection (5. A)(a)(i) (exception where consent unreasonably refused does not apply where there is residence order in favour of person refusing consent) substitute—
"(i)named in a child arrangements order as a person with whom the child is to live;".
(6) In subsection (7)(a) (interpretation) for " "residence" substitute " "child arrangements".
Commencement Information
I47. Sch. 2 para. 47 in force at 22.4.2014 by S.I. 2014/889, art. 4. (f) (with transitional provisions in S.I. 2014/1042, arts. 3, 4, 6-10)

Child Abduction and Custody Act 1985 (c. 60)

48. For paragraph 1. (b) of Schedule 3 to the Child Abduction and Custody Act 1985 (orders mentioned in section 27. (1) include a residence order) substitute—
"(b)a child arrangements order (as defined by section 8 of the Act of 1989) if the arrangements regulated by the order consist of, or include, arrangements relating to either or both of the following—
(i) with whom a child is to live, or
(ii) when a child is to live with any person;".
Commencement Information

148. Sch. 2 para. 48 in force at 22.4.2014 by S.I. 2014/889, art. 4. (f) (with transitional provisions in S.I. 2014/1042, arts. 3, 4, 6-10)

Family Law Act 1986 (c. 55)

49. The Family Law Act 1986 is amended as follows.
Commencement Information
149. Sch. 2 para. 49 in force at 22.4.2014 by S.I. 2014/889, art. 4. (f) (with transitional provisions in S.I. 2014/1042, arts. 3, 4, 6-10)
50. (1)Section 5 (which contains references to contact activity directions) is amended as follows.
(2) In subsection (2. A)—
(a) for "a contact" substitute " an ", and
(b) for "the contact" substitute " the ".
(3) In subsection (3. B) for "a contact" substitute " an ".
Commencement Information
150. Sch. 2 para. 50 in force at 22.4.2014 by S.I. 2014/889, art. 4. (f) (with transitional provisions in S.I. 2014/1042, arts. 3, 4, 6-10)
51. (1)Section 6 (which includes provision for a family assistance order to cease to have effect where a related residence order is superseded by an order made in Scotland or Northern Ireland) is amended as follows.
(2) After subsection (5) insert—
"(5. A)Subsection (7) below applies where a Part I order which is a child arrangements order (within the meaning of section 8. (1) of the Children Act 1989) ceases by virtue of subsection (1) above to name a person as someone with whom a child is to live."
(3) In subsection (6) (circumstances in which subsection (7) applies)—
(a) after "Subsection (7) below" insert " also ", and
(b) omit paragraph (a) (residence order ceasing to have effect by virtue of subsection (1)).
Commencement Information
151. Sch. 2 para. 51 in force at 22.4.2014 by S.I. 2014/889, art. 4. (f) (with transitional provisions in S.I. 2014/1042, arts. 3, 4, 6-10)

Child Support Act 1991 (c. 48)

52. For section 3. (4)(c) of the Child Support Act 1991 (persons with residence orders in their favour may not be prescribed as persons who are not "persons with care") substitute—
"(c)persons named, in a child arrangements order under section 8 of the Children Act 1989, as persons with whom a child is to live;".
Commencement Information
152. Sch. 2 para. 52 in force at 22.4.2014 by S.I. 2014/889, art. 4. (f) (with transitional provisions in S.I. 2014/1042, arts. 3, 4, 6-10)

Armed Forces Act 1991 (c. 62)

53. The Armed Forces Act 1991 is amended as follows.
Commencement Information
153. Sch. 2 para. 53 in force at 22.4.2014 by S.I. 2014/889, art. 4. (f) (with transitional provisions in S.I. 2014/1042, arts. 3, 4, 6-10)
54. In section 17. (4) (persons who may apply for assessment order) after paragraph (d) insert—
"(da)any person who is named in a child arrangements order as a person with whom the child is to live, spend time or otherwise have contact;".
Commencement Information

I54. Sch. 2 para. 54 in force at 22.4.2014 by S.I. 2014/889, art. 4. (f) (with transitional provisions in S.I. 2014/1042, arts. 3, 4, 6-10)

55. In section 18. (7) (persons who may apply to vary or discharge an assessment order) after paragraph (d) insert—

"(da)any person who is named in a child arrangements order as a person with whom the child is to live, spend time or otherwise have contact;".

Commencement Information

I55. Sch. 2 para. 55 in force at 22.4.2014 by S.I. 2014/889, art. 4. (f) (with transitional provisions in S.I. 2014/1042, arts. 3, 4, 6-10)

56. In section 20. (8) (persons who are to be allowed reasonable contact with a child subject to a protection order) after paragraph (c) insert—

"(ca)any person who is named in a child arrangements order as a person with whom the child is to live, spend time or otherwise have contact;".

Commencement Information

I56. Sch. 2 para. 56 in force at 22.4.2014 by S.I. 2014/889, art. 4. (f) (with transitional provisions in S.I. 2014/1042, arts. 3, 4, 6-10)

57. In section 22. A(7) (persons who are to be allowed reasonable contact with a child in service police protection) after paragraph (c) insert—

"(ca)any person who is named in a child arrangements order as a person with whom the child is to live, spend time or otherwise have contact,".

Commencement Information

I57. Sch. 2 para. 57 in force at 22.4.2014 by S.I. 2014/889, art. 4. (f) (with transitional provisions in S.I. 2014/1042, arts. 3, 4, 6-10)

58. (1)Section 23. (1) (interpretation of Part 3) is amended as follows.

(2) After the definition of "child" insert—

""child arrangements order" has the meaning given by section 8. (1) of the Children Act 1989;".

(3) In the definition of "contact order"—

(a) omit "section 8. (1) of the Children Act 1989 or", and

(b) omit "as the case may be".

Commencement Information

I58. Sch. 2 para. 58 in force at 22.4.2014 by S.I. 2014/889, art. 4. (f) (with transitional provisions in S.I. 2014/1042, arts. 3, 4, 6-10)

Adoption and Children Act 2002 (c. 38)

59. The Adoption and Children Act 2002 is amended as follows.

Commencement Information

I59. Sch. 2 para. 59 in force at 22.4.2014 by S.I. 2014/889, art. 4. (f) (with transitional provisions in S.I. 2014/1042, arts. 3, 4, 6-10)

60. (1)Section 26 (placement of children by adoption agency for adoption: contact) is amended as follows.

(2) In subsection (1) (provision for contact under the 1989 Act ceases to have effect and any contact activity direction is discharged) for the words from "any provision for contact" to the end substitute "—

(a) any contact provision in a child arrangements order under section 8 of the 1989 Act ceases to have effect,

(b) any order under section 34 of that Act (parental etc contact with children in care) ceases to have effect, and

(c) any activity direction made in proceedings for the making, variation or discharge of a child arrangements order with respect to the child, or made in other proceedings that relate to such an order, is discharged."

(3) In subsection (2)(a) (no application may be made for provision for contact under the 1989 Act)

for "any provision for contact under that Act, but" substitute "—
(i) a child arrangements order under section 8 of the 1989 Act containing contact provision, or
(ii) an order under section 34 of that Act, but".
(4) In subsection (3)(c) (application for contact may be made by person in whose favour provision for contact was made)—
(a) omit "for contact under the 1989 Act", and
(b) for "(1)" substitute " (1)(a) or an order which ceased to have effect by virtue of subsection (1)(b) ".
(5) In subsection (3)(d) (application for contact may be made by person in whose favour residence order was made)—
(a) for "residence" substitute " child arrangements ", and
(b) for "the person in whose favour the order was made" substitute " any person named in the order as a person with whom the child was to live ".
(6) In subsection (5) (application for contact order that is to be heard together with application for adoption order) for "contact order under section 8 of the 1989 Act" substitute " child arrangements order under section 8 of the 1989 Act containing only contact provision ".
(7) For subsection (6) (interpretation) substitute—
"(5. A)In this section "contact provision" means provision which regulates arrangements relating to—
   (a) with whom a child is to spend time or otherwise have contact, or
   (b) when a child is to spend time or otherwise have contact with any person;
but in paragraphs (a) and (b) a reference to spending time or otherwise having contact with a person is to doing that otherwise than as a result of living with the person.
(6) In this section "activity direction" has the meaning given by section 11. A of the 1989 Act."
Commencement Information
I60. Sch. 2 para. 60 in force at 22.4.2014 by S.I. 2014/889, art. 4. (f) (with transitional provisions in S.I. 2014/1042, arts. 3, 4, 6-10)
61. (1)Section 28 (further consequences of placement) is amended as follows.
(2) In subsection (1)(a) (restrictions on applying for residence order) for "residence order" substitute " child arrangements order regulating the child's living arrangements ".
(3) After subsection (4) insert—
"(5)For the purposes of subsection (1)(a), a child arrangements order regulates a child's living arrangements if the arrangements regulated by the order consist of, or include, arrangements which relate to either or both of the following—
   (a) with whom the child is to live, and
   (b) when the child is to live with any person."
Commencement Information
I61. Sch. 2 para. 61 in force at 22.4.2014 by S.I. 2014/889, art. 4. (f) (with transitional provisions in S.I. 2014/1042, arts. 3, 4, 6-10)
62. (1)Section 29 (further consequences of placement orders) is amended as follows.
(2) In subsection (3)(a) (residence order etc may not be made if placement order is in force) omit ", residence order".
(3) In subsection (4) (residence orders to which subsection (3) does not apply)—
(a) for "Subsection (3)(a) does not apply in respect of a residence order if—" substitute " Where a placement order is in force, a child arrangements order may be made with respect to the child's living arrangements only if— ", and
(b) in paragraph (b), for "residence" substitute " child arrangements ".
(4) After subsection (4) insert—
"(4. A)For the purposes of subsection (4), a child arrangements order is one made with respect to a child's living arrangements if the arrangements regulated by the order consist of, or include, arrangements which relate to either or both of the following—
   (a) with whom the child is to live, and
   (b) when the child is to live with any person."

Commencement Information

I62. Sch. 2 para. 62 in force at 22.4.2014 by S.I. 2014/889, art. 4. (f) (with transitional provisions in S.I. 2014/1042, arts. 3, 4, 6-10)

63. (1)Section 32 (recovery of child from placement) is amended as follows.

(2) In subsection (5) (effect of undecided application for residence order etc on duty to return child) for paragraphs (a) and (b) substitute—

"(a)before the notice was given, an application—

(i) for an adoption order (including a Scottish or Northern Irish adoption order),

(ii) for a special guardianship order,

(iii) for a child arrangements order to which subsection (6) applies, or

(iv) for permission to apply for an order within sub-paragraph (ii) or (iii),

was made in respect of the child, and

(b) the application (and, in a case where permission is given on an application to apply for an order within paragraph (a)(ii) or (iii), the application for the order) has not been disposed of,".

(3) After that subsection insert—

"(6)A child arrangements order is one to which this subsection applies if it is an order regulating arrangements that consist of, or include, arrangements which relate to either or both of the following—

(a) with whom a child is to live, and

(b) when the child is to live with any person."

Commencement Information

I63. Sch. 2 para. 63 in force at 22.4.2014 by S.I. 2014/889, art. 4. (f) (with transitional provisions in S.I. 2014/1042, arts. 3, 4, 6-10)

64. (1)Section 35 (return of placed child in certain cases) is amended as follows.

(2) In subsection (5) (effect of undecided application for residence order etc on duty to return child) for paragraphs (b) and (c) substitute—

"(b)before the notice was given, an application—

(i) for an adoption order (including a Scottish or Northern Irish adoption order),

(ii) for a special guardianship order,

(iii) for a child arrangements order to which subsection (5. A) applies, or

(iv) for permission to apply for an order within sub-paragraph (ii) or (iii),

was made in respect of the child, and

(c) the application (and, in a case where permission is given on an application to apply for an order within paragraph (b)(ii) or (iii), the application for the order) has not been disposed of,".

(3) After that subsection insert—

"(5. A)A child arrangements order is one to which this subsection applies if it is an order regulating arrangements that consist of, or include, arrangements which relate to either or both of the following—

(a) with whom a child is to live, and

(b) when a child is to live with any person."

Commencement Information

I64. Sch. 2 para. 64 in force at 22.4.2014 by S.I. 2014/889, art. 4. (f) (with transitional provisions in S.I. 2014/1042, arts. 3, 4, 6-10)

65. (1)Schedule 6 (glossary) is amended as follows.

(2) At the appropriate place insert—

"child arrangements order | section 8(1) of the 1989 Act" |

(3) Omit the entry for "residence order".

Commencement Information

I65. Sch. 2 para. 65 in force at 22.4.2014 by S.I. 2014/889, art. 4. (f) (with transitional provisions in S.I. 2014/1042, arts. 3, 4, 6-10)

Civil Partnership Act 2004 (c. 33)

66. (1)Schedule 2 to the Civil Partnership Act 2004 (civil partnerships of persons under 18) is amended as follows.
(2) In paragraph 1 (persons whose consent is required), in each of items 4 and 8 in the first column of the table, for "residence order" substitute " child arrangements order to which paragraph 2. A applies ".
(3) In paragraph 2 (interpretation of paragraph 1) for " "residence order"," substitute " "child arrangements order", ".
(4) In Part 1 (appropriate persons) after paragraph 2 insert—
"2. AA child arrangements order (as defined by section 8 of the Children Act 1989) is one to which this paragraph applies if the order regulates arrangements that consist of, or include, arrangements which relate to either or both of the following—
(a) with whom the child is to live, and
(b) when the child is to live with any person."
Commencement Information
I66. Sch. 2 para. 66 in force at 22.4.2014 by S.I. 2014/889, art. 4. (f) (with transitional provisions in S.I. 2014/1042, arts. 3, 4, 6-10)

Income Tax (Trading and Other Income) Act 2005 (c. 5)

67. The Income Tax (Trading and Other Income) Act 2005 is amended as follows.
Commencement Information
I67. Sch. 2 para. 67 in force at 22.4.2014 by S.I. 2014/889, art. 4. (f) (with transitional provisions in S.I. 2014/1042, arts. 3, 4, 6-10)
68. (1)Section 744 (payments to adopters, etc: England and Wales) is amended as follows.
(2) In subsection (1)(g) (no income tax on payments under section 17 of the Children Act 1989 made to a person as a result of a residence order being in force in the person's favour) for "in whose favour a residence order with respect to a child is in force" substitute " named in a child arrangements order as a person with whom a child is to live ".
(3) In subsection (1)(h) (no income tax on payments under paragraph 15 of Schedule 1 to the 1989 Act made to person with whom child is living, or is to live, as a result of a residence order) for "in whose favour residence order is in force" substitute " with whom child is living, or is to live, as a result of a child arrangements order ".
(4) In subsection (1)(i) (no income tax on other payments under maintenance agreements or under orders under Schedule 1 to the 1989 Act) for "in whose favour a residence order with respect to the child is in force" substitute " named in a child arrangements order as a person with whom the child is to live ".
(5) For subsection (2)(c) (payment not exempt from tax if made to a person in whose favour a residence order is in force where that order is also in favour of an excluded relative) substitute—
"(c)it is made to a person ("P") named in a child arrangements order as a person with whom the child is to live and an excluded relative who lives in the same household as P is also named in that order as a person with whom the child is to live."
(6) In subsection (3) (interpretation) for " "residence" substitute " "child arrangements".
Commencement Information
I68. Sch. 2 para. 68 in force at 22.4.2014 by S.I. 2014/889, art. 4. (f) (with transitional provisions in S.I. 2014/1042, arts. 3, 4, 6-10)
69. In section 806. (5) (persons who are not foster carers for purposes of Chapter 2 of Part 7) after paragraph (b) insert—
"(ba)where the child is in care and there was a child arrangements order in force with respect to the child immediately before the care order was made, a person named in the child arrangements order as a person with whom the child was to live,
(bb) (in Scotland) where the child is in care and there was a child arrangements order in force

with respect to the child immediately before the child was placed in care, a person named in the child arrangements order as a person with whom the child was to live, spend time or otherwise have contact,".
Commencement Information
I69. Sch. 2 para. 69 in force at 22.4.2014 by S.I. 2014/889, art. 4. (f) (with transitional provisions in S.I. 2014/1042, arts. 3, 4, 6-10)

Legal Aid, Sentencing and Punishment of Offenders Act 2012 (c. 10)

70. In paragraph 13. (1)(c) of Schedule 1 to the Legal Aid, Sentencing and Punishment of Offenders Act 2012 (civil legal services: orders mentioned in section 8. (1) of the Children Act 1989) for "residence, contact" substitute " child arrangements orders ".
Commencement Information
I70. Sch. 2 para. 70 in force at 22.4.2014 by S.I. 2014/889, art. 4. (f) (with transitional provisions in S.I. 2014/1042, arts. 3, 4, 6-10)

Schedule 3. Special educational needs: consequential amendments

Section 82

PART 1 Amendments to the Education Act 1996

1. The Education Act 1996 is amended as follows.
Commencement Information
I1. Sch. 3 para. 1 in force at 1.9.2014 by S.I. 2014/889, art. 7. (a) (with savings and transitional provisions in S.I. 2014/2270 (as amended (1.4.2015) by S.I. 2015/505 and (1.9.2015) by S.I. 2015/1619)
2. (1)Section 6 (nursery schools and special schools) is amended as follows.
(2) Omit subsection (2).
(3) In the title, omit "and special schools".
Commencement Information
I2. Sch. 3 para. 2 in force at 1.9.2014 by S.I. 2014/889, art. 7. (a) (with savings and transitional provisions in S.I. 2014/2270 (as amended (1.4.2015) by S.I. 2015/505 and (1.9.2015) by S.I. 2015/1619)
3. (1)Section 13 (general responsibility for education) is amended as follows.
(2) In subsection (3)(b) for "but under 25 and are subject to learning difficulty assessment" substitute " and for whom an EHC plan is maintained ".
(3) Omit subsections (4) and (5).
Commencement Information
I3. Sch. 3 para. 3 in force at 1.9.2014 by S.I. 2014/889, art. 7. (a) (with savings and transitional provisions in S.I. 2014/2270 (as amended (1.4.2015) by S.I. 2015/505 and (1.9.2015) by S.I. 2015/1619)
4. In section 13. A (duty to promote high standards and fulfilment of potential), in subsection (2)(b) for "but under 25 who are subject to learning difficulty assessment" substitute " and for whom an EHC plan is maintained ".
Commencement Information
I4. Sch. 3 para. 4 in force at 1.9.2014 by S.I. 2014/889, art. 7. (a) (with savings and transitional

provisions in S.I. 2014/2270 (as amended (1.4.2015) by S.I. 2015/505 and (1.9.2015) by S.I. 2015/1619)

5. (1)Section 15.ZA (duty in respect of education and training for persons over compulsory school age: England) is amended as follows.

(2) In subsection (1) for "but under 25 and are subject to learning difficulty assessment" substitute " and for whom an EHC plan is maintained ".

(3) In subsection (3)(b) after "learning difficulties" insert " or disabilities ".

(4) In subsections (6) and (7) after "learning difficulty" insert " or disability ".

(5) For subsection (9) substitute—

"(9)The duty in subsection (1) does not apply in relation to persons in a local authority's area who are subject to a detention order."

Commencement Information

I5. Sch. 3 para. 5 in force at 1.9.2014 by S.I. 2014/889, art. 7. (a) (with savings and transitional provisions in S.I. 2014/2270 (as amended (1.4.2015) by S.I. 2015/505 and (1.9.2015) by S.I. 2015/1619)

6. In section 15.A (powers in respect of education and training for 16 to 18 year olds), in subsection (3) for the words from "a local authority" to the end substitute "—

(a) a local authority in England must in particular have regard to the needs of persons with learning difficulties or disabilities (within the meaning of section 15.ZA(6) and (7));

(b) a local authority in Wales must in particular have regard to the needs of persons with learning difficulties (within the meaning of section 41.(5) and (6) of the Learning and Skills Act 2000)."

Commencement Information

I6. Sch. 3 para. 6 in force at 1.9.2014 by S.I. 2014/889, art. 7. (a) (with savings and transitional provisions in S.I. 2014/2270 (as amended (1.4.2015) by S.I. 2015/505 and (1.9.2015) by S.I. 2015/1619)

7. In section 15.B (functions in respect of education for persons aged over 19), in subsection (3) for the words from "a local authority" to the end substitute "—

(a) a local authority in England must in particular have regard to the needs of persons with learning difficulties or disabilities (within the meaning of section 15.ZA(6) and (7));

(b) a local authority in Wales must in particular have regard to the needs of persons with learning difficulties (within the meaning of section 41.(5) and (6) of the Learning and Skills Act 2000)."

Commencement Information

I7. Sch. 3 para. 7 in force at 1.9.2014 by S.I. 2014/889, art. 7. (a) (with savings and transitional provisions in S.I. 2014/2270 (as amended (1.4.2015) by S.I. 2015/505 and (1.9.2015) by S.I. 2015/1619)

8. In section 18.A (provision of education for persons subject to youth detention), in subsection (2)—

(a) in paragraph (b) omit "or learning difficulties (within the meaning of section 15.ZA(6) and (7))", and

(b) after that paragraph insert—

"(ba)in the case of a local authority in England, any learning difficulties or disabilities (within the meaning of section 15.ZA(6) and (7)) the persons may have;

(bb) in the case of a local authority in Wales, any learning difficulties (within the meaning of section 41.(5) and (6) of the Learning and Skills Act 2000) the persons may have;".

Commencement Information

I8. Sch. 3 para. 8 in force at 1.9.2014 by S.I. 2014/889, art. 7. (a) (with savings and transitional provisions in S.I. 2014/2270 (as amended (1.4.2015) by S.I. 2015/505 and (1.9.2015) by S.I. 2015/1619)

9. In the title of Chapter 1 of Part 4 (children with special educational needs) after "children" insert " in Wales ".

Commencement Information

I9. Sch. 3 para. 9 in force at 1.9.2014 by S.I. 2014/889, art. 7. (a) (with savings and transitional provisions in S.I. 2014/2270 (as amended (1.4.2015) by S.I. 2015/505 and (1.9.2015) by S.I. 2015/1619)

10. Before section 312 (meaning of special educational needs etc) insert—

"311. AApplication of this Chapter: children in Wales

This Chapter applies only in relation to children in the area of a local authority in Wales."

Commencement Information

I10. Sch. 3 para. 10 in force at 1.9.2014 by S.I. 2014/889, art. 7. (a) (with savings and transitional provisions in S.I. 2014/2270 (as amended (1.4.2015) by S.I. 2015/505 and (1.9.2015) by S.I. 2015/1619)

11. (1)Section 312 (meaning of "special educational needs" and "special educational provision" etc) is amended as follows.
(2) In subsections (1) and (2), after "child" insert " in the area of a local authority in Wales ".
(3) In subsection (3. A)—
(a) in paragraph (a)—
(i) omit "15. ZA", and
(ii) for ", 15. B and 507. B" substitute " and 15. B ", and
(b) in paragraph (b), before "determining" substitute "a local authority in Wales".
(4) In subsection (4), after " "special educational provision"" insert " , in relation to a child in the area of a local authority in Wales, ".

Commencement Information

I11. Sch. 3 para. 11 in force at 1.9.2014 by S.I. 2014/889, art. 7. (a) (with savings and transitional provisions in S.I. 2014/2270 (as amended (1.4.2015) by S.I. 2015/505 and (1.9.2015) by S.I. 2015/1619)

12. (1)Section 313 (code of practice) is amended as follows.
(2) In subsections (1) and (4) for "Secretary of State" substitute " Welsh Ministers ".
(3) In subsection (5)—
(a) after "means" insert " the Special Educational Needs Tribunal for Wales. ", and
(b) omit paragraphs (a) and (b).

Commencement Information

I12. Sch. 3 para. 12 in force at 1.9.2014 by S.I. 2014/889, art. 7. (a) (with savings and transitional provisions in S.I. 2014/2270 (as amended (1.4.2015) by S.I. 2015/505 and (1.9.2015) by S.I. 2015/1619)

13. (1)Section 314 (making and approval of code) is amended as follows.
(2) In subsection (1)—
(a) for "Secretary of State proposes" substitute " Welsh Ministers propose ", and
(b) for "he" substitute " they ".
(3) In subsection (2)—
(a) for "Secretary of State" substitute " Welsh Ministers ",
(b) for "he thinks" substitute " they think ", and
(c) for "them" substitute " those persons ".
(4) For subsection (3) substitute—
"(3)If the Welsh Ministers determine to proceed with the draft (either in its original form or with such modifications as they think fit) they shall lay it before the National Assembly for Wales."
(5) In subsection (4)—
(a) for "each house, the Secretary of State" substitute " the National Assembly for Wales, the Welsh Ministers ", and
(b) for "the Secretary of State may" substitute " the Welsh Ministers may ".

Commencement Information

I13. Sch. 3 para. 13 in force at 1.9.2014 by S.I. 2014/889, art. 7. (a) (with savings and transitional

provisions in S.I. 2014/2270 (as amended (1.4.2015) by S.I. 2015/505 and (1.9.2015) by S.I. 2015/1619)

14. (1)Section 316. A (education otherwise than in mainstream schools) is amended as follows.
(2) In subsection (2)—
(a) in paragraph (a), for sub-paragraph (ii) substitute—
"(ii)the governing body of the school or, if the school is in England, its head teacher,", and
(b) in paragraph (c), for sub-paragraph (ii) substitute—
"(ii)the governing body of the school or, if the school is in England, its head teacher,".
(3) In subsection (8)—
(a) after "issued" insert " by the Welsh Ministers ", and
(b) omit paragraphs (a) and (b).
(4) In subsection (10)—
(a) omit ", in relation to Wales,", and
(b) for "National Assembly for Wales" substitute " Welsh Ministers ".
Commencement Information
I14. Sch. 3 para. 14 in force at 1.9.2014 by S.I. 2014/889, art. 7. (a) (with savings and transitional provisions in S.I. 2014/2270 (as amended (1.4.2015) by S.I. 2015/505 and (1.9.2015) by S.I. 2015/1619)

15. In section 317 (duties of governing body or local authority in relation to pupils with special educational needs), in subsection (5)—
(a) after "foundation special school shall" insert "include special needs information in the report prepared under section 30. (1) of the Education Act 2002 (governors' report).", and
(b) omit paragraphs (a) and (b).
Commencement Information
I15. Sch. 3 para. 15 in force at 1.9.2014 by S.I. 2014/889, art. 7. (a) (with savings and transitional provisions in S.I. 2014/2270 (as amended (1.4.2015) by S.I. 2015/505 and (1.9.2015) by S.I. 2015/1619)

16. (1)Section 318 (provision of goods and services in connection with special educational needs) is amended as follows.
(2) Omit subsections (3) and (3. A).
(3) In subsection (3. B) omit "in Wales" (in the first place it occurs).
(4) In consequence of the repeal made by sub-paragraph (2)—
(a) in Schedule 30 to the School Standards and Framework Act 1998 omit paragraph 75. (4),
(b) in the Education Act 2002, in section 194 omit subsection (2)(a), and
(c) in Schedule 2 to the Childcare Act 2006, omit paragraph 21.
Commencement Information
I16. Sch. 3 para. 16 in force at 1.9.2014 by S.I. 2014/889, art. 7. (a) (with savings and transitional provisions in S.I. 2014/2270 (as amended (1.4.2015) by S.I. 2015/505 and (1.9.2015) by S.I. 2015/1619)

17. In section 326 (appeal against contents of statement), in subsection (4)(c) for the words from "in the case" to "in the proceedings" substitute " in the proceedings the child has proposed the school ".
Commencement Information
I17. Sch. 3 para. 17 in force at 1.9.2014 by S.I. 2014/889, art. 7. (a) (with savings and transitional provisions in S.I. 2014/2270 (as amended (1.4.2015) by S.I. 2015/505 and (1.9.2015) by S.I. 2015/1619)

18. (1)Section 326. A (unopposed appeals) is amended as follows.
(2) In subsection (1), for paragraph (a) substitute—
"(a)the parent of a child, or a child, has appealed to the Tribunal under section 325, 328, 329 or 329. A or paragraph 8. (3) of Schedule 27 against a decision of a local authority, and".
(3) In subsection (6)—
(a) after "regulations made" insert " by the Welsh Ministers ", and
(b) omit paragraphs (a) and (b).

Commencement Information

I18. Sch. 3 para. 18 in force at 1.9.2014 by S.I. 2014/889, art. 7. (a) (with savings and transitional provisions in S.I. 2014/2270 (as amended (1.4.2015) by S.I. 2015/505 and (1.9.2015) by S.I. 2015/1619)

19. (1)Section 328. A (appeal against determination of local authority in England not to amend statement following review) is repealed.

(2) In consequence of the repeal made by sub-paragraph (1), section 2 of the Children, Schools and Families Act 2010 is repealed.

Commencement Information

I19. Sch. 3 para. 19 in force at 1.9.2014 by S.I. 2014/889, art. 7. (a) (with savings and transitional provisions in S.I. 2014/2270 (as amended (1.4.2015) by S.I. 2015/505 and (1.9.2015) by S.I. 2015/1619)

20. (1)Section 329. A (review or assessment of educational needs at request of responsible body) is amended as follows.

(2) In subsection (14)—

(a) after " "Relevant early years education"" insert " has the same meaning as it has (in relation to Wales) in section 123 of the School Standards and Framework Act 1998 except that it does not include early years education provided by a local authority at a maintained nursery school. ", and

(b) omit paragraphs (a) and (b).

(3) In subsection (15)—

(a) omit ", in relation to Wales,", and

(b) for "National Assembly for Wales" substitute " Welsh Ministers ".

(4) In consequence of the amendments made by sub-paragraph (2), in paragraph 22 of Schedule 2 to the Childcare Act 2006, omit sub-paragraph (4).

(5) Until the coming into force in relation to Wales of the amendments made by paragraph 22. (2) and (3) of Schedule 2 to the Childcare Act 2006, section 329. A of EA 1996 has effect as if for subsection (14) (as amended by sub-paragraph (2)) there were substituted—

"(14)Relevant nursery education" has the same meaning as in section 123 of the School Standards and Framework Act 1998, except that it does not include nursery education provided by a local authority at a maintained nursery school."

Commencement Information

I20. Sch. 3 para. 20 in force at 1.9.2014 by S.I. 2014/889, art. 7. (a) (with savings and transitional provisions in S.I. 2014/2270 (as amended (1.4.2015) by S.I. 2015/505 and (1.9.2015) by S.I. 2015/1619)

21. (1)Section 332. ZA (right of a child to appeal to the Welsh Tribunal) is amended as follows.

(2) In subsection (1) omit "Welsh".

(3) In the title omit "Welsh".

Commencement Information

I21. Sch. 3 para. 21 in force at 1.9.2014 by S.I. 2014/889, art. 7. (a) (with savings and transitional provisions in S.I. 2014/2270 (as amended (1.4.2015) by S.I. 2015/505 and (1.9.2015) by S.I. 2015/1619)

22. In section 332. ZB (notice and service of documents on a child in relation to an appeal by the child), in subsection (1) omit "in Wales".

Commencement Information

I22. Sch. 3 para. 22 in force at 1.9.2014 by S.I. 2014/889, art. 7. (a) (with savings and transitional provisions in S.I. 2014/2270 (as amended (1.4.2015) by S.I. 2015/505 and (1.9.2015) by S.I. 2015/1619)

23. (1)Section 332. ZC (case friends—Wales) is amended as follows.

(2) In subsection (1), in paragraph (a) omit "in Wales".

(3) In subsection (3), in paragraph (a) omit "Welsh".

(4) In the title, omit "—Wales".

Commencement Information

I23. Sch. 3 para. 23 in force at 1.9.2014 by S.I. 2014/889, art. 7. (a) (with savings and transitional

provisions in S.I. 2014/2270 (as amended (1.4.2015) by S.I. 2015/505 and (1.9.2015) by S.I. 2015/1619)

24. (1) Section 332. A (advice and information for parents—England) is repealed.

(2) In consequence of the repeal made by sub-paragraph (1), section 2 of the Special Educational Needs and Disability Act 2001 is repealed.

(3) The repeals made by sub-paragraphs (1) and (2) do not affect the application for the time being of section 332. A to certain local authorities in Wales by virtue of article 4. (a) of the Education (Wales) Measure 2009 (Commencement No 3 and Transitional Provisions) Order 2012 (SI 2012/320).

Commencement Information

I24. Sch. 3 para. 24 in force at 1.9.2014 by S.I. 2014/889, art. 7. (a) (with savings and transitional provisions in S.I. 2014/2270 (as amended (1.4.2015) by S.I. 2015/505 and (1.9.2015) by S.I. 2015/1619)

25. (1) Section 332. AA (advice and information— Wales) is amended as follows.

(2) In subsection (1) omit "in Wales".

(3) In the title, omit "— Wales".

Commencement Information

I25. Sch. 3 para. 25 in force at 1.9.2014 by S.I. 2014/889, art. 7. (a) (with savings and transitional provisions in S.I. 2014/2270 (as amended (1.4.2015) by S.I. 2015/505 and (1.9.2015) by S.I. 2015/1619)

26. (1) Section 332. B (resolution of disputes—England) is repealed.

(2) In consequence of the repeal made by sub-paragraph (1), section 3 of the Special Educational Needs and Disability Act 2001 is repealed.

(3) The repeals made by sub-paragraphs (1) and (2) do not affect the application for the time being of section 332. B to certain local authorities in Wales by virtue of article 4. (b) of the Education (Wales) Measure 2009 (Commencement No 3 and Transitional Provisions) Order 2012 (SI 2012/320).

Commencement Information

I26. Sch. 3 para. 26 in force at 1.9.2014 by S.I. 2014/889, art. 7. (a) (with savings and transitional provisions in S.I. 2014/2270 (as amended (1.4.2015) by S.I. 2015/505 and (1.9.2015) by S.I. 2015/1619)

27. (1) Section 332. BA (resolution of disputes—Wales) is amended as follows.

(2) In subsections (1) and (2) omit "in Wales".

(3) In the title, omit "—Wales".

Commencement Information

I27. Sch. 3 para. 27 in force at 1.9.2014 by S.I. 2014/889, art. 7. (a) (with savings and transitional provisions in S.I. 2014/2270 (as amended (1.4.2015) by S.I. 2015/505 and (1.9.2015) by S.I. 2015/1619)

28. (1) Section 332. BB (independent advocacy services—Wales) is amended as follows.

(2) In subsections (1) and (5) omit "in Wales".

(3) In the title, omit "—Wales".

Commencement Information

I28. Sch. 3 para. 28 in force at 1.9.2014 by S.I. 2014/889, art. 7. (a) (with savings and transitional provisions in S.I. 2014/2270 (as amended (1.4.2015) by S.I. 2015/505 and (1.9.2015) by S.I. 2015/1619)

29. (1) Sections 332. C to 332. E (information about children in England with special educational needs) are repealed, and the cross-heading which precedes section 332. C is omitted.

(2) In consequence of the repeals made by sub-paragraph (1), section 1 of the Special Educational Needs (Information) Act 2008 is repealed.

Commencement Information

I29. Sch. 3 para. 29 in force at 1.9.2014 by S.I. 2014/889, art. 7. (a) (with savings and transitional provisions in S.I. 2014/2270 (as amended (1.4.2015) by S.I. 2015/505 and (1.9.2015) by S.I. 2015/1619)

30. In the cross-heading which precedes section 333 (Special Educational Needs Tribunal) after "Tribunal" insert " for Wales ".
Commencement Information
I30. Sch. 3 para. 30 in force at 1.9.2014 by S.I. 2014/889, art. 7. (a) (with savings and transitional provisions in S.I. 2014/2270 (as amended (1.4.2015) by S.I. 2015/505 and (1.9.2015) by S.I. 2015/1619)

31. (1)Section 333 (constitution of Welsh Tribunal) is amended as follows.
(2) Omit subsection (1. ZB).
(3) In the following provisions, omit "Welsh"—
(a) subsection (1),
(b) in subsection (2), paragraphs (a), (b) and (c),
(c) in subsection (5), paragraph (a), and paragraph (b) (in the first place it occurs), and
(d) subsection (6) (in the second place it occurs).
(4) In the title, omit "Welsh".
Commencement Information
I31. Sch. 3 para. 31 in force at 1.9.2014 by S.I. 2014/889, art. 7. (a) (with savings and transitional provisions in S.I. 2014/2270 (as amended (1.4.2015) by S.I. 2015/505 and (1.9.2015) by S.I. 2015/1619)

32. In section 335 (remuneration and expenses), in subsection (1) and (2) omit "Welsh" (in each case, in the second place it occurs).
Commencement Information
I32. Sch. 3 para. 32 in force at 1.9.2014 by S.I. 2014/889, art. 7. (a) (with savings and transitional provisions in S.I. 2014/2270 (as amended (1.4.2015) by S.I. 2015/505 and (1.9.2015) by S.I. 2015/1619)

33. (1)Section 336 (Tribunal procedure) is amended as follows.
(2) In the following provisions omit "Welsh"—
(a) subsection (1) (in the second place it occurs),
(b) in subsection (2), paragraphs (b), (o) and (p),
(c) subsection (2. A),
(d) subsection (3) (in the second place it occurs), and
(e) subsection (4) (in the first place it occurs).
(2) Omit subsection (5. A).
(3) In subsection (6) omit "or (5. A)".
Commencement Information
I33. Sch. 3 para. 33 in force at 1.9.2014 by S.I. 2014/889, art. 7. (a) (with savings and transitional provisions in S.I. 2014/2270 (as amended (1.4.2015) by S.I. 2015/505 and (1.9.2015) by S.I. 2015/1619)

34. (1)Section 336. ZB (appeals from the Welsh Tribunal to the Upper Tribunal) is amended as follows.
(2) In the following provisions, omit "Welsh"—
(a) subsection (1) (in both places it occurs),
(b) subsection (2), and
(c) subsection (3).
(3) In the title, omit "Welsh".
Commencement Information
I34. Sch. 3 para. 34 in force at 1.9.2014 by S.I. 2014/889, art. 7. (a) (with savings and transitional provisions in S.I. 2014/2270 (as amended (1.4.2015) by S.I. 2015/505 and (1.9.2015) by S.I. 2015/1619)

35. In section 336. A (compliance with orders), in subsection (2)—
(a) after "made" insert " by the Welsh Ministers with the agreement of the Secretary of State. ", and
(b) omit paragraphs (a) and (b).
Commencement Information

I35. Sch. 3 para. 35 in force at 1.9.2014 by S.I. 2014/889, art. 7. (a) (with savings and transitional provisions in S.I. 2014/2270 (as amended (1.4.2015) by S.I. 2015/505 and (1.9.2015) by S.I. 2015/1619)

36. For section 337 (special schools) substitute—

"337. Special schools

A school is a special school if it is specially organised to make special educational provision for pupils with special educational needs, and it is—
  (a) maintained by a local authority,
  (b) an Academy school, or
  (c) a non-maintained special school."

Commencement Information

I36. Sch. 3 para. 36 in force at 1.9.2014 by S.I. 2014/889, art. 7. (a) (with savings and transitional provisions in S.I. 2014/2270 (as amended (1.4.2015) by S.I. 2015/505 and (1.9.2015) by S.I. 2015/1619)

37. In section 342 (approval of non-maintained special schools), in subsection (1)(b) after "community or foundation special school" insert " or an Academy school ".

Commencement Information

I37. Sch. 3 para. 37 in force at 1.9.2014 by S.I. 2014/889, art. 7. (a) (with savings and transitional provisions in S.I. 2014/2270 (as amended (1.4.2015) by S.I. 2015/505 and (1.9.2015) by S.I. 2015/1619)

38. (1)Section 348 (provision of special education at non-maintained schools) is amended as follows.

(2) In subsection (1) after paragraph (a) (and before the "and" which follows it) insert—
  "(aa)the child is in the area of a local authority in Wales,".

(3) In the title, at the end insert " —Wales ".

Commencement Information

I38. Sch. 3 para. 38 in force at 1.9.2014 by S.I. 2014/889, art. 7. (a) (with savings and transitional provisions in S.I. 2014/2270 (as amended (1.4.2015) by S.I. 2015/505 and (1.9.2015) by S.I. 2015/1619)

39. (1)Section 438 (choice of school: child without statement of special educational needs) is amended as follows.

(2) In subsection (1)—
(a) after "maintain" insert " an EHC plan (in the case of a local authority in England) or ", and
(b) after "section 324" insert " (in the case of a local authority in Wales) ".

(3) In the title, after "without" insert " EHC plan or ".

Commencement Information

I39. Sch. 3 para. 39 in force at 1.9.2014 by S.I. 2014/889, art. 7. (a) (with savings and transitional provisions in S.I. 2014/2270 (as amended (1.4.2015) by S.I. 2015/505 and (1.9.2015) by S.I. 2015/1619)

40. (1)Section 440 (amendment of order at request of parent: child without statement of special educational needs) is amended as follows.

(2) In subsection (1)—
(a) after "maintain" insert " an EHC plan (in the case of a local authority in England) or ", and
(b) after "section 324" insert " (in the case of a local authority in Wales) ".

(3) In the title, after "without" insert " EHC plan or ".

Commencement Information

I40. Sch. 3 para. 40 in force at 1.9.2014 by S.I. 2014/889, art. 7. (a) (with savings and transitional provisions in S.I. 2014/2270 (as amended (1.4.2015) by S.I. 2015/505 and (1.9.2015) by S.I. 2015/1619)

41. (1)Section 441 (choice of school: child with statement of special educational needs) is

amended as follows.
(2) In subsection (1)—
(a) after "maintain" insert " an EHC plan (in the case of a local authority in England) or ", and
(b) after "section 324" insert " (in the case of a local authority in Wales) ".
(3) In subsection (2) after "Where the" insert " EHC plan or ".
(4) In subsection (3)—
(a) after "Where the" insert " EHC plan or ", and
(b) after "amend the" insert " EHC plan or ".
(5) After subsection (3. A) insert—
"(3. B)An amendment to an EHC plan required to be made under subsection (3)(a) shall be treated as if it were an amendment made following a review under section 44 of the Children and Families Act 2014, and that section and regulations made under it apply accordingly."
(6) In subsection (4)—
(a) in paragraph (a) after "maintain" insert " an EHC plan or ", and
(b) in paragraph (b) after "specified in the" insert " plan or ".
(7) In the title, after "with" insert " EHC plan or ".
Commencement Information
I41. Sch. 3 para. 41 in force at 1.9.2014 by S.I. 2014/889, art. 7. (a) (with savings and transitional provisions in S.I. 2014/2270 (as amended (1.4.2015) by S.I. 2015/505 and (1.9.2015) by S.I. 2015/1619)
42. In section 442 (revocation of order at request of parent), in subsection (5)—
(a) after "maintain" insert " an EHC plan (in the case of a local authority in England) or ",
(b) after "section 324" insert " (in the case of a local authority in Wales) ",
(c) in paragraph (a) after "specified in" insert " the EHC plan or ", and
(d) in paragraph (b) after "in the" insert " plan or the ".
Commencement Information
I42. Sch. 3 para. 42 in force at 1.9.2014 by S.I. 2014/889, art. 7. (a) (with savings and transitional provisions in S.I. 2014/2270 (as amended (1.4.2015) by S.I. 2015/505 and (1.9.2015) by S.I. 2015/1619)
43. In section 463 (meaning of "independent school")—
(a) in subsection (1)(b), after "for whom" insert " an EHC plan is maintained or for whom ", and
(b) in subsection (1), for "or a special school not so maintained" substitute " non-maintained special school ".
Commencement Information
I43. Sch. 3 para. 43 in force at 1.9.2014 by S.I. 2014/889, art. 7. (a) (with savings and transitional provisions in S.I. 2014/2270 (as amended (1.4.2015) by S.I. 2015/505 and (1.9.2015) by S.I. 2015/1619)
44. (1)Section 483. A (city colleges and academies: special educational needs) is amended as follows.
(2) In subsection (2), in paragraph (a) for "a statement is maintained under section 324" substitute " an EHC plan or a statement under section 324 is maintained ".
(3) In subsection (3), in paragraph (a) for "the statement" substitute " the EHC plan ".
(4) In subsection (4), in paragraphs (a) and (b) after "specified in" insert " the plan or ".
Commencement Information
I44. Sch. 3 para. 44 in force at 1.9.2014 by S.I. 2014/889, art. 7. (a) (with savings and transitional provisions in S.I. 2014/2270 (as amended (1.4.2015) by S.I. 2015/505 and (1.9.2015) by S.I. 2015/1619)
45. In section 507. B (local authorities in England: functions in respect of leisure-time activities etc for persons aged 13 to 19 and certain persons aged 20 to 24), in subsection (2)(b) after "learning difficulty" insert " or disability ".
Commencement Information
I45. Sch. 3 para. 45 in force at 1.9.2014 by S.I. 2014/889, art. 7. (a) (with savings and transitional provisions in S.I. 2014/2270 (as amended (1.4.2015) by S.I. 2015/505 and (1.9.2015) by S.I.

2015/1619)
46. In section 508.F (local authorities in England: provision of transport etc for adult learners), in subsection (9) in the definition of "relevant young adult" for "who is aged under 25 and is subject to learning difficulty assessment" substitute " for whom an EHC plan is maintained ".
Commencement Information
I46. Sch. 3 para. 46 in force at 1.9.2014 by S.I. 2014/889, art. 7. (a) (with savings and transitional provisions in S.I. 2014/2270 (as amended (1.4.2015) by S.I. 2015/505 and (1.9.2015) by S.I. 2015/1619)
47. In the title of section 508.I (complaints about transport arrangements etc for young adults subject to learning difficulty assessment: England), for "adults subject to learning difficulty assessment" substitute " adult for whom EHC plan is maintained ".
Commencement Information
I47. Sch. 3 para. 47 in force at 1.9.2014 by S.I. 2014/889, art. 7. (a) (with savings and transitional provisions in S.I. 2014/2270 (as amended (1.4.2015) by S.I. 2015/505 and (1.9.2015) by S.I. 2015/1619)
48. (1)Section 509.AB (local authorities in England: further provision about transport policy statements for persons of sixth form age) is amended as follows.
(2) In subsection (1) after "difficulties" insert " or disabilities ".
(3) In subsection (2)(b) after "difficulties" (in each place it occurs) insert " or disabilities ".
Commencement Information
I48. Sch. 3 para. 48 in force at 1.9.2014 by S.I. 2014/889, art. 7. (a) (with savings and transitional provisions in S.I. 2014/2270 (as amended (1.4.2015) by S.I. 2015/505 and (1.9.2015) by S.I. 2015/1619)
49. In section 509.AC (interpretation of sections 509.AA and 509.AB), in subsection (4) after "learning difficulties" insert " or disabilities ".
Commencement Information
I49. Sch. 3 para. 49 in force at 1.9.2014 by S.I. 2014/889, art. 7. (a) (with savings and transitional provisions in S.I. 2014/2270 (as amended (1.4.2015) by S.I. 2015/505 and (1.9.2015) by S.I. 2015/1619)
50. (1)Section 514.A (provision of boarding accommodation for persons subject to learning difficulty assessment) is amended as follows.
(2) In subsection (1)—
(a) after "who is" insert " over compulsory school age and for whom an EHC plan is maintained. ", and
(b) omit paragraphs (a) and (b).
(3) In the title, for "persons subject to learning difficulty assessment" substitute " person for whom an EHC plan is maintained ".
Commencement Information
I50. Sch. 3 para. 50 in force at 1.9.2014 by S.I. 2014/889, art. 7. (a) (with savings and transitional provisions in S.I. 2014/2270 (as amended (1.4.2015) by S.I. 2015/505 and (1.9.2015) by S.I. 2015/1619)
51. In section 517 (payment of fees at schools not maintained by a local authority), in subsection (1), for "or Part IV (special educational needs)" substitute " , Part 4 (special educational needs) or Part 3 of the Children and Families Act 2014 (children and young people in England with special educational needs or disabilities) ".
Commencement Information
I51. Sch. 3 para. 51 in force at 1.9.2014 by S.I. 2014/889, art. 7. (a) (with savings and transitional provisions in S.I. 2014/2270 (as amended (1.4.2015) by S.I. 2015/505 and (1.9.2015) by S.I. 2015/1619)
52. (1)Section 532.A (direct payments: persons with special educational needs or subject to learning difficulty assessment) is amended as follows.
(2) In subsection (1)—
(a) after "("the beneficiary")" insert " for whom the authority maintain an EHC plan. ", and

(b) omit paragraphs (a) and (b).
(3) In subsection (2)—
(a) for paragraph (a) substitute—
"(a)special educational provision specified in the EHC plan;", and
(b) omit paragraph (b).
(4) In the title, omit "or subject to learning difficulty assessment".
Commencement Information
I52. Sch. 3 para. 52 in force at 1.9.2014 by S.I. 2014/889, art. 7. (a) (with savings and transitional provisions in S.I. 2014/2270 (as amended (1.4.2015) by S.I. 2015/505 and (1.9.2015) by S.I. 2015/1619)
53. In section 532. B (direct payments: pilot schemes), in subsection (9) for paragraph (a) substitute—
"(a)section 42. (2) of the Children and Families Act 2014 (duty to secure special educational provision in accordance with EHC plan);".
Commencement Information
I53. Sch. 3 para. 53 in force at 1.9.2014 by S.I. 2014/889, art. 7. (a) (with savings and transitional provisions in S.I. 2014/2270 (as amended (1.4.2015) by S.I. 2015/505 and (1.9.2015) by S.I. 2015/1619)
54. In section 560. A (work experience for persons over compulsory school age), in subsection (1)(b) for "but under 25 and are subject to learning difficulty assessment" substitute " and for whom an EHC plan is maintained ".
Commencement Information
I54. Sch. 3 para. 54 in force at 1.9.2014 by S.I. 2014/889, art. 7. (a) (with savings and transitional provisions in S.I. 2014/2270 (as amended (1.4.2015) by S.I. 2015/505 and (1.9.2015) by S.I. 2015/1619)
55. (1)Section 562. C (detained persons with special educational needs) is amended as follows.
(2) In subsection (1), after "local authority" insert " in Wales ".
(3) In the title, after "with" insert " statement of ".
Commencement Information
I55. Sch. 3 para. 55 in force at 1.4.2015 by S.I. 2015/375, art. 2. (e)
56. In section 562. D (appropriate special educational provision: arrangements between local authorities), in subsection (2) after "local authority" insert " in Wales ".
Commencement Information
I56. Sch. 3 para. 56 in force at 1.4.2015 by S.I. 2015/375, art. 2. (e)
57. (1)Section 562. G (information to be provided where statement of special educational needs previously maintained) is amended as follows.
(2) In subsection (1) after "local authority" insert " in Wales ".
(3) In subsection (2) after "home authority" insert " , where they are a local authority in Wales, ".
(4) In subsection (4) after "local authority" insert " in Wales ".
(5) In subsection (5) after "local authority" insert " in Wales ".
(6) In subsection (7)—
(a) in paragraph (a) after "home authority" insert " , where they are a local authority in Wales ", and
(b) in paragraph (b) after "authority" insert " in Wales ".
(7) In subsection (8)—
(a) after "home authority", where it first occurs insert " , where they are a local authority in Wales ", and
(b) in paragraph (a) after "local authority" insert " in Wales ".
Commencement Information
I57. Sch. 3 para. 57 in force at 1.4.2015 by S.I. 2015/375, art. 2. (e)
58. (1)Section 562. H (release of detained person appearing to host authority to require assessment) is amended as follows.
(2) In subsection (1)—

(a) after "person" insert "—
    (a) ", and
(b) after "apply" insert ", and
    (b) for whom the home authority are a local authority in Wales."
(3) In subsection (4), for "Subsections (5) and (6) apply" substitute " Subsection (6) applies ".
(4) Omit subsection (5).
(5) In subsection (6), omit paragraph (b) and the "and" preceding it.
Commencement Information
I58. Sch. 3 para. 58 in force at 1.4.2015 by S.I. 2015/375, art. 2. (e)
59. In section 579 (general interpretation)—
(a) in subsection (1), after the definition of "education functions" insert—
""EHC plan" means a plan within section 37. (2) of the Children and Families Act 2014;",
(b) in subsection (1), after the definition of "school year" insert—
""special educational needs"—
    (a) in relation to a child or person over compulsory school age but under 25 in the area of a local authority in England, has the meaning given by section 20. (1) of the Children and Families Act 2014;
    (b) in relation to a child in the area of a local authority in Wales, has the meaning given by section 312;
"special educational provision"—
    (a) in relation to a person in the area of a local authority in England, has the meaning given by section 21. (1) and (2) of the Children and Families Act 2014;
    (b) in relation to a child in the area of a local authority in Wales, has the meaning given by section 312. (4);",
(c) after subsection (1) insert—
"(1. A)For the purposes of this Act a person is subject to learning difficulty assessment if—
    (a) an assessment under section 140 of the Learning and Skills Act 2000 (learning difficulty assessments: Wales) has been conducted in respect of the person, or
    (b) arrangements for such an assessment to be conducted in respect of the person have been made or are required to be made.", and
(d) before subsection (4) insert—
"(3. A)References in this Act to a person who is "in the area" of a local authority in England do not include a person who is wholly or mainly resident in the area of a local authority in Wales.
(3. B)References in this Act to a person who is "in the area" of a local authority in Wales do not include a person who is wholly or mainly resident in the area of a local authority in England."
Commencement Information
I59. Sch. 3 para. 59 in force at 1.9.2014 by S.I. 2014/889, art. 7. (a) (with savings and transitional provisions in S.I. 2014/2270 (as amended (1.4.2015) by S.I. 2015/505 and (1.9.2015) by S.I. 2015/1619)
60. In section 580 (index)—
(a) after the entry for "education functions" insert—
"EHC plan | section 579(1)", |
(b) after the entry for "interest in land" insert—
"in the area of a local authority in England | section 579(3A) |
in the area of a local authority in Wales | section 579(3B)", |
(c) for the entry for "learning difficulty" substitute—
"learning difficulty (in relation to a child in the area of a local authority in Wales) | section 312(2) and (3) (subject to subsection (3A))", |
(d) in the entry for "special educational needs", in the second column for "section 312. (1)" substitute " section 579. (1) ",
(e) in the entry for "special educational provision", in the second column for "section 312. (4)" substitute " section 579. (1) ",
(f) in the entry for "special school", in the second column for "sections 6. (2) and" substitute "

section ", and
(g) in the entry for "subject to learning difficulty assessment", in the second column for "section 13. (4)" substitute " section 579. (1. A) ".
Commencement Information
I60. Sch. 3 para. 60 in force at 1.9.2014 by S.I. 2014/889, art. 7. (a) (with savings and transitional provisions in S.I. 2014/2270 (as amended (1.4.2015) by S.I. 2015/505 and (1.9.2015) by S.I. 2015/1619)
61. In Schedule 35. B (meaning of "eligible child" for purposes of section 508. B), in paragraph 15. (3)—
(a) in paragraph (a) for "statement maintained for the child under section 324" substitute " EHC plan maintained for the child ", and
(b) in paragraph (b) for "statement" substitute " plan ".
Commencement Information
I61. Sch. 3 para. 61 in force at 1.9.2014 by S.I. 2014/889, art. 7. (a) (with savings and transitional provisions in S.I. 2014/2270 (as amended (1.4.2015) by S.I. 2015/505 and (1.9.2015) by S.I. 2015/1619)
62. (1)In Schedule 36. A (education functions), the table in paragraph 2 is amended as follows.
(2) In the entry for the Disabled Persons (Services, Consultation and Representation) Act 1986, in the second column after "child with" insert " an EHC plan or ".
(3) In the entry for the Learning and Skills Act 2000, omit the entry for section 139. A.
Commencement Information
I62. Sch. 3 para. 62 in force at 1.9.2014 by S.I. 2014/889, art. 7. (a) (with savings and transitional provisions in S.I. 2014/2270 (as amended (1.4.2015) by S.I. 2015/505 and (1.9.2015) by S.I. 2015/1619)

PART 2 Amendments to other Acts

Local Government Act 1974 (c. 7)

63. In Schedule 5 to the Local Government Act 1974 (matters not subject to investigation by Local Commissioners), in paragraph 5. (2)(b) for "by section 312" substitute " by section 579. (1) ".
Commencement Information
I63. Sch. 3 para. 63 in force at 1.9.2014 by S.I. 2014/889, art. 7. (a)

Disabled Persons (Services, Consultation and Representation) Act 1986 (c. 33)

64. (1)In the Disabled Persons (Services, Consultation and Representation) Act 1986, section 5 (disabled persons leaving special education) is amended as follows.
(2) In subsection (1)—
(a) in paragraph (a) after "needs)" insert " , or have maintained an EHC plan under section 37 of the Children and Families Act 2014, ", and
(b) in paragraph (b) after "statement" (in both places) insert " or plan ".
(3) In subsection (2)—
(a) in paragraph (a) after "statement" insert " , or secure the preparation of an EHC plan, ",
(b) in paragraph (b) after "statement" insert " or plan ", and
(c) after "making the statement" insert " , securing the preparation of the plan ".
(4) After subsection (8) insert—
"(8. A)Regulations under section 47 of the Children and Families Act 2014 (transfer of EHC plans) may make such provision as appears to the Secretary of State to be necessary or expedient

in connection with subsections (1) to (7) of this section."
(5) In subsection (9), in paragraph (a) of the definition of "the responsible authority", after "1996" insert " or (as the case may be) Part 3 of the Children and Families Act 2014 ".
Commencement Information
I64. Sch. 3 para. 64 in force at 1.9.2014 by S.I. 2014/889, art. 7. (a)

Children Act 1989 (c. 41)

65. (1)The Children Act 1989 is amended as follows.
(2) In section 23. E (pathway plans), in subsection (1. A)(a) after "Education Act 1996" insert " or Part 3 of the Children and Families Act 2014 ".
(3) In Part 1 of Schedule 2 (provision of services to families) in paragraph 3 (assessment of children's needs) after paragraph (b) insert—
"(ba)Part 3 of the Children and Families Act 2014;".
Commencement Information
I65. Sch. 3 para. 65 in force at 1.9.2014 by S.I. 2014/889, art. 7. (a)

Value Added Tax Act 1994 (c. 23)

66. (1)In Schedule 9 to the Value Added Tax Act 1994, in Part 2 (groups of goods and services the supply of which is exempt from VAT), group 6 (education) is amended as follows.
(2) In item 5. B—
(a) after paragraph (b) insert—
   "(ba)aged 19 or over and for whom an EHC plan is maintained,", and
(b) in paragraph (d), after "paragraph" insert " (ba) or ".
(3) in note (5. B), after "item (5. B)," insert " "EHC plan" and " and for "has the same meaning" substitute " have the same meanings ".
Commencement Information
I66. Sch. 3 para. 66 in force at 1.9.2014 by S.I. 2014/889, art. 7. (a)

School Standards and Framework Act 1998 (c. 31)

67. The School Standards and Framework Act 1998 is amended as follows.
Commencement Information
I67. Sch. 3 para. 67 in force at 1.9.2014 by S.I. 2014/889, art. 7. (a)
68. (1)Section 98 (admission for nursery education or to nursery or special school: children with statements of special educational needs) is amended as follows.
(2) In subsection (7) after "for whom" insert " EHC plans are maintained under section 37 of the Children and Families Act 2014 or ".
(3) In the title after "special education needs" insert " or EHC plans ".
Commencement Information
I68. Sch. 3 para. 68 in force at 1.9.2014 by S.I. 2014/889, art. 7. (a)
69. (1)Section 123 (nursery education: children with special educational needs) is amended as follows.
(2) In subsection (1), for the words from "(except" to the end substitute " to have regard to the provisions of the code of practice issued under section 77 of the Children and Families Act 2014 (in the case of education in England) or section 313. (2) of the Education Act 1996 (in the case of education in Wales). "
(3) After subsection (1) insert—
"(1. A)Subsection (1) does not apply in so far as the person in question is already under a duty to have regard to the provisions of the code of practice in question."

(4) In subsection (2)—
(a) for "That code of practice" substitute " The code of practice in question ", and
(b) after "functions under" insert " Part 3 of the Children and Families Act 2014 or (as the case may be) ".
(5) In subsection (3)—
(a) for "that code of practice" substitute " the code of practice in question ", and
(b) after "functions under" insert " Part 3 of the Children and Families Act 2014 or (as the case may be) ".
(6) In subsection (3. A)(b) after "no" insert " EHC plan or ".
Commencement Information
I69. Sch. 3 para. 69 in force at 1.9.2014 by S.I. 2014/889, art. 7. (a)
70. In Part A1 of Schedule 22 (disposals of land in case of foundation, voluntary and foundation special schools in England), in paragraph A23. (9), in paragraph (d) of the definition of "children's services"—
(a) after "learning difficulty" insert " or disability ", and
(b) omit "66,".
Commencement Information
I70. Sch. 3 para. 70 in force at 1.9.2014 by S.I. 2014/889, art. 7. (a)

Learning and Skills Act 2000 (c. 21)

71. The Learning and Skills Act 2000 is amended as follows.
Commencement Information
I71. Sch. 3 para. 71 in force at 1.9.2014 by S.I. 2014/889, art. 7. (a) (with savings and transitional provisions in S.I. 2014/2270 (as amended (1.4.2015) by S.I. 2015/505 and (1.9.2015) by S.I. 2015/1619)
72. In section 35 (conditions imposed by Welsh Ministers on financial resources provided by them), in subsection (3)(f) omit "139. A or".
Commencement Information
I72. Sch. 3 para. 72 in force at 1.9.2014 by S.I. 2014/889, art. 7. (a) (with savings and transitional provisions in S.I. 2014/2270 (as amended (1.4.2015) by S.I. 2015/505 and (1.9.2015) by S.I. 2015/1619)
73. In section 41 (discharge by the Welsh Ministers of certain functions in relation to persons with learning difficulties), in subsection (1)(b) omit "139. A or".
Commencement Information
I73. Sch. 3 para. 73 in force at 1.9.2014 by S.I. 2014/889, art. 7. (a) (with savings and transitional provisions in S.I. 2014/2270 (as amended (1.4.2015) by S.I. 2015/505 and (1.9.2015) by S.I. 2015/1619)
74. Sections 139. A, 139. B and 139. C (assessments relating to learning difficulties: England) are repealed.
Commencement Information
I74. Sch. 3 para. 74 in force at 1.9.2014 by S.I. 2014/889, art. 7. (a) (with savings and transitional provisions in S.I. 2014/2270 (as amended (1.4.2015) by S.I. 2015/505 and (1.9.2015) by S.I. 2015/1619)
75. In consequence of the repeals made by paragraphs 72, 73 and 74—
(a) omit paragraph 76 of Schedule 1 to the Education and Skills Act 2008;
(b) section 80 of the Education and Skills Act 2008 is repealed.
Commencement Information
I75. Sch. 3 para. 75 in force at 1.9.2014 by S.I. 2014/889, art. 7. (a) (with savings and transitional provisions in S.I. 2014/2270 (as amended (1.4.2015) by S.I. 2015/505 and (1.9.2015) by S.I. 2015/1619)

Education Act 2002 (c. 32)

76. The Education Act 2002 is amended as follows.
Commencement Information
I76. Sch. 3 para. 76 in force at 1.9.2014 by S.I. 2014/889, art. 7. (a)
77. In section 92 (pupils with statements of special educational needs: application of National Curriculum for England)—
(a) for the words from "a statement" to "special educational needs" substitute " an EHC plan maintained for the pupil ",
(b) for "the statement" substitute " the plan ", and
(c) in the heading for "statements of special educational needs" substitute " EHC plans ".
Commencement Information
I77. Sch. 3 para. 77 in force at 1.9.2014 by S.I. 2014/889, art. 7. (a)
78. (1)Section 94 (information concerning directions under section 93) is amended as follows.
(2) In subsection (3), for the words from "by virtue of" to the end substitute " and the responsible authority ought to be required to secure an EHC needs assessment for the pupil under section 36 of the Children and Families Act 2014 (or, if an EHC plan is maintained for the pupil, a re-assessment under section 44 of that Act). "
(3) In subsection (5), for the words from "consider" to the end substitute " make a determination in respect of the pupil under section 36. (3) of the Children and Families Act 2014 (or, if an EHC plan is maintained for the pupil, under that section as it applies to re-assessments by virtue of regulations under section 44. (7)). "
(4) In subsection (6), for "Part 4 of the Education Act 1996" substitute " Part 3 of the Children and Families Act 2014 (see section 24 of that Act) ".
Commencement Information
I78. Sch. 3 para. 78 in force at 1.9.2014 by S.I. 2014/889, art. 7. (a)

Nationality, Immigration and Asylum Act 2002 (c. 41)

79. (1)Section 36 of the Nationality, Immigration and Asylum Act 2002 (education of children who are residents of accommodation centres) is amended as follows.
(2) In subsection (3)(b), after "named in" insert " an EHC plan maintained for the child under section 37 of the Children and Families Act 2014 or ".
(3) In subsection (5), omit the "and" after paragraph (d) and after paragraph (e) insert—
    "(f)sections 33 and 34 of the Children and Families Act 2014 (mainstream education for children with special educational needs), and
    (g) sections 38 and 39 of that Act (EHC plan: request of parent for named school etc)."
(4) After subsection (5) insert—
"(5. A)The powers of the First-tier Tribunal on determining an appeal under section 51. (2)(c) of the Children and Families Act 2014 (appeals against certain aspects of content of EHC plan) are subject to subsection (2) above."
(5) In subsection (6), omit "the First-tier Tribunal or".
(6) In subsection (7)—
(a) after "function under this Act" insert " , Part 3 of the Children and Families Act 2014 ", and
(b) in paragraph (a), after "special educational provision" insert " called for by his special educational needs or ".
(7) In subsection (9), after paragraph (a) insert—
    "(aa)section 36 of the Children and Families Act 2014 (assessment of education, health and care needs: England) shall have effect as if an accommodation centre were a school,".
Commencement Information
I79. Sch. 3 para. 79 in force at 1.9.2014 by S.I. 2014/889, art. 7. (a)

Children Act 2004 (c. 31)

80. In section 10. (9) of the Children Act 2004 (co-operation arrangements in respect of children may include arrangements in respect of certain young people), in paragraph (c)—
(a) after "but under the age of 25" insert "—
(i) for whom an EHC plan is maintained, or
(ii) ", and
(b) after "learning difficulty" insert " or disability ".
Commencement Information
I80. Sch. 3 para. 80 in force at 1.9.2014 by S.I. 2014/889, art. 7. (a)

Education and Inspections Act 2006 (c. 40)

81. In section 16 of the Education and Inspections Act 2006 (consultation before publishing proposals for discontinuance of maintained schools), in subsection (1)(c), after "maintain" insert " an EHC plan or ".
Commencement Information
I81. Sch. 3 para. 81 in force at 1.9.2014 by S.I. 2014/889, art. 7. (a)

Education and Skills Act 2008 (c. 25)

82. The Education and Skills Act 2008 is amended as follows.
Commencement Information
I82. Sch. 3 para. 82 in force at 1.9.2014 by S.I. 2014/889, art. 7. (a)
83. In section 4 (meaning of appropriate full-time education or training)—
(a) in subsection (1)(b), for "learning difficulty" substitute " special educational needs ", and
(b) omit subsection (3).
Commencement Information
I83. Sch. 3 para. 83 in force at 1.9.2014 by S.I. 2014/889, art. 7. (a)
84. In section 17 (sharing and use of information held for purposes of support services or functions under Part 1), in subsection (8)(b)—
(a) for "a learning difficulty" substitute " special educational needs ", and
(b) omit the words from "and subsections (6) and (7)" to the end.
Commencement Information
I84. Sch. 3 para. 84 in force at 1.9.2014 by S.I. 2014/889, art. 7. (a)
85. In section 47 (attendance notice: description of education or training)—
(a) in subsection (5)(b)(ii), for "learning difficulty" substitute " special educational needs ", and
(b) omit subsection (6).
Commencement Information
I85. Sch. 3 para. 85 in force at 1.9.2014 by S.I. 2014/889, art. 7. (a)
86. In section 78. (1) (Part 2: supplementary), in the definition of "relevant young adult"—
(a) for "a learning difficulty" substitute " special educational needs (within the meaning given by section 579. (1) of the Education Act 1996) ", and
(b) omit the words from "and subsections (6) and (7)" to the end.
Commencement Information
I86. Sch. 3 para. 86 in force at 1.9.2014 by S.I. 2014/889, art. 7. (a)
87. In section 132 (providers of independent education or training for 16 to 18 year olds)—
(a) in subsection (4)(a), for the words from "a statement" to "needs" substitute " an EHC plan is maintained ",
(b) in subsection (4)(b), for "a statement was so" substitute " an EHC plan was ",
(c) in subsection (4)(b)(i), after "school" insert " or (if later) the person ceased to be a student at

his or her last post-16 institution ",
(d) in subsection (4)(b)(ii), after "institution" insert " in England mentioned in subsection (2) ", and
(e) in subsection (6), after the definition of "an academic year" insert—
""post-16 institution" has the meaning given by section 83. (2) of the Children and Families Act 2014;".
Commencement Information
I87. Sch. 3 para. 87 in force at 1.9.2014 by S.I. 2014/889, art. 7. (a)

Apprenticeships, Skills, Children and Learning Act 2009 (c. 22)

88. The Apprenticeships, Skills, Children and Learning Act 2009 is amended as follows.
Commencement Information
I88. Sch. 3 para. 88 in force at 1.9.2014 by S.I. 2014/889, art. 7. (a)
89. In section 83 (power to secure provision of apprenticeship training)—
(a) in subsection (1)(b), for "are subject to learning difficulty assessment" substitute " for whom an EHC plan is maintained ",
(b) in subsection (2)(b), for "learning difficulties" substitute " special educational needs ", and
(c) omit subsection (4).
Commencement Information
I89. Sch. 3 para. 89 in force at 1.9.2014 by S.I. 2014/889, art. 7. (a)
90. In section 86 (education and training for persons aged 19 or over etc), in subsection (1)(a), for "who are subject to learning difficulty assessment" substitute " for whom an EHC plan is maintained ".
Commencement Information
I90. Sch. 3 para. 90 in force at 1.9.2014 by S.I. 2014/889, art. 7. (a)
91. In section 87 (learning aims for persons aged 19 or over: provision of facilities), in subsection (3)(a), for "who are subject to learning difficulty assessment" substitute " for whom an EHC plan is maintained ".
Commencement Information
I91. Sch. 3 para. 91 in force at 1.9.2014 by S.I. 2014/889, art. 7. (a)
92. In section 101 (financial resources: conditions), in subsection (5)(f)—
(a) after "specified in" insert " an EHC plan or ", and
(b) omit "139. A or".
Commencement Information
I92. Sch. 3 para. 92 in force at 1.9.2014 by S.I. 2014/889, art. 7. (a)
93. In section 115 (persons with learning difficulties)—
(a) in subsection (1), for "learning difficulties" substitute " special educational needs ",
(b) in subsection (2)(a), for "who are subject to learning difficulty assessment" substitute " for whom an EHC plan is maintained ",
(c) omit subsections (3) and (4), and
(d) in the title, for "learning difficulties" substitute " special educational needs ".
Commencement Information
I93. Sch. 3 para. 93 in force at 1.9.2014 by S.I. 2014/889, art. 7. (a)
94. In section 129 (general duties of Ofqual)—
(a) in subsection (2)(b) and (c), for "learning difficulties" substitute " special educational needs ", and
(b) omit subsections (9) and (10).
Commencement Information
I94. Sch. 3 para. 94 in force at 1.9.2014 by S.I. 2014/889, art. 7. (a)

Academies Act 2010 (c. 32)

95. In section 1 of the Academies Act 2010 (Academy arrangements), omit subsections (7) and (8).
Commencement Information
I95. Sch. 3 para. 95 in force at 1.9.2014 by S.I. 2014/889, art. 7. (a)

Legal Aid, Sentencing and Punishment of Offenders Act 2012 (c. 10)

96. In paragraph 2 of Schedule 1 to the Legal Aid, Sentencing and Punishment of Offenders Act 2012 (civil legal services: special educational needs)—
(a) in sub-paragraph (1)(a), after "1996" insert " or Part 3 of the Children and Families Act 2014 ", and
(b) in sub-paragraph (1)(b), for "sections 139. A and" substitute " section ".
Commencement Information
I96. Sch. 3 para. 96 in force at 1.9.2014 by S.I. 2014/889, art. 7. (a)

Schedule 4. Childminder agencies: amendments

Section 84

PART 1 The childcare registers

1. The Childcare Act 2006 is amended as follows.
Commencement Information
I1. Sch. 4 para. 1 in force at 1.4.2014 for specified purposes by S.I. 2014/889, art. 3. (m)
I2. Sch. 4 para. 1 in force at 1.9.2014 in so far as not already in force by S.I. 2014/889, art. 7. (e)
2. (1)Section 32 (childcare registration in England: maintenance of the two childcare registers) is amended as follows.
(2) In subsection (2)—
(a) after "register of" insert "—
   (a) ",
(b) omit "who are", and
(c) for "under Chapter 2" substitute " by the Chief Inspector for the purposes of Chapter 2 ".
(3) At the end of that subsection insert ", and
   (b) all persons registered as early years childminder agencies under Chapter 2. A (which provides for the compulsory registration of persons with whom early years childminders and certain other early years providers may register for the purposes of Chapter 2)."
(4) In subsection (4)—
(a) after "register of" insert "—
   (a) ",
(b) omit "who are", and
(c) for "under Chapter 3" substitute " by the Chief Inspector for the purposes of Chapter 3 ".
(5) At the end of that subsection insert ", and
   (b) all persons registered as later years childminder agencies under Chapter 3. A (which provides for the compulsory registration of persons with whom later years childminders and certain other later years providers may register for the purposes of Chapter 3)."
(6) In subsection (5), for "under Chapter 4" substitute " by the Chief Inspector for the purposes of Chapter 4 ".
Commencement Information

I3. Sch. 4 para. 2 in force at 1.4.2014 for specified purposes by S.I. 2014/889, art. 3. (m)
I4. Sch. 4 para. 2 in force at 1.9.2014 in so far as not already in force by S.I. 2014/889, art. 7. (e)

PART 2 Early years childminder agencies

3. The Childcare Act 2006 is amended as follows.
Commencement Information
I5. Sch. 4 para. 3 in force at 1.4.2014 for specified purposes by S.I. 2014/889, art. 3. (m)
I6. Sch. 4 para. 3 in force at 1.9.2014 in so far as not already in force by S.I. 2014/889, art. 7. (e)
4. In section 33 (requirement to register: early years childminders), in subsection (1) for "in the early years register as an early years childminder" substitute "as an early years childminder—
    (a) in the early years register, or
    (b) with an early years childminder agency."
Commencement Information
I7. Sch. 4 para. 4 in force at 1.4.2014 for specified purposes by S.I. 2014/889, art. 3. (m)
I8. Sch. 4 para. 4 in force at 1.9.2014 in so far as not already in force by S.I. 2014/889, art. 7. (e)
5. (1)Section 34 (requirement to register: other early years providers) is amended as follows.
(2) For subsection (1) substitute—
"(1)A person may not provide early years provision on premises in England which are not domestic premises unless the person is registered in the early years register in respect of the premises.
(1. A)A person may not provide early years provision on domestic premises in England which would be early years childminding but for section 96. (5) unless the person is registered—
    (a) in the early years register in respect of the premises, or
    (b) with an early years childminder agency in respect of the premises."
(3) In subsection (2) for "Subsection (1) does" substitute " Subsections (1) and (1. A) do ".
(4) In subsection (3) for "subsection (1) does" substitute " subsections (1) and (1. A) do ".
(5) In subsection (5) after "subsection (1)" insert " or (1. A) ".
Commencement Information
I9. Sch. 4 para. 5 in force at 1.4.2014 for specified purposes by S.I. 2014/889, art. 3. (m)
I10. Sch. 4 para. 5 in force at 1.9.2014 in so far as not already in force by S.I. 2014/889, art. 7. (e)
6. (1)Section 35 (applications for registration: early years childminders) is amended as follows.
(2) In subsection (1) for "to the Chief Inspector for registration as an early years childminder" substitute "—
    (a) to the Chief Inspector for registration as an early years childminder in the early years register, or
    (b) to an early years childminder agency for registration with that agency as an early years childminder."
(3) In subsection (2)—
(a) in paragraph (b) after "Chief Inspector" insert " or (as the case may be) the early years childminder agency ", and
(b) in paragraph (c) at the beginning insert " if it is an application to the Chief Inspector, ".
(4) In subsections (3) and (4), after "subsection (1)" insert " (a) ".
(5) After subsection (4) insert—
"(4. A)An early years childminder agency may grant an application under subsection (1)(b) only if—
    (a) the applicant is not disqualified from registration by regulations under section 75,
    (b) it appears to the agency that the prescribed requirements for registration are satisfied and are likely to continue to be satisfied, and
    (c) it appears to the agency that any other reasonable requirements it has imposed are satisfied and are likely to continue to be satisfied."
(6) In subsection (5), after paragraph (a) insert—

"(aa) prohibiting the applicant from being registered in the early years register as an early years childminder if the applicant is registered with a childminder agency;

(ab) prohibiting the applicant from being registered with an early years childminder agency as an early years childminder if the applicant is registered—

(i) with another childminder agency;

(ii) in the early years register or the general childcare register;".

Commencement Information

I11. Sch. 4 para. 6 in force at 1.4.2014 for specified purposes by S.I. 2014/889, art. 3. (m)

I12. Sch. 4 para. 6 in force at 1.9.2014 in so far as not already in force by S.I. 2014/889, art. 7. (e)

7. (1) Section 36 (applications for registration: other early years providers) is amended as follows.

(2) After subsection (1) insert—

"(1. A) A person who proposes to provide on any premises early years provision in respect of which the person is required by section 34. (1. A) to be registered may make an application—

(a) to the Chief Inspector for registration as an early years provider in respect of the premises, or

(b) to an early years childminder agency for registration with that agency as an early years provider in respect of the premises."

(3) In subsection (2)—

(a) after "subsection (1)" insert " or (1. A) ",

(b) in paragraph (b) after "Chief Inspector" insert " or (as the case may be) the early years childminder agency ", and

(c) in paragraph (c) at the beginning insert " if it is an application to the Chief Inspector, ".

(4) In subsections (3) and (4), after "subsection (1)" insert " or (1. A)(a) ".

(5) After subsection (4) insert—

"(4. A) An early years childminder agency may grant an application under subsection (1. A)(b) only if—

(a) the applicant is not disqualified from registration by regulations under section 75,

(b) it appears to the agency that the prescribed requirements for registration are satisfied and are likely to continue to be satisfied, and

(c) it appears to the agency that any other reasonable requirements it has imposed are satisfied and are likely to continue to be satisfied."

(6) In subsection (5), after paragraph (a) insert—

"(aa) prohibiting the applicant from being registered in the early years register as an early years provider other than a childminder if the applicant is registered with a childminder agency;

(ab) prohibiting the applicant from being registered with an early years childminder agency as an early years provider other than a childminder if the applicant is registered—

(i) with another childminder agency;

(ii) in the early years register or the general childcare register;".

Commencement Information

I13. Sch. 4 para. 7 in force at 1.4.2014 for specified purposes by S.I. 2014/889, art. 3. (m)

I14. Sch. 4 para. 7 in force at 1.9.2014 in so far as not already in force by S.I. 2014/889, art. 7. (e)

8. (1) Section 37 (entry on the register and certificates) is amended as follows.

(2) In subsection (1) after "section 35. (1)" insert " (a) ".

(3) In subsection (2) after "section 36. (1)" insert " or (1. A)(a) ".

Commencement Information

I15. Sch. 4 para. 8 in force at 1.4.2014 for specified purposes by S.I. 2014/889, art. 3. (m)

I16. Sch. 4 para. 8 in force at 1.9.2014 in so far as not already in force by S.I. 2014/889, art. 7. (e)

9. After section 37 insert—

"37. A Early years childminder agencies: registers and certificates

(1) If an application under section 35. (1)(b) is granted, the early years childminder agency must—

(a) register the applicant in the register maintained by the agency as an early years childminder, and

(b) give the applicant a certificate of registration stating that he or she is so registered.

(2) If an application under section 36. (1. A)(b) is granted, the early years childminder agency must—

(a) register the applicant in the register maintained by the agency as an early years provider other than a childminder, in respect of the premises in question, and

(b) give the applicant a certificate of registration stating that he or she is so registered.

(3) A certificate of registration given to the applicant in pursuance of subsection (1) or (2) must contain prescribed information about prescribed matters.

(4) If there is a change of circumstances which requires the amendment of a certificate of registration, the early years childminder agency must give the registered early years provider an amended certificate."

Commencement Information

I17. Sch. 4 para. 9 in force at 1.4.2014 for specified purposes by S.I. 2014/889, art. 3. (m)

I18. Sch. 4 para. 9 in force at 1.9.2014 in so far as not already in force by S.I. 2014/889, art. 7. (e)

10. In section 38 (conditions on registration), in subsections (1) and (5) for "under this Chapter" substitute " in the early years register ".

Commencement Information

I19. Sch. 4 para. 10 in force at 1.4.2014 for specified purposes by S.I. 2014/889, art. 3. (m)

I20. Sch. 4 para. 10 in force at 1.9.2014 in so far as not already in force by S.I. 2014/889, art. 7. (e)

11. (1)Section 44 (instruments specifying learning and development or welfare requirements) is amended as follows.

(2) In subsection (2)—

(a) after "Chief Inspector" insert " or early years childminder agencies ", and

(b) omit "his".

(3) In subsection (3) after "Chief Inspector" insert " or early years childminder agencies ".

(4) In subsection (4) after paragraph (a) (and before the "or" which follows it) insert—

"(aa)by early years childminder agencies in the exercise of functions under this Part,".

Commencement Information

I21. Sch. 4 para. 11 in force at 1.4.2014 for specified purposes by S.I. 2014/889, art. 3. (m)

I22. Sch. 4 para. 11 in force at 1.9.2014 in so far as not already in force by S.I. 2014/889, art. 7. (e)

12. In section 49 (inspections), in subsection (1) for "under this Chapter" substitute " in the early years register ".

Commencement Information

I23. Sch. 4 para. 12 in force at 1.4.2014 for specified purposes by S.I. 2014/889, art. 3. (m)

I24. Sch. 4 para. 12 in force at 1.9.2014 in so far as not already in force by S.I. 2014/889, art. 7. (e)

13. After Chapter 2 (regulation of early years provision) insert—

"CHAPTER 2. ARegulation of early years childminder agencies

Process of registration

51. AApplications for registration

(1) A person may make an application to the Chief Inspector for registration as an early years childminder agency.

(2) An application under subsection (1) must—

(a) give any prescribed information about prescribed matters,

(b) give any other information which the Chief Inspector reasonably requires the applicant to give, and

(c) be accompanied by any prescribed fee.

(3) The Chief Inspector must grant an application under subsection (1) if—
    (a) the applicant is not disqualified from registration by regulations under section 76. A, and
    (b) it appears to the Chief Inspector that any requirements prescribed for the purposes of this subsection ("the prescribed requirements for registration") are satisfied and are likely to continue to be satisfied.
(4) The Chief Inspector must refuse any application under subsection (1) which subsection (3) does not require the Chief Inspector to grant.
(5) The prescribed requirements for registration may include requirements relating to—
    (a) the applicant;
    (b) any persons employed by the applicant;
    (c) management and control of the applicant (where the applicant is not an individual);
    (d) the provision to the Chief Inspector of information about early years providers registered with the applicant;
    (e) the applicant's arrangements for registering early years providers;
    (f) the applicant's arrangements in relation to training and monitoring early years providers and providing such persons with information, advice and assistance;
    (g) the applicant's arrangements for ensuring that early years provision is of a sufficient standard.

51. BEntry on the register and certificates
(1) If an application under section 51. A is granted, the Chief Inspector must—
    (a) register the applicant in the early years register as an early years childminder agency, and
    (b) give the applicant a certificate of registration stating that the applicant is so registered.
(2) A certificate of registration given to the applicant in pursuance of subsection (1) must contain prescribed information about prescribed matters.
(3) If there is a change of circumstances which requires the amendment of a certificate of registration, the Chief Inspector must give the early years childminder agency an amended certificate.
(4) If the Chief Inspector is satisfied that a certificate of registration has been lost or destroyed, the Chief Inspector must give the early years childminder agency a copy, on payment by the agency of any prescribed fee.

51. CConditions on registration
(1) The Chief Inspector may impose such conditions as the Chief Inspector thinks fit on the registration of an early years childminder agency under this Chapter.
(2) The power conferred by subsection (1) may be exercised at the time when the Chief Inspector registers the person in pursuance of section 51. B or at any subsequent time.
(3) The Chief Inspector may at any time vary or remove any condition imposed under subsection (1).
(4) An early years childminder agency commits an offence if, without reasonable excuse, the agency fails to comply with any condition imposed under subsection (1).
(5) A person guilty of an offence under subsection (4) is liable on summary conviction to a fine not exceeding level 5 on the standard scale.

Inspections
51. DInspections of early years childminder agencies
(1) The Chief Inspector—
    (a) must inspect an early years childminder agency at any time when the Secretary of State requires the Chief Inspector to secure its inspection, and
    (b) may inspect an early years childminder agency at any other time when the Chief Inspector considers that it would be appropriate for it to be inspected.
(2) For the purposes of an inspection under this section, the Chief Inspector may inspect early years provision provided by early years providers who are registered with the early years childminder agency for the purposes of Chapter 2.
(3) The Chief Inspector may charge a prescribed fee for conducting an inspection of an early years childminder agency where—

(a) the inspection is conducted at the request of the agency, and

(b) the Chief Inspector is required by the Secretary of State under subsection (1)(a) to conduct that inspection.

(4) Regulations may make provision requiring an early years childminder agency to notify prescribed persons of the fact that it is to be inspected under this section.

51. EReports of inspections

(1) After conducting an inspection under section 51. D, the Chief Inspector must make a report in writing on—

(a) the quality and standards of the services offered by the early years childminder agency to early years providers registered with it,

(b) the quality of leadership and management in the early years childminder agency, and

(c) the effectiveness of the arrangements of the early years childminder agency for assuring itself of the quality of the care and education provided by the early years providers registered with it.

(2) The Chief Inspector—

(a) may send a copy of the report to the Secretary of State and must do so without delay if the Secretary of State requests a copy,

(b) must ensure that a copy of the report is sent without delay to the early years childminder agency,

(c) must ensure that copies of the report, or such parts of it as the Chief Inspector considers appropriate, are sent to such other persons as may be prescribed, and

(d) may arrange for the report (or parts of it) to be further published in any manner the Chief Inspector considers appropriate.

(3) Regulations may make provision—

(a) requiring the early years childminder agency to make a copy of any report sent to it under subsection (2)(b) available for inspection by prescribed persons;

(b) requiring the agency, except in prescribed cases, to provide a copy of the report to prescribed persons;

(c) authorising the agency in prescribed cases to charge a fee for providing a copy of the report.

False representations

51. FFalse representations

(1) A person who without reasonable excuse falsely represents that the person is an early years childminder agency commits an offence.

(2) A person guilty of an offence under subsection (1) is liable on summary conviction to a fine not exceeding level 5 on the standard scale."

Commencement Information

I25. Sch. 4 para. 13 in force at 1.4.2014 for specified purposes by S.I. 2014/889, art. 3. (m)

I26. Sch. 4 para. 13 in force at 1.9.2014 in so far as not already in force by S.I. 2014/889, art. 7. (e)

PART 3 Later years childminder agencies

14. The Childcare Act 2006 is amended as follows.

Commencement Information

I27. Sch. 4 para. 14 in force at 1.4.2014 for specified purposes by S.I. 2014/889, art. 3. (m)

I28. Sch. 4 para. 14 in force at 1.9.2014 in so far as not already in force by S.I. 2014/889, art. 7. (e)

15. In section 52 (requirement to register: later years childminders for children under 8), in subsection (1) for "in Part A of the general childcare register as a childminder" substitute "as a later years childminder—

(a) in Part A of the general childcare register, or

(b) with a later years childminder agency."

Commencement Information

I29. Sch. 4 para. 15 in force at 1.4.2014 for specified purposes by S.I. 2014/889, art. 3. (m)
I30. Sch. 4 para. 15 in force at 1.9.2014 in so far as not already in force by S.I. 2014/889, art. 7. (e)

16. (1)Section 53 (requirement to register: other later years providers for children under 8) is amended as follows.
(2) For subsection (1) substitute—
"(1)A person may not provide, for a child who has not attained the age of eight, later years provision on premises in England which are not domestic premises unless the person is registered in Part A of the general childcare register in respect of the premises.
(1. A)A person may not provide, for a child who has not attained the age of eight, later years provision on domestic premises in England which would be later years childminding but for section 96. (9) unless the person is registered—
    (a) in Part A of the general childcare register in respect of the premises, or
    (b) with a later years childminder agency in respect of the premises."
(3) In subsection (2) for "Subsection (1) does" substitute " Subsections (1) and (1. A) do ".
(4) In subsection (3) for "subsection (1) does" substitute " subsections (1) and (1. A) do ".
(5) In subsection (5) after "subsection (1)" insert " or (1. A) ".

Commencement Information

I31. Sch. 4 para. 16 in force at 1.4.2014 for specified purposes by S.I. 2014/889, art. 3. (m)
I32. Sch. 4 para. 16 in force at 1.9.2014 in so far as not already in force by S.I. 2014/889, art. 7. (e)

17. (1)Section 54 (applications for registration: later years childminders) is amended as follows.
(2) In subsection (1) for "to the Chief Inspector for registration as a later years childminder" substitute "—
    (a) to the Chief Inspector for registration as a later years childminder in Part A of the general childcare register, or
    (b) to a later years childminder agency for registration with that agency as a later years childminder."
(3) In subsection (2)—
(a) in paragraph (b) after "Chief Inspector" insert " or (as the case may be) the later years childminder agency ", and
(b) in paragraph (c) at the beginning insert " if it is an application to the Chief Inspector, ".
(4) In subsections (3) and (4), after "subsection (1)" insert " (a) ".
(5) After subsection (4) insert—
"(4. A)A later years childminder agency may grant an application under subsection (1)(b) only if—
    (a) the applicant is not disqualified from registration by regulations under section 75,
    (b) it appears to the agency that the prescribed requirements for registration are satisfied and are likely to continue to be satisfied, and
    (c) it appears to the agency that any other reasonable requirements it has imposed are satisfied and are likely to continue to be satisfied."
(6) In subsection (5), after paragraph (a) insert—
"(aa)prohibiting the applicant from being registered in Part A of the general childcare register as a later years childminder if the applicant is registered with a childminder agency;
(ab) prohibiting the applicant from being registered with a later years childminder agency as a later years childminder if the applicant is registered—
(i) with another childminder agency;
(ii) in the early years register or the general childcare register;".

Commencement Information

I33. Sch. 4 para. 17 in force at 1.4.2014 for specified purposes by S.I. 2014/889, art. 3. (m)
I34. Sch. 4 para. 17 in force at 1.9.2014 in so far as not already in force by S.I. 2014/889, art. 7. (e)

18. (1) Section 55 (applications for registration: other later years providers) is amended as follows.
(2) After subsection (1) insert—
"(1. A) A person who proposes to provide on any premises later years provision in respect of which the person is required by section 53. (1. A) to be registered may make an application—
    (a) to the Chief Inspector for registration as a later years provider in respect of the premises, or
    (b) to a later years childminder agency for registration with that agency as a later years provider in respect of the premises."
(3) In subsection (2)—
(a) after "subsection (1)" insert " or (1. A) ",
(b) in paragraph (b) after "Chief Inspector" insert " or (as the case may be) the later years childminder agency ", and
(c) in paragraph (c) at the beginning insert " if it is an application to the Chief Inspector, ".
(4) In subsections (3) and (4), after "subsection (1)" insert " or (1. A)(a) ".
(5) After subsection (4) insert—
"(4. A) A later years childminder agency may grant an application under subsection (1. A)(b) only if—
    (a) the applicant is not disqualified from registration by regulations under section 75,
    (b) it appears to the agency that the prescribed requirements for registration are satisfied and are likely to continue to be satisfied, and
    (c) it appears to the agency that any other reasonable requirements it has imposed are satisfied and are likely to continue to be satisfied."
(6) In subsection (5), after paragraph (a) insert—
"(aa) prohibiting the applicant from being registered in Part A of the general childcare register as a later years provider other than a childminder if the applicant is registered with a childminder agency;
(ab) prohibiting the applicant from being registered with a later years childminder agency as a later years provider other than a childminder if the applicant is registered—
(i) with another childminder agency;
(ii) in the early years register or the general childcare register;".
Commencement Information
I35. Sch. 4 para. 18 in force at 1.4.2014 for specified purposes by S.I. 2014/889, art. 3. (m)
I36. Sch. 4 para. 18 in force at 1.9.2014 in so far as not already in force by S.I. 2014/889, art. 7. (e)
19. (1) Section 56 (entry on the register and certificates) is amended as follows.
(2) In subsection (1) after "section 54. (1)" insert " (a) ".
(3) In subsection (2) after "section 55. (1)" insert " or (1. A)(a) ".
Commencement Information
I37. Sch. 4 para. 19 in force at 1.4.2014 for specified purposes by S.I. 2014/889, art. 3. (m)
I38. Sch. 4 para. 19 in force at 1.9.2014 in so far as not already in force by S.I. 2014/889, art. 7. (e)
20. After section 56 insert—

"56. A Later years childminder agencies: registers and certificates

(1) If an application under section 54. (1)(b) is granted, the later years childminder agency must—
    (a) register the applicant in the register maintained by the agency as a later years childminder, and
    (b) give the applicant a certificate of registration stating that he or she is so registered.
(2) If an application under section 55. (1. A)(b) is granted, the later years childminder agency must—
    (a) register the applicant in the register maintained by the agency as a later years provider other than a childminder, in respect of the premises in question, and

(b) give the applicant a certificate of registration stating that he or she is so registered.

(3) A certificate of registration given to the applicant in pursuance of subsection (1) or (2) must contain prescribed information about prescribed matters.

(4) If there is a change of circumstances which requires the amendment of a certificate of registration, the later years childminder agency must give the registered later years provider an amended certificate."

Commencement Information

I39. Sch. 4 para. 20 in force at 1.4.2014 for specified purposes by S.I. 2014/889, art. 3. (m)

I40. Sch. 4 para. 20 in force at 1.9.2014 in so far as not already in force by S.I. 2014/889, art. 7. (e)

21. In section 57 (special procedure for registered early years providers), in the title for "registered early years providers" substitute " providers registered in the early years register ".

Commencement Information

I41. Sch. 4 para. 21 in force at 1.4.2014 for specified purposes by S.I. 2014/889, art. 3. (m)

I42. Sch. 4 para. 21 in force at 1.9.2014 in so far as not already in force by S.I. 2014/889, art. 7. (e)

22. After section 57 insert—

"57. ASpecial procedure for providers registered with early years childminder agencies

(1) Subsection (2) applies where—

(a) a person is registered with an early years childminder agency as an early years childminder, and

(b) that agency is also a later years childminder agency.

(2) If the person gives notice to the agency that he or she proposes to provide later years childminding in respect of which he or she is required to be registered under this Chapter, the agency must—

(a) register the person in the register maintained by the agency as a later years childminder, and

(b) give the person a certificate of registration stating that he or she is so registered.

(3) Subsection (4) applies where—

(a) a person is registered with an early years childminder agency in respect of particular premises as an early years provider other than a childminder, and

(b) that agency is also a later years childminder agency.

(4) If the person gives notice to the agency that he or she proposes to provide later years provision in respect of which he or she is required to be registered under this Chapter on the same premises, the agency must—

(a) register the person in the register maintained by the agency as a later years provider other than a childminder, in respect of the premises, and

(b) give the person a certificate of registration stating that he or she is so registered.

(5) Subsections (3) and (4) of section 56. A apply in relation to a certificate of registration given in pursuance of subsection (2) or (4) of this section as they apply in relation to a certificate of registration given in pursuance of subsection (1) or (2) of that section."

Commencement Information

I43. Sch. 4 para. 22 in force at 1.4.2014 for specified purposes by S.I. 2014/889, art. 3. (m)

I44. Sch. 4 para. 22 in force at 1.9.2014 in so far as not already in force by S.I. 2014/889, art. 7. (e)

23. In section 58 (conditions on registration), in subsections (1) and (5) for "under this Chapter" substitute " in Part A of the general childcare register ".

Commencement Information

I45. Sch. 4 para. 23 in force at 1.4.2014 for specified purposes by S.I. 2014/889, art. 3. (m)

I46. Sch. 4 para. 23 in force at 1.9.2014 in so far as not already in force by S.I. 2014/889, art. 7.

(e)

24.—(1) Section 59 (regulations governing activities) is amended as follows.

(2) In subsection (4)—

(a) after "Chief Inspector" insert " or later years childminder agencies ", and

(b) omit "his".

(3) In subsection (5)—

(a) after "Chief Inspector" insert " or later years childminder agencies ", and

(b) omit "his".

(4) In subsection (6) after paragraph (a) (and before the "or" which follows it) insert—

"(aa) by later years childminder agencies in the exercise of functions under this Part,".

Commencement Information

I47. Sch. 4 para. 24 in force at 1.4.2014 for specified purposes by S.I. 2014/889, art. 3. (m)

I48. Sch. 4 para. 24 in force at 1.9.2014 in so far as not already in force by S.I. 2014/889, art. 7. (e)

25. In section 60 (inspections), in subsection (1) for "under this Chapter" substitute " in Part A of the general childcare register ".

Commencement Information

I49. Sch. 4 para. 25 in force at 1.4.2014 for specified purposes by S.I. 2014/889, art. 3. (m)

I50. Sch. 4 para. 25 in force at 1.9.2014 in so far as not already in force by S.I. 2014/889, art. 7. (e)

26. After Chapter 3 (regulation of later years provision for children under 8) insert—

"CHAPTER 3. A Regulation of later years childminder agencies

Process of registration

61. A Applications for registration

(1) A person may make an application to the Chief Inspector for registration as a later years childminder agency.

(2) An application under subsection (1) must—

(a) give any prescribed information about prescribed matters,

(b) give any other information which the Chief Inspector reasonably requires the applicant to give, and

(c) be accompanied by any prescribed fee.

(3) The Chief Inspector must grant an application under subsection (1) if—

(a) the applicant is not disqualified from registration by regulations under section 76. A, and

(b) it appears to the Chief Inspector that any requirements prescribed for the purposes of this subsection ("the prescribed requirements for registration") are satisfied and are likely to continue to be satisfied.

(4) The Chief Inspector must refuse any application under subsection (1) which subsection (3) does not require the Chief Inspector to grant.

(5) The prescribed requirements for registration may include requirements relating to—

(a) the applicant;

(b) any persons employed by the applicant;

(c) management and control of the applicant (where the applicant is not an individual);

(d) the provision to the Chief Inspector of information about later years providers registered with the applicant;

(e) the applicant's arrangements for registering later years providers;

(f) the applicant's arrangements in relation to training and monitoring later years providers, and providing such persons with information, advice and assistance;

(g) the applicant's arrangements for ensuring that later years provision is of a sufficient standard.

61. B Entry on the register and certificates

(1) If an application under section 61.A is granted, the Chief Inspector must—

(a) register the applicant in Part A of the general childcare register as a later years childminder agency, and

(b) give the applicant a certificate of registration stating that the applicant is so registered.

(2) A certificate of registration given to the applicant in pursuance of subsection (1) must contain prescribed information about prescribed matters.

(3) If there is a change of circumstances which requires the amendment of a certificate of registration, the Chief Inspector must give the later years childminder agency an amended certificate.

(4) If the Chief Inspector is satisfied that a certificate of registration has been lost or destroyed, the Chief Inspector must give the later years childminder agency a copy, on payment by the agency of any prescribed fee.

61.C Special procedure for registered early years childminder agencies

(1) If an early years childminder agency gives notice to the Chief Inspector of a wish to be a later years childminder agency the Chief Inspector must—

(a) register the early years childminder agency in Part A of the general childcare register as a later years childminder agency, and

(b) give the agency a certificate of registration stating that it is so registered.

(2) Subsections (2) to (4) of section 61.B apply in relation to a certificate of registration given in pursuance of subsection (1) of this section as they apply in relation to a certificate of registration given in pursuance of subsection (1) of that section.

61.D Conditions on registration

(1) The Chief Inspector may impose such conditions as the Chief Inspector thinks fit on the registration of a later years childminder agency under this Chapter.

(2) The power conferred by subsection (1) may be exercised at the time when the Chief Inspector registers the person in pursuance of section 61.B or 61.C or at any subsequent time.

(3) The Chief Inspector may at any time vary or remove any condition imposed under subsection (1).

(4) A later years childminder agency commits an offence if, without reasonable excuse, the agency fails to comply with any condition imposed under subsection (1).

(5) A person guilty of an offence under subsection (4) is liable on summary conviction to a fine not exceeding level 5 on the standard scale.

Inspections

61.E Inspections of later years childminder agencies

(1) The Chief Inspector—

(a) must inspect a later years childminder agency at any time when the Secretary of State requires the Chief Inspector to secure its inspection, and

(b) may inspect a later years childminder agency at any other time when the Chief Inspector considers that it would be appropriate for it to be inspected.

(2) For the purposes of an inspection under this section, the Chief Inspector may inspect later years provision provided by later years providers who are registered with the later years childminder agency for the purposes of Chapter 3.

(3) The Chief Inspector may charge a prescribed fee for conducting an inspection of a later years childminder agency where—

(a) the inspection is conducted at the request of the agency, and

(b) the Chief Inspector is required by the Secretary of State under subsection (1)(a) to conduct that inspection.

(4) Regulations may make provision requiring a later years childminder agency to notify prescribed persons of the fact that it is to be inspected under this section.

61.F Reports of inspections

(1) After conducting an inspection under section 61.E, the Chief Inspector must make a report in writing on—

(a) the quality and standards of the services offered by the later years childminder agency to later years providers registered with it,

(b) the quality of leadership and management in the later years childminder agency, and

(c) the effectiveness of the arrangements of the later years childminder agency for assuring itself of the quality of the care and education provided by the later years providers registered with it.

(2) The Chief Inspector—

(a) may send a copy of the report to the Secretary of State and must do so without delay if the Secretary of State requests a copy,

(b) must ensure that a copy of the report is sent without delay to the later years childminder agency,

(c) must ensure that copies of the report, or such parts of it as the Chief Inspector considers appropriate, are sent to such other persons as may be prescribed, and

(d) may arrange for the report (or parts of it) to be further published in any manner the Chief Inspector considers appropriate.

(3) Regulations may make provision—

(a) requiring the later years childminder agency to make a copy of any report sent to it under subsection (2)(b) available for inspection by prescribed persons;

(b) requiring the agency, except in prescribed cases, to provide a copy of the report to prescribed persons;

(c) authorising the agency in prescribed cases to charge a fee for providing a copy of the report.

False representations

61. GFalse representations

(1) A person who without reasonable excuse falsely represents that the person is a later years childminder agency commits an offence.

(2) A person guilty of an offence under subsection (1) is liable on summary conviction to a fine not exceeding level 5 on the standard scale."

Commencement Information

I51. Sch. 4 para. 26 in force at 1.4.2014 for specified purposes by S.I. 2014/889, art. 3. (m)

I52. Sch. 4 para. 26 in force at 1.9.2014 in so far as not already in force by S.I. 2014/889, art. 7. (e)

PART 4 Voluntary registration with childminder agency

27. The Childcare Act 2006 is amended as follows.

Commencement Information

I53. Sch. 4 para. 27 in force at 1.4.2014 for specified purposes by S.I. 2014/889, art. 3. (m)

I54. Sch. 4 para. 27 in force at 1.9.2014 in so far as not already in force by S.I. 2014/889, art. 7. (e)

28. In section 65 (special procedure for persons already registered), in the title, at the end insert " in a childcare register ".

Commencement Information

I55. Sch. 4 para. 28 in force at 1.4.2014 for specified purposes by S.I. 2014/889, art. 3. (m)

I56. Sch. 4 para. 28 in force at 1.9.2014 in so far as not already in force by S.I. 2014/889, art. 7. (e)

29. After section 65 insert—

65. AProcedure for persons already registered with a childminder agency

(1) A person who is registered as an early years childminder with an early years childminder agency or as a later years childminder with a later years childminder agency may give notice to the agency that he or she wishes to be registered with the agency in respect of the provision in England of—

(a) later years childminding for a child who has attained the age of eight;

(b) early years childminding or later years childminding for a child who has not attained that age but in respect of which the person is not required to be registered under Chapter 2 or 3.

(2) If a person gives notice to an agency under subsection (1), the agency must—
(a) register the person in the register maintained by the agency as a childminder registered under this Chapter, and
(b) give the person a certificate of registration stating that he or she is so registered.
(3) A person who is registered as an early years provider (other than a childminder) with an early years childminder agency or as a later years provider (other than a childminder) with a later years childminder agency in respect of particular premises may give notice to the agency that he or she wishes to be registered with the agency in respect of the provision on the same premises of—
(a) later years provision (other than later years childminding) for a child who has attained the age of eight;
(b) early years provision or later years provision (other than early years or later years childminding) for a child who has not attained that age but in respect of which the person is not required to be registered under Chapter 2 or 3.
(4) If a person gives notice to an agency under subsection (3), the agency must—
(a) register the person in the register maintained by the agency as a provider of childcare (other than a childminder) registered under this Chapter, in respect of the premises, and
(b) give the person a certificate of registration stating that he or she is so registered.
(5) A certificate of registration given to the applicant in pursuance of subsection (2) or (4) must contain prescribed information about prescribed matters.
(6) If there is a change of circumstances which requires the amendment of a certificate of registration, the agency must give the registered person an amended certificate."

Commencement Information

I57. Sch. 4 para. 29 in force at 1.4.2014 for specified purposes by S.I. 2014/889, art. 3. (m)
I58. Sch. 4 para. 29 in force at 1.9.2014 in so far as not already in force by S.I. 2014/889, art. 7. (e)

30. In section 66 (conditions on registration), in subsections (1) and (5) for "under this Chapter" substitute " in Part B of the general childcare register ".

Commencement Information

I59. Sch. 4 para. 30 in force at 1.4.2014 for specified purposes by S.I. 2014/889, art. 3. (m)
I60. Sch. 4 para. 30 in force at 1.9.2014 in so far as not already in force by S.I. 2014/889, art. 7. (e)

31. (1) Section 67 (regulations governing activities) is amended as follows.
(2) In subsection (4)—
(a) after "Chief Inspector" insert " , early years childminder agencies or later years childminder agencies ", and
(b) omit "his".
(3) In subsection (5)—
(a) after "Chief Inspector" insert " , early years childminder agencies or later years childminder agencies ", and
(b) omit "his".
(4) In subsection (6) after paragraph (a) (and before the "or" which follows it) insert—
"(aa) by early years childminder agencies or later years childminder agencies in the exercise of functions under this Part,".

Commencement Information

I61. Sch. 4 para. 31 in force at 1.4.2014 for specified purposes by S.I. 2014/889, art. 3. (m)
I62. Sch. 4 para. 31 in force at 1.9.2014 in so far as not already in force by S.I. 2014/889, art. 7. (e)

PART 5 Provisions applying in relation to all childminder agencies

32. The Childcare Act 2006 is amended as follows.

Commencement Information

I63. Sch. 4 para. 32 in force at 1.4.2014 for specified purposes by S.I. 2014/889, art. 3. (m)

I64. Sch. 4 para. 32 in force at 1.9.2014 in so far as not already in force by S.I. 2014/889, art. 7. (e)

33. (1)Section 68 (cancellation of registration) is amended as follows.

(2) In subsection (1) after "or 4" insert " in the early years register or the general childcare register ".

(3) In subsection (2)—

(a) after "or 4" insert " in the early years register or the general childcare register ", and

(b) in paragraph (d) after "Chapter 2" insert " in the early years register ".

(4) In subsection (3) for "as an early years childminder under Chapter 2" substitute " under Chapter 2 in the early years register as an early years childminder ".

(5) In subsection (4) for "as a later years childminder under Chapter 3" substitute " under Chapter 3 in Part A of the general childcare register as a later years childminder ".

(6) In subsection (5) for "as a childminder under Chapter 4" substitute " under Chapter 4 in Part B of the general childcare register as a childminder ".

(7) In subsection (6) after "or 4" insert " in the early years register or the general childcare register ".

(8) In the title, at the end insert " in a childcare register: early years and later years providers ".

Commencement Information

I65. Sch. 4 para. 33 in force at 1.4.2014 for specified purposes by S.I. 2014/889, art. 3. (m)

I66. Sch. 4 para. 33 in force at 1.9.2014 in so far as not already in force by S.I. 2014/889, art. 7. (e)

34. (1)Section 69 (suspension of registration) is amended as follows.

(2) In subsection (1) after "or 4" insert " in the early years register or the general childcare register ".

(3) In subsection (3) for "as an early years childminder under Chapter 2" substitute " under Chapter 2 in the early years register as an early years childminder ".

(4) In subsection (4) for "as a later years childminder under Chapter 3" substitute " under Chapter 3 in Part A of the general childcare register as a later years childminder ".

(5) In subsection (6) for "as an early years provider (other than an early years childminder) under Chapter 2" substitute " under Chapter 2 in the early years register as an early years provider (other than an early years childminder) ".

(6) In subsection (7) for "as a later years provider (other than a later years childminder) under Chapter 3" substitute " under Chapter 3 in Part A of the general childcare register as a later years provider (other than a later years childminder) ".

(7) In the title, at the end insert " in a childcare register: early years and later years providers ".

Commencement Information

I67. Sch. 4 para. 34 in force at 1.4.2014 for specified purposes by S.I. 2014/889, art. 3. (m)

I68. Sch. 4 para. 34 in force at 1.9.2014 in so far as not already in force by S.I. 2014/889, art. 7. (e)

35. After section 69 insert—

"69. ACancellation, termination and suspension of registration with a childminder agency

(1) Regulations may make provision about the cancellation, termination and suspension of the registration of an early years provider or a later years provider with an early years childminder agency or a later years childminder agency for the purposes of Chapter 2, 3 or 4, in particular—

(a) about the termination by an early years provider or a later years provider of his or her registration;

(b) for the creation of offences relating to things done while a registration is suspended;

(c) about the resolution of disputes between an early years provider or a later years provider and an early years childminder agency or a later years childminder agency.

(2) Regulations by virtue of subsection (1) which make provision about the suspension of the registration of an early years provider or a later years provider with a childminder agency must include provision conferring on the registered provider a right of appeal to the Tribunal against suspension.

(3) Regulations made by virtue of subsection (1)(b) may only create offences which are—

(a) triable only summarily, and

(b) punishable only with a fine not exceeding the level specified in the regulations, which may not exceed level 5 on the standard scale."

Commencement Information

I69. Sch. 4 para. 35 in force at 1.4.2014 for specified purposes by S.I. 2014/889, art. 3. (m)

I70. Sch. 4 para. 35 in force at 1.9.2014 in so far as not already in force by S.I. 2014/889, art. 7. (e)

36. After section 69. A (as inserted by paragraph 35) insert—

"69. BCancellation of registration: childminder agencies

(1) The Chief Inspector must cancel the registration of a person registered under Chapter 2. A or 3. A as an early years childminder agency or a later years childminder agency if it appears to the Chief Inspector that the person has become disqualified from registration by regulations under section 76. A.

(2) The Chief Inspector may cancel the registration of a person registered under Chapter 2. A or 3. A as an early years childminder agency or a later years childminder agency if it appears to the Chief Inspector—

(a) that the prescribed requirements for registration which apply in relation to the person's registration under that Chapter have ceased, or will cease, to be satisfied,

(b) that the person has failed to comply with a condition imposed on the registration under that Chapter,

(c) that the person has failed to comply with a requirement imposed by regulations under that Chapter,

(d) that the person has failed to comply with a requirement imposed by this Chapter, or by regulations under this Chapter, or

(e) that the person has failed to pay a prescribed fee.

(3) Where a requirement to make any changes or additions to any services has been imposed on a person registered under Chapter 2. A or 3. A as an early years childminder agency or a later years childminder agency, the person's registration may not be cancelled on the ground of any defect or insufficiency in the services, if—

(a) the time set for complying with the requirements has not expired, and

(b) it is shown that the defect or insufficiency is due to the changes or additions not having been made.

(4) Regulations may make provision about the effect of the cancellation under this section of the registration under Chapter 2. A or 3. A of an early years childminder agency or a later years childminder agency on an early years provider or a later years provider registered with the agency for the purposes of Chapter 2, 3 or 4.

69. CSuspension of registration: childminder agencies

(1) Regulations may provide for the registration of a person registered under Chapter 2. A or 3. A as an early years childminder agency or a later years childminder agency to be suspended for a prescribed period in prescribed circumstances.

(2) Regulations under subsection (1) must include provision conferring on the registered person a

right of appeal to the Tribunal against suspension.

(3) Regulations under subsection (1) may make provision about the effect of the suspension of the registration of an early years childminder agency or a later years childminder agency on an early years provider or a later years provider registered with the agency for the purposes of Chapter 2, 3 or 4.

(4) A person registered under Chapter 2. A as an early years childminder agency may not, at any time when the person's registration under that Chapter is suspended in accordance with regulations under this section—

    (a) exercise any functions of an early years childminder agency, or

    (b) represent that the person may exercise such functions.

(5) A person registered under Chapter 3. A as a later years childminder agency may not, at any time when the person's registration under that Chapter is suspended in accordance with regulations under this section—

    (a) exercise any functions of a later years childminder agency, or

    (b) represent that the person may exercise such functions.

(6) A person commits an offence if, without reasonable excuse, the person contravenes subsection (4) or (5).

(7) A person guilty of an offence under subsection (6) is liable on summary conviction to a fine not exceeding level 5 on the standard scale."

Commencement Information

I71. Sch. 4 para. 36 in force at 1.4.2014 for specified purposes by S.I. 2014/889, art. 3. (m)

I72. Sch. 4 para. 36 in force at 1.9.2014 in so far as not already in force by S.I. 2014/889, art. 7. (e)

37. (1)Section 70 (voluntary removal from register) is amended as follows.

(2) In subsection (1) for "any of Chapters 2 to 4" substitute " Chapter 2, 3 or 4 ".

(3) In the title for "register" substitute " a childcare register: early years and later years providers ".

Commencement Information

I73. Sch. 4 para. 37 in force at 1.4.2014 for specified purposes by S.I. 2014/889, art. 3. (m)

I74. Sch. 4 para. 37 in force at 1.9.2014 in so far as not already in force by S.I. 2014/889, art. 7. (e)

38. After section 70 insert—

"70. AVoluntary removal from a childcare register: childminder agencies

(1) A person registered under Chapter 2. A or 3. A as an early years childminder agency or a later years childminder agency may give notice to the Chief Inspector of a wish to be removed from the early years register or (as the case may be) from Part A of the general childcare register.

(2) If a person gives notice under subsection (1) the Chief Inspector must remove the person from the early years register or (as the case may be) from Part A of the general childcare register.

(3) The Chief Inspector must not act under subsection (2) if—

    (a) the Chief Inspector has sent the person a notice (in pursuance of section 73. (2)) of the Chief Inspector's intention to cancel the person's registration, and

    (b) the Chief Inspector has not decided that he or she no longer intends to take that step.

(4) The Chief Inspector must not act under subsection (2) if—

    (a) the Chief Inspector has sent the person a notice (in pursuance of section 73. (7)) of the Chief Inspector's decision to cancel the person's registration, and

    (b) the time within which an appeal under section 74 may be brought has not expired or, if such an appeal has been brought, it has not been determined."

Commencement Information

I75. Sch. 4 para. 38 in force at 1.4.2014 for specified purposes by S.I. 2014/889, art. 3. (m)

176. Sch. 4 para. 38 in force at 1.9.2014 in so far as not already in force by S.I. 2014/889, art. 7. (e)

39. In section 71 (termination of voluntary registration on expiry of prescribed period), in the title after "registration" insert " in Part B of the general childcare register ".

Commencement Information

177. Sch. 4 para. 39 in force at 1.4.2014 for specified purposes by S.I. 2014/889, art. 3. (m)

178. Sch. 4 para. 39 in force at 1.9.2014 in so far as not already in force by S.I. 2014/889, art. 7. (e)

40. In section 72 (protection of children in an emergency), in subsection (1) after "or 4" insert " in the early years register or the general childcare register ".

Commencement Information

179. Sch. 4 para. 40 in force at 1.4.2014 for specified purposes by S.I. 2014/889, art. 3. (m)

180. Sch. 4 para. 40 in force at 1.9.2014 in so far as not already in force by S.I. 2014/889, art. 7. (e)

41. (1) Section 73 (procedure for taking certain steps) is amended as follows.

(2) In subsection (3)(b) for "his" substitute "the person's".

(3) In subsection (4) for "he" substitute " the applicant or registered person ".

(4) In subsection (5)—

(a) for "he" substitute " the recipient ", and

(b) for "him" substitute " the recipient ".

(5) In subsection (6) for "his" substitute "the recipient's".

(6) In subsection (7) for "he" (in the second place it occurs) substitute " the recipient ".

(7) In subsection (9) for "he" substitute " the person ".

(8) In subsection (10) for "his" substitute " the ".

Commencement Information

181. Sch. 4 para. 41 in force at 1.4.2014 for specified purposes by S.I. 2014/889, art. 3. (m)

182. Sch. 4 para. 41 in force at 1.9.2014 in so far as not already in force by S.I. 2014/889, art. 7. (e)

42. (1) Section 74 (appeals) is amended as follows.

(2) In subsection (1)—

(a) in paragraph (a) for "his" substitute " the ",

(b) in paragraph (b) for "his" substitute "the person's",

(c) in paragraph (c) for "his" substitute "the person's", and

(d) in paragraph (e) for "his" substitute "the person's".

(3) In subsection (5)(b) for "his" substitute " the ".

(4) In the title, at the end insert " relating to registration in a childcare register ".

Commencement Information

183. Sch. 4 para. 42 in force at 1.4.2014 for specified purposes by S.I. 2014/889, art. 3. (m)

184. Sch. 4 para. 42 in force at 1.9.2014 in so far as not already in force by S.I. 2014/889, art. 7. (e)

43. In the italic heading before section 75 (disqualification from registration), at the end insert " : early years and later years providers ".

Commencement Information

185. Sch. 4 para. 43 in force at 1.4.2014 for specified purposes by S.I. 2014/889, art. 3. (m)

186. Sch. 4 para. 43 in force at 1.9.2014 in so far as not already in force by S.I. 2014/889, art. 7. (e)

44. In the title of section 75, at the end insert " : early years and later years providers ".

Commencement Information

187. Sch. 4 para. 44 in force at 1.4.2014 for specified purposes by S.I. 2014/889, art. 3. (m)

188. Sch. 4 para. 44 in force at 1.9.2014 in so far as not already in force by S.I. 2014/889, art. 7. (e)

45. (1) Section 76 (consequences of disqualification) is amended as follows.

(2) In subsection (1)—

(a) in paragraph (a) after "34. (1)" insert " or (1. A) ", and
(b) in paragraph (c) after "53. (1)" insert " or (1. A) ".
(3) After subsection (3) insert—
"(3. A)An early years childminder agency must not register for the purposes of Chapter 2 a person who is disqualified from registration by regulations under section 75.
(3. B)A later years childminder agency must not register for the purposes of Chapter 3 a person who is disqualified from registration by regulations under section 75.
(3. C)An early years childminder agency or a later years childminder agency must not register for the purposes of Chapter 4 a person who is disqualified from registration by regulations under section 75."
(4) In subsection (4), for "or (3)" substitute " , (3), (3. A), (3. B) or (3. C) ".
(5) In subsection (6)—
(a) after "A person" insert " ("A") ", and
(b) for "he" (in each place it occurs) substitute " A ".
(6) After subsection (6) insert—
"(6. A)A person ("A") who contravenes subsection (3. A), (3. B) or (3. C) is not guilty of an offence under subsection (4) if A proves that A did not know, and had no reasonable grounds for believing, that the person registered by A was disqualified from registration."
(7) In the title, at the end insert " : early years and later years providers ".
Commencement Information
I89. Sch. 4 para. 45 in force at 1.4.2014 for specified purposes by S.I. 2014/889, art. 3. (m)
I90. Sch. 4 para. 45 in force at 1.9.2014 in so far as not already in force by S.I. 2014/889, art. 7. (e)
46. After section 76 insert—
76. ADisqualification from registration: childminder agencies
(1) In this section, "registration" means registration under Chapter 2. A or 3. A.
(2) Regulations may provide for a person to be disqualified from registration.
(3) Regulations under subsection (2) may provide for a person not to be disqualified from registration (and in particular may provide for a person not to be disqualified from registration for the purposes of section 76. B) by reason of any fact which would otherwise cause the person to be disqualified if—
    (a) the person has disclosed the fact to the Chief Inspector, and
    (b) the Chief Inspector has consented in writing to the person's not being disqualified from registration and has not withdrawn the consent.
76. BConsequences of disqualification: childminder agencies
(1) A person who is disqualified from registration by regulations under section 76. A must not—
    (a) exercise any functions of an early years childminder agency or a later years childminder agency,
    (b) represent that the person can exercise such functions,
    (c) be a director, manager or other officer of, or partner in, an early years childminder agency or a later years childminder agency, be a member of the governing body of such an agency, or otherwise be directly concerned in the management of such an agency, or
    (d) work for such an agency in any capacity which involves entering premises on which early years provision or later years provision is being provided.
(2) No early years childminder agency or later years childminder agency may employ a person who is disqualified from registration by regulations under section 76. A in any capacity which involves—
    (a) being directly concerned in the management of an early years childminder agency or a later years childminder agency, or
    (b) entering premises on which early years provision or later years provision is being provided.
(3) A person who contravenes subsection (1) or (2) commits an offence.
(4) A person ("P") who contravenes subsection (2) is not guilty of an offence under subsection (3) if P proves that P did not know, and had no reasonable grounds for believing, that the person

whom P was employing was disqualified from registration.

(5) A person guilty of an offence under subsection (3) is liable on summary conviction to imprisonment for a term not exceeding 51 weeks, or to a fine not exceeding level 5 on the standard scale, or to both.

(6) In relation to an offence committed before the commencement of section 281. (5) of the Criminal Justice Act 2003 (c. 44) (alteration of penalties for summary offences), the reference in subsection (5) to 51 weeks is to be read as a reference to 6 months."

Commencement Information

I91. Sch. 4 para. 46 in force at 1.4.2014 for specified purposes by S.I. 2014/889, art. 3. (m)

I92. Sch. 4 para. 46 in force at 1.9.2014 in so far as not already in force by S.I. 2014/889, art. 7. (e)

47. (1)Section 77 (powers of entry) is amended as follows.

(2) In subsection (1)—

(a) after "34. (1)" insert " or (1. A) ", and

(b) after "53. (1)" insert " or (1. A) ".

(3) In subsection (2)(a) for "or 60" substitute " , 51. D(2), 60 or 61. E(2) ".

(4) For the title substitute " Chief Inspector's powers of entry: early years provision and later years provision ".

Commencement Information

I93. Sch. 4 para. 47 in force at 1.4.2014 for specified purposes by S.I. 2014/889, art. 3. (m)

I94. Sch. 4 para. 47 in force at 1.9.2014 in so far as not already in force by S.I. 2014/889, art. 7. (e)

48. For the title of section 78 substitute " Powers of entry under section 77: requirement for consent ".

Commencement Information

I95. Sch. 4 para. 48 in force at 1.4.2014 for specified purposes by S.I. 2014/889, art. 3. (m)

I96. Sch. 4 para. 48 in force at 1.9.2014 in so far as not already in force by S.I. 2014/889, art. 7. (e)

49. After section 78 insert—

"78. AChief Inspector's powers of entry: childminder agencies

(1) The Chief Inspector may at any reasonable time enter any premises in England if the Chief Inspector has reasonable cause to believe that a person on the premises is falsely representing—
    (a) that the person is an early years childminder agency, or
    (b) that the person is a later years childminder agency.

(2) The Chief Inspector may at any reasonable time enter any premises in England which is registered in—
    (a) the early years register as premises of an early years childminder agency, or
    (b) Part A of the general childcare register as premises of a later years childminder agency,
for any of the purposes in subsection (3).

(3) Those purposes are—
    (a) conducting an inspection under section 51. D(1) or 61. E(1);
    (b) determining whether any conditions or requirements imposed by or under this Part are being complied with.

(4) An authorisation given by the Chief Inspector under paragraph 9. (1) of Schedule 12 to the Education and Inspections Act 2006 in relation to the functions under subsection (1) or (2)—
    (a) may be given for a particular occasion or period;
    (b) may be given subject to conditions.

(5) A person entering premises under this section may (subject to any conditions imposed under subsection (4)(b))—
    (a) inspect the premises;

(b) inspect, and take copies of—
(i) any records kept concerning early years providers or later years providers, and
(ii) any other documents containing information relating to such providers;
(c) seize and remove any document or other material or thing found there which the person has reasonable grounds to believe may be evidence of a failure to comply with any condition or requirement imposed by or under this Part;
(d) take measurements and photographs or make recordings;
(e) interview in private any person present on the premises who works there.
(6) A person entering premises under this section may (subject to any conditions imposed under subsection (4)(b)) require any person to afford such facilities and assistance with respect to matters within the person's control as are necessary to enable the powers under this section to be exercised.
(7) Section 58 of the Education Act 2005 (inspection of computer records for the purposes of Part 1 of that Act) applies for the purposes of this section as it applies for the purposes of Part 1 of that Act.
(8) It is an offence intentionally to obstruct a person exercising any power under this section.
(9) A person guilty of an offence under subsection (8) is liable on summary conviction to a fine not exceeding level 4 on the standard scale.
(10) In this section, "documents" and "records" each include information recorded in any form.

78. BPowers of entry under section 78. A: requirement for consent

(1) This section applies where a person ("the authorised person") proposes to enter domestic premises in pursuance of a power of entry conferred by section 78. A(2).
(2) If the authorised person has reasonable cause to believe that the premises are the home of a person who—
(a) is not employed by the early years childminder agency or (as the case may be) the later years childminder agency, or
(b) is not a director, manager or other officer of, or partner in, the agency, a member of its governing body or otherwise directly concerned in the management of the agency,
the authorised person may not enter the premises without the consent of an adult who is an occupier of the premises and who falls within paragraph (a) or (b)."
Commencement Information
I97. Sch. 4 para. 49 in force at 1.4.2014 for specified purposes by S.I. 2014/889, art. 3. (m)
I98. Sch. 4 para. 49 in force at 1.9.2014 in so far as not already in force by S.I. 2014/889, art. 7. (e)
50. In section 79 (power of constable to assist in exercise of powers of entry), in subsection (2), in paragraph (a) after "77" insert " or 78. A ".
Commencement Information
I99. Sch. 4 para. 50 in force at 1.4.2014 for specified purposes by S.I. 2014/889, art. 3. (m)
I100. Sch. 4 para. 50 in force at 1.9.2014 in so far as not already in force by S.I. 2014/889, art. 7. (e)
51. (1)Section 82 (supply of information to the Chief Inspector), is amended as follows.
(2) The existing provision becomes subsection (1).
(3) In that subsection, after "later years provider" insert " , or (as the case may be) as an early years childminder agency or later years childminder agency, ".
(4) After subsection (1) insert—
"(2)The Chief Inspector's power under subsection (1) includes a power to require an early years childminder agency or a later years childminder agency to provide the Chief Inspector with information about an early years provider or a later years provider registered with the agency for the purposes of Chapter 2, 3 or 4."
Commencement Information
I101. Sch. 4 para. 51 in force at 1.4.2014 for specified purposes by S.I. 2014/889, art. 3. (m)

I102. Sch. 4 para. 51 in force at 1.9.2014 in so far as not already in force by S.I. 2014/889, art. 7. (e)
52. (1)Section 83 (supply of information to HMRC and local authorities) is amended as follows.
(2) In subsection (4)—
(a) after "in which" insert "—
   (a) ", and
(b) after "registered" insert ";
   (b) registered premises of the early years childminder agency or later years childminder agency are (or, as the case may be, were) located."
(3) In the title, at the end insert " by the Chief Inspector ".
Commencement Information
I103. Sch. 4 para. 52 in force at 1.4.2014 for specified purposes by S.I. 2014/889, art. 3. (m)
I104. Sch. 4 para. 52 in force at 1.9.2014 in so far as not already in force by S.I. 2014/889, art. 7. (e)
53. After section 83 insert—

"83. ASupply of information to the Secretary of State, HMRC and local authorities by childminder agencies

(1) An early years childminder agency or a later years childminder agency must provide prescribed information to the Secretary of State, Her Majesty's Revenue and Customs, and each relevant local authority, if it—
   (a) grants a person's application for registration for the purposes of Chapter 2, 3 or 4;
   (b) takes any other steps under this Part of a prescribed description.
(2) The information which may be prescribed for the purposes of this section is—
   (a) in the case of information to be provided to the Secretary of State, information which the Secretary of State may require for the purposes of the Secretary of State's functions in relation to universal credit under Part 1 of the Welfare Reform Act 2012;
   (b) in the case of information to be provided to Her Majesty's Revenue and Customs, information which Her Majesty's Revenue and Customs may require for the purposes of their functions in relation to tax credits;
   (c) in the case of information to be provided to a relevant local authority, information which would assist the local authority in the discharge of their functions under section 12.
(3) In this section, "relevant local authority" means an English local authority for an area in which a person who is (or, as the case may be, was) registered with the early years childminder agency or later years childminder agency for the purposes of Chapter 2 or 3 provides (or has provided) early years provision or later years provision in respect of which he or she is (or was) registered."
Commencement Information
I105. Sch. 4 para. 53 in force at 1.4.2014 for specified purposes by S.I. 2014/889, art. 3. (m)
I106. Sch. 4 para. 53 in force at 1.9.2014 in so far as not already in force by S.I. 2014/889, art. 7. (e)
54. In the title of section 84 (disclosure of information for certain purposes), at the end insert " : the Chief Inspector ".
Commencement Information
I107. Sch. 4 para. 54 in force at 1.4.2014 for specified purposes by S.I. 2014/889, art. 3. (m)
I108. Sch. 4 para. 54 in force at 1.9.2014 in so far as not already in force by S.I. 2014/889, art. 7. (e)
55. After section 84 insert—

"84. ADisclosure of information for certain purposes: childminder agencies

(1) An early years childminder agency or a later years childminder agency may arrange for prescribed information held by the agency in relation to persons registered with the agency under this Part to be made available for the purpose of—
  (a) assisting parents or prospective parents in choosing an early years provider or later years provider, or
  (b) protecting children from harm or neglect.
(2) The information may be made available in such manner and to such persons as the agency considers appropriate.
(3) Regulations may require an early years childminder agency or a later years childminder agency to provide prescribed information held by the agency in relation to persons registered with the agency under this Part to prescribed persons for either of the purposes mentioned in subsection (1)."

Commencement Information

I109. Sch. 4 para. 55 in force at 1.4.2014 for specified purposes by S.I. 2014/889, art. 3. (m)
I110. Sch. 4 para. 55 in force at 1.9.2014 in so far as not already in force by S.I. 2014/889, art. 7. (e)

56. In section 85 (offence of making false or misleading statement), in subsection (1) for "he" substitute " the person ".

Commencement Information

I111. Sch. 4 para. 56 in force at 1.4.2014 for specified purposes by S.I. 2014/889, art. 3. (m)
I112. Sch. 4 para. 56 in force at 1.9.2014 in so far as not already in force by S.I. 2014/889, art. 7. (e)

57. (1) Section 87 (offences by bodies corporate) is amended as follows.
(2) In subsection (1) for "This section" substitute " Subsection (2) ".
(3) After subsection (2) insert—
"(3) Subsection (4) applies where any offence under this Part is committed by a partnership.
(4) If the offence is proved to have been committed with the consent or connivance of, or to be attributable to any neglect on the part of, any partner, that partner (as well as the partnership) is guilty of the offence and liable to be proceeded against and punished accordingly."
(4) In the title, at the end insert " and partnerships ".

Commencement Information

I113. Sch. 4 para. 57 in force at 1.4.2014 for specified purposes by S.I. 2014/889, art. 3. (m)
I114. Sch. 4 para. 57 in force at 1.9.2014 in so far as not already in force by S.I. 2014/889, art. 7. (e)

58. In section 89 (fees), in subsection (1) after "to 4" insert " in the early years register or the general childcare register ".

Commencement Information

I115. Sch. 4 para. 58 in force at 1.4.2014 for specified purposes by S.I. 2014/889, art. 3. (m)
I116. Sch. 4 para. 58 in force at 1.9.2014 in so far as not already in force by S.I. 2014/889, art. 7. (e)

59. (1) Section 90 (cases where consent to disclosure is withheld) is amended as follows.
(2) In subsection (1)—
(a) in paragraph (a) for "Chapter 2, 3 or 4" substitute " any of Chapters 2 to 4 ", and
(b) in paragraph (b) after "68. (2)(a)" insert " or 69. B(2)(a) ".
(3) In subsection (2)(b) omit "his" in both places it occurs.

Commencement Information

I117. Sch. 4 para. 59 in force at 1.4.2014 for specified purposes by S.I. 2014/889, art. 3. (m)
I118. Sch. 4 para. 59 in force at 1.9.2014 in so far as not already in force by S.I. 2014/889, art. 7. (e)

60. (1) Section 93 (notices) is amended as follows.
(2) In subsection (1)—
(a) after paragraph (a) insert—

"(aa)section 57. A(2) and (4);
(ab) section 61. C(1);", and
(b) after paragraph (b) insert—
"(ba)section 65. A(1) and (3);".
(3) In subsection (2)(a) for "him" substitute " the person ".
(4) In subsection (4)—
(a) in paragraph (a) for "his" substitute " a ", and
(b) in paragraph (b) omit "by him".
Commencement Information
I119. Sch. 4 para. 60 in force at 1.4.2014 for specified purposes by S.I. 2014/889, art. 3. (m)
I120. Sch. 4 para. 60 in force at 1.9.2014 in so far as not already in force by S.I. 2014/889, art. 7. (e)
61. In section 94 (power to amend Part 3: applications in respect of multiple premises), in paragraph (a)—
(a) after "36. (1)" insert " or (1. A) ", and
(b) after "55. (1)" insert " or (1. A) ".
Commencement Information
I121. Sch. 4 para. 61 in force at 1.4.2014 for specified purposes by S.I. 2014/889, art. 3. (m)
I122. Sch. 4 para. 61 in force at 1.9.2014 in so far as not already in force by S.I. 2014/889, art. 7. (e)
62. (1)Section 98 (interpretation of Part 3) is amended as follows.
(2) In subsection (1)—
(a) after the definition of "childcare" insert—
""childminder agency" means—
  (a) an early years childminder agency;
  (b) a later years childminder agency;",
(b) after the definition of "domestic premises" insert—
""early years childminder agency" means a person registered in the early years register as an early years childminder agency;", and
(c) before the definition of "later years provision" insert—
""later years childminder agency" means a person registered in Part A of the general childcare register as a later years childminder agency;".
(3) After that subsection insert—
"(1. A)A person is registered for the purposes of this Part if that person is registered—
  (a) in the early years register,
  (b) in the general childcare register, or
  (c) with an early years childminder agency or a later years childminder agency."
Commencement Information
I123. Sch. 4 para. 62 in force at 1.4.2014 for specified purposes by S.I. 2014/889, art. 3. (m)
I124. Sch. 4 para. 62 in force at 1.9.2014 in so far as not already in force by S.I. 2014/889, art. 7. (e)

PART 6 Other amendments

63. In section 99 of the Childcare Act 2006 (provision of information about young children: England), in subsection (1) after paragraph (a) (and before the "and" which follows it) insert—
"(aa)a person registered as an early years childminder agency under Chapter 2. A of Part 3,".
Commencement Information
I125. Sch. 4 para. 63 in force at 1.4.2014 for specified purposes by S.I. 2014/889, art. 3. (m)
I126. Sch. 4 para. 63 in force at 1.9.2014 in so far as not already in force by S.I. 2014/889, art. 7. (e)
64. In the Employment Agencies Act 1973, in section 13. (7) (exemptions) after paragraph (c)

insert—

"(ca)an early years childminder agency or a later years childminder agency (as defined in section 98 of the Childcare Act 2006);".

Commencement Information

I127. Sch. 4 para. 64 in force at 1.4.2014 for specified purposes by S.I. 2014/889, art. 3. (m)
I128. Sch. 4 para. 64 in force at 1.9.2014 in so far as not already in force by S.I. 2014/889, art. 7. (e)

Schedule 5. Children's Commissioner: minor and consequential amendments

Section 115

Inquiries

1. (1)Section 3 of the Children Act 2004 (inquiries initiated by Commissioner) is amended as follows.
(2) Omit subsection (3) (requirement to consult the Secretary of State before holding an inquiry).
(3) In subsection (7) for "under any enactment" substitute " of a public nature ".
2. (1)Section 4 of the Children Act 2004 (inquiries held on the direction of the Secretary of State) is repealed.
(2) In consequence of sub-paragraph (1), omit the following provisions of the Children Act 2004—
(a) section 5. (6) and (7) (inquiries in Wales),
(b) section 6. (7) to (9) (inquiries in Scotland), and
(c) section 7. (7) to (9) (inquiries in Northern Ireland).

Functions of Commissioner: children in Wales, Scotland and Northern Ireland

3. (1)Section 5 of the Children Act 2004 (functions of Commissioner in Wales) is amended as follows.
(2) In subsection (1), for "promoting awareness of the views and interests of children in Wales" substitute " promoting and protecting the rights of children in Wales ".
(3) After subsection (1) insert—
"(1. A)The function under subsection (1) includes promoting awareness of the views and interests of children in Wales."
(4) For subsection (2) substitute—
"(2)Subsections (3) to (5) of section 2 and sections 2. A to 2. C, 2. E and 2. F apply in relation to the Children's Commissioner's function under subsection (1) as in relation to the Commissioner's primary function.
(2. A)For the purposes of subsection (2)—
    (a) section 2. (3)(i) has effect as if for "in England" there were substituted " in Wales, except in so far as relating to any matter falling within the remit of the Children's Commissioner for Wales under section 72. B, 73 or 74 of the Care Standards Act 2000, ",
    (b) sections 2. (4) and 2. B(3) have effect as if for "children who are within section 8. A (children living away from home or receiving social care) and other groups of children" there were substituted " groups of children ",
    (c) section 2. E(1) has effect as if "and the function under section 2. D" were omitted, and

(d) section 2. F(1) has effect as if "or the function under section 2. D" were omitted."

4. (1)Section 6 of the Children Act 2004 (functions of Commissioner in Scotland) is amended as follows.

(2) In subsection (1), for "promoting awareness of the views and interests of children in Scotland in relation to reserved matters" substitute " promoting and protecting the rights of children in Scotland where those rights are or may be affected by reserved matters ".

(3) After subsection (1) insert—

"(1. A)The function under subsection (1) includes promoting awareness of the views and interests of children in Scotland."

(4) For subsection (2) substitute—

"(2)Subsections (3) to (5) of section 2 and sections 2. A to 2. C, 2. E and 2. F apply in relation to the Children's Commissioner's function under subsection (1) as in relation to the Commissioner's primary function.

(2. A)For the purposes of subsection (2)—

(a) section 2. (3)(i) has effect as if for "in England" there were substituted " in Scotland, in relation to reserved matters, ",

(b) sections 2. (4) and 2. B(3) have effect as if for "children who are within section 8. A (children living away from home or receiving social care) and other groups of children" there were substituted " groups of children ",

(c) section 2. E(1) has effect as if "and the function under section 2. D" were omitted, and

(d) section 2. F(1) has effect as if "or the function under section 2. D" were omitted."

5. (1)Section 7 of the Children Act 2004 (functions of Commissioner in Northern Ireland) is amended as follows.

(2) In subsection (1), for "promoting awareness of the views and interests of children in Northern Ireland in relation to excepted matters" substitute " promoting and protecting the rights of children in Northern Ireland where those rights are or may be affected by excepted matters ".

(3) After subsection (1) insert—

"(1. A)The function under subsection (1) includes promoting awareness of the views and interests of children in Northern Ireland."

(4) For subsection (2) substitute—

"(2)Subsections (3) to (5) of section 2 and sections 2. A to 2. C, 2. E and 2. F apply in relation to the Children's Commissioner's function under subsection (1) as in relation to the Commissioner's primary function.

(2. A)For the purposes of subsection (2)—

(a) section 2. (3)(i) has effect as if for "in England" there were substituted " in Northern Ireland, in relation to excepted matters, ",

(b) sections 2. (4) and 2. B(3) have effect as if for "children who are within section 8. A (children living away from home or receiving social care) and other groups of children" there were substituted " groups of children ",

(c) section 2. E(1) has effect as if "and the function under section 2. D" were omitted, and

(d) section 2. F(1) has effect as if "or the function under section 2. D" were omitted."

Young persons

6. (1)For section 9 of the Children Act 2004 (care leavers and young persons with learning disabilities) substitute—

"9. Commissioner's functions in relation to certain young people

(1) This section applies for the purposes of this Part, other than sections 2. A and 8. A (and references in this Part to a child who is within section 8. A).

(2) For the purposes of the Children's Commissioner's functions in respect of children in England,

a reference to a child includes, in addition to a person under the age of 18—
  (a) a person aged 18 or over for whom an EHC plan is maintained by a local authority,
  (b) a person aged 18 or over and under 25 to whom a local authority in England has provided services under any of sections 23. C to 24. D of the Children Act 1989 at any time after reaching the age of 16, or
  (c) a person aged 18 or over and under 25 who has been looked after by a local authority (in Wales, Scotland or Northern Ireland) at any time after reaching the age of 16.
(3) For the purposes of the Children's Commissioner's functions in respect of children in Wales, Scotland and Northern Ireland, a reference to a child includes, in addition to a person under the age of 18, a person aged 18 or over and under 25—
  (a) who has a learning disability,
  (b) who has been looked after by a local authority (in Wales, Scotland or Northern Ireland) at any time after reaching the age of 16, or
  (c) to whom a local authority in England has provided services under any of sections 23. C to 24. D of the Children Act 1989 at any time after reaching the age of 16.
(4) For the purposes of this section—
"EHC plan" means a plan within section 37. (2) of the Children and Families Act 2014 (education, health and care plans);
"learning disability" means a state of arrested or incomplete development of mind which induces significant impairment of intelligence and social functioning;
a person is "looked after by a local authority" if—
  - for the purposes of the Children Act 1989, he or she is looked after by a local authority in Wales;
  - for the purposes of the Children (Scotland) Act 1995, he or she is looked after by a local authority in Scotland;
  - for the purposes of the Children (Northern Ireland) Order 1995, he or she is looked after by an authority in Northern Ireland."
(2) Until the coming into force of Part 3 of this Act, section 9 of the Children Act 2004 (as substituted by sub-paragraph (1)) has effect as if—
(a) in subsection (2) for paragraph (a) there were substituted—
"(a)a person aged 18 or over and under 25 in respect of whom an assessment under section 139. A of the Learning and Skills Act 2000 (a learning difficulty assessment) has been conducted,", and
(b) in subsection (4) the definition of "EHC plan" were omitted.

Appointment and tenure of Children's Commissioner

7. In Schedule 1 to the Children Act 2004, in paragraph 3 (appointment and tenure of office)—
(a) in sub-paragraph (2) for ", to such extent and in such manner as he thinks fit," substitute " take reasonable steps to ",
(b) in sub-paragraph (4) for "five years" substitute " six years ", and
(c) in sub-paragraph (5) for "is eligible for reappointment once only" substitute " is not eligible for reappointment ".
8. In Schedule 1 to the Children Act 2004, after paragraph 3 insert—

"Interim appointments

3. A(1)Where there is a vacancy in the office of Children's Commissioner, the Secretary of State may appoint a person as interim Children's Commissioner.
(2) Subject to the provisions of this paragraph, a person holds and vacates office as interim Children's Commissioner in accordance with the terms and conditions of the appointment as determined by the Secretary of State.
(3) An appointment as interim Children's Commissioner is for a term ending—

(a) with the appointment of a person as the Children's Commissioner under paragraph 3, or
(b) if sooner, at the end of the period of six months beginning with the date on which the appointment as interim Children's Commissioner was made.
(4) A person who has held office as interim Children's Commissioner—
(a) is eligible for reappointment, and
(b) is eligible for appointment as the Children's Commissioner.
(5) An interim Children's Commissioner may at any time resign by notice in writing to the Secretary of State.
(6) The Secretary of State may remove an interim Children's Commissioner from office if satisfied that the interim Commissioner has—
(a) become unfit or unable properly to discharge his or her functions; or
(b) behaved in a way that is not compatible with continuing in office."

Deputy Children's Commissioner

9. (1)In Schedule 1 to the Children Act 2004, in paragraph 5 (staff)—
(a) in sub-paragraph (1) omit ", one of whom shall be appointed as deputy Children's Commissioner",
(b) omit sub-paragraph (2), and
(c) in sub-paragraph (3) omit "Without prejudice to sub-paragraph (2),".
(2) In consequence of sub-paragraph (1), in section 36. (6) of the Criminal Justice and Court Services Act 2000 (meaning of "regulated position"), in paragraph (fa) omit "and deputy Children's Commissioner".

Schedule 6. Repeal of requirement to appoint Children's Rights Director: transfer schemes

Section 116

Staff transfer schemes

1. (1)The Secretary of State may make a scheme (a "staff transfer scheme") providing for designated members of staff of the Office for Standards in Education, Children's Services and Skills ("the Office") to become members of the Children's Commissioner's staff.
(2) A staff transfer scheme may provide—
(a) for the terms and conditions of service of a member of staff of the Office to have effect (subject to any necessary modifications) as the terms and conditions of service as a member of the Children's Commissioner's staff;
(b) for the transfer to the Children's Commissioner of the rights, powers, duties and liabilities of the Office under or in connection with the contract of employment of the member of staff;
(c) for anything done (or having effect as if done) before that transfer by or in relation to the Office in respect of such a contract or the member of staff to be treated as having been done by or in relation to the Children's Commissioner.
(3) A staff transfer scheme may provide for a period before a person became a member of the Children's Commissioner's staff to count as a period during which he or she was a member of the Commissioner's staff (and for the operation of the scheme not to be treated as having interrupted the continuity of that period).
(4) A staff transfer scheme may provide for a person who would be treated (by an Act or otherwise) as being dismissed by the operation of the scheme not to be so treated.

(5) A staff transfer scheme may provide for a person who is a member of staff of the Office not to become a member of the Children's Commissioner's staff if the person gives notice objecting to the operation of the scheme in relation to him or her.

Property transfer schemes

2. (1)The Secretary of State may make a scheme (a "property transfer scheme") providing for the transfer to the Children's Commissioner of designated property, rights or liabilities of the Office.
(2) A property transfer scheme may—
(a) create rights, or impose liabilities, in relation to property or rights transferred by virtue of the scheme;
(b) provide for anything done by or in relation to the Office in connection with any property, rights or liabilities transferred by the scheme to be treated as done, or to be continued, by or in relation to the Children's Commissioner;
(c) apportion property, rights and liabilities;
(d) make provision about the continuation of legal proceedings.
(3) The things that may be transferred by a property transfer scheme include—
(a) property, rights and liabilities that could not otherwise be transferred;
(b) property acquired, and rights and liabilities arising, after the making of the scheme.

The Chief Inspector

3. In the following provisions of this Schedule, a reference to the Office includes a reference to the Chief Inspector—
(a) paragraph 1. (2)(b) (to the extent that the Chief Inspector has rights, powers, duties or liabilities under or in connection with the contract of employment of a member of staff of the Office);
(b) paragraph 1. (2)(c) (to the extent that anything has been done (or has effect as if done) by or in relation to the Chief Inspector in respect of such a contract or member of staff before a transfer);
(c) paragraph 2. (1) (to the extent that the Chief Inspector has property, rights or liabilities);
(d) paragraph 2. (2)(b) (to the extent that anything has been done by or in relation to the Chief Inspector in respect of any property, rights or liabilities transferred by a property transfer scheme).

Continuity

4. A transfer by virtue of a staff transfer scheme or a property transfer scheme does not affect the validity of anything done by or in relation to the Office or the Chief Inspector before the transfer takes effect.

Supplementary provisions

5. A staff transfer scheme or a property transfer scheme may include supplementary, incidental, transitional and consequential provision.

Interpretation

6. In this Schedule—
"the Chief Inspector" means Her Majesty's Chief Inspector of Education, Children's Services and Skills;
"designated", in relation to a staff transfer scheme or a property transfer scheme, means specified in, or determined in accordance with, the scheme;
"the Office" has the meaning given in paragraph 1. (1).

Schedule 7. Statutory rights to leave and pay: further amendments

Section 126

Social Security Act 1989 (c. 24)

1. Schedule 5 to the Social Security Act 1989 (employment-related schemes for pensions or other benefits to comply with the principle of equal treatment for men and women) is amended as follows.
Commencement Information
I1. Sch. 7 para. 1 in force at 30.6.2014 by S.I. 2014/1640, art. 3. (2)(a)
2. (1)Paragraph 5. A (schemes that contain unfair paternity leave provisions) is amended as follows.
(2) In sub-paragraph (3) (how scheme affected), in the words following paragraph (b), for ", ordinary statutory paternity pay or additional statutory paternity pay" there is substituted " or statutory paternity pay ".
(3) In sub-paragraph (4) (definitions), in the definition of "period of paid paternity leave"—
(a) in paragraph (a), after "(6), (7)" there is inserted " , (7. A) or (7. B) ";
(b) in paragraph (a), the words "or (8)" are repealed;
(c) in paragraph (b), for ", ordinary statutory paternity pay or additional statutory paternity pay" there is substituted " or statutory paternity pay ".
(4) In sub-paragraph (7) (type of paid paternity leave: where adoption does not involve placement for adoption under the law of any part of the United Kingdom), for "section 171. ZK" there is substituted " section 171. ZK(1) ".
(5) After sub-paragraph (7) there is inserted—
"(7. A)This sub-paragraph applies if—
    (a) the member's absence from work is due to the placement or expected placement of a child under section 22. C of the Children Act 1989, and
    (b) in relation to that child, the member satisfies the conditions prescribed under section 171. ZB(2)(a)(i) and (ii) of the Social Security Contributions and Benefits Act 1992, as modified by section 171. ZB(8) of that Act (cases involving the placing of a child by a local authority in England with a local authority foster parent who has been approved as a prospective adopter).
(7. B)This sub-paragraph applies if—
    (a) the member's absence from work is due to the birth or expected birth of a child, and
    (b) in relation to that child, the member satisfies the conditions prescribed under section 171. ZB(2)(a)(i) and (ii) of the Social Security Contributions and Benefits Act 1992, as applied by virtue of section 171. ZK(2) of that Act (cases involving applicants for parental orders under section 54 of the Human Fertilisation and Embryology Act 2008)."
(6) Sub-paragraph (8) (absence from work in circumstances where certain conditions for payment of additional statutory paternity pay are satisfied) is repealed.
Commencement Information
I2. Sch. 7 para. 2. (1)(4) in force at 30.6.2014 by S.I. 2014/1640, art. 3. (2)(b)
I3. Sch. 7 para. 2. (2)(3)(b)(c)(6) in force at 5.4.2015 by S.I. 2014/1640, art. 7. (a) (with art. 16)
I4. Sch. 7 para. 2. (3)(a) in force at 1.12.2014 by S.I. 2014/1640, art. 5. (2)(a)
I5. Sch. 7 para. 2. (5) in force at 1.12.2014 for specified purposes by S.I. 2014/1640, art. 5. (2)(a)
I6. Sch. 7 para. 2. (5) in force at 5.4.2015 for specified purposes by S.I. 2014/1640, art. 7. (a) (with art. 16)
3. (1)Paragraph 5. B (schemes that contain unfair adoption leave provisions) is amended as

follows.

(2) In sub-paragraph (4) (definitions), in the definition of "period of paid adoption leave", in paragraph (a), for "or (6)" there is substituted " , (6), (7) or (8) ".

(3) After sub-paragraph (6) there is inserted—

"(7)This sub-paragraph applies if—

(a) the member's absence from work is due to the placement or expected placement of a child under section 22. C of the Children Act 1989, and

(b) in relation to that child, the member satisfies the condition in section 171. ZL(2)(a) of the Social Security Contributions and Benefits Act 1992, as modified by section 171. ZL(9) of that Act (cases involving the placing of a child by a local authority in England with a local authority foster parent who has been approved as a prospective adopter).

(8) This sub-paragraph applies if—

(a) the member's absence from work is due to the birth or expected birth of a child, and

(b) in relation to that child, the member satisfies the condition in section 171. ZL(2)(a) of the Social Security Contributions and Benefits Act 1992, as applied by virtue of section 171. ZT(2) of that Act (cases involving applicants for parental orders under section 54 of the Human Fertilisation and Embryology Act 2008)."

Commencement Information

17. Sch. 7 para. 3. (1)(2) in force at 1.12.2014 by S.I. 2014/1640, art. 5. (2)(b)

18. Sch. 7 para. 3. (3) in force at 1.12.2014 for specified purposes by S.I. 2014/1640, art. 5. (2)(b)

19. Sch. 7 para. 3. (3) in force at 5.4.2015 for specified purposes by S.I. 2014/1640, art. 7. (b) (with art. 16)

4. After paragraph 5. B there is inserted—

5. C(1)Where an employment-related benefit scheme includes any unfair shared parental leave provisions (irrespective of any differences on the basis of sex in the treatment accorded to members under those provisions), then—

(a) the scheme shall be regarded to that extent as not complying with the principle of equal treatment; and

(b) subject to sub-paragraph (3), this Schedule shall apply accordingly.

(2) In this paragraph "unfair shared parental leave provisions", in relation to an employment-related benefit scheme, means any provision—

(a) which relates to continuing membership of, or the accrual of rights under, the scheme during any period of paid shared parental leave in the case of any member who is (or who, immediately before the commencement of such a period, was) an employed earner and which treats such a member otherwise than in accordance with the normal employment requirement; or

(b) which requires the amount of any benefit payable under the scheme to or in respect of any such member, to the extent that it falls to be determined by reference to earnings during a period which included a period of paid shared parental leave, to be determined otherwise than in accordance with the normal employment requirement.

(3) In the case of any unfair shared parental leave provision—

(a) the more favourable treatment required by paragraph 3. (1) is treatment no less favourable than would be accorded to the member in accordance with the normal employment requirement; and

(b) paragraph 3. (2) does not authorise the making of any such election as is there mentioned;

but, in respect of any period of paid shared parental leave, a member shall only be required to pay contributions on the amount of contractual remuneration or statutory shared parental pay actually paid to or for the member in respect of that period.

(4) In this paragraph—

"the normal employment requirement" is the requirement that any period of paid shared parental leave shall be treated as if it were a period throughout which the member in question works normally and receives the remuneration likely to be paid for doing so;

"period of paid adoption leave" has the same meaning as in paragraph 5. B;

"period of paid paternity leave" has the same meaning as in paragraph 5. A;

"period of paid shared parental leave", in the case of a member, means a period—

- throughout which the member is absent from work in circumstances where sub-paragraph (5), (6), (7), (8), (9) or (10) applies, and
- for which the employer (or if the member is no longer in that person's employment, his former employer) pays the member any contractual remuneration or statutory shared parental pay.

(5) This sub-paragraph applies if—
(a) the member's absence from work is due to the birth of a child,
(b) the member is the mother of the child, and
(c) the absence from work is not absence on maternity leave (within the meaning of the Equality Act 2010).

(6) This sub-paragraph applies if—
(a) the member's absence from work is due to the birth of a child,
(b) the member is a person who satisfies the conditions prescribed under section 171. ZU(4)(b)(i) or (ii) of the Social Security Contributions and Benefits Act 1992 in relation to the child, and
(c) the member's absence from work is not absence during a period of paid paternity leave.

(7) This sub-paragraph applies if—
(a) the member's absence from work is due to the placement of a child for adoption under the law of any part of the United Kingdom,
(b) the member is—
(i) a person with whom a child is placed for adoption under the law of any part of the United Kingdom, or
(ii) a person who satisfies the conditions prescribed under section 171. ZV(4)(b)(i) or (ii) of the Social Security Contributions and Benefits Act 1992 in relation to the child, and
(c) the member's absence from work is not absence during—
(i) a period of paid paternity leave, or
(ii) a period of paid adoption leave.

(8) This sub-paragraph applies if—
(a) the member's absence from work is due to the placement of a child under section 22. C of the Children Act 1989 by a local authority in England with a local authority foster parent who has been approved as a prospective adopter,
(b) the member is—
(i) the local authority foster parent with whom the child in question is placed under section 22. C of the Children Act 1989, or
(ii) a person who satisfies the conditions prescribed under section 171. ZV(4)(b)(i) or (ii) of the Social Security Contributions and Benefits Act 1992, as modified by section 171. ZV(18) of that Act (cases involving the placing of a child by a local authority in England with a local authority foster parent who has been approved as a prospective adopter), in relation to the child, and
(c) the member's absence from work is not absence during—
(i) a period of paid paternity leave, or
(ii) a period of paid adoption leave.

(9) This sub-paragraph applies if—
(a) the member's absence from work is due to the adoption or expected adoption of a child who has entered the United Kingdom in connection with or for the purposes of adoption which does not involve placement of the child for adoption under the law of any part of the United Kingdom,
(b) the member is—
(i) the person who has adopted or expects to adopt the child in question, or
(ii) a person who satisfies the conditions prescribed under section 171. ZV(4)(b)(i) or (ii) of the Social Security Contributions and Benefits Act 1992, as applied by virtue of section 171. ZZ5. (1) of that Act (adoption cases not involving placement under the law of the United Kingdom), in relation to the child, and
(c) the member's absence from work is not absence during—
(i) a period of paid paternity leave, or
(ii) a period of paid adoption leave.

(10) This sub-paragraph applies if—

(a) the member's absence from work is due to the birth of a child,
(b) the member is a person who has applied, or intends to apply, for a parental order under section 54 of the Human Fertilisation and Embryology Act 2008 in relation to the child, and
(c) the member's absence from work is not absence during—
(i) a period of paid paternity leave, or
(ii) a period of paid adoption leave."
Commencement Information
110. Sch. 7 para. 4 in force at 1.12.2014 by S.I. 2014/1640, art. 5. (2)(c)

Finance Act 1989 (c. 26)

5. (1)Section 182 of the Finance Act 1989 (offences relating to disclosure of information relating to social security functions etc) is amended as follows.
(2) In subsection (1) (offence where official discloses information relating to an individual's tax affairs etc), in paragraph (c) (an individual's statutory pay)—
(a) for "ordinary statutory paternity pay, additional statutory paternity pay or" there is substituted " statutory paternity pay, ";
(b) after "statutory adoption pay" there is inserted " or statutory shared parental pay ".
(3) In subsection (2. A) (meaning of "social security functions"), in paragraph (a)—
(a) for "ordinary statutory paternity pay, additional statutory paternity pay or" there is substituted " statutory paternity pay, ";
(b) after "statutory adoption pay" there is inserted " or statutory shared parental pay ".
(4) In subsection (4)(c) (offence where person discloses information relating to an individual's tax affairs etc), in sub-paragraph (iii) (an individual's statutory benefits and statutory pay)—
(a) for "ordinary statutory paternity pay, additional statutory paternity pay or" there is substituted " statutory paternity pay, ";
(b) after "statutory adoption pay" there is inserted " or statutory shared parental pay ".
(5) In subsection (5)(b) (exception to offence: disclosure with consent)—
(a) for "ordinary statutory paternity pay, additional statutory paternity pay or" there is substituted " statutory paternity pay, ";
(b) after "statutory adoption pay" there is inserted " or statutory shared parental pay ".
(6) In subsection (11. A) (references to Great Britain statutory pay to include references to statutory pay under corresponding Northern Ireland legislation)—
(a) for "ordinary statutory paternity pay, additional statutory paternity pay or" there is substituted " statutory paternity pay, ";
(b) after "statutory adoption pay" there is inserted " or statutory shared parental pay ";
(c) for "or Part 12. ZB" there is substituted " , Part 12. ZB or Part 12. ZC ".
Commencement Information
111. Sch. 7 para. 5. (1)(2)(b)(3)(b)(4)(b)(5)(b) in force at 1.12.2014 by S.I. 2014/1640, art. 5. (2)(d) (with art. 12)
112. Sch. 7 para. 5. (2)(a)(3)(a)(4)(a)(5)(a) in force at 5.4.2015 by S.I. 2014/1640, art. 7. (c) (with arts. 16, 17)
113. Sch. 7 para. 5. (6) in force at 15.3.2015 being the date on which 1992 c. 7, Pt. 12. ZC comes into force by virtue of S.R. 2015/86, art. 3. (1)(d) by S.I. 2014/1640, art. 8. (a) (with art. 18)

Social Security Contributions and Benefits Act 1992 (c. 4)

6. The Social Security Contributions and Benefits Act 1992 is amended as follows.
Commencement Information
114. Sch. 7 para. 6 in force at 1.12.2014 by S.I. 2014/1640, art. 5. (2)(e)
7. In section 1 (outline of contributory system), in subsection (5) (money provided by Parliament applied in relation to statutory pay)—

(a) for "ordinary statutory paternity pay, additional statutory paternity pay and" there is substituted " statutory paternity pay, ";
(b) after "statutory adoption pay" there is inserted " and statutory shared parental pay ".
Commencement Information
I15. Sch. 7 para. 7. (a) in force at 5.4.2015 by S.I. 2014/1640, art. 7. (d) (with art. 16)
I16. Sch. 7 para. 7. (b) in force at 1.12.2014 by S.I. 2014/1640, art. 5. (2)(f)
8. In section 4 (payments treated as remuneration and earnings), in subsection (1)(a)—
(a) in sub-paragraph (iii), the word "ordinary" is repealed;
(b) sub-paragraph (iv) (additional statutory paternity pay) and the "or" following it are repealed;
(c) for the "and" following sub-paragraph (v) there is substituted "or
(vi) statutory shared parental pay; and".
Commencement Information
I17. Sch. 7 para. 8. (a) in force at 5.4.2015 by S.I. 2014/1640, art. 7. (e) (with art. 16)
I18. Sch. 7 para. 8. (b)(c) in force at 1.12.2014 by S.I. 2014/1640, art. 5. (2)(g)
9. In section 4. C (power to make provision in consequence of provision made by or by virtue of section 4. B etc), in subsection (11), in the definition of "statutory payment", in paragraph (a)—
(a) for "ordinary statutory paternity pay, additional statutory paternity pay or" there is substituted " statutory paternity pay, ";
(b) after "statutory adoption pay" there is inserted " or statutory shared parental pay ".
Commencement Information
I19. Sch. 7 para. 9. (a) in force at 5.4.2015 by S.I. 2014/1640, art. 7. (f) (with art. 16)
I20. Sch. 7 para. 9. (b) in force at 30.6.2014 by S.I. 2014/1640, art. 3. (2)(c)
10. In the title of Part 12. ZA, the words "Ordinary and additional" are repealed.
Commencement Information
I21. Sch. 7 para. 10 in force at 5.4.2015 by S.I. 2014/1640, art. 7. (g) (with art. 16)
11. The italic cross-heading preceding section 171. ZA is repealed.
Commencement Information
I22. Sch. 7 para. 11 in force at 5.4.2015 by S.I. 2014/1640, art. 7. (g) (with art. 16)
12. (1)Section 171. ZA (entitlement to ordinary statutory paternity pay: birth) is amended as follows.
(2) In subsection (1), for " "ordinary statutory paternity pay"" there is substituted " "statutory paternity pay" ".
(3) In subsection (4), the word "ordinary" is repealed.
Commencement Information
I23. Sch. 7 para. 12 in force at 5.4.2015 by S.I. 2014/1640, art. 7. (g) (with art. 16)
13. (1)Section 171. ZB (entitlement to ordinary statutory paternity pay: adoption) is amended as follows.
(2) In subsection (1), for " "ordinary statutory paternity pay"" there is substituted " "statutory paternity pay" ".
(3) In subsection (4), the word "ordinary" is repealed.
(4) In subsection (6), the word "ordinary" is repealed.
Commencement Information
I24. Sch. 7 para. 13 in force at 5.4.2015 by S.I. 2014/1640, art. 7. (g) (with art. 16)
14. (1)Section 171. ZC (entitlement to ordinary statutory paternity pay: general) is amended as follows.
(2) In subsection (1), the word "ordinary", in both places it occurs, is repealed.
(3) In subsection (2), the word "ordinary" is repealed.
Commencement Information
I25. Sch. 7 para. 14 in force at 5.4.2015 by S.I. 2014/1640, art. 7. (g) (with art. 16)
15. (1)Section 171. ZD (liability to pay ordinary statutory paternity pay) is amended as follows.
(2) In subsection (1), the word "ordinary" is repealed.
(3) In subsection (2)—
(a) the word "ordinary", in both places it occurs, is repealed;

(b) the words "or additional statutory paternity pay (or both)" are repealed.
Commencement Information
I26. Sch. 7 para. 15 in force at 5.4.2015 by S.I. 2014/1640, art. 7. (g) (with art. 16)
16. (1)Section 171. ZE (rate and period of pay) is amended as follows.
(2) In subsection (1), the word "Ordinary" is repealed.
(3) In subsection (2)—
(a) in the words preceding paragraph (a), the word "Ordinary" is repealed;
(b) in paragraph (b), the word "ordinary" is repealed.
(4) In subsection (4), the word "Ordinary" is repealed.
(5) In subsection (5), the word "ordinary" is repealed.
(6) In subsection (7), the word "ordinary", in both places it occurs, is repealed.
(7) In subsection (8), the word "ordinary" is repealed.
(8) In subsection (10. A), the word "ordinary", in both places it occurs, is repealed.
(9) In subsection (11), in the definition of "statutory pay week", the word "ordinary", in both places it occurs, is repealed.
Commencement Information
I27. Sch. 7 para. 16 in force at 5.4.2015 by S.I. 2014/1640, art. 7. (g) (with art. 16)
17. The italic cross-heading preceding section 171. ZEA is repealed.
Commencement Information
I28. Sch. 7 para. 17 in force at 5.4.2015 by S.I. 2014/1640, art. 7. (g) (with art. 16)
18. The italic cross-heading preceding section 171. ZF is repealed.
Commencement Information
I29. Sch. 7 para. 18 in force at 5.4.2015 by S.I. 2014/1640, art. 7. (g) (with art. 16)
19. In section 171. ZF (restrictions on contracting out), in subsection (2) (agreements which are not void for contracting out), for "ordinary statutory paternity pay or additional statutory paternity pay" there is substituted " statutory paternity pay ".
Commencement Information
I30. Sch. 7 para. 19 in force at 5.4.2015 by S.I. 2014/1640, art. 7. (g) (with art. 16)
20. In section 171. ZG (relationship with contractual remuneration), subsection (4) is repealed.
Commencement Information
I31. Sch. 7 para. 20 in force at 5.4.2015 by S.I. 2014/1640, art. 7. (g) (with art. 16)
21. (1)Section 171. ZJ (provision supplementary to Part 12. ZA) is amended as follows.
(2) In subsection (5) (meaning of "week"), for "sections 171. ZE and 171. ZEE" there is substituted " section 171. ZE ".
(3) In subsection (10)(f) (regulations relating to NHS contracts treated as a single contract: provision for identifying the employer under the single contract), for "ordinary statutory paternity pay or additional statutory paternity pay" there is substituted " statutory paternity pay ".
Commencement Information
I32. Sch. 7 para. 21 in force at 5.4.2015 by S.I. 2014/1640, art. 7. (g) (with art. 16)
22. In section 176 (Parliamentary control of subordinate legislation), in subsection (1) (affirmative procedure), in paragraph (a), the words "171. ZEA to 171. ZEE;" are repealed.
Commencement Information
I33. Sch. 7 para. 22 in force at 5.4.2015 by S.I. 2014/1640, art. 7. (g) (with art. 16)

Social Security Administration Act 1992 (c. 5)

23. The Social Security Administration Act 1992 is amended as follows.
Commencement Information
I34. Sch. 7 para. 23 in force at 30.6.2014 by S.I. 2014/1640, art. 3. (2)(d)
24. In section 5 (regulations about claims for and payments of benefits), in subsection (5) (application of provisions of subsection (1) to statutory pay)—
(a) for "ordinary statutory paternity pay, additional statutory paternity pay and" there is substituted

" statutory paternity pay, ";
(b) after "statutory adoption pay" there is inserted " and statutory shared parental pay ".
Commencement Information
I35. Sch. 7 para. 24. (a) in force at 5.4.2015 by S.I. 2014/1640, art. 7. (h) (with art. 16)
I36. Sch. 7 para. 24. (b) in force at 30.6.2014 by S.I. 2014/1640, art. 3. (2)(e)
25. In section 122. AA (disclosure of contributions information etc by HMRC), in subsection (1) (disclosure to HSE etc or because of reciprocal agreements with other countries)—
(a) for "ordinary statutory paternity pay, additional statutory paternity pay or" there is substituted " statutory paternity pay, ";
(b) after "statutory adoption pay" there is inserted " or statutory shared parental pay ".
Commencement Information
I37. Sch. 7 para. 25. (a) in force at 5.4.2015 by S.I. 2014/1640, art. 7. (i) (with art. 16)
I38. Sch. 7 para. 25. (b) in force at 1.12.2014 by S.I. 2014/1640, art. 5. (2)(h)
26. In section 150 (annual up-rating of benefits), in subsection (1) (sums to be reviewed), in paragraph (j), for "171. ZEE(1) or 171. ZN(1)" there is substituted " 171. ZN(2. E)(b) or 171. ZY(1) ".
Commencement Information
I39. Sch. 7 para. 26 in force at 5.4.2015 by S.I. 2014/1640, art. 7. (j) (with art. 16)
27. In section 163 (general financial arrangements), in subsection (1) (payments to be made out of the National Insurance Fund), in paragraph (d) (sums falling to be paid etc by HMRC under regulations relating to forms of statutory pay)—
(a) for "ordinary statutory paternity pay or additional statutory paternity pay" there is substituted " statutory paternity pay ";
(b) before the words ", falls to be" there is inserted "or statutory shared parental pay".
Commencement Information
I40. Sch. 7 para. 27. (a) in force at 5.4.2015 by S.I. 2014/1640, art. 7. (k) (with art. 16)
I41. Sch. 7 para. 27. (b) in force at 1.12.2014 by S.I. 2014/1640, art. 5. (2)(i)
28. (1)Section 165 (adjustments between the National Insurance Fund and the Consolidated Fund) is amended as follows.
(2) In subsection (1) (payments from National Insurance Fund into Consolidated Fund), in paragraph (b) (payments by way of adjustment in consequence of the operation of legislation relating to forms of statutory pay)—
(a) in sub-paragraph (iii) (ordinary statutory paternity pay), the word "ordinary" is repealed;
(b) sub-paragraph (iv) (additional statutory paternity pay) and the "and" following it are repealed;
(c) in sub-paragraph (v), at the end there is inserted "; and
(vi) statutory shared parental pay."
(3) In subsection (5) (payments from National Insurance Fund into Consolidated Fund), in paragraph (a) (sums in respect of HMRC administrative expenses)—
(a) for "ordinary statutory paternity pay, additional statutory paternity pay or" there is substituted " statutory paternity pay, ";
(b) after "statutory adoption pay" there is inserted " or statutory shared parental pay ".
Commencement Information
I42. Sch. 7 para. 28. (1)(2)(c)(3)(b) in force at 1.12.2014 by S.I. 2014/1640, art. 5. (2)(j)
I43. Sch. 7 para. 28. (2)(a)(b)(3)(a) in force at 5.4.2015 by S.I. 2014/1640, art. 7. (l) (with art. 16)

Employment Rights Act 1996 (c. 18)

29. The Employment Rights Act 1996 is amended as follows.
Commencement Information
I44. Sch. 7 para. 29 in force at 30.6.2014 by S.I. 2014/1640, art. 3. (2)(f)
30. In section 27 (meaning of "wages"), in subsection (1) (sums included)—
(a) in paragraph (ca), for "ordinary statutory paternity pay or additional statutory paternity pay"

there is substituted " statutory paternity pay ";
(b) after paragraph (cb) there is inserted—
"(cc)statutory shared parental pay under Part 12. ZC of that Act,".
Commencement Information
145. Sch. 7 para. 30. (a) in force at 5.4.2015 by S.I. 2014/1640, art. 7. (m) (with art. 16)
146. Sch. 7 para. 30. (b) in force at 1.12.2014 by S.I. 2014/1640, art. 5. (2)(k)
31. In section 47. C (right not to be subjected to detriment in connection with leave for family and domestic reasons), in subsection (2) (reasons that may be prescribed)—
(a) after paragraph (ba) there is inserted—
"(bb)shared parental leave,";
(b) in paragraph (ca) (paternity leave), the words "ordinary or additional" are repealed.
Commencement Information
147. Sch. 7 para. 31. (a) in force at 30.6.2014 by S.I. 2014/1640, art. 3. (2)(g)
148. Sch. 7 para. 31. (b) in force at 5.4.2015 by S.I. 2014/1640, art. 7. (n) (with art. 16)
32. In section 80. A (entitlement to ordinary paternity leave: birth), in the title, the word "ordinary" is repealed.
Commencement Information
149. Sch. 7 para. 32 in force at 5.4.2015 by S.I. 2014/1640, art. 7. (o) (with art. 16)
33. In section 80. B (entitlement to ordinary paternity leave: adoption), in the title, the word "ordinary" is repealed.
Commencement Information
150. Sch. 7 para. 33 in force at 5.4.2015 by S.I. 2014/1640, art. 7. (o) (with art. 16)
34. (1)Section 80. C (rights during and after ordinary and additional paternity leave) is amended as follows.
(2) In subsection (1) (provision as to rights under section 80. A or 80. AA), the words "or 80. AA" are repealed.
(3) In subsection (2) (absence on leave under section 80. A or 80. AA may include a period of other statutory leave)—
(a) the words "or 80. AA" are repealed;
(b) paragraph (za) (leave under section 80. AA) is repealed;
(c) the "and" following paragraph (b) is repealed;
(d) after paragraph (b) there is inserted—
"(ba)shared parental leave, and".
(4) In subsection (3) (provision as to rights under section 80. B or 80. BB)—
(a) the words "or 80. BB" are repealed;
(b) the words "or 80. AA" are repealed.
(5) In subsection (4) (absence on leave under section 80. B or 80. BB may include a period of other statutory leave)—
(a) the words "or 80. BB" are repealed;
(b) paragraph (za) (leave under section 80. BB) is repealed;
(c) after paragraph (b) there is inserted—
"(ba)shared parental leave,";
(d) in paragraph (d) (leave under section 80. A or 80. AA), the words "or 80. AA" are repealed.
(6) In subsection (6) (provision as to remuneration), for "any of sections 80. A to 80. BB" there is substituted " section 80. A or 80. B ".
(7) In subsection (7) (provision as to seniority on return etc), for "any of sections 80. A to 80. BB" there is substituted " section 80. A or 80. B ".
Commencement Information
151. Sch. 7 para. 34. (1)(3)(c)(d)(5)(c) in force at 30.6.2014 by S.I. 2014/1640, art. 3. (2)(h)
152. Sch. 7 para. 34. (2)(3)(a)(b)(4)(5)(a)(b)(d)(6)(7) in force at 5.4.2015 by S.I. 2014/1640, art. 7. (p) (with art. 16)
35. In section 80. D (provision as to redundancy or dismissal), in subsection (1), for ", 80. AA, 80. B or 80. BB" there is substituted " or 80. B ".

Commencement Information

I53. Sch. 7 para. 35 in force at 5.4.2015 by S.I. 2014/1640, art. 7. (q) (with art. 16)

36. (1)Section 80. E (supplemental to Chapter 3 of Part 8) is amended as follows.

(2) In subsection (1) (provision that may be made by regulations), for "any of sections 80. A to 80. BB", in each place it occurs, there is substituted " section 80. A or 80. B ".

(3) Subsection (2) (persons who may be subjected to duties in connection with employees exercising rights under section 80. AA or 80. BB) is repealed.

Commencement Information

I54. Sch. 7 para. 36 in force at 5.4.2015 by S.I. 2014/1640, art. 7. (q) (with art. 16)

37. (1)Section 88 (liability of employer to pay employee during period of notice: employments with normal working hours) is amended as follows.

(2) In subsection (1)(c) (liability to employee who is absent from work because of pregnancy etc)—

(a) after "adoption leave," there is inserted " shared parental leave, ";

(b) for "ordinary or additional paternity leave" there is substituted " paternity leave ".

(3) In subsection (2) (certain payments during the period of notice treated as meeting employer's liability)—

(a) for "ordinary statutory paternity pay, additional statutory paternity pay" there is substituted " statutory paternity pay ";

(b) after "statutory adoption pay," there is inserted " shared parental pay, statutory shared parental pay, ".

Commencement Information

I55. Sch. 7 para. 37. (1)(2)(a)(3)(b) in force at 1.12.2014 by S.I. 2014/1640, art. 5. (2)(l)

I56. Sch. 7 para. 37. (2)(b)(3)(a) in force at 5.4.2015 by S.I. 2014/1640, art. 7. (r) (with art. 16)

38. (1)Section 89 (effect of notice of termination: employments without normal working hours) is amended as follows.

(2) In subsection (3)(b) (effect of absence from work because of pregnancy etc during the period of notice)—

(a) after "adoption leave," there is inserted " shared parental leave, ";

(b) for "ordinary or additional paternity leave" there is substituted " paternity leave ".

(3) In subsection (4) (certain payments during the period of notice treated as remuneration)—

(a) for "ordinary statutory paternity pay, additional statutory paternity pay" there is substituted " statutory paternity pay ";

(b) after "statutory adoption pay," there is inserted " shared parental pay, statutory shared parental pay, ".

Commencement Information

I57. Sch. 7 para. 38. (1)(2)(a)(3)(b) in force at 1.12.2014 by S.I. 2014/1640, art. 5. (2)(m)

I58. Sch. 7 para. 38. (2)(b)(3)(a) in force at 5.4.2015 by S.I. 2014/1640, art. 7. (s) (with art. 16)

39. In section 99 (dismissal to be regarded as unfair where the dismissal relates to leave for family reasons), in subsection (3) (reasons or sets of circumstances that may be prescribed)—

(a) after paragraph (ba) there is inserted—

"(bb)shared parental leave,";

(b) in paragraph (ca), for "ordinary or additional paternity leave" there is substituted " paternity leave ".

Commencement Information

I59. Sch. 7 para. 39. (a) in force at 30.6.2014 by S.I. 2014/1640, art. 3. (2)(i)

I60. Sch. 7 para. 39. (b) in force at 5.4.2015 by S.I. 2014/1640, art. 7. (t) (with art. 16)

40. In section 106 (dismissal of employee engaged as replacement for person absent from work because of pregnancy etc), in subsection (2)(a), for "leave under section 80. AA or 80. BB (additional paternity leave)" there is substituted " shared parental leave ".

Commencement Information

I61. Sch. 7 para. 40 in force at 1.12.2014 by S.I. 2014/1640, art. 5. (2)(n) (with art. 12)

41. In section 230 (meaning of "employee", etc), after subsection (6) there is inserted—

"(7)This section has effect subject to section 75. K(3) and (5)."
Commencement Information
162. Sch. 7 para. 41 in force at 30.6.2014 by S.I. 2014/1640, art. 3. (2)(j)
42. In section 235 (other definitions), in subsection (1)—
(a) for the definition of "ordinary or additional paternity leave" there is substituted—
""paternity leave" means leave under section 80. A or 80. B,";
(b) in the definition of "week", in paragraph (b), after "in sections" there is inserted " 75. F, 75. H, ";
(c) at the appropriate place there is inserted—
""shared parental leave" means leave under section 75. E or 75. G,".
Commencement Information
163. Sch. 7 para. 42. (a) in force at 5.4.2015 by S.I. 2014/1640, art. 7. (u) (with art. 16)
164. Sch. 7 para. 42. (b)(c) in force at 30.6.2014 by S.I. 2014/1640, art. 3. (2)(k)
43. In section 236 (orders and regulations), in subsection (3) (affirmative procedure), the following are repealed—
(a) "80. AA,";
(b) "80. BB,".
Commencement Information
165. Sch. 7 para. 43 in force at 5.4.2015 by S.I. 2014/1640, art. 7. (v) (with art. 16)

Social Security Contributions (Transfer of Functions, etc.) Act 1999 (c. 2)

44. The Social Security Contributions (Transfer of Functions, etc.) Act 1999 is amended as follows.
Commencement Information
166. Sch. 7 para. 44 in force at 1.12.2014 by S.I. 2014/1640, art. 5. (2)(o)
45. (1)Section 8 (decisions by officers of Revenue and Customs) is amended as follows.
(2) In subsection (1)—
(a) in paragraph (f), for "ordinary statutory paternity pay, additional statutory paternity pay or" there is substituted " statutory paternity pay, ";
(b) in paragraph (f), after "statutory adoption pay" there is inserted " or statutory shared parental pay ";
(c) in paragraph (g), for "to 12. ZB" there is substituted " to 12. ZC ";
(d) in paragraph (g), for "ordinary statutory paternity pay, additional statutory paternity pay and" there is substituted " statutory paternity pay, ";
(e) in paragraph (g), after "statutory adoption pay" there is inserted " and statutory shared parental pay ";
(f) in paragraph (ga), for "ordinary statutory paternity pay, additional statutory paternity pay or" there is substituted " statutory paternity pay, ";
(g) in paragraph (ga), after "statutory adoption pay" there is inserted " or statutory shared parental pay ".
(3) In subsection (3)(b)—
(a) for "ordinary statutory paternity pay, additional statutory paternity pay or" there is substituted " statutory paternity pay, ";
(b) after "statutory adoption pay" there is inserted " or statutory shared parental pay ".
Commencement Information
167. Sch. 7 para. 45. (1)(2)(b)(c)(e)(g)(3)(b) in force at 1.12.2014 by S.I. 2014/1640, art. 5. (2)(p)
168. Sch. 7 para. 45. (2)(a)(d)(f)(3)(a) in force at 5.4.2015 by S.I. 2014/1640, art. 7. (w) (with art. 16)
46. In section 11 (appeals against decisions of officers of Revenue and Customs), in subsection (2)(a)—

(a) for "ordinary statutory paternity pay, additional statutory paternity pay or" there is substituted " statutory paternity pay, ";
(b) after "statutory adoption pay" there is inserted " or statutory shared parental pay ".
Commencement Information
I69. Sch. 7 para. 46. (a) in force at 5.4.2015 by S.I. 2014/1640, art. 7. (x) (with art. 16)
I70. Sch. 7 para. 46. (b) in force at 1.12.2014 by S.I. 2014/1640, art. 5. (2)(q)
47. (1)Section 14 (matters arising as respects decisions) is amended as follows.
(2) In subsection (1) (regulations as to matters arising pending a decision etc), in paragraph (a)(i)—
(a) for "ordinary statutory paternity pay, additional statutory paternity pay or" there is substituted " statutory paternity pay, ";
(b) after "statutory adoption pay" there is inserted " or statutory shared parental pay ".
(3) In subsection (3) (regulations requiring concurrence of the Secretary of State)—
(a) for "ordinary statutory paternity pay, additional statutory paternity pay or" there is substituted " statutory paternity pay, ";
(b) after "statutory adoption pay" there is inserted " or statutory shared parental pay ".
Commencement Information
I71. Sch. 7 para. 47. (1)(2)(b)(3)(b) in force at 30.6.2014 by S.I. 2014/1640, art. 3. (2)(l)
I72. Sch. 7 para. 47. (2)(a)(3)(a) in force at 5.4.2015 by S.I. 2014/1640, art. 7. (y) (with art. 16)

Finance Act 1999 (c. 16)

48. (1)Sections 132 and 133 of the Finance Act 1999 have effect as if statutory shared parental pay were a matter which is under the care and management of the Commissioners for Revenue and Customs.
(2) In this paragraph "statutory shared parental pay" includes statutory pay under Northern Ireland legislation corresponding to the provisions of Part 12. ZC of the Social Security Contributions and Benefits Act 1992.
Commencement Information
I73. Sch. 7 para. 48. (1) in force at 30.6.2014 by S.I. 2014/1640, art. 3. (2)(m)
I74. Sch. 7 para. 48. (2) in force at 15.3.2015 being the date on which 1992 c. 7, Pt. 12. ZC comes into force by virtue of S.R. 2015/86, art. 3. (1)(d) by S.I. 2014/1640, art. 8. (b)

Finance Act 2000 (c. 17)

49. In Schedule 15 to the Finance Act 2000 (the corporate venturing scheme), in paragraph 22. A (qualifying issuing company: full-time equivalent employee number to be less than 50), in sub-paragraph (4) (who is an employee), in paragraph (b)(i) (exception relating to certain leave), for "or paternity" there is substituted " , paternity or shared parental ".
Commencement Information
I75. Sch. 7 para. 49 in force at 1.12.2014 by S.I. 2014/1640, art. 5. (2)(r)

Employment Act 2002 (c. 22)

50. The Employment Act 2002 is amended as follows.
Commencement Information
I76. Sch. 7 para. 50 in force at 30.6.2014 by S.I. 2014/1640, art. 3. (2)(n)
51. (1)Section 7 (funding of employers' liabilities as regards certain statutory pay) is amended as follows.
(2) In subsection (1) (power to make regulations regarding the funding of statutory pay by Her Majesty's Revenue and Customs)—

(a) for "ordinary statutory paternity pay, additional statutory paternity pay and" there is substituted " statutory paternity pay, ";
(b) after "statutory adoption pay" there is inserted " and statutory shared parental pay ".
(3) In subsection (2) (recovery relating to small employers' relief)—
(a) in paragraph (a)—
(i) for "ordinary statutory paternity pay, additional statutory paternity pay or" there is substituted " statutory paternity pay, ";
(ii) after "statutory adoption pay" there is inserted " or statutory shared parental pay ";
(b) in paragraph (b)—
(i) for "ordinary statutory paternity pay, additional statutory paternity pay or" there is substituted " statutory paternity pay, ";
(ii) after "statutory adoption pay" there is inserted " or statutory shared parental pay ".
(4) In subsection (3) (payments treated as qualifying for small employers' relief)—
(a) for "ordinary statutory paternity pay, additional statutory paternity pay or" there is substituted " statutory paternity pay, ";
(b) after "statutory adoption pay", in the first place it occurs, there is inserted " or statutory shared parental pay ";
(c) for the words from "treating the period" to the end there is substituted "treating—
"(a)the period for which the payment of statutory paternity pay is made,
(b) the payee's adoption pay period, or
(c) the period for which the payment of statutory shared parental pay is made,
as the maternity pay period."
Commencement Information
I77. Sch. 7 para. 51. (1)(2)(b)(3)(a)(ii)(b)(ii)(4)(b)(c) in force at 30.6.2014 by S.I. 2014/1640, art. 3. (2)(o) (with art. 9)
I78. Sch. 7 para. 51. (2)(a)(i)(b)(i)(4)(a) in force at 5.4.2015 by S.I. 2014/1640, art. 7. (z) (with art. 16)
52. (1)Section 8 (regulations about payment) is amended as follows.
(2) In subsection (1) (power to make regulations with respect to payment by employers of statutory pay)—
(a) for "ordinary statutory paternity pay, additional statutory paternity pay and" there is substituted " statutory paternity pay, ";
(b) after "statutory adoption pay" there is inserted " and statutory shared parental pay ".
(3) In subsection (2) (further provision as to regulations)—
(a) in paragraph (a)—
(i) for "ordinary statutory paternity pay, additional statutory paternity pay and" there is substituted " statutory paternity pay, ";
(ii) after "statutory adoption pay" there is inserted " and statutory shared parental pay ";
(b) in paragraph (b)—
(i) for "ordinary statutory paternity pay, additional statutory paternity pay and" there is substituted " statutory paternity pay, ";
(ii) after "statutory adoption pay" there is inserted " and statutory shared parental pay ";
(c) in paragraph (d)—
(i) for "ordinary statutory paternity pay, additional statutory paternity pay and" there is substituted " statutory paternity pay, ";
(ii) after "statutory adoption pay" there is inserted " and statutory shared parental pay ".
Commencement Information
I79. Sch. 7 para. 52. (1)(2)(b)(3)(a)(ii)(b)(ii)(c)(ii) in force at 30.6.2014 by S.I. 2014/1640, art. 3. (2)(p)
I80. Sch. 7 para. 52. (2)(a)(3)(a)(i)(b)(i)(c)(i) in force at 5.4.2015 by S.I. 2014/1640, art. 7. (aa) (with art. 16)
53. (1)Section 10 (powers to require information) is amended as follows.
(2) In subsection (1) (power to make regulations requiring the production of information or

documents)—
(a) for "ordinary statutory paternity pay, additional statutory paternity pay or" there is substituted " statutory paternity pay, ";
(b) after "statutory adoption pay" there is inserted " or statutory shared parental pay ".
(3) In subsection (2) (persons who may be specified as liable to produce information or documents), in paragraph (a)—
(a) for "ordinary statutory paternity pay, additional statutory paternity pay or" there is substituted " statutory paternity pay, ";
(b) after "statutory adoption pay" there is inserted " or statutory shared parental pay ".
Commencement Information
I81. Sch. 7 para. 53. (1)(2)(b)(3)(b) in force at 30.6.2014 by S.I. 2014/1640, art. 3. (2)(q)
I82. Sch. 7 para. 53. (2)(a)(3)(a) in force at 5.4.2015 by S.I. 2014/1640, art. 7. (bb) (with art. 16)
54. In section 11 (penalties for failure to comply), in subsection (6) (failures to make payments)—
(a) for "ordinary statutory paternity pay, additional statutory paternity pay or" there is substituted " statutory paternity pay, ";
(b) after "statutory adoption pay" there is inserted " or statutory shared parental pay ".
Commencement Information
I83. Sch. 7 para. 54. (a) in force at 5.4.2015 by S.I. 2014/1640, art. 7. (cc) (with art. 16)
I84. Sch. 7 para. 54. (b) in force at 1.12.2014 by S.I. 2014/1640, art. 5. (2)(s)
55. (1)Section 12 (penalties for fraud or negligence) is amended as follows.
(2) In subsection (1) (incorrect statement or declaration: ordinary statutory paternity pay)—
(a) in paragraph (a), the word "ordinary" is repealed;
(b) in paragraph (b), the word "ordinary" is repealed.
(3) In subsection (2) (incorrect statement or declaration: statutory adoption pay or additional statutory paternity pay)—
(a) in paragraph (a), for "additional statutory paternity pay" there is substituted " statutory shared parental pay ";
(b) in paragraph (b), for "additional statutory paternity pay" there is substituted " statutory shared parental pay ".
(4) In subsection (3) (incorrect payment: ordinary statutory paternity pay), the word "ordinary" is repealed.
(5) In subsection (4) (incorrect payment: statutory adoption pay or additional statutory paternity pay), for "additional statutory paternity pay" there is substituted " statutory shared parental pay ".
(6) In subsection (5) (fraudulently or negligently providing incorrect information or receiving incorrect payments), the word "ordinary" is repealed.
Commencement Information
I85. Sch. 7 para. 55. (1)(3)(5) in force at 1.12.2014 by S.I. 2014/1640, art. 5. (2)(t) (with art. 12)
I86. Sch. 7 para. 55. (2)(4)(6) in force at 5.4.2015 by S.I. 2014/1640, art. 7. (dd) (with art. 16)
56. In section 13 (supply of information held by Her Majesty's Revenue and Customs), in subsection (1)—
(a) for "ordinary statutory paternity pay, additional statutory paternity pay or" there is substituted " statutory paternity pay, ";
(b) after "statutory adoption pay" there is inserted " or statutory shared parental pay ".
Commencement Information
I87. Sch. 7 para. 56. (a) in force at 5.4.2015 by S.I. 2014/1640, art. 7. (ee) (with arts. 16, 19)
I88. Sch. 7 para. 56. (b) in force at 1.12.2014 by S.I. 2014/1640, art. 5. (2)(u)
57. (1)Section 14 (supply of information held by the Secretary of State) is amended as follows.
(2) In subsection (1)—
(a) for "ordinary statutory paternity pay, additional statutory paternity pay or" there is substituted " statutory paternity pay, ";
(b) after "statutory adoption pay" there is inserted " or statutory shared parental pay ".
(3) In subsection (2)—
(a) for "ordinary statutory paternity pay, additional statutory paternity pay or" there is substituted "

statutory paternity pay, ";
(b) after "statutory adoption pay" there is inserted " or statutory shared parental pay ".
Commencement Information
I89. Sch. 7 para. 57. (1)(2)(b)(3)(b) in force at 1.12.2014 by S.I. 2014/1640, art. 5. (2)(v)
I90. Sch. 7 para. 57. (2)(a)(3)(a) in force at 5.4.2015 by S.I. 2014/1640, art. 7. (ff) (with arts. 16, 19)
58. In section 15 (use of information by Her Majesty's Revenue and Customs), in subsection (2) (functions for the purposes of which information may be used)—
(a) in paragraph (a) (functions relating to ordinary statutory paternity pay), the word "ordinary" is repealed;
(b) paragraph (aa) (functions relating to additional statutory paternity pay) is repealed;
(c) the "and" following paragraph (b) is repealed;
(d) after paragraph (b) there is inserted—
"(ba)their functions in relation to statutory shared parental pay; and".
Commencement Information
I91. Sch. 7 para. 58. (a)(b) in force at 5.4.2015 by S.I. 2014/1640, art. 7. (gg) (with arts. 16, 19)
I92. Sch. 7 para. 58. (c)(d) in force at 1.12.2014 by S.I. 2014/1640, art. 5. (2)(w)
59. In section 55 (short title etc), in subsection (8) (references to Great Britain statutory pay to include statutory pay under corresponding Northern Ireland legislation)—
(a) for "ordinary statutory paternity pay, additional statutory paternity pay or" there is substituted " statutory paternity pay, ";
(b) after "statutory adoption pay" there is inserted " or statutory shared parental pay ";
(c) for "or Part 12. ZB" there is substituted " , Part 12. ZB or Part 12. ZC ".
Commencement Information
I93. Sch. 7 para. 59 in force at 15.3.2015 being the date on which 1992 c. 7, Pt. 12. ZC comes into force by virtue of S.R. 2015/86, art. 3. (1)(d) by S.I. 2014/1640, art. 8. (c) (with art. 18)
I94. Sch. 7 para. 59. (a) in force at 5.4.2015 by S.I. 2014/1640, art. 7. (hh) (with art. 16)

Proceeds of Crime Act 2002 (c. 29)

60. (1)Section 323 of the Proceeds of Crime Act 2002 (Revenue functions) is amended as follows.
(2) In subsection (1) (general Revenue functions)—
(a) in paragraph (g) (ordinary statutory paternity pay), the word "ordinary" is repealed;
(b) paragraph (ga) (additional statutory paternity pay) is repealed;
(c) after paragraph (h) there is inserted—
"(ha)statutory shared parental pay;".
(3) In subsection (4) (interpretation: Great Britain)—
(a) in paragraph (d), for " "ordinary statutory paternity pay"" there is substituted " "statutory paternity pay" ";
(b) paragraph (da) (meaning of "additional statutory paternity pay") is repealed;
(c) after paragraph (e) there is inserted—
"(ea)statutory shared parental pay" must be construed in accordance with sections 171. ZU and 171. ZV of that Act;".
(4) In subsection (5) (interpretation: Northern Ireland)—
(a) in paragraph (d) (construction of "ordinary statutory paternity pay" and "additional statutory paternity pay"), for " "ordinary statutory paternity pay" and "additional statutory paternity pay"" there is substituted " "statutory paternity pay"";
(b) after paragraph (e) there is inserted—
"(ea)statutory shared parental pay" must be construed in accordance with any Northern Ireland legislation which corresponds to Part 12. ZC of that Act;".
Commencement Information
I95. Sch. 7 para. 60. (1)(2)(c)(3)(c) in force at 1.12.2014 by S.I. 2014/1640, art. 5. (2)(x)

I96. Sch. 7 para. 60. (2)(a)(b)(3)(a)(b) in force at 5.4.2015 by S.I. 2014/1640, art. 7. (ii) (with arts. 16, 19)

I97. Sch. 7 para. 60. (4) in force at 15.3.2015 being the date on which 1992 c. 7, Pt. 12. ZC comes into force by virtue of S.R. 2015/86, art. 3. (1)(d) by S.I. 2014/1640, art. 8. (d) (with art. 18)

Income Tax (Earnings and Pensions) Act 2003 (c. 1)

61. The Income Tax (Earnings and Pensions) Act 2003 is amended as follows.
Commencement Information
I98. Sch. 7 para. 61 in force at 1.12.2014 by S.I. 2014/1640, art. 5. (2)(y)
62. (1)Section 660 (taxable benefits: UK benefits - Table A) is amended as follows.
(2) In subsection (1), in Table A, the entry relating to additional statutory paternity pay is repealed.
(3) In subsection (1), in Table A, in the entry relating to ordinary statutory paternity pay, in the left hand column, for "Ordinary statutory" there is substituted " Statutory ".
(4) In subsection (1), in Table A, after the entry relating to statutory maternity pay there is inserted—
"Statutory shared parental pay | SSCBA 1992 | Section 171ZU or 171ZV |
Any provision made for Northern Ireland which corresponds to section 171ZU or 171ZV of SSCBA 1992". |
(5) In subsection (2)—
(a) the entry relating to additional statutory paternity pay is repealed;
(b) in the entry relating to ordinary statutory paternity pay, the word "ordinary" is repealed;
(c) after the entry relating to statutory maternity pay there is inserted— " statutory shared parental pay; ".
Commencement Information
I99. Sch. 7 para. 62. (1)(4)(5)(c) in force at 1.12.2014 by S.I. 2014/1640, art. 5. (2)(z)
I100. Sch. 7 para. 62. (2)(3)(5)(a)(b) in force at 5.4.2015 by S.I. 2014/1640, art. 7. (jj) (with art. 16)
63. (1)Schedule 5 (enterprise management incentives) is amended as follows.
(2) In paragraph 12. A (the number of employees requirement), in sub-paragraph (4) (who is an employee), in paragraph (b)(i) (exception relating to certain leave), for "or paternity" there is substituted " , paternity or shared parental ".
(3) In paragraph 26 (eligible employees: requirement as to commitment of working time), in sub-paragraph (3) (what is committed time), after "paternity leave" there is inserted " , shared parental leave ".
Commencement Information
I101. Sch. 7 para. 63 in force at 1.12.2014 by S.I. 2014/1640, art. 5. (2)(aa)

Commissioners for Revenue and Customs Act 2005 (c. 11)

64. (1)Schedule 1 to the Commissioners for Revenue and Customs Act 2005 (former Inland Revenue matters where functions vest in officers of Revenue and Customs) is amended as follows.
(2) In paragraph 26 (ordinary statutory paternity pay), for "Ordinary statutory" there is substituted " Statutory ".
(3) Paragraph 26. A (additional statutory paternity pay) is repealed.
(4) After paragraph 26. A there is inserted—
"26. BStatutory shared parental pay."
Commencement Information
I102. Sch. 7 para. 64. (1)(4) in force at 1.12.2014 by S.I. 2014/1640, art. 5. (2)(bb)
I103. Sch. 7 para. 64. (2)(3) in force at 5.4.2015 by S.I. 2014/1640, art. 7. (kk) (with arts. 16, 19)

Work and Families Act 2006 (c. 18)

65. The Work and Families Act 2006 is amended as follows.
Commencement Information
I104. Sch. 7 para. 65 in force at 5.4.2015 by S.I. 2014/1640, art. 7. (ll) (with art. 16)
66. Sections 3 to 10 (additional paternity leave and additional statutory paternity pay) are repealed.
Commencement Information
I105. Sch. 7 para. 66 in force at 5.4.2015 by S.I. 2014/1640, art. 7. (ll) (with art. 16)
67. Section 11. (2) (treatment of references to statutory paternity pay) is repealed.
Commencement Information
I106. Sch. 7 para. 67 in force at 5.4.2015 by S.I. 2014/1640, art. 7. (ll) (with art. 16)
68. In Schedule 1 (leave and pay related to birth or adoption: further amendments), paragraphs 1. (4), 11, 17, 19, 22, 38. (3), 49 and 57. (b) are repealed.
Commencement Information
I107. Sch. 7 para. 68 in force at 15.3.2015 for specified purposes, that being the date on which 1992 c. 7, Pt. 12. ZC comes into force by virtue of S.R. 2015/86, art. 3. (1)(d) by S.I. 2014/1640, art. 8. (e)
I108. Sch. 7 para. 68 in force at 5.4.2015 for specified purposes by S.I. 2014/1640, art. 7. (mm) (with art. 16)

Income Tax Act 2007 (c. 3)

69. The Income Tax Act 2007 is amended as follows.
Commencement Information
I109. Sch. 7 para. 69 in force at 1.12.2014 by S.I. 2014/1640, art. 5. (2)(cc)
70. In section 186. A (enterprise investment schemes: the number of employees requirement for an issuing company), in subsection (4) (who is an employee), in paragraph (b)(i) (exception relating to certain leave), for "or paternity" there is substituted " , paternity or shared parental ".
Commencement Information
I110. Sch. 7 para. 70 in force at 1.12.2014 by S.I. 2014/1640, art. 5. (2)(cc)
71. In section 257. DJ (seed enterprise investment schemes: the number of employees requirement for an issuing company), in subsection (4) (who is an employee), in paragraph (b)(i), for "or paternity" there is substituted " , paternity or shared parental ".
Commencement Information
I111. Sch. 7 para. 71 in force at 1.12.2014 by S.I. 2014/1640, art. 5. (2)(cc)
72. In section 297. A (venture capital trusts: the number of employees requirement for a qualifying holding), in subsection (4) (who is an employee), in paragraph (b)(i), for "or paternity" there is substituted " , paternity or shared parental ".
Commencement Information
I112. Sch. 7 para. 72 in force at 1.12.2014 by S.I. 2014/1640, art. 5. (2)(cc)

Welfare Reform Act 2007 (c. 5)

73. (1)Section 20 of the Welfare Reform Act 2007 (relationship with statutory payments) is amended as follows.
(2) In subsection (6) (no entitlement to an employment and support allowance during an additional paternity pay period)—
(a) for "additional statutory paternity pay" there is substituted " statutory shared parental pay ";
(b) for "a day that falls within the additional paternity pay period" there is substituted " a day that falls within a period in respect of which statutory shared parental pay is payable ".
(3) In subsection (7) (regulations providing for exceptions to subsection (6)), in paragraph (a), for

"additional statutory paternity pay for a period" there is substituted " statutory shared parental pay for a period ".

(4) In subsection (8) (definitions), the definition of "the additional paternity pay period" is repealed.

Commencement Information

I113. Sch. 7 para. 73. (1)(2)(3) in force at 30.6.2014 by S.I. 2014/1640, art. 3. (2)(r) (with art. 9)

I114. Sch. 7 para. 73. (4) in force at 5.4.2015 by S.I. 2014/1640, art. 7. (nn) (with art. 16)

Pensions Act 2008 (c. 30)

74. In section 13 of the Pensions Act 2008 (qualifying earnings), in subsection (3) (meaning of "earnings")—

(a) in paragraph (d), for "ordinary statutory paternity pay or additional statutory paternity pay" there is substituted " statutory paternity pay ";

(b) after paragraph (e) there is inserted—

"(ea)statutory shared parental pay under Part 12. ZC of that Act;".

Commencement Information

I115. Sch. 7 para. 74. (a) in force at 5.4.2015 by S.I. 2014/1640, art. 7. (oo) (with art. 16)

I116. Sch. 7 para. 74. (b) in force at 1.12.2014 by S.I. 2014/1640, art. 5. (2)(dd)

Welfare Reform Act 2012 (c. 5)

75. In the Welfare Reform Act 2012, in section 63 (entitlement to be in employment as condition for receiving maternity allowance or statutory pay), subsections (6) and (7) are repealed.

Commencement Information

I117. Sch. 7 para. 75 in force at 5.4.2015 by S.I. 2014/1640, art. 7. (pp) (with art. 16)

Open Government Licence v3.0

Contains public sector information licensed under the Open Government Licence v3.0.
The full licence if available at the following address:
http://www.nationalarchives.gov.uk/doc/open-government-licence/version/3/

Printed in Great Britain
by Amazon